Educational Assessments in the Age of Generative AI

Patrick W. Wachira
Cleveland State University, USA

Xiongyi Liu
Cleveland State University, USA

Selma Koc
Cleveland State University, USA

IGI Global
Scientific Publishing
Publishing Tomorrow's Research Today

Vice President of Editorial Melissa Wagner
Managing Editor of Acquisitions Mikaela Felty
Managing Editor of Book Development Jocelynn Hessler
Production Manager Mike Brehm
Cover Design Phillip Shickler

Published in the United States of America by
IGI Global Scientific Publishing
701 East Chocolate Avenue
Hershey, PA, 17033, USA
Tel: 717-533-8845
Fax: 717-533-8661
E-mail: cust@igi-global.com
Website: https://www.igi-global.com

Library of Congress Cataloging-in-Publication Data

Names: Wachira, Patrick, editor. | Liu, Xiongyi, editor. | Koç, Selma, editor.
Title: Educational assessments in the age of generative AI / Edited by Patrick Wachira, Xiongyi Liu, Selma Koc.
Description: Hershey, PA : IGI Global, [2025] | Includes bibliographical references and index. | Summary: "The book explores how the use of generative AI tools and applications can transform and revolutionize assessment practices"-- Provided by publisher.
Identifiers: LCCN 2024048800 (print) | LCCN 2024048801 (ebook) | ISBN 9798369363515 (hardcover) | ISBN 9798369363553 (paperback) | ISBN 9798369363522 (ebook)
Subjects: LCSH: Educational tests and measurements--Technological innovations. | Artificial intelligence--Educational applications.
Classification: LCC LB3060.5 .E38 2025 (print) | LCC LB3060.5 (ebook) | DDC 371.26/1--dc23/eng/20241107
LC record available at https://lccn.loc.gov/2024048800
LC ebook record available at https://lccn.loc.gov/2024048801
ISBN:979-8-3693-6351-5
eISBN:979-8-3693-6352-2

British Cataloguing in Publication Data
A Cataloguing in Publication record for this book is available from the British Library.

Table of Contents

Detailed Table of Contents

In this chapter, I begin with a contextualization of a college writing course and a brief review of scholarship related to writing pedagogy. I then provide a discussion detailing various ways that I have seen my ENG 100 students using (and misusing) generative AI. Following these observations, I share two assignments and related supplemental materials that can be used to resist the unethical use of AI in writing classrooms and that embrace process over product pedagogy. I argue for the use of process over product pedagogy to resist, challenge, and counter-act this paradigm as well as a way to respond to students' misuse of generative AI.

This chapter examines the impact of Generative AI tools on higher education (HE). The authors explore how these tools, while enhancing learning experiences, pose significant challenges to academic integrity and higher education by fostering a false sense of achievement among students. The chapter delves into the complexities of using generative AI in academic settings, highlighting the ease with which students can produce passable assignments with minimal effort, thus bypassing critical thinking and deep engagement with the subject matter. It critically analyzes the inadequacy of traditional assessment methods in distinguishing genuine student work from AI-generated content. The authors discuss the implications of this reliance on AI tools for the development of essential cognitive skills and the authenticity of academic qualifications. Furthermore, the chapter proposes assessment strategies and policy recommendations to ensure the responsible and ethical use of AI in HE.

Educational assessments are essential for evaluating student learning and academic achievement. Generative Artificial Intelligence (GAI), a branch of AI that generates content based on natural-language prompts, offers new possibilities in education, particularly in the areas of content design, delivery, and student support. With GAI, there is growing interest in leveraging AI-driven assessments to enhance formative and summative evaluation processes. This chapter explores the benefits of GAI in promoting personalised learning, improving student engagement, and optimising feedback. While GAI holds promise in transforming educational assessments, its implementation also raises important challenges, such as algorithmic bias, data privacy concerns, and issues of fairness, particularly within the African context where infrastructural disparities and digital divides remain significant barriers. Addressing these challenges is critical to ensuring that AI-driven tools are used responsibly and equitably in African educational systems.

This chapter explores integrating generative AI tools in first-year writing courses, proposing a dual framework for balanced AI integration and AI literacy development. It addresses the challenges that come from the widespread student use of AI tools and presents new approaches to assessment design. The dual framework can help educators create AI-powered assessments that enhance learning outcomes, promote critical thinking, and build student confidence. A case study on thesis development illustrates how AI can be used to teach foundational writing skills while developing AI literacy. The chapter argues for a transformation of writing instruction that prepares students by instilling both discipline specific skills and critical AI skills. This approach turns potential challenges into opportunities for deeper learning, and positions AI as a tool rather than a replacement for human skills. The chapter concludes by discussing the implications for educational practice, curriculum redesign, instructor training, and assessment methods.

This chapter explores the transformative impact of generative artificial intelligence on inquiry-based learning in educational assessment. Generative AI technologies have revolutionized traditional assessment methods, enabling dynamic, individualized learning experiences that meet individual student needs. By harnessing the power of artificial intelligence, teachers can create assessments that promote critical thinking, conceptual understanding, and deeper engagement with content. The chapter begins with an overview of the theoretical foundations of generative artificial intelligence and its integration into educational frameworks such as constructivism and technology-enhanced learning. It discusses practical applications of artificial intelligence in creating dynamic assessment environments. Examples include tools like Knewton and MATH from Carnegie Learning, which adapt learning methods based on student performance.

This chapter examines the transformative potential of AI-enhanced formative assessment in higher education, focusing on fostering inspirational learning experiences. The authors explore how artificial intelligence can revolutionize traditional assessment practices, enabling more personalized, efficient, and effective learning environments. The chapter discusses benefits and challenges of implementation, including potential improvements in student engagement, motivation, and academic achievement. It analyzes AI's role in facilitating real-time feedback, automating grading, and enhancing teacher-student interactions. A comprehensive review of the current state of AI-enhanced formative assessment in higher education is provided, highlighting best practices, strategies, and challenges. The chapter concludes by outlining future research directions, emphasizing collaboration among educators, policymakers, and technologists to harness AI's potential in inspiring and empowering learners.

Preface

In recent times, artificial intelligence (AI) has been at the frontier of both industry and academia. The rapid permeation of generative AI technology into all aspects of modern society has profoundly changed the landscape of higher education. Integrating AI unto education has become one of the critical issues in this field (Zawacki-Richter, et al, 2019; Hwang et al., 2021). To underscore its importance, several governments, institutions, and industries have invested a lot of money to facilitate the integration of AI in education to support teaching and learning (Chen et al, 2020).

Generative AI specifically has presented immense opportunities to transform education. These AI tools offer remarkable assistance in enhancing the learning process by providing personalized responses, generating written content, and solving complex problems (Song, 2024). One of the most significant areas of opportunity offered by generative-AI, is in the assessment of learning but with these opportunities also comes challenges. For instance, with the improved capabilities of generative AI tools and students increasingly turning to generative AI tools to aid them in completing assignments educators, the value of take-home assessments especially, is taken into question. As noted by Cotton et al., (2023) assessment is an integral part of higher education, serving as a means of evaluating student learning and progress and therefore if students can pass assessment tasks by submitting work that is not their own, then the purpose and integrity of education is undermined. Thus, while there are robust discussions and ongoing projects on the use and impact of AI as valuable tools to improve learning, there needs to be parallel discussions on the methods used to assess teaching and learning in the context of generative AI use. Assessments must be reimagined in this new era to ensure that they remain an effective and an equitable way to gauge student learning. A goal of assessment is to foster learning essential for success beyond the classroom, and this can only be possible with well-designed assessments that have the potential for determining whether students have truly learned. As the use of AI becomes ubiquitous, rethinking assessments could also mean harnessing the power of AI tools to (re) design them to address especially the limitations of traditional assessments which remain persistent in education. Traditional assessments are limited in measuring the sophisticated knowledge and skills students needed for 21st century careers. Multiple-choice assessments, common in traditional assessments or instance, have been more widely associated with lower level of knowledge on Blooms Taxonomy rather than with higher-order skills.

Beyond using AI to rethink traditional assessments, it is important to note that AI offers other benefits which educators can leverage when it comes to the process of assessment. According to Swiecki et al. (2022), AI may assist teachers for instance through creation of assessment tasks and support peer assessment especially as class sizes increase thus becoming more challenging for instructors to provide rich and timely feedback. Teacher may also use AI for automated grading of students work providing accurate and timely feedback thus helping to make assessments practices more feasible to maintain. AI can also create more adaptive and personalized assessments that adjust the task to the student's abilities, giving them tailored assessment experiences (Swiecki et al., 2022). For instance, AI tools can be used to generate customized tests or quizzes for each student based on their individual needs and abilities which is essential as a differentiated learning and assessments has become more important in the classroom in recent times. Other benefits include using AI to evaluate student engagement and academic integrity (Zawacki-Richter et al., 2019) and facilitate collaboration among students. Zhai et al. (2021) also noted the facilitation of interactive role-play and to support gamification as another benefit of using AI in the class. Creation of interactive, game-based assessments could be a fun and engaging way for students to demonstrate their knowledge and skills and could also help to teach them valuable communication and problem-solving skills (Cotton et. al., 2023)

While generative AI tools can potentially offer many benefits for assessment practices, there are also challenges to using these tools, including the sidelining of expertise, deferral of accountability, adoption of surveillance pedagogy, and a potentially unproductive separation of humans and machines in the assessment process (Swiecki et al., 2022). As noted previously, with increased access to generative AI tools, there are also concerns about identity, plagiarism, and assurance of learning (Hisan & Amri, 2023). However if institutions are able to address these challenges by for instance, putting in place policies and procedures on the responsible and ethical use of AI tools, using various means to detect and prevent the use of these tools to cheat or plagiarize and providing professional development and support to faculty, then they can take advantage of the immense opportunities offered by generative AI in both teaching and assessment.

As the use of generative AI becomes ubiquitous, this book *Educational Assessments in the age of Generative AI* contributes to the effort to bring generative AI to the forefront of assessing students' learning. Thus, the motivation for writing this book is to provide an avenue to share and learn from professionals, effective practices and pedagogies for designing and assessing learning in the context of teaching and learning in the era of AI. Specifically, the main objectives are to share research and pedagogies with respect to assessments in the context of generative AI, identify generative AI-enabled tools and applications for the effective assessment of learning, to share strategies and models of generative AI-based assessments and to identify promising areas and directions for future innovations in generative AI-based assessments.

The book explores how the use of generative AI tools and applications can transform and revolutionize assessment practices. The content within this publication covers such topics as, generative AI-enabled tools and applications for the effective assessment of learning, strategies and models of generative AI-based assessments, design and modifications of assessment items in the context of AI-learning, research and pedagogies with respect to assessments in the context of generative AI, generative AI and assessments for leaners with disabilities, AI-enabled assessments in face to face, online and blended learning environments, promising areas and directions for future innovations in generative AI-based assessments among others. Generative AI holds an immense potential to support all aspects of the assessment process, however this is contingent on the responsible use by both educators and learners.

This book is a valuable resource for faculty interested in generative AI, its assessment and research applications in the classroom and beyond, pre- and in-service teachers, higher education administrators and staff, policy makers, information technology support specialists, students interested in using generative AI for learning, publishing companies, tests, assessments developers, educational services agencies and organizations, and the general public.

ORGANIZATION OF THE BOOK

The book is organized into eleven chapters. A brief description of each of the chapters follows.

Chapter 1 provides a discussion of the various ways that the students of the author and researcher for this chapter use and misuse generative AI. Based on her observations the author shares two assignments and related supplemental materials that can be used to resist the unethical use of AI in writing classrooms. The chapter argues for the use of process over product pedagogy to resist, challenge, and counteract this paradigm as well as a way to respond to students' misuse of generative AI.

Chapter 2 explores how generative AI tools while enhancing learning experiences, pose significant challenges to academic integrity and higher education by fostering a false sense of achievement among students. The author highlights the ease with which students can produce passable assignments with minimal effort, thus bypassing critical thinking and deep engagement with the subject matter. The inadequacy of traditional assessments in distinguishing genuine student work from AI-generated content is critically analyzed. The authors propose assessment strategies and policy recommendations to ensure the responsible and ethical use of AI in higher education.

Chapter 3 explores the benefits of generative AI in promoting personalised learning, improving student engagement, and optimizing feedback. The chapter also raises important concerns such as algorithmic bias, data privacy concerns, and issues of fairness, particularly within the context of Africa where infrastructural disparities and digital divides remain significant barriers. The authors posit that it is critical to address these challenges to ensure that AI-driven tools are used responsibly and equitably in African educational systems.

Chapter 4 explores integrating generative AI tools in first year writing courses, proposing a dual framework for balanced AI integration and AI literacy development. The chapter addresses the challenges that come from the widespread student use of AI tools and presents new approaches to assessment design. Using a case study on thesis development, the author illustrates how AI can be used to teach foundational writing skills while developing AI literacy. The author argues for a transformation of writing instruction that prepares students by instilling both discipline specific skills and critical AI skills. The chapter concludes by discussing the implications for educational practice, curriculum redesign, instructor training, and assessment methods

Chapter 5 sheds some light on discussions on the use of generative AI in Chinese language assessment in the Hong Kong educational context. The author by critically analyzing the views on the use of generative artificial intelligence in Chinese language education and investigating the different views of the stakeholders in Chinese education expressed in Hong Kong newspapers, discusses the development of AI-adaptive Chinese language learning environments and assessments, as well as innovations, future directions and assessments in the AI era.

Chapter 6 explores the impact of AI on traditional assessment methods, particularly the take-home essay. The authors argue that the rise of AI-generated content challenges the efficacy and integrity of conventional writing assignments. The chapter calls for educators to reconsider their assessment strategies in such a way that integrates AI tools in ways that enhance critical thinking and learning outcomes. The author notes that by adapting assignments to incorporate AI-generated responses and emphasizing evaluation and synthesis, educators can maintain academic rigor and better prepare students for the evolving demands of the working world. This approach leverages the potential of AI to foster deeper engagement and understanding among students while mitigating the risks associated with AI use in education.

Chapter 7 explores the impact of generative AI on inquiry-based learning in educational assessment including enabling dynamic, individualized learning experiences that meet individual student needs. The chapter calls for teachers to harness the power of AI, to create assessments that promote critical thinking, conceptual understanding, and deeper engagement with content. The chapter provides an overview of the theoretical foundations of generative AI and its integration into educational frameworks such as constructivism and technology-enhanced learning. The chapter concludes by discussing practical applications of AI in creating dynamic assessment environments.

Chapter 8 examines the transformative potential of AI-enhanced formative assessment in higher education, focusing on fostering inspirational learning experiences. The authors explore how AI can revolutionize traditional assessment practices, enabling more personalized, efficient, and effective learning environments. The chapter then discusses benefits and challenges of implementation of AI. The authors also provide a comprehensive review of the current state of AI-enhanced formative assessment in higher education, highlighting best practices, strategies, and challenges. The chapter concludes by outlining future research directions.

Chapter 9 discusses the emergence of AI within management education, owing to its profound transformative potential in reshaping the paradigms of assessment methodology and evaluation in this area. The chapter discusses how the implementation of AI tools into management education has opened new horizons for learning and pedagogy. The chapter addresses the need for comprehensive exploration into the characteristics and significance of ChatGPT within the context of management education. The chapter offers a practical approach to addressing the prevalent challenges encountered by educators in the management education field and offers actionable guidelines for integrating AI.

Chapter 10 discusses the development and assessment of higher-order and critical thinking skills in the context of AI-enhanced learning environments. It examines the effectiveness of various AI tools and methodologies in fostering the development of complex cognitive abilities, including problem-solving, critical analysis, and decision-making. The chapter further explores the potential implications of AI on the traditional assessment of higher-order skills and discusses the challenges and opportunities that arise in its integration in educational settings.

Chapter 11 examines the perspectives and user experiences of faculty and elementary school preservice mathematics teachers using generative AI tools in solving mathematics problems. With the improved capabilities of generative AI tools and students increasingly turning to generative AI tools to aid them in completing assignments, the study calls for educators to rethink teaching and assessment. The study concludes with some recommended practices to reimagine and redesign assessments, moving away from 'shallow' assessments that can be easily completed with AI to assessments that support inquiry-based learning and the development of a deeper conceptual understanding of mathematics.

Patrick Wachira
Cleveland State University, USA

REFERENCES

Chen, L., Chen, P., & Lin, Z. (2020). Artificial intelligence in education: A review. *IEEE Access : Practical Innovations, Open Solutions*, 8, 75264–75278. DOI: 10.1109/ACCESS.2020.2988510

Cotton, D. R. E., Cotton, P. A., & Shipway, J. R. (2023). Chatting and cheating: Ensuring academic integrity in the era of ChatGPT. *Innovations in Education and Teaching International, 61*(2), 228-239. . 2023. 21901 48DOI: 10. 1080/ 14703 297

Hisan, U. K., & Amri, M. M. (2023). ChatGPT and medical education: A double-edged sword. *Journal of Pedagogy and Education Science, 2*(1), 71–89. . v2i01. 302DOI: 10.56741/jpes

Hwang, G.-J., Sung, H.-Y., Chang, S.-C., & Huang, X.-C. (2020). A fuzzy expert system-based adaptive learning approach to improving students' learning performances by considering affective and cognitive factors. *Computers and Education: Artificial.Intelligence*, 1, 100003. DOI: 10.1016/j.caeai.2020.100003

Song, N. (2024). Higher education crisis: Academic misconduct with generative AI. *Journal of Contingencies and Crisis Management*, 32(1), e12532. Advance online publication. DOI: 10.1111/1468-5973.12532

Swiecki, Z., Khosravi, H., Chen, G., Martinez-Maldonado, R., Lodge, J. M., Milligan, S., Selwyn, N., & Gašević, D. (2022). Assessment in the age of artificial intelligence. *Computers and Education: Artificial Intelligence, 3*, 100075. . caeai. 2022. 100075DOI: 10. 1016/j

Zawacki-Richter, O., Marn, V. I., Bond, M., & Gouverneur, F. (2019). Systematic review of research on artificial intelligence applications in higher education – where are the educators? *International Journal of Educational Technology in Higher Education*, 16(39), 39. Advance online publication. DOI: 10.1186/s41239-019-0171-0

Zhai, X., Chu, X., Chai, C. S., Jong, M. S. Y., Istenic, A., Spector, M., Liu, J. B., Yuan, J., & Li, Y. (2021). A review of Artificial Intelligence (AI) in education from 2010 to 2020. *Complexity*, 2021(1), 1–18. DOI: 10.1155/2021/8812542

Chapter 1
Using Process-Based Pedagogical Assessment Practices to Challenge Generative AI in the Writing Classroom

Melanie Gagich
Cleveland State University, USA

ABSTRACT

In this chapter, I begin with a contextualization of a college writing course and a brief review of scholarship related to writing pedagogy. I then provide a discussion detailing various ways that I have seen my ENG 100 students using (and misusing) generative AI. Following these observations, I share two assignments and related supplemental materials that can be used to resist the unethical use of AI in writing classrooms and that embrace process over product pedagogy. I argue for the use of process over product pedagogy to resist, challenge, and counter-act this paradigm as well as a way to respond to students' misuse of generative AI.

INTRODUCTION

In 1806, Harvard College created the Boylston Professorship of Rhetoric and Oratory, thus cementing its place in the field of writing studies and becoming the "dominant influence of the development of rhetoric [and writing] at other American colleges" (Reynolds, Dolmage, Bizzell, & Hertzberg, 2012). The 1874 entrance requirement for English composition illustrates how Harvard's approach to com-

DOI: 10.4018/979-8-3693-6351-5.ch001

position emphasized grammar, structure, and literature and became the model for many freshman composition requirements. In the time since, academic writing and rhetoric have evolved beyond their origins in a class for elite male college students, relying on pen and paper, studying grammar, mechanics, and literature. Students and instructors have grappled with the invention of the typewriter, then word processing programs, the internet, and now generative artificial intelligence (GenAI). Yet too often, new technologies have been viewed as merely assisting students toward the same outcomes, rather than challenging the paradigm that values Standard American English (SAE) over any other variations of English and/or other languages.

As a First-Year Writing (FYW) instructor at a public four-year institution for over twelve years at the time of writing, I have had the opportunity to develop composition strategies that help students respond to changing expectations and technologies. In this chapter, I focus on a four-credit course, ENG 100: Intensive College Writing, which I have been teaching since 2012. This course is composed of traditional and nontraditional students and native and non-native English speakers who have been placed into the course by either GPA, SAT/ACT scores, or placement exam. In these classes, I have witnessed many students, especially those who perceive their writing as poor or weak, enter my classroom full of writing apprehension. Often they fear that their writing will be overly edited, marked with red pen, and torn apart by their instructor. Consequently, in the past, some students have resorted to seeking assistance from friends, family members, or even online markets to produce their essays, driven by a desire for perfection that has likely been instilled in them since high school or even elementary school.

Most recently, students have been turning to GenAI tools such as ChatGPT to help them write their essays. In their timely article, Mills, Bali, and Eaton (2023) point out that in 2022 academia became aware of the ways that generative AI could help students "complete or assist in many of the kinds of tasks traditionally used for assessment" (para. 1). This raises the questions: How can instructors create assessment practices that help students resist the temptation to use AI to complete their writing? How can we help students recognize both the benefits and the pitfalls of using tools such as ChatGPT?

Using the ENG 100 classroom as the context for this chapter allows me to challenge traditional educational paradigms in higher education that privilege Standard American English (SAE) and normative discourses and that often view non-native or non-standard English languages, accents, and dialects as lesser than or as problems that need to be remedied. GenAI, with its ability to produce polished academic prose in response to traditional prompts, supports this problematic paradigm. In this chapter, I argue for the use of "process over product" pedagogy to resist, challenge, and counteract this paradigm, as well to respond to students' misuse of generative AI.

While the idea of process over product is not new in the field of writing studies (Murray, 1972), I offer it in this context as a way for any instructor who teaches, or assigns, writing to innovate and alter their assessment practices so that the focus is no longer on the final product but instead on how students got to their final text. Moving away from assessment practices that promote final products solely emphasizing SAE also provides an entryway for students to use their own languages, dialects, and experiences in academic prose (Alvarez, Wan, & Lee, 2021; CCCC, 2014), which offers opportunities for students to embrace and enact differences rather striving for homogeneous writing style and tone (Matsuda, 2006).

Further, as an instructor who has been teaching this course since the emergence of ChatGPT and its similar tools, ENG 100 provides a rich space for me to introduce and reflect on assignments meant to help students critically approach their use (or non-use) of generative AI. Embracing process over product pedagogy helps instructors teach students to resist generative AI. By emphasizing the importance of critical thinking and personal engagement in the writing process, instructors can help students embrace their own unique voices and styles, while also making them less reliant on tools such as ChatGPT that prioritize conformity to standardized norms and SAE. Process-based assessments help students recognize that meaningful learning occurs through exploration, experimentation, and reflection, rather than simply aiming for a polished final product. In this way, process-oriented approaches not only foster linguistic diversity and inclusivity but also serve as a powerful tool to resist AI in academic writing.

A Brief Review of Writing Studies Scholarship

In Donald Murray's 1972 foundational text, "Teach Writing as a Process Not Product," he questions and argues against the idea of product-driven writing and advocates process-driven approaches to writing. Additionally, he places focus and importance on the student as writer. Flower and Hayes (1981) relate to Murray's foundational work but propose a more detailed and nuanced model of the writing process. While they also advocate for a process-driven approach, they argue that writing is a hierarchical and recursive process rather than a linear one. Their "Cognitive Process Theory of Writing" introduces three key elements: "the task environment, the writer's long-term memory, and the writing processes" (Flower & Hayes, p. 277). They argue that writing involves planning, translating, and reviewing, and that these processes are interconnected and nonlinear. In contrast to Murray's stage-based model, Flower and Hayes emphasize flexibility and constant movement between these processes as writers compose.

Mike Rose's (1985) work also critiques traditional approaches to teaching writing, particularly at the university level. In his essay "The Language of Exclusion: Writing Instruction at the University," Rose challenges the language used within higher education that positions writing as a skill separate from critical thinking. He argues that this exclusionary language misrepresents the nature of writing and the challenges students face. Rose advocates for a reconceptualization of writing instruction that places writing at the center of the undergraduate curriculum. His critique aligns with later scholars like Bizzell (2006) and Berthoff (2003), who question how traditional academic discourse focuses on finding and correcting errors, rather than fostering students' voices and their ability to effect change. Other early composition and rhetoric scholars also advocated for pedagogical approaches to teaching writing that de-emphasized grammar and placed emphasis on the student-writers themselves (Elbow, 1995). While not all scholars at the time (Bartholomae, 1995) agreed with this approach to writing instruction (and we still see many proponents of grammar-based instruction, such as Stanley Fish in his 2009 New York Times article, "What Colleges Should Teach," promoting the need to go back to basic sentence-writing), writing process has become a mainstay in college writing classes across the country.

These foundational scholars helped shift writing studies from a product-centered approach to one that recognizes the complexity of writing as a cognitive and social process. Together, they advocate for a writing pedagogy that emphasizes creativity, self-discovery, and inclusivity, while pushing against traditional formalist approaches that prioritize correctness over the development of writers. This work continues in our current educational, intra- and interdisciplinary landscape.

More recently, scholars in writing studies argue for the disruption of traditional paradigms within educational contexts to provide opportunities to challenge and counteract normative discourses. Scholars such as Faltis (2014) also point out that academic language is not well-defined and does not have a universally accepted definition, but the "...belief that academic language is cognitively and inherently superior to social language has become deeply woven into the social fabric of contemporary educational thought" (p.4). Arguably, in English language and composition classrooms, native English-speaking students are seen as more equipped than their non-native English-speaking peers.[1] Extending this idea is the recognition that even within the privileged circle of native-English speakers, there is still a hierarchal system: academic English is preferred to dialectal English, "no accent" is better than strong accents, language varieties associated with whiteness are preferred to other types of racialized language, and the list goes on. One can see the predominance of the history associated not only with English's status as a colonial language but, specifically in the U.S., with English associated with the dominant status quo (white, male, and educated) (Motha, 2014). GenAI produces prose that aligns with these status quo expectations and thus reinforces this problematic hierarchy. Paradoxically, this creates an opportunity for instructors to help students resist this paradigm and to empower non-normative discourses."

What is the Writing Process? In this chapter, writing process refers broadly to Murray's (1972) three stages of writing: "prewriting, writing, and rewriting" (p. 4). According to Murray, prewriting should constitute 85% of the writing process and should focus "on the subject, spot[] an audience, choose a form which may carry his [her/their] subject to his [her/their] audience. Prewriting may include research and daydreaming, note-making and outlining, title-writing and lead-writing" (p. 4). He describes the "writing" portion as the act of creating a first draft and as the "fastest part" and "most frightening," while the last stage, rewriting, includes editing and "reconsideration of subject, form, and audience."

Writing Process and Generative AI

In a pre-printed article, Campbell (2024) briefly examines the history of writing process in composition pedagogy and articulates the recognition that prior to ChatGPT the invention and ubiquitousness of computers and writing process programs such as Microsoft Word represented a drastic shift in how students write. Campbell argues that the invention and arrival of generative AI is yet another step in the evolution of writing practices and writing instructors should rethink their approaches to writing and writing assignments. The rapid development of GenAI tools such as ChatGPT, CoPilot, Gemini, etc. are transforming the landscape of writing education and processes, eliciting both excitement and concern among educators.

The debate around whether ChatGPT represents an opportunity or a threat to education is ongoing. Rudolph, Tan, and Tan (2022) point out the feeling of panic in academia, especially when ChatGPT first debuted, and explain that "the advent of new education technology often engenders strong emotions, ranging from doomsday predictions to unbridled euphoria" (p.342). Their study showed that ChatGPT produced an essay that "lacked structure and was grammatically poor" (p.349), though they also note some benefits of ChatGPT usage, including flexibility, speed, and cost-effectiveness (among others)—all benefits that would appeal to college writing students. As Leiter et al. (2023) observe, the field of education has expressed mixed views about this innovation, with concerns about academic integrity and fears that AI could diminish students' investment in their own writing processes. Some educators argue that ChatGPT could be a valuable tool for improving student writing, while others worry that it may enable a culture of academic dishonesty and lead to a devaluation of writing skills.

In terms of writing process, the potential for generative AI to enhance or disrupt student learning is still under investigation. Researchers have long emphasized the importance of focusing on writing process, as it allows students to better understand their own writing habits and develop strategies for overcoming challenges (Kamehameha Schools, 2007). However, as Campbell (2024) points out, the ease with which students can use ChatGPT, and other similar programs and tools, to bypass this process poses a significant threat to established writing pedagogy. AI tools like ChatGPT encourage students to rely on externally generated content rather than engaging with the cognitive and reflective processes necessary for skill development.

Nevertheless, I see the integration of AI into writing instruction as an opportunity to shift focus toward more dynamic and iterative processes. As writing instructors and educators debate the role of AI in the classroom, it becomes clear that a rethinking of writing assignments and assessment methods is necessary. This chapter aims to introduce readers to the writing process pedagogical approach to teaching in college writing classrooms, share assignments that address the increasing usage of generative AI, and reflect on the benefits and challenges of implementing such assignments. In this chapter, I argue that for educators, understanding how to effectively integrate these new technologies is crucial for enhancing student learning outcomes and preparing students for a future in which AI will be a ubiquitous part of their professional and personal lives.

IMPLEMENTING ASSESSMENTS IN THE FIRST-YEAR WRITING CLASSROOM

In the following sections, I present two assignments that not only promote process but also challenge the misuse of generative AI in the college classroom. The work here is based on the author's own experiences in their ENG 100 classroom in spring 2024 and fall 2024. I chose to focus on ENG 100 because this course offers a rich context to explore the (mis)usage of generative AI, argue for assessment practices that promote process, and suggest that this approach promotes writing diversity.

Contextualizing the Course

At my university, there were approximately 9,518 undergraduate students in 2023. As reported in the university's 2023 Book of Trends, published by the Office of Institutional Research and Analysis. Of this student body, 57.1% identified as white, 16.3% as Black/African American, 8.85% as Asian, 6.33% as non-resident alien, 5% as Hispanic/Latino, 4.24% as two or more races, 4.71% as unknown, 0.2% as

American Indian/Alaskan Native, and 0.1% as Native Hawaiian or Pacific Islander (Cleveland State University, 2023).

Essentially, the first-year writing program at my university considers students in ENG 100 to be "developmental" or basic writers. ENG 100 is a four-credit-hour course that includes eleven mandatory visits to the Writing Center, but only three credits count towards graduation. The classes usually contain a diverse population of traditional and nontraditional students and native and non-native speakers. Like Mina P. Shaughnessy in her "Diving In: An Introduction to Basic Writing" (1977), I am concerned by how some students' learning needs may be labeled as "remedial" and how academic writing insists on Standard American English in the writing classroom. Shaughnessy highlights the disconnect between formal written English and students' spoken languages, particularly for those whose first language is not English, an insight that is especially relevant in ENG 100. Students in this class are often diverse not in only their languages but also in writing preparedness. While this can be a challenge, it also provides an opportunity to promote diversity by sharing experiences with language, writing, and reading.

Students Using and Misusing Generative AI

I began conducting discussions and offering assignments integrating generative AI into ENG 100 in spring of 2023. This choice came as a result of conversations with colleagues across campus, as well as reading varying opinions in publications such as the *Chronicle of Higher Education* on writing and AI, and whether AI is the "death of student writing" (Lieberman, 2024) or an opportunity for higher education to "reimagine learning in an AI world" (McMurtie, 2024). The feeling I perceived from most publications was that of fear. Conversations centered on questions such as "will AI replace writing?" and "will students use AI to cheat?" Since I knew that students have been using tools such as CourseHero to buy essays and/or have copied and pasted whole sections of Wikipedia for years, I decided to approach generative AI with an open mind. At first, it looked as though many students did not know how to use GenAI and/or were unfamiliar with its limitations or its benefits. In response to informal surveys asking students about their experiences with GenAI, many reported that they never used it, or if they did, only used it for "fun." This made me think about how to incorporate this new tool into a writing classroom in a way that helped students see its potential benefits while also recognizing its many limitations.

One of the most common and egregious mistakes I saw students making when it came to GenAI was asking it to write entire essays for them. Many writing instructors have anecdotes that include recognizing that a student used AI to cheat because their essay includes the words "although I am a machine…" or something along those lines. Beginning in spring 2023, I began to see quite a number of my

ENG 100 students using AI as a way to complete an assignment quickly, though, much to their chagrin, these essays almost always produced failing grades because the AI-generated essay did not adhere to assignment guidelines.

Other ways I saw students using AI were intriguing, and for me, less problematic. I saw several students whose first language was not English beginning with their home language, using Google Translate to help them translate their work to English, and finally using ChatGPT or other AI tools to help them edit and revise. To me, this seemed like an excellent use of the tool: the ideas were the student's, and the cognitive and critical work they were doing went above and beyond simply writing sentences, in my opinion. The issue was convincing students to tell me in some formal way if and how they were using GenAI.

I also observed many students actively avoiding any type of GenAI. They would remark that they were too scared to try to use it and did not want to use it incorrectly for fear of failing and/or being accused of plagiarism. After observing the varying responses of students who were using and not using AI, I decided to embrace this new tool and create an initial assignment that would hopefully clear the way for students to learn when and how to use this tool while also recognizing its limitations. What follows are descriptions of these assignments.

Generative AI Assignments

I created two assignments and related supplemental materials that can be used to resist the unethical use of AI in writing classrooms and that embrace process over product pedagogy. To support my argument for using process over product pedagogy, I will discuss and reflect on these two practical and revisable assignments. The first is a process-based assignment I integrated in spring 2024 (Appendix A). It asked ENG 100 students to directly engage with and critique a generative AI tool such as ChatGPT. This assignment promotes an emphasis on process in that it constitutes students' first experience with the writing process and includes multiple steps including outlining, drafting, peer review, and reflection. Figure 1 outlines the process-driven approach I used for the first essay unit (e.g., the Critique of Generative AI assignment).

Figure 1. Learning Module 1 Process-Driven Steps

Figure 1. Learning Module 1 Process-Driven Steps

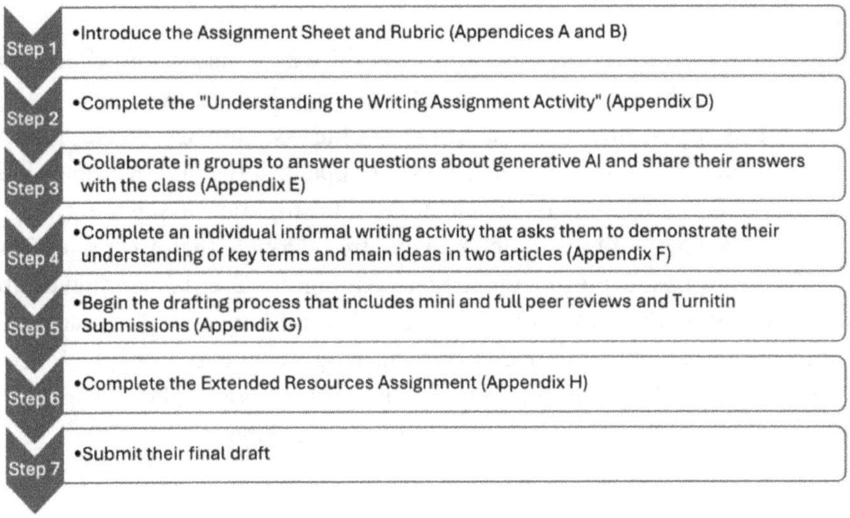

Critiquing Generative AI Assignment

As stated above, I began integrating GenAI into my ENG 100/101 curricula in spring 2023. As I describe in the case study “Creation and Implementation of Two GenAI Activities,” (Gagich, 2023) my first attempt asked students to “choose one of two articles provided” (e.g., Donald Murray’s “Teach Writing as a Process Not Product” or Anne Lamott’s essay “Shitty First Drafts”), ask ChatGPT to write a “brief summary” of the article, and then critique that summary’s accuracy, neutrality, and tone. I go on to discuss that while this assignment did help students recognize issues related to tone and accuracy, the assignment failed to achieve my goals due to how well tools such as ChatGPT are able to produce perfectly fine summaries. So I decided to broaden the scope of the assignment, and in spring 2024 I created a broader “Critiquing GenAI Output” assignment prompt.

One of the most important aspects of process-driven assignments is creating a system that students can use no matter the assignment. The Critiquing Generative AI Assignment (Appendix A) was the first assignment in my ENG 100 course, so it set the stage for all of the writing assignments to follow. During the first two weeks of the semester, classes included “getting to know you and the class” assignments such as taking surveys, completing a diagnostic, and reading about the writing process. For example, we begin the semester reading Murray’s (1972) “Teach Writing as a Process Not Product" and Lamott's (2005) "Shitty First Drafts," in addition to short chapters from our free textbook related to reading effectively. The goal was to help students begin thinking of writing as a process rather than a linear skill that can be mastered quickly.

The GenAI essay assignment began in Week 2 with a discussion of Generative AI— questions such as "what is it?" and "what experience do you have with it?" helped students begin thinking about the topic of the assignment. Students then read the Assignment Sheet (Appendix A), rubric (Appendix B), and instructor model (Appendix C). To reinforce their understanding of the topic and assignment, students completed a Jamboard (a free whiteboard app from Google that was retired in October 2024) in groups, exploring the topic of AI. Figures 2 and 3 show an example of the Jamboard work from spring 2024 and illustrate my use of "jigsawing" to help students work together to understand the assignment and concepts. Since the removal of Jamboard, I have moved this activity to a Google Slide (Appendix E) so that students still have the opportunity to engage anonymously.

Figure 2. Screenshot of ENG 100 spring 2024 Jamboard with jigsaw groups 1 and 2.

Figure 2. Screenshot of ENG 100 spring 2024 Jamboard with jigsaw groups 1 and 2.

Figure 3. Screenshot of ENG 100 spring 2024 Jamboard with jigsaw groups 3 and 4.

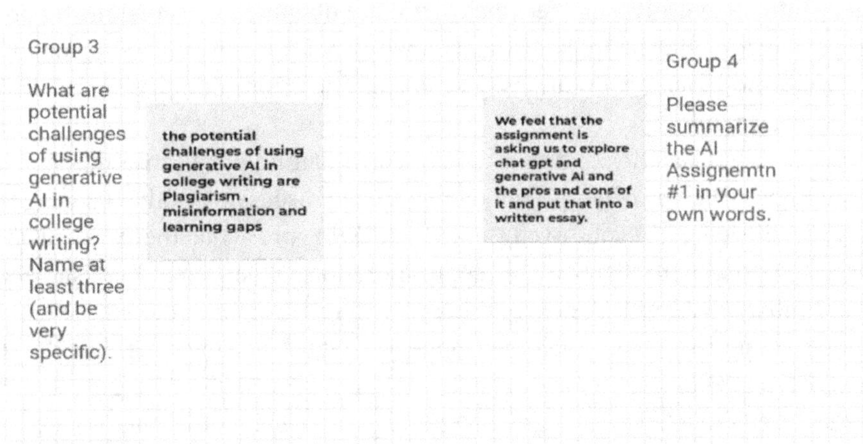

Figure 3. Screenshot of ENG 100 spring 2024 Jamboard with jigsaw groups 3 and 4.

In addition to using jigsawing, Jamboard, and now Google Slides, I also asked student to complete an "Understanding your Writing Assignment Activity" (Appendix D) from our free textbook. I required students to complete this activity for every writing assignment over the course of the semester because it asked them to scour their writing assignments to look for key components such as audience, voice, purpose, sources, and documentation. For this first writing assignment, I walked students through each question in class and discussed each answer thoroughly.

Students were also given a brief review of how to use ChatGPT, though they were able to use a different AI tool if they preferred. I did not go into much detail as they explored the tool; however, I assigned them two readings to complete, "How Do Students Feel about OpenAI's ChatGPT?" in the Wall Street Journal Opinion (2023) and "How ChatGPT Robs Students of Motivation to Think and Write for Themselves" by Naomi S. Baron (2023), before starting their drafting of the assignment. These readings were also the basis for discussions about the pros and cons of GenAI. Finally, students began drafting their essays. This took place in- and outside of class, so that students had time to write with me in the room so that I could answer questions, and I would often assign light homework such as adding one or two more paragraphs to their essays.

The assignment is not necessarily complicated or groundbreaking. Many other instructors have discovered the need to introduce GenAI into their writing classrooms and it's a fairly common practice to critique the tool. What separates my approach from others' is, first, that I use this assignment as a way to introduce students to a writing process that will now often include the use of some sort of AI, as these tools continue to evolve and become even more ubiquitous. Second, my approach here also helps students think critically about what it means to "write" in college and why some voices, conventions, grammatical structures, etc. are elevated above others in academia.

Essentially, ChatGPT and other tools like it can produce prose that emulates that of SAE, which provides yet another avenue to discuss why other languages are not so privileged. I have observed students changing prose that they worked on and that was written with their own voice, to more formal academic English because they felt that the AI was "better." Watching and responding to these moments and urging students to embrace their own languages rather than the rather bland style of ChatGPT, makes for exciting opportunities to discuss academic writing as hierarchal. Further, even though there is a growing multicultural and multilingual environment in our classrooms, the "myth of linguistic homogeneity" (Matsuda, 2006) is still prevalent in many FYW classrooms. This myth is reflected in the common image many assignments and instructors reinforce that their imagined audience/students as white and native speakers of privileged varieties of English. However, adding discussions and assignments like the one described above give students an opportunity to think about what a real audience might look like and reflect on whether GenAI can target an audience as successfully as they can.

Challenges with Integrating Generative AI Assignments

One of the major components missing in this assignment is the lack of opportunity for students to practice more refined prompt engineering. Learning how to produce a critical prompt is a valuable skill that can help students use AI tools in ways that go beyond that of a grammar checker or even essay-writer. However, I found that the placement of this assignment into my curriculum did not allow enough time to discuss and practice this important skill. I would also argue that prompt engineering requires more time than I could devote to it, in order for students to connect the critical thinking skills required for successful prompt engineering with the writing process and communicating in general.

Further, another missing component is a more nuanced and practical discussion of what AI actually is. I provide a cursory, and inexpert, review of these tools at the very beginning of the unit, but students are by no means given a comprehensive review of how generative AI tools actually work. In light of this, I hope to invite at least one expert speaker into the class to help students understand how these tools actually work and that they are not actually "thinking" or producing content. I am likely to encounter the same issue related to time with this approach, but I think it will be a worthwhile endeavor, not only to help students understand but also to create a collaborative environment.

Extending the Resources Assignment

The second assignment that showcases the writing process is an Extended Resources page (Blair Van Dam, 2024; see Appendix H). I advocate for instructors to include it as part of their assessment strategy for each writing assignment over the course of the semester. This type of assignment promotes critical usage of GenAI and also reinforces an emphasis on the writing process. This assignment asks students to include not only their Works Cited entries, which align with content they quote or paraphrase in the essay, but also all resources used, including GenAI and more traditional resources, such as the Writing Center, friends, and family. For each resource used, students must answer the following questions:

1. What resource did you use? How did you learn about the tool? How did you access it?
2. Why did you use the resource?
3. How did you use the resource? This is very important so be sure to be very specific.
4. Include any other comments you would like me to know.

This is then collected as part of the final draft of any given essay assignment. I implemented this assignment as part of each essay unit in spring 2024. As I write this chapter, students have completed three Extended Resources assignments (see Appendix J for an instructor model).

Benefits of the Extended Works Cited Assignment. In my experience, the benefit of this assignment is that it allows students to think critically about sources that they use and to reflect on all the various resources available to them. Students often forget resources that they have drawn upon as they write and asking them to share their experience builds their understanding of writing as a process and encourages a collaborative mindset. In terms of GenAI, students have the opportunity to be very open and thorough, which seems to make many of them feel less anxiety related to accidentally cheating. I also urge them to include the links to their prompts and output to further demonstrate how they are using the tool. While these are just some of the benefits I am seeing, I also discovered that there are some pitfalls and challenges.

Challenges of the Extended Works Cited Assignment. Some students seem to treat this assignment as a "throwaway" activity and/or busywork at the end of an essay. I have experienced this in the past when I asked students to write reflections because students may not understand the importance of the assignment. As such,

I urge instructors to fully integrate the Extended Resources assignment into their writing process and/or assignment sheet. This way students will see it as part of the learning process and as a space to really think about and share experiences with their resources. I also made the mistake of not making the assignment worth very many points, so placing enough grade-based incentive (while not overly alarming students) is also an important consideration.

While many of my students are becoming more comfortable sharing that they did in fact use GenAI, they still struggle to explain how they used it with integrity and ethically. Many students will honestly explain that they used the tool to, for instance, write a summary paragraph, but then they do not elaborate and explain how they made it their own, fact-checked it, etc. While I maintain that this assignment can be an important part of a process-driven approach to assessing GenAI usage, I urge instructors to consider ways to model critical reflective practices related to using GenAI as a resource.

CONCLUSION

The adoption of a process-oriented approach to writing assignments offers an important avenue for resisting the homogenizing influence of generative AI in academic writing. Classrooms in higher education continue to proliferate hegemonic pedagogies and practices that seek to "fix" students who do not conform to standardizations connected to language and writing. McLaren (2009) points out the "hidden curriculums" in classrooms whose hegemonic dynamics "shape students both through standardized learning situations, and through other agendas including rules of conduct, classroom organization, and informal pedagogical procedures used by teachers with specific groups of students" (p. 75). This hidden curriculum is still evident in many FYW classrooms and in the common focus on teaching students what are believed to be "college writing skills." These skills often privilege academic language, conventions, and forms while adhering to writing conventions that Horner and Selfe (2013) define as SLMN or "single, uniform ('standard') language and modality." This context is problematic for all students, not only those students whose heritage language may or may not be English.

By shifting the focus away from polished final products and toward the various stages of the writing process—prewriting, drafting, revising, and reflecting—students are empowered to engage more deeply with their work. In my opinion, embracing a recursive writing process allows students to begin achieving agency as writers, which in turn will help them turn away from misusing generative AI tools.

As AI technology becomes increasingly prevalent in education, it is essential for writing pedagogy to evolve in ways that prepare students to critically engage with these tools. While generative AI can offer certain advantages in brainstorming or providing surface-level assistance, it cannot replicate the depth of human creativity, critical thinking, or the emotional nuance that process-oriented writing can foster. By teaching students to value the journey of writing over the destination, we equip them with the tools to question and resist over-reliance on AI in their academic and professional lives.

REFERENCES

Alvarez, S. P., Wan, A. J., & Lee, E. (2021). Workin' languages: Who we are matters in our writing. *Writing Spaces: Readings on Writing, 4*, 1-17. https://writingspaces.org/past-volumes/workin-languages-who-we-are-matters-in-our-writing/

Aneja, G. A. (2016). (Non)native speakered: Rethinking (non)nativeness and teacher identity in TESOL teacher education. *TESOL Quarterly*, 50(3), 572–596. DOI: 10.1002/tesq.315

Baron, S. N. (19 Jan. 2023). How ChatGPT robs students of motivation to think and write for themselves. The Conversation. Retrieved from https://theconversation.com/how-chatgpt-robs-students-of-motivation-to-write-and-think-for-themselves-197875

Bartholomae, D. (1995). Writing with teachers: A conversation with Peter Elbow. *College Composition and Communication*, 46(1), 62–71. DOI: 10.58680/ccc19958754

Berthoff, A. E. (2003). Is Teaching Still Possible? Writing, Meaning, and Higher Order Reasoning. In Villanueva, V. (Ed.), *Cross-Talk in Comp Theory: A Reader* (pp. 329–343). NCTE. Print

Bizzell, P. (2006). The Intellectual Work of 'Mixed' Forms of Academic Discourses. In Vandenberg, P., Hum, S., & Clary-Lemon, J. (Eds.), *Relations, Locations, Positions: Composition Theory for Writing Teachers* (pp. 72–83). NCTE. Print

Campbell, H. S. (2023). What is human about writing?: Writing process theory and ChatGPT. *Research Square*. DOI: 10.21203/rs.3.rs-3208562/v1

Conference on College Composition and Communication. (2014). *Students right to their own languages.* Retrieved from https://prod-ncte cdn.azureedge.net/nctefiles/groups/cccc/newsrtol.pdf

Elbow, P. (1995, February). Being a writer vs. being an academic. *College Composition and Communication*, 46(1), 72–83. DOI: 10.58680/ccc19958755

Ellis, E. (2016). "I may not be a native speaker but I'm not monolingual": Reimagining all teachers linguistic identities in TESOL. *TESOL Quarterly*, 50(3), 597–630. DOI: 10.1002/tesq.314

Faltis, C. J. (2013). Demystifying and questioning the power of academic language. In Arias, M. B., & Faltis, C. J. (Eds.), *Academic language in second language learning* (pp. 3–26). Information Age Publishing.

Fish, S. (24 Aug. 2009). What should colleges teach? *New York Times*, https://archive.nytimes.com/opinionator.blogs.nytimes.com/2009/08/24/what-should-colleges-teach/

Flower, L., & Hayes, J. R. (2003). A Cognitive Process Theory of Writing. In Villanueva, V. (Ed.), *Cross-Talk in Comp Theory: A Reader* (pp. 273–297). NCTE. Print

Gagich, M. (Mar. 2023). Creation and implementation of two GenAI activities. CLE Teaching Collaborative. https://cleteaching.org/gagich-ai/

Horner, B., & Selfe, C. (2013). Translinguality/transmodality relations: Snapshots from a dialogue. Retrieved from University of Louisville website: https://louisville.edu/workingpapers/copy_of_working-papers

How do students feel about OpenAI's ChatGPT? (3 Jan. 2023). *Wall Street Journal*. Retrieved from https://www.wsj.com/articles/how-do-students-feel-about-openais-chatgpt-education-openai-exams-testing-essay-learning-plagiarism-cheating-11672780587

Lamott, A. (2005). Shitty First Drafts. In Eschholz, P., Rosa, A., & Clark, V. (Eds.), *Language Awareness: Readings for College Writers* (9th ed., pp. 93–96). Bedford/St. Martin's.

Leiter, C., ... (2023). ChatGPT: A meta-analysis after 2.5 months. arXiv preprint arXiv:2302.13795.

Lieberman, L. (7 Jun. 2024). AI and the death of student writing. *The Chronicle of Higher Education*. Retrieved from https://www.chronicle.com/article/ai-and-the-death-of-student-writing

Matsuda, P. K. (2006). The myth of linguistic homogeneity in U.S. college composition. *College English, 68*(6), 637-651. Retrieved from https://www.jstor.org/stable/pdf/25472180.pdf?refreqid=excelsior%3A6ae835ff602e9cc74091c0b833274ddbAlvarez, Wan, & Lee, 2021

McLaren, P. (2009). Critical pedagogy: A look at the major concepts. A. Darder, M. Baltodano, R.D. Torres (Eds), *The Critical Pedagogy Reader*. New York: NY: Routledge.

McMurtrie, B. (3 Oct. 2024). The future is hybrid. *The Chronicle of Higher Education*. Retrieved from https://www.chronicle.com/article/the-future-is-hybrid

Mills, A., Bali, M., & Eaton, L. (2023). How do we respond to generative AI in education? Open educational practices give us a framework for an ongoing process. *Journal of Applied Learning and Teaching*, 6(1), 16–30. https://journals.sfu.ca/jalt/index.php/jalt/article/view/843/597

Motha, S. (2014). *Race, empire, and English language teaching: Creating responsible and ethical anti-racist practice.* Teachers College Press.

Murray, D. (2003). Teach writing as a process not product. Villanueva, Victor (Ed.) *Cross-Talk in comp theory: A reader.* Urbana, IL: NCTE. 3-6.

Reynolds, N., Dolmage, J., Bizzell, P., & Herzberg, B. (2012). *A brief history of rhetoric in composition in The Bedford Bibliography for Teachers of Writing* (Reynolds, N., Dolmage, J., Bizzell, P., & Herzberg, B., Eds.).

Rose, M. (1985). The language of exclusion: Writing instruction at the university. *College English*, 47(4), 341–359. https://www.jstor.org/stable/376957?origin=JSTOR-pdf. DOI: 10.58680/ce198513275

Rudolph, J., Tan, S., & Tan, S. (2023). ChatGPT: Bullshit spewer or the end of traditional assessments in higher education? *Journal of Applied Learning & Teaching*, 6(1), 342–263. https://journals.sfu.ca/jalt/index.php/jalt/article/view/689/539

Schools, K. (2007). The writing process: An overview of research on teaching writing as a process. https://www.ksbe.edu/assets/research/collection/07_0237_.pdf

Shaughnessy, M. P. (2003). Diving. In Villanueva, V. (Ed.), *An Introduction to Basic Writing." Cross-Talk in Comp Theory: A Reader* (pp. 311–319). National Council of Teachers of English.

Thomas, A., Hodges, A., & Blair Van Dam, C. (April 2024). An abundance of "resources": Teaching digital literacy & academic integrity to help students navigate a complex information ecosystem. *Conference on College Composition and Communication*, Spokane, WA._https://drive.google.com/file/d/1XvKnbI5QJ_mnDcfq2eOiVnPICU42ed2_/view?usp=sharing

Appendix A: Assignment Sheet

AI Exploration Assignment: Critiquing Generative AI Output

Essay Genre: You are being asked to write a short critical reflective essay examining AI output. Specifically, you will analyze its accessibility, accuracy, and style/tone.

Genre Expectations: The essay must include your AI prompt (word-for-word) and the AI output (also word-for-word). Following this, your examination should include clear and edited paragraphs answering the questions below. Ideally, the essay should include an introduction, body paragraphs, a conclusion, and a Works Cited. The Works Cited should include at least one article and ChatGPT.

The Assignment: We have discussed AI and OpenAI's ChatGPT in class and you completed an activity, Project 1 Activity 2, that asked you to examine potential issues related to using these types of resources in college and, more specifically, college writing classes.

This assignment asks you to continue exploring Generative AI such as ChatGPT. You will create a prompt (on a topic of your choice) for ChatGPT (or another generative AI tool) and record its output. Using this experience, you will then answer the following questions in your essay:

Critique the Accessibility:

- Describe the experience of using and interacting with the AI tool focusing on its accessibility (or lack of).
- Was your experience similar to or different from experiences described in the articles (see below)?

Critique the Output:

- What kind of information were you looking for? Was the output useful?
- What, if anything, is inaccurate, problematic, confusing, etc. about the output?
- Is your opinion similar to or different from opinions described in the articles (see below)?

Critique the Style:

- Does the output "sound" like you? How does the tone "sound"? Do you like it?

- Is your opinion similar to or different from experiences described in the articles (see below)?

Article Options:

- "How do Students Feel about OpenAI's ChatGPT?" in the Wall Street Journal Opinion (PDF here)
- "How ChatGPT Robs Students of Motivation to Think and Write for Themselves" by Naomi S. Baron

Using These Skills Over the Course of the Semester: AI is here to stay and as such, we all (students, professors, employers, etc.) need to determine the limitations of the tool and when it is appropriate to use it.

AI Guidelines: This assignment directly asks you to engage with AI. As such, you should use and cite it. We will discuss how to cite AI in MLA during class. However, be sure to keep track of your prompts and outputs because they will need to be part of your final essay.

Table 1. Student Learning Outcome Learning Module

Student Learning Outcomes Practiced Over the Course of the Semester
Knowledge of Writing Processes • Organize assignments with the steps of the writing process in mind • Distinguish between higher- and lower- order concerns in the writing process • Model the writing process in various formal essays • Prioritize higher- and lower-order issues in the revision stage of the writing process • Compose formal academic prose in a variety of genres by utilizing the writing process Knowledge of Conventions • Choose appropriate documentation style for academic writing • Employ academic writing conventions in essays of various genres • Illustrate mastery of conventions of style, voice, correctness, and citation • Compose essays in various genres that are error-free, organized, and clear Critical Reflection • Rewrite essays based on feedback and self-reflection\ • Demonstrate effective strategies for rewriting and revision • Modify ineffective writing strategies and processes • Prioritize revision choices based on both external feedback and personal choice
Student Learning Outcomes for Learning Module 1
• *Identify* various rhetorical features of an academic text • *Recognize* bias/subjectivity in an academic text • *Restate* the major and supportive claims in an academic text • *Describe* the writing processes in various ways

Submission Guidelines

- Length: 1-3 pages double-spaced, not counting the Works Cited page
- Documentation Style: MLA
- Source Requirements: at least 2 (one article from above, and ChatGPT)
- Submission Requirement: Post an editable Google Doc to Blackboard
- Due Date: Post by 11:59 p.m. on Sunday XXX
- Required Process Work (due dates TBA):
    - o Peer response workshop

Resources:

- AI Critique Assignment Presentation

Appendix B: Rubric

Table 2. Rubric (created using ChaptGPT 4.0)

Criteria	Excellent (A)	Good (B)	Satisfactory (C)	Needs Improvement (D)	Poor (F)
MLA Formatting (5 points)	Correct MLA format throughout, including AI prompt, summary, essay, and a properly formatted Works Cited page.	Minor errors in MLA formatting, but includes AI prompt, summary, essay, and Works Cited.	Several MLA formatting errors, but all required components (AI prompt, summary, etc.) are present.	Numerous MLA formatting issues; some required components may be missing.	Significant MLA errors and missing multiple required components.
AI Generated Material (5 points)	Includes the AI prompt and accurately integrates in-text citation for the AI summary within the essay.	Includes the AI prompt with a minor issue in citing the AI summary.	Includes the AI prompt but fails to correctly cite or summarize the AI output.	AI prompt or citation missing or improperly done.	No AI prompt or citation included.
Works Cited (5 points)	Includes correct entries for both ChatGPT and the article in MLA format.	Minor errors in MLA citation for ChatGPT or the article.	Several errors in citation entries, but both sources are listed.	One of the required sources is missing or has significant errors.	Works Cited is incomplete or missing entirely.

continued on following page

Table 2. Continued

Criteria	Excellent (A)	Good (B)	Satisfactory (C)	Needs Improvement (D)	Poor (F)
Introductory Paragraph (10 points)	Engages the reader with a clear introduction to the original article, mentioning author, title, year, and publication.	Clearly introduces the article but lacks engagement or depth.	Adequately introduces the article but missing some essential details (e.g., year or publication).	Introduction is unclear or missing key information (e.g., title, author).	No clear introduction to the article provided.
Thesis Statement (5 points)	Thesis is clear, debatable, argumentative, and directly focused on the critique of the AI summary.	Thesis is present and debatable, though could be more focused or clearly related to AI critique.	Thesis is somewhat unclear or not sufficiently focused on AI critique.	Thesis is weak, lacks a clear argument, or is unrelated to the AI critique.	No clear thesis present.
Body Paragraphs (10 points)	At least three well-organized paragraphs, each with a clear topic sentence, examples, and thorough explanations.	At least three paragraphs, generally well-organized with clear examples and explanations, but may lack depth.	Three paragraphs present but organization or explanations are unclear or lack development.	Fewer than three paragraphs or significant issues in paragraph structure and coherence.	Body paragraphs are poorly structured or missing.
Conclusion (10 points)	Thoughtful conclusion, reflecting on what was learned about AI, personal views, and its broader challenges/benefits.	Strong conclusion but may not fully engage with personal reflection on AI or its broader implications.	Conclusion is present but lacks depth or fails to clearly address AI and its implications.	Weak conclusion with little reflection or focus on AI.	Conclusion is absent or does not relate to the AI critique.

Appendix C: Instructor Model with Directions

Critiquing Generative AI

ChatGPT Prompt: "Are cats better pets than dogs?"

ChatGPT Output: "The preference for cats versus dogs as pets is subjective and depends on individual preferences, lifestyle, and needs. Both cats and dogs can make wonderful companions, but they have different characteristics that may appeal to different people.

Cats are often seen as more independent and low-maintenance. They are generally more self-sufficient and can be left alone for longer periods. Cats are also known for being cleaner and requiring less attention and exercise than dogs. They are often well-suited for individuals with busier lifestyles or those who prefer a more laid-back pet.

On the other hand, dogs are known for their loyalty, companionship, and social nature. They often require more attention, exercise, and training compared to cats. Dogs can be great for people who enjoy outdoor activities, exercise, and want a pet that is highly interactive and responsive.

Ultimately, the choice between a cat and a dog as a pet depends on your personal preferences, lifestyle, and the amount of time and effort you can dedicate to a pet. Some people may find that they prefer one over the other based on their individual needs and circumstances. It's essential to consider factors such as living space, daily routine, and the level of commitment you are willing to provide when deciding which pet is better suited for you" ("Are cats better pets than dogs?").

Reflective Essay Paragraph Breakdown:

Introduction. In the introduction you should describe your experience using your AI tool and also conclude with a thesis. This section might also include a reference to one of the articles. For example, my thesis is "While I found Open AI's ChatGPT easy to use, its answer to my question was very vague and does not match my writing style."

Critique of Accessibility. The first body paragraph should describe your experience using the tool. You might consider questions like, was it easy to navigate? How accessible was it? Feel free to share your experience.

Critique of Output. The next body paragraph should critique the output. You might address whether the output is accurate, clear, vague, helpful, etc. Also feel free to fact check its work. This paragraph might also include a reference to one of the articles.

Critique of Style. The last body paragraph should critique the style and tone of the output. You might address whether you think it "sounds" like you, whether you like how it sounds, etc. This paragraph might also include a reference to one of the articles.

Conclusion. The last paragraph is your conclusion. You might consider ending with ideas about how you would or would not use AI in your college writing class.

Works Cited

"Are cats better pets than dogs?" prompt. *ChatGPT 4.0 mini*, 14 Mar. 2023 version, OpenAI, 29 Jan. 2024, chat.openai.com

Appendix D: Understanding the Writing Assignment

Students are asked to complete the following activity that is embedded in the free textbook, *A Guide to Rhetoric, Genre, and Success in First-Year Writing (the Interactive 2nd edition)*. The digital textbook was adopted by the entire First-Year Writing Program in fall 2019 and was updated to include interactive activities in fall 2024. This activity was created by H5P and added to our Pressbook, so students complete the activity, "A Guide for Understanding Your Writing Assignment" (Excelsior OWL and Zickel) in the textbook chapter, "Understanding the Writing Assignment," export their document, and submit to our LMS.

Purpose

1. What is the purpose of this assignment? What learning or knowledge are you, the student, being asked to showcase in this assignment?

Assignment Type

2. What kind of text are you being asked to produce in order to achieve the assignment's purpose?
   a. Personal text (narrative, reflection)
   b. Analytical text (closely examining a topic; "breaking it down")
   c. Argumentative text (you take a position and defend it)
   d. Research-based text (you incorporate source material to support a perspective on a topic)
   e. Report (you must report the results of an activity, experience, study, etc.)
   f. Description (you must provide a detailed explanation of a process, event, object, etc)
   g. Multimodal text (conveys information via image, sound, color, video, gesture, words, and more)

**if you are not sure, write that down! But then make sure you speak with your professor to get clarification. It is important to clarify the type of assignment with your professor!

Audience

3. Who is the audience for your text? Who will be reading your work?
   a. Formal, academic audience (professor, scholars in the field)
   b. Formal, professional audience (writing for the workplace; technical terms associated with the job are used)
   c. Informal audience (available to a broad audience)

Voice

4. Based on the assignment purpose and the audience you are writing for, what kind of voice should you adopt as the creator of this text? Why do you think this voice is appropriate for the purpose and audience?
   a. formal?
   b. informal?
   c. authoritative, knowledgeable?
   d. curious, exploratory, but maybe a little unsure?
   e. persuasive and aggressive?
   f. impartial, passive?
   g. explanatory?
   h. friendly and entertaining?

Source Materials

5. Does this assignment require you to use sources? If so:
   a. why do you need sources?
   b. how many sources do you need to use?
   c. what kind of sources do they need to be?
   d. where can you find the sources that you will need?
   e. what type of citation style do you need to use?
   f. do you need a Works Cited/Reference page?

Style

6. Does the assignment require you to use any specific style guidelines? (MLA, APA, Chicago, etc?) If so, list resources you can use to help with
   a. document formatting
   b. in-text citations
   c. reference formatting/Works Cited

Connection to Previous Compositions

7. How does this assignment sound similar to previous assignments you have done or other assignments (in other classes) that you are working on? What elements from previous writing activities or assignments can you use to complete this assignment? Make a list of what skills, resources, or knowledge you have that can inform this project:

Questions or Concerns

8. What questions do you have about this assignment at this point? (always ask your professor about questions that you have!)

Appendix E: Jigsaw Activity using Google Slides

Directions: In groups, answer the question associated with your group number There should be at least one of the following:

- Speaker, they will share your answers with the class
- Note taker, they will write the answers in the slides document
- Researcher, they oversee helping to find the necessary materials

Group 1 - What is generative AI? Please give at least two examples.

Group 2 - What are potential benefits of using generative AI in college writing? Name at least three and be very specific.

Group 3 - What are potential challenges of using generative AI in college writing? Name at least three (and be very specific).

Group 4 - Please summarize the AI Assignment in your own words.

Group 5 - Why did I assign you an AI assignment to start the semester? Do you think this is a good idea?

Appendix F: Informal Activity: Practicing Rhetorical Reading and AI Review

Table 3. Module directions

Directions
• Create a new editable Google Doc in your Google Drive (I strongly suggest creating an ENG 100/101 folder to help you stay organized). • Copy and paste the contents of this activity into your Google Doc. Title it "Project 1. Activity 2." • When you are finished, copy your editable Google Doc Link and paste it in Blackboard • Paste your content in Project-based Writing Activities Posting Areas (on the Homepage) → Project 1. Activity 2.

Part I: Rhetorical Reading

Complete a quick rhetorical reading for "How ChatGPT Robs Students of Motivation to Think and Write for Themselves" by Naomi S. Baron (be sure to refer to our textbook chapter, "How to Read Rhetorically"):

- What is the topic of the article?
- Who is the author? Is the author a credible source on this subject?
- What is the purpose of the article?
- Who is the audience? How can you tell?
- When was this originally published? Is it too old or is it still relevant?
- Where was this originally published? Does that tell you anything about the essay?
- Were there any words you did not know? What are they? Look at least one up to share.

Part II: AI Review of Terms and Readings

Please use the following resources to help you answer the questions:

- "What is ChatGPT (in about a minute)" (video)
- "How do Students Feel about OpenAI's ChatGPT?" in the Wall Street Journal Opinion (PDF here)
- "How ChatGPT Robs Students of Motivation to Think and Write for Themselves" by Naomi S. Baron
- Our AI syllabus policy

What is ChatGPT and generative AI?

Have you used generative AI? What was your experience like?

What does it mean when folks say that ChatGPT "hallucinates"? Why might this be problematic?

Part III: Applying Reading Strategies to the Articles (chart created by ChatGPT 4.0)

Table 4. Reading Strategies Activity

Categories	**Article 1: "How do Students Feel about OpenAI's ChatGPT?"**	**Article 2: "How ChatGPT Robs Students of Motivation to Think and Write for Themselves"**
Main Idea (Summarize central argument) and provide 3-4 Key Points		
Author's Perspective (Positive, Negative, Neutral)		
3-4 Key Concepts/Terms		
Questions Raised (at least one per article)		

continued on following page

Table 4. Continued

Categories	Article 1: "How do Students Feel about OpenAI's ChatGPT?"	Article 2: "How ChatGPT Robs Students of Motivation to Think and Write for Themselves"
Personal Response ((Brief reflection on article)		
Connection to Writing (How it influences your thinking)		
Differing Opinions: (Note any differences in perspectives or arguments)		
Common Themes: (List any themes shared by the articles)		
Overall Impact on Understanding AI: (Summarize how the articles collectively shape your view on AI)		

Part IV: Reflecting on AI Use

What benefits do you see related to generative AI? What are some of the challenges?

What are some of the potential ethical issues related to us generative AI?

What are some of the potential issues related to using generative AI in college writing classes?

Appendix G: Peer Review

Table 5. Mini Peer Review: Please follow the directions below

Mini Peer Review (Context Paragraph and MLA Formatting) • Choose a peer and open their draft • Answer the questions below on their draft (in comments, at the bottom) or on a separate doc)
1. Is the MLA formatting correct? (Header, Heading, Times New Roman, 12-point font, double-spaced) 2. Do they include the ChatGPT prompt? 3. Do they include the ChatGPT output? Do they have an in-text citation for the output? 4. Does the first essay paragraph include the title of the summarized article, the author's name, year, and publication? 5. Is their thesis argumentative? 6. What are their main points (should be at least three in the thesis) 7. Do they have a paragraph for each main point? 8. Do they have a conclusion wrapping up about how they feel about using ChatGPT? 9. Do they have a Works Cited page? Is the formatting correct? 10. What are they doing well? 11. What needs work?

Appendix H: Extended Resources Assignment

Extended Resources Assignment

Essay Genre: This assignment is not an essay. In fact, it is an extended resources activity, similar to a Works Cited page, but in this case, you will address every source that you use in your essay AND every resource you used to help you complete each assignment.

Genre Expectations: The genre expectations for this assignment is to use MLA to create a classic Works Cited page for each assignment that includes the relevant sources used in your essay. You will also include a list of resources that you used as well as brief descriptions of how you used them.

The Assignment: This assignment will accompany every essay that you write in the course. It will serve not only as your Works Cited page but also as a compilation of resources you used. The purpose of this assignment is to help you see how resources, both in-person and online, can help you achieve your writing goals, promote the use of the writing process, and allow you to share various ways that you solved writing-based problems (e.g., editing, revision, grammar, mechanics, etc.).

Each Extended Resource assignment will include the following:

- A Works Cited page that aligns with the specific assignment
- A list and discussion of the use (or not use) of Generative AI
- A list and discussion of any other resources which may include the following:
    - The Writing Center
    - The Academic Support Hub
    - The Michael Schwartz Library/Librarians
    - Parents/Family
    - Friends

For each resource, please answer the following questions:

5. What resource did you use? How did you learn about the tool? How did you access it?
6. Why did you use the resource?
7. How did you use the resource? This is very important so be sure to be very specific.
8. Include any other comments you would like me to know.

Using These Skills Over the Course of the Semester: As stated above, this assignment will accompany each essay you write in this course and will help you practice the writing process.

AI Guidelines: This assignment directly asks you to engage with AI. As such, you should use and cite it. We will discuss how to cite AI in MLA during class. However, be sure to keep track of your prompts and outputs because they will need to be part of your Extended Resource Assignment.

Table 6. Learning Outcomes

Student Learning Outcomes Practiced Over the Course of the Semester
Knowledge of Writing Processes • Organize assignments with the steps of the writing process in mind • Distinguish between higher- and lower- order concerns in the writing process • Model the writing process in various formal essays • Prioritize higher- and lower-order issues in the revision stage of the writing process • Compose formal academic prose in a variety of genres by utilizing the writing process
Knowledge of Conventions • Choose appropriate documentation style for academic writing • Employ academic writing conventions in essays of various genres • Illustrate mastery of conventions of style, voice, correctness, and citation • Compose essays in various genres that are error-free, organized, and clear
Critical Reflection • Rewrite essays based on feedback and self-reflection\ • Demonstrate effective strategies for rewriting and revision • Modify ineffective writing strategies and processes • Prioritize revision choices based on both external feedback and personal choice

Submission Guidelines:

- Length: your Works Cited page (depended on the assignment) and a description of each resource you used
- Documentation Style: MLA
- Submission Requirement: Post an editable Google Doc to Blackboard
- Due Date: Due with the final draft of each essay

Table 7. Extended Resources Assignment Rubric

Criteria	Excellent (A)	Good (B)	Satisfactory (C)	Needs Improvement (D)	Poor (F)
Works Cited in MLA Format	Accurate and complete Works Cited in MLA format for all relevant sources used in the essay. No errors.	Works Cited is mostly accurate, with minor MLA formatting errors.	Works Cited includes most relevant sources but contains several MLA formatting errors.	Works Cited is missing sources or has major MLA errors.	Works Cited is incomplete or not in MLA format.
Inclusion of Generative AI Use	Clearly discusses the use (or decision not to use) Generative AI. Provides specific examples and how they impacted the writing process.	Discusses the use of Generative AI, but lacks depth or specific examples.	Mentions Generative AI use, but lacks a clear explanation or detail on its impact on the writing process.	Limited discussion of Generative AI, missing key details or examples.	No mention of Generative AI or unclear discussion of its role.
Discussion of Other Resources	Provides a comprehensive list of resources (Writing Center, Librarians, Friends, etc.) and explains in detail how each was used. Reflects deeply on the purpose and impact of each resource.	Includes a list of resources used with some explanations, but lacks depth or specificity in discussing how each was used.	Lists some resources but offers minimal explanation of how they were used, or how they contributed to the writing process.	Provides an incomplete list of resources, with vague or unclear explanations of their use.	Little to no discussion of resources used or unclear how they contributed to the writing process.
Answering Reflection Questions	Thoughtfully answers all reflection questions for each resource, offering specific details on access, use, and how the resource helped solve specific writing challenges.	Answers all reflection questions, but with limited detail or specificity.	Answers most of the reflection questions but lacks depth or skips key questions.	Answers some of the questions, but provides vague or minimal responses.	Does not answer reflection questions or provides incomplete answers.
Submission Guidelines	Submitted as an editable Google Doc on time, following all submission guidelines.	Submitted as an editable Google Doc with minor issues in following submission guidelines.	Submitted late or not following all submission guidelines.	Submitted late with significant issues in submission guidelines.	Not submitted or does not meet guidelines.

Appendix J: Extended Resources Assignment Model

Work Cited

"Are cats better than dogs?" prompt. *ChapGPT 4.0 mini*, 14 Mar. 2023 version, OpenAI, 9

Sept 2024, https://chatgpt.com/c/66df29b2-0a64-8010-aa2b-d67c7951589e

Joffre, Therese. "The New Google". *The Wall Street Journal*, 3 Jan 2023, https://www.wsj.com/articles/how-do-students-feel-about-openais-chatgpt-education-openai-exams-testing-essay-learning-plagiarism-cheating-11672780587 (Joffre, para. 2)

Resources:

Writing Center. I used the Writing Center as a resource for my essay. I learned about the Writing Center during the first week of class when my professor introduced it as a helpful place for students who need assistance with writing assignments. To access it, I made an appointment online through their website, where I selected a time slot to meet with a tutor via Zoom. I used the Writing Center because I was struggling with organizing my ideas for the body paragraphs of my essay and needed help refining my thesis statement. During my session, the tutor helped me break down my ideas into clearer topic sentences and explained how to develop each point more effectively. They also reviewed my thesis, suggesting a more specific direction that tied all of my points together, making my argument more cohesive.

ChatGPT 4.0. I used ChatGPT as a resource to help me edit my essay. I first heard about it from a class discussion where we talked about using AI tools to assist in the writing process. To access it, I visited the ChatGPT website, typed in my prompt, and shared the part of my essay that needed editing. I used ChatGPT because I wanted feedback on the clarity and flow of my ideas, as well as help identifying any grammar or sentence structure issues. Specifically, I asked it to suggest improvements to a few paragraphs where I was unsure about the wording. ChatGPT provided alternative phrasing for several awkward sentences and pointed out repetitive word choices. It also highlighted areas where I could improve transitions between ideas, which helped make my essay more readable and polished.

My parents. I used my parents as a resource to help me proofread my essay. I decided to ask them for help because they both have strong writing backgrounds, and I've often turned to them for advice on school assignments. I simply printed out a copy of my essay and asked them to read through it over the weekend. I used this resource because I wanted a fresh set of eyes to catch any minor grammar mistakes or awkward phrasing that I might have missed. They went through the essay line by line, pointing out areas where I needed clearer word choices and catching some small punctuation errors I hadn't noticed. My parents also gave me feedback on the overall flow of the essay, suggesting a few ways I could reorder sentences to improve coherence.

[1] Although I find the labels "native English speaker" and "nonnative English speakers" problematic, there are often still common terms used within the existing literature. Aneja, 2016; Ellis, 2016; Motha, 2014 argue for the removal and/or revision of such labels.

Chapter 2
The False Sense of Achievement:
Navigating Academic Integrity and Assessment Challenges of GenAI

Edyta Kostanek
https://orcid.org/0000-0002-2854-2587
University College London, UK

Fujia Li
https://orcid.org/0000-0003-4060-4899
University of Exeter Business School, UK

ABSTRACT

This chapter examines the impact of Generative AI tools on higher education (HE). The authors explore how these tools, while enhancing learning experiences, pose significant challenges to academic integrity and higher education by fostering a false sense of achievement among students. The chapter delves into the complexities of using generative AI in academic settings, highlighting the ease with which students can produce passable assignments with minimal effort, thus bypassing critical thinking and deep engagement with the subject matter. It critically analyzes the inadequacy of traditional assessment methods in distinguishing genuine student work from AI-generated content. The authors discuss the implications of this reliance on AI tools for the development of essential cognitive skills and the authenticity of academic qualifications. Furthermore, the chapter proposes assessment strategies and policy recommendations to ensure the responsible and ethical use of AI in HE.

DOI: 10.4018/979-8-3693-6351-5.ch002

INTRODUCTION

The advent of generative artificial intelligence (AI) technologies, such as OpenAI's ChatGPT, has rapidly transformed various sectors, including higher education (HE). These AI tools offer remarkable assistance in enhancing the learning process by providing personalized responses, generating written content, and solving complex problems. However, they also present significant challenges to academic integrity and the authenticity of student achievements (Simms 2024; Song 2024). Generative AI tools have been integrated into many industries beyond education, significantly impacting fields such as healthcare, business, and law. In healthcare, AI systems like ChatGPT have been employed in passing medical licensing exams and aiding diagnostic processes, highlighting their increasing role in professional training (Wójcik et al., 2024). Similarly, in business, AI tools have been adopted to automate customer service interactions and generate personalized marketing content, demonstrating their efficiency in routine tasks (Aler Tubela et al., 2024). In law, AI has even been used to pass bar exams, raising concerns about how such tools might undermine the rigor of traditional assessment methods (Rodriguez-Echeverría et al., 2021). These interdisciplinary applications underscore the transformative potential of AI across different sectors, prompting a critical reassessment of its role in education.

In HE, the rise of generative AI tools poses profound challenges for maintaining academic integrity. These technologies allow students to complete assignments with minimal effort, often bypassing essential learning processes such as critical thinking, analysis, and problem-solving (Currie 2023). The increasing use of AI-generated content has made it difficult for educators to distinguish between genuine student work and AI-assisted submissions, raising concerns about the validity of academic achievements (Zeb et al., 2024). This creates what can be described as a "false sense of achievement," where students meet academic standards without fully mastering the material, undermining the core objectives of education.

As these tools become more sophisticated and accessible, educational institutions face the challenge of balancing the benefits of AI with the need to uphold academic standards. This chapter delves into these complexities, exploring the impact of AI on academic integrity, the risks of fostering a false sense of achievement, and the strategies that can be employed to address these challenges in the evolving educational landscape.

AI and Higher Education

The scholarly discourse surrounding AI in education reveals a landscape of both opportunities and challenges. For example, Chen et al., (2020) discuss the efficiencies AI brings to personalized learning experiences and content delivery, while Fowler

(2023) warns of the risks to academic integrity and originality. As AI continues to evolve, so too must the strategies employed by educational institutions to safeguard the authenticity of academic achievements and maintain the rigorous standards upon which HE is built (Tang, 2024; Widodo et al., 2023).

Artificial Intelligence (AI) has been increasingly integrated into various aspects of HE, offering numerous benefits and opportunities for improvement. Studies have highlighted the advantages of AI adoption in HE, such as improved efficiency, global learning opportunities, personalized learning experiences, enhanced content delivery, and more effective administration (Chen et al., 2020). AI technologies have the potential to revolutionize the internal structure of HE institutions by facilitating investigations into teaching methods, student learning processes, and decision-making processes (Wu et al., 2024). By implementing holistic AI strategies, institutions can enhance operational efficiency, learning quality, and research contributions, fostering innovation and adaptability in the educational environment (Aldosari, 2020; Widodo et al., 2023). Moreover, AI has the potential to enhance conceptual understanding, provide personalised instruction, facilitate social interaction, and improve assessment methods in various disciplines, including STEM fields (Mahligawati et al., 2023). Therefore, AI has significantly transformed teaching and learning approaches, shifting towards student-centred education models (Tang, 2024).

The interdisciplinary nature of HE also allows for the diverse applications of AI tools beyond writing, influencing various academic fields. GenAI, which can create content such as text, images, and code, is increasingly used in disciplines such as design, engineering, and healthcare education. These tools help students produce innovative designs efficiently, expanding creative possibilities. In engineering education, GenAI tools are being explored for their potential to transform teaching and learning by facilitating simulation, design, and data analysis, enabling students to engage with complex engineering concepts through more interactive and personalized learning experiences (Kumar et al., 2024).

In healthcare, AI tools like IBM Watson help analyse vast datasets to assist in diagnostics and treatment recommendations, thus enhancing clinical decision-making (Topol, 2019). Additionally, AI-driven virtual reality (VR) simulations provide medical students with immersive, risk-free environments where they can practice surgeries and clinical procedures, thereby improving their practical skills in controlled settings (Pottle, 2019). These interdisciplinary uses of AI demonstrate its potential to enhance creativity, automate routine tasks, and facilitate experiential learning, transforming education across multiple fields beyond traditional text-based approaches.

However, the evolving landscape of academic integrity within HE has been significantly influenced by AI tools, impacting academic practices and pedagogical approaches (Fowler, 2023). Despite the benefits AI is believed to offer in the HE context, it also poses challenges such as the potential for plagiarism, the suppression of critical thinking, and the erosion of originality in teaching, research, and scholarship (Kharti & Karki, 2023). More specifically, AI has brought new challenges to upholding academic honesty and rigour as it empowers students with unprecedented resources and automates the process of plagiarism (Fowler, 2023; Tahir & Tahir, 2023). Universities are seeing burgeoning instances of plagiarism caused by AI-generated essays, which puts academics in an ethical dilemma due to the lack of clear policies or reliable detecting tools (Tahir & Tahir, 2023).

AI-driven grade inflation is another pressing issue. The rise of generative AI tools, such as advanced language models and content generators, has revolutionised many aspects of academia. These tools offer unprecedented assistance in producing essays, solving complex problems, and generating high-quality academic content. However, this convenience has brought about a significant concern: grade inflation at universities. Grade inflation, the tendency to award higher academic grades for work that would have received lower grades in the past, has become a pervasive issue in universities worldwide (Foster, 2024).

Generative AI tools can produce text that is grammatically correct, well-structured, and rich in content. Students using these tools can submit assignments that appear more polished and sophisticated than their unaided efforts would have been. Consequently, instructors may award higher grades based on the perceived improvement in the quality of work, leading to grades inflation. The use of AI tools reduces the amount of effort required by students to achieve high grades. With AI-generated content, students can meet assignment criteria with minimal personal input, undermining the traditional measures of effort and understanding. AI-generated content is becoming increasingly sophisticated and harder to detect. Detection tools lag behind the rapid advancements in generative AI, making it challenging for educators to identify when a piece of work has been produced by AI. This leads to a scenario where students may consistently receive higher grades for AI-generated content without being caught, contributing to overall marks inflation (Johnson et al., 2023).

One of the most significant consequences of grade inflation is the erosion of academic standards. Universities are meant to be bastions of rigorous academic assessment, where grades are an accurate reflection of a student's understanding and mastery of the subject matter. When grades are inflated, this standard is compromised. Professors may feel pressured to award higher grades due to student expectations, administrative policies, or a desire to maintain positive evaluations. This results in a situation where the actual academic achievements of students are misrepresented. Over time, the credibility of the university's grading system is undermined, leading to a devaluation of its academic credentials (Karger & Stoesz, 2024).

Grade inflation also negatively affects student motivation and learning. When students receive high grades for mediocre work, they are less likely to be motivated to strive for excellence. The challenge and rigour that are essential for intellectual growth are diminished. Students may become complacent, knowing that they can achieve high grades without putting in the necessary effort. This not only hampers their academic development but also ill-prepares them for the challenges of the real world, where high performance is often required to succeed (Kim, 2023). Moreover, students who are genuinely high achievers may feel disillusioned when their exceptional efforts are not adequately distinguished from those of their peers. This can lead to a decrease in their motivation and a sense of injustice as the differentiation between levels of achievement becomes blurred.

This erosion of learning outcomes can have long-term implications for students' professional and personal growth (Henderson et al., 2023). Additionally, the reputation of institutions known for grade inflation may suffer. Prospective students and faculty may be less inclined to join a university with a reputation for inflated grades, viewing it as less rigorous and prestigious. This can have long-term effects on the institution's ability to attract high-quality students and staff, further perpetuating the cycle of declining academic standards (Thompson, 2023).

Generative AI tools can create an uneven playing field where students who use these tools have an unfair advantage over those who do not. This disparity can foster resentment and demotivate students who strive to achieve high grades through their efforts, further complicating the academic integrity landscape (Davidson, 2023). Grade inflation also exacerbates issues of inequality and fairness within the education system. Students from more privileged backgrounds often have access to resources and support systems that can help them navigate and excel in an inflated grading environment. In contrast, students from less privileged backgrounds may not have the same level of support, making it harder for them to achieve inflated grades. This can widen the gap between different socioeconomic groups, undermining efforts to create a more equitable educational landscape (Miller, 2023).

THE FALSE SENSE OF LEARNING AND ACHIEVEMENT

Generative AI tools, both free and paid versions, are increasingly being utilised by students to aid in their coursework. These tools can produce high-quality written content, solve complex problems, and generate creative works (Chung, 2023; Conde et al., 2024). Students increasingly rely on AI tools like ChatGPT to complete their assessments due to a combination of academic pressure, time constraints, and the ease of access to these technologies. Many students face high workloads and tight deadlines, leaving them with limited time to engage deeply with their coursework.

AI tools provide a convenient solution, allowing students to generate coherent, well-structured responses quickly, thereby managing multiple academic obligations. Research by Abbas et al. (2024) highlights that students often use AI to save time, particularly for tasks that require substantial writing or repetitive work.

Another significant factor driving AI usage is the growing familiarity and accessibility of these tools. Unlike complex technologies, AI chatbots are easy to use and increasingly seen as legitimate aids for tasks like drafting papers or summaries. Consuegra-Fernández et al. (2024) emphasize that many students do not view AI usage as unethical, especially when the distinction between tools like Grammarly and generative AI is unclear. A lack of institutional guidance further blurs the lines, leading students to perceive AI as a practical tool rather than one that undermines academic integrity.

Additionally, the use of AI is often motivated by a lack of engagement or perceived irrelevance of course material. Doshi and Hauser (2024) found that when students feel disconnected from their studies, they are more likely to use AI to meet academic requirements with minimal effort. For some, particularly those with language barriers, AI acts as a cognitive equalizer, helping them produce grammatically correct work (Wojcik et al., 2024). These trends are exacerbated by traditional assessment methods that focus on rote tasks rather than fostering higher-order thinking, making AI seem like a legitimate way to complete simpler assignments while focusing on more meaningful aspects of learning (Abbas et al. 2024). While AI tools can help some students save time and achieve higher grades, it also allows others who might otherwise fail to submit passable assignments. This raises significant concerns about academic integrity and the authenticity of student achievements (Currie, 2023).

Students who rely heavily on AI-generated content can easily bypass the traditional learning process. Instead of engaging deeply with the material, developing critical thinking skills, and mastering the subject matter, they can produce assignments that meet minimum passing standards with minimal effort. This situation undermines the educational process, as the expected learning outcomes are not met (Jose & Jayaron Jose, 2024). Studies have shown that such reliance on AI diminishes the development of essential cognitive skills, leading to a superficial understanding of the content (Thorp, 2023).

The implications of this reliance on AI tools are profound. Students who would normally fail their assignments, and thus would have the opportunity to resubmit or retake assessments, are now passing with the help of AI-generated content. This situation means that learning is not taking place, and students are not developing the essential skills needed for their future careers. The lack of effective detection tools for AI-generated work means that these cases often go unnoticed (Khalil & Er, 2023). Current academic integrity processes are not equipped to identify AI-assisted submissions reliably, especially when these submissions are just barely passable.

As a result, students can progress through their courses and even graduate without having acquired the necessary critical thinking, analytical skills, and subject-specific knowledge (Zeb et al., 2024).

For instance, a student might use AI tools to generate essays or solve mathematical problems, submitting work that appears competent but lacks personal understanding and critical thinking. This reliance on AI can lead to significant gaps in knowledge and skills, which become apparent when these students enter the workforce. Employers may find that graduates are ill-prepared for professional challenges, as their academic credentials do not accurately reflect their actual competencies. This issue not only diminishes the value of HE degrees but also poses significant risks in professions where precision and expertise are critical, such as engineering and healthcare (Zaharia, 2023).

The implications of this reliance on generative AI are far-reaching. Students who use AI tools to bypass traditional learning processes miss out on developing essential skills such as critical thinking, problem-solving, and the ability to apply knowledge in practical settings. This reliance on AI can lead to decreased motivation to learn, reduced memory retention, and a diminished ability to engage deeply with educational material (Bai et al., 2023). Furthermore, it creates an uneven playing field where students with access to advanced AI tools have an unfair advantage over those who do not, potentially exacerbating educational inequities (Davidson, 2023). The ethical dilemma and the need for clear policies on AI usage in education are crucial to address these challenges (Henderson, 2023).

Moreover, the psychological impact on students who rely on AI for their academic work can be detrimental. These students may develop a false sense of confidence in their abilities, believing that they have mastered the material when, in fact, they have only mastered the use of AI tools. This can lead to a rude awakening when they are faced with situations that require genuine understanding and application of knowledge, such as during exams or in real-world job scenarios (Brown & Smith, 2024). Additionally, the overreliance on AI can hinder the development of self-regulation skills, which are critical for lifelong learning and professional growth (Garcia et al., 2023).

To combat the false sense of learning and achievement fostered by AI tools, educators must emphasize the importance of the learning process over the final product. This can be achieved by incorporating more formative assessments, which focus on student progress and understanding rather than just summative assessments that evaluate the final output. By providing continuous feedback and encouraging students to reflect on their learning, educators can help students develop a deeper understanding of the material and foster intrinsic motivation (Vygotsky, 1978; Nicol & Macfarlane-Dick, 2006).

Furthermore, the role of educators must evolve to guide students in the ethical use of AI tools. This involves educating students on the limitations of AI, the importance of personal effort in learning, and the ethical implications of using AI to complete academic work. By fostering a culture of integrity and responsibility, institutions can help students understand that while AI can be a valuable aid, it should not replace their efforts and engagement with the material (Busch, 2023; Kimmerle et al., 2023).

IMPLICATIONS FOR EDUCATORS AND EMPLOYERS

In addition to the immediate academic concerns, there are broader implications for future employability. The increasing use of generative AI tools in HE poses significant challenges for employers who rely on academic credentials to assess the suitability of potential employees (Davidovitch & Eckhaus, 2020). When students graduate with a degree that does not accurately reflect their knowledge and skills, it undermines the value of academic qualifications and can lead to several problems in the workplace.

The overreliance on AI tools like ChatGPT can lead to decreased motivation to learn and reduced memory retention, ultimately hindering the development of critical thinking skills (Bai et al., 2023). Employers may find that these graduates also lack the highly valued ability to apply their knowledge in practical settings, solve real-life problems (Stăiculescu et al., 2021), and demonstrate the depth of understanding that their degrees purportedly signify due to their limited engagement with the industry beyond AI assistance. For instance, a graduate with a degree in engineering might struggle with basic technical tasks or fail to solve complex engineering problems, leading to subpar job performance and potentially costly mistakes.

Graduates who have not genuinely earned their degrees may enter the workforce ill-prepared for the challenges of their professions. Graduates who have used AI to complete their coursework without truly understanding the material may enter the workforce with significant skill gaps (Alshurafat et al., 2023), leading to increased training costs for employers. Employers may need to invest additional time and resources into training new hires who are not as competent as their qualifications suggest. This can include remedial training in fundamental skills, mentoring, and more intensive onboarding processes. For example, a tech company that hires a software developer who cannot code effectively due to reliance on AI tools during their studies might need to provide extensive training to bring the new hire up to the expected standard, resulting in increased operational costs and delayed project timelines (Johnson et al., 2023).

In professions where safety and reliability are paramount, such as healthcare or engineering, the consequences of skill deficiencies can be severe (Sharples et al., 2017). For example, a medical graduate who relied on AI for coursework may lack the diagnostic skills needed to provide safe patient care, or an engineer may be unable to perform essential technical tasks, leading to safety hazards and operational inefficiencies (Kim, 2023). In the field of healthcare, this could result in misdiagnoses or improper treatment plans, endangering patient lives and potentially leading to legal liabilities for both the practitioner and the institution (Zaharia, 2023). Moreover, the disconnection between academic qualifications and actual competencies could harm the reputation of educational institutions and diminish the value of HE degrees. Employers depend on the credibility of educational institutions to guarantee a certain level of competence in their hires. When graduates are ill-prepared, it can damage the reputation of the hiring company, especially if these employees fail to meet professional standards. For instance, a law firm hiring graduates who are unable to construct coherent legal arguments due to their reliance on AI-generated coursework could suffer reputational harm and lose clients.

Furthermore, this phenomenon may lead to a broader scepticism regarding the reliability of academic credentials. Employers might start placing less trust in degrees from institutions known to have issues with AI-related academic dishonesty, which can affect the employability of all graduates from those institutions, not just those who rely on AI. This devaluation of academic credentials can undermine the overall trust in HE systems and complicate the hiring process for employers, who may have to develop additional measures to assess the true competencies of their candidates (Davidson, 2023).

Employers may also face challenges in maintaining a cohesive and skilled workforce if employees lack fundamental skills due to their reliance on AI during their education. This can lead to increased turnover rates, lower job satisfaction, and higher operational costs as companies repeatedly invest in training and development to compensate for these deficiencies. In industries where continuous learning and adaptation are crucial, such as technology and finance, the inability of employees to independently acquire and apply new knowledge can severely impact organizational growth and innovation (Thompson, 2023).

This chapter has so far discussed the development of GenAI in the context of HE, including the various issues it brings and its impact on various stakeholders such as students, educators, and employers. In the following section, we turn to the call for assessment review to address the issues brought by GenAI discussed above.

RECOMMENDATION FOR ASSESSMENT DESIGN

Educational institutions are currently facing a complex landscape where the integration of AI tools in academic work challenges traditional notions of learning and assessment. Universities must grapple with the dual responsibilities of harnessing the benefits of AI to enhance learning while safeguarding academic integrity. Students need to understand that while AI can be a valuable tool, it should not replace their learning and personal effort (Busch, et al., 2023; Kimmerle et al., 2023). Assessments should be used to cultivate and test students' creative and critical thinking skills through methods such as presentations, multimedia content, and stealth assessments (Schön et al., 2023).

Traditional methods such as essays and problem sets are easily completed with the help of AI tools. Instead, assessments should be more analytical, focusing on problem-solving and requiring a higher degree of individualization and innovation (Xiang, 2023). By designing assessments that demand deeper engagement and original thought, educators can better differentiate between students' genuine abilities and AI-assisted outputs. To achieve this, integrating frameworks like Bloom's Taxonomy can be instrumental. By adapting Bloom's Taxonomy to emphasize higher-order cognitive skills and personal engagement, educators can harness the benefits of AI while safeguarding the authenticity of student learning. This approach not only preserves the core objectives of education but also prepares students for the complexities and challenges of the modern world. Following the discussion above, we hereby make our recommendations for HE providers based on the design principle of Authentic Assessment accompanied by interactive and/or multimedia content as the design format for assessments.

Although written assessments are easy for AI to produce, authentic assessments that are designed based on the module-specific context and content, meaningful to students, relevant to real-life problems, and with reflective elements based on experiential learning should still be the design principle of assessments as they offer students the chance to demonstrate their learning based on their experience (Wiewiora and Kowalkiewicz, 2018). This type of assessment can be the way forward as AI-generated work can be distinguished from student-written ones due to its personalised nature. This design principle we argue could be implemented throughout entire programmes or across various modules to offer students an all-rounded learning experience.

Assessments that are interactive in their format, such as oral examinations or presentations, are likely to be AI-proof because students have to articulate the learning process or the learning outcome in front of an audience and demonstrate the capability of understanding by answering questions from the assessors. Multimedia content, such as videos, posters, websites, or animation, cultivates students' multidimensional cognitive capabilities which is something AI (LLMs) in its current form cannot easily produce. If designed with the principle of authenticity, it is very likely to be AI-proof for the foreseeable future (Akbari et al., 2022; Schön et al., 2023).

One potential approach is to incorporate more cognitively challenging, open-ended, complex problem-solving tasks that cannot be easily replicated by AI tools (Rebello et al., 2011). These tasks should require students to apply their knowledge in novel ways, demonstrating their understanding and creativity. Additionally, oral examinations and presentations can be effective in assessing students' comprehension and ability to articulate their thoughts clearly (Käng et al., 2019). These methods not only challenge students to engage more deeply with the material but also make it more difficult for AI-generated content to suffice. To expand on the above, we present Table 2 which includes different types of assessments with their benefits, challenges, and how they can be adapted in the context of the evolution of generative AI.

Table 1. Analysis of assessment types in the era of Generative AI

Type of Assessment	Benefits	Challenges	Adaptation in the Context of Generative AI	Bloom's Taxonomy
Creative Projects (e.g. Video Assessments, Multimedia presentations)	• Engages multiple learning styles • Demonstrates practical skills and creativity • Allows for a more personal and engaging presentation	• Requires technical skills and access to technology • Can be time-consuming to create and assess	• Develop rubrics to assess creativity, technical skills, and content comprehension	• **Create**: Students produce original content • **Apply**: Students demonstrate practical skills in real-world contexts
Written Essays and Research Papers	• Develops critical thinking and writing skills • Allows for deep exploration of topics • Encourages synthesis and evaluation of information	• Susceptible to plagiarism and AI-generated content • Time-consuming to grade • Difficult to ensure originality	• Implement AI detection tools to identify AI-generated content • Use plagiarism detection software • Encourage the inclusion of personal reflection and experiences that are difficult for AI to replicate	• **Understand**: Students explain concepts • **Evaluate**: Students critically appraise information and provide justifications
Case Studies and Simulations	• Promotes application of theoretical knowledge • Develops problem-solving and analytical skills • Encourages critical thinking	• Risk of students using AI to generate solutions • Time-intensive to grade • Ensuring originality and depth of analysis	• Require students to present multiple solutions and justify their choices • Include oral defence as part of the assessment	• **Analyse**: Students break down complex scenarios • **Apply**: Students use knowledge in practical situations
Group Projects	• Fosters collaboration and teamwork skills • Allows for division of labour and varied perspectives • Develops project management skills	• Difficulty in assessing individual contributions • Potential for unequal participation • Risk of using AI for major parts of the project	• Incorporate peer evaluations • Require presentations and reflective components to assess understanding	• **Apply**: Students collaborate to solve problems • **Evaluate**: Peer review and feedback mechanisms assess contributions

continued on following page

Table 1. Continued

Type of Assessment	Benefits	Challenges	Adaptation in the Context of Generative AI	Bloom's Taxonomy
Viva (Oral Defence)	• Assesses real-time understanding and critical thinking • Reduces chances of AI assistance • Provides immediate feedback	• Can be stressful for students • Requires significant time for both students and examiners • Potential for examiner bias	• Record sessions for review and moderation • Incorporate structured rubrics to ensure consistency	• **Understand**: Students explain and defend their knowledge • **Evaluate**: Immediate critical appraisal of student responses
Presentations	• Develops public speaking and communication skills • Allows for creative expression • Demonstrates understanding and synthesis of information	• Requires access to presentation tools and technology • Can be anxiety inducing for students • Potential for overreliance on AI tools for creation	• Develop rubrics that focus on delivery, content, and engagement • Include Q&A sessions to assess depth of understanding	• **Create**: Students create and deliver original content • **Understand**: Students explain and synthesize information clearly
Peer Reviews, Self-Assessment, Reflections	• Students explain concepts in their own words or reflect on personal experiences. • Allows for personal reflection and evaluation of ideas • Allows to develop feedback giving skills • AI tools lack the depth of human judgment and personal reflection	• Risk of AI used for generic feedback • AI tools struggle with personal and authentic reflection, but students may still rely on AI to structure or outline reflections.	• Encourage detailed, critical engagement in peer feedback, emphasizing reasoning behind evaluation choices • Incorporate reflective prompts that require personal examples, self-assessment, or deep engagement with course content.	• **Evaluate**: Students assess and provide justifications for their own or others' work • **Analyse**: Students critically assess feedback • **Analyse**: Students break down concepts in a personalized manner • **Reflect**: Students critically engage with their learning and personal experiences
Quizzes	• Can be used to quickly assess recall of key facts or concepts.	• Risk of AI easily responding to these tasks, providing instant feedback that could misrepresent learning without deep engagement.	• Use adaptive quizzes that change based on student responses • Integrate follow-up questions that require explanation or application.	• **Remember**: Students recall factual information • **Apply**: Students demonstrate understanding through follow-up questions requiring application

One of the primary benefits of these assessments is their encouragement of higher-order thinking skills. Traditional essays often focus on students' ability to recall and synthesize information. While these are valuable skills, alternative assessments such as video projects, presentations, and group projects require students to engage in deeper cognitive processes, including analysis, evaluation, and creation. These skills are essential for deep learning and are emphasized in the revised Bloom's Taxonomy (Anderson & Krathwohl, 2001). Furthermore, alternative assessments promote the application of theoretical knowledge to real-world scenarios. This practical application is critical for developing problem-solving and critical-thinking skills, which traditional essays do not always effectively assess. For instance, case studies and simulations compel students to utilise their theoretical understanding in practical settings, thereby enhancing their ability to think critically and solve problems (Kolb, 2015).

Another significant advantage of these assessments is their reduced susceptibility to plagiarism and AI-generated content. Formats such as video projects and oral exams necessitate personal engagement and real-time responses, making it difficult for students to rely solely on AI tools. These formats often include unique, personalised elements that AI cannot easily replicate, ensuring a more authentic demonstration of student capabilities (Denny et al., 2023). Moreover, alternative assessments provide a more accurate reflection of a student's abilities. Traditional essays and individual coursework often overlook skills such as collaboration, communication, and technical proficiency. By incorporating diverse assessment methods, educators can obtain a comprehensive understanding of a student's abilities. Group projects, for example, assess collaboration and teamwork skills, while presentations evaluate public speaking and communication abilities (Brown & Race, 2012).

Increased student engagement is another key benefit of alternative assessments. Multimedia projects and interactive presentations tend to be more stimulating for students than traditional essays, providing opportunities for creativity and innovation. This engagement can enhance motivation and lead to better learning outcomes (Prince, 2004). Additionally, alternative assessments cater to diverse learning styles. Students have different strengths and preferences; some excel in written tasks, while others thrive in oral presentations or practical projects. By offering a variety of assessment types, educators can ensure that all students have the opportunity to demonstrate their strengths (Felder & Brent, 2005). These types of assessments also develop transferable skills that are directly applicable to the professional world. Creating a video project, for instance, enhances technical skills, project management, and creativity, while participating in a group project fosters teamwork and leadership abilities. These skills are invaluable in the modern workplace and are not typically developed through traditional essays (Jackson, 2010).

Moreover, assessments such as oral exams and presentations allow for immediate feedback. This real-time interaction helps students quickly identify areas for improvement and fosters a more dynamic and interactive learning environment (Nicol & Macfarlane-Dick, 2006). The adaptability of alternative assessments to technological advances is another significant advantage. AI tools can assist in the creation and evaluation of multimedia content, providing students and educators with innovative ways to enhance learning and assessment processes (Denny et al., 2023). Encouraging originality and creativity is another critical benefit of alternative assessments. Tasks that require students to create unique content, such as authentic assessments and creative projects, promote innovative thinking.

These assessments push students to develop their ideas and think outside the box, which is crucial for fostering innovation (Wiggins, 1998). In addition, alternative assessments prepare students for real-world challenges. By simulating real-life scenarios, these assessments provide students with practical experience and a better understanding of how to apply their knowledge. This preparation is essential for students' success in their professional lives (Kolb, 2015). Lastly, incorporating a variety of assessment methods ensures fairness and equity in education. This approach provides opportunities for students who may not perform well in traditional written assessments to demonstrate their understanding and skills in other ways. By offering multiple assessment formats, educators can create a more inclusive and equitable learning environment (Sadler, 1989).

These types of assessments offer a more holistic and comprehensive evaluation of student learning. They address the limitations of traditional essays and individual coursework, particularly in the context of generative AI, by promoting higher-order thinking, reducing the risk of plagiarism, and enhancing student engagement. Furthermore, these assessments develop practical and professional skills, cater to diverse learning styles, and prepare students for real-world challenges. By adopting these diverse assessment methods, educators can create a more dynamic, fair, and effective educational environment.

Another effective solution could involve the use of incremental assessments, where students are required to demonstrate progress in real time, reducing the possibility of reliance on AI tools for final submissions (Jonas, 2024). Incremental assessments can be structured in ways that allow educators to track the development of a student's work overtime, ensuring that each stage of the learning process is thoroughly evaluated. For example, universities could implement in-class assignments or oral defences of written work. In-class assignments can be designed to test a student's immediate understanding of a topic, minimizing the potential for AI tools to interfere, while oral defences require students to articulate and justify their written work in real-time. This interactive element makes it more challenging for students to rely solely on AI-generated content, as they must demonstrate their understanding and reasoning in a dynamic setting (Gamage et al. 2023).

Additionally, adopting project-based assessments that evaluate students on iterative processes can further mitigate the risks posed by AI. Projects that span an entire semester, for example, require students to submit multiple drafts, outlines, and progress reports. These drafts can be reviewed incrementally, allowing instructors to assess not only the final product but also the student's evolving understanding and engagement with the subject matter. Such iterative assessments are particularly effective for evaluating competencies like research design, implementation, and problem-solving (Consuegra-Fernández et al., 2024). This approach shifts the focus away from the final product and toward the entire learning process, ensuring that students are deeply engaged at every step of their academic journey.

Furthermore, peer reviews and collaborative assessments can also act as AI-proof mechanisms. By incorporating peer feedback into the grading process, students are required to critically evaluate the work of their peers, while simultaneously receiving critiques of their own work. This interactive process encourages accountability and reduces the reliance on AI by ensuring that students engage with the content on a deeper level. Moreover, collaborative assessments, such as group projects, require students to work together and communicate effectively—skills that cannot be outsourced to AI (Amabile, 1996; Akbari et al., 2022).

Together, these strategies emphasize the importance of personal engagement, real-time feedback, and iterative learning, all of which are essential for creating AI-resistant assessments. By designing assessments that focus on the process of learning rather than just the final product, educators can better ensure that students develop the necessary critical thinking, analytical, and problem-solving skills.

RECOMMENDATIONS FOR EDUCATIONAL POLICIES

The integration of generative AI in HE presents a complex blend of opportunities and challenges that necessitate robust policy responses. Policymakers and educational institutions are increasingly recognizing the need for clear guidelines and strategies to manage the impact of generative AI on grade inflation and educational equity. This includes developing policies that regulate the use of AI tools in academic work (Vasoya, 2023) and implementing educational programs to improve digital literacy among students (Rafi et al., 2019). By ensuring that all students have a basic understanding of how to use AI responsibly and effectively, universities can help mitigate the risks of grade inflation while still leveraging the benefits of these technologies.

Firstly, it is essential to establish clear policies regulating the use of AI tools in academic work. These policies should delineate acceptable and unacceptable uses, outline consequences for misuse, and provide illustrative examples to guide student behaviour. Clear guidelines help students understand boundaries and encourage ethical conduct. Existing frameworks, such as the IEEE Global Initiative on Ethics of Autonomous and Intelligent Systems, can offer valuable insights for developing these policies (IEEE, 2021).

Enhancing digital literacy programs is another crucial step. Institutions should integrate digital literacy education across all disciplines to ensure students understand the capabilities and limitations of AI tools, the ethical implications of their use, and the importance of academic integrity. These programs should educate students on how to use AI responsibly and effectively, reducing the risk of misuse. The European Commission's Digital Education Action Plan provides a comprehensive model for integrating digital literacy into HE (European Commission, 2020).

Investing in advanced AI detection tools is also imperative as these tools can help educators differentiate between human-generated and AI-generated content, thus preserving the integrity of assessments. Given the rapid advancement of AI, detection tools must be continuously updated and improved. Collaborative efforts between universities and tech companies could lead to the development of more sophisticated detection mechanisms. Research by Turnitin and other companies demonstrates the potential effectiveness of such tools in identifying AI-generated content (Turnitin, 2023). Moreover, there is a growing recognition that assessment design must evolve to keep pace with technological advancements. Universities are being encouraged to design assessments that are more reflective of real-world tasks and that require students to apply their knowledge in practical, meaningful ways. This approach not only helps to maintain academic standards but also ensures that graduates are better prepared for the complexities of the modern workforce.

Redesigning assessment strategies to emphasise higher order thinking skills, creativity, and practical application of knowledge is vital. Traditional assessments, such as essays, are easily susceptible to AI manipulation. In contrast, assessments like oral exams, presentations, and authentic tasks require personal engagement and original thought, making it difficult for students to rely solely on AI. Innovative assessment models, such as project-based learning and competency-based education, focus on real-world application and critical thinking, aligning well with this approach (Thomas, 2000).

Encouraging originality and creativity through policies that reward innovative thinking and unique problem-solving approaches is crucial. Institutions can implement innovation grants, competitions, and recognition programs to incentivize students to develop original work. Educators should design assignments that require students to incorporate personal experiences and perspectives, which are challenging for AI to replicate (Amabile, 1996). Strengthening academic integrity frameworks to address AI-related challenges is necessary. This includes updating honour codes to explicitly mention AI misuse, training faculty on detecting and addressing AI-generated content and establishing clear procedures for handling violations.

Educational institutions should work with AI developers to ensure that AI tools are designed with educational integrity in mind. This collaboration can involve codeveloping features that help educators identify AI-generated content and create tools that support authentic learning. Partnerships with organizations like the AI Ethics Lab can facilitate these collaborations (AI Ethics Lab, 2022). Aler Tubella and colleagues (2024) emphasize the need for HE providers across Europe to teach the responsible use of AI so that it can be used ethically. One of the recent projects that may be worth noting is the "Co-Creating AI Best Practices in Higher Education" project by Queen Mary University of London academics, which focuses on exploring and developing effective approaches to integrating artificial intelligence (AI) in HE, with a strong emphasis on co-creation, involving students, educators, and researchers to collaboratively develop best practices for AI use. A key objective was the creation of an inclusive and ethical framework for AI adoption, enhancing learning without compromising academic standards. Educators were encouraged to rethink pedagogical approaches, including AI-proof assessments and responsible teaching practices. Additionally, the project focuses on educating students about the ethical use of AI, equipping them with the necessary skills to navigate AI-assisted learning responsibly. Through workshops, discussions, and shared resources, the project promotes proactive integration of AI while addressing potential risks like plagiarism and misuse of AI tools (Queen Mary University of London, 2024).

All HE institutions should play a significant role in ensuring the safe and ethical use of AI, promoting positive applications while mitigating potential risks. Advocacy for supportive policies at national and international levels is essential. Institutions should engage with policymakers to create regulations that prevent AI misuse and promote transparency in AI development. Collaborative efforts, such as the UNESCO Recommendation on the Ethics of Artificial Intelligence, provide a framework for advocating ethical AI use globally (UNESCO, 2021).

Promoting the responsible and ethical use of AI through targeted campaigns and educational initiatives is another essential measure. Institutions should integrate discussions about AI ethics into the curriculum and provide workshops and seminars on the topic. The Responsible AI initiative by the Partnership on AI offers valuable resources and guidelines for promoting ethical AI use (Partnership on AI, 2019). Finally, continuous monitoring and evaluation of policies and strategies are crucial to ensure their effectiveness. Institutions should establish committees or task forces dedicated to overseeing the implementation of AI-related policies and making necessary adjustments. Regular assessments and feedback from students and faculty can help refine these policies and address emerging challenges (Banta & Palomba, 2014).

Addressing the challenges posed by generative AI in HE requires a multifaceted approach. Developing clear guidelines, enhancing digital literacy, implementing advanced detection tools, redesigning assessment strategies, promoting ethical AI use, encouraging originality, strengthening academic integrity frameworks, collaborating with AI developers, advocating for supportive policies, and continuously monitoring and evaluating strategies are all essential measures. These actions will help maintain the integrity and value of academic achievements while leveraging the benefits of AI to enhance learning and assessment processes.

CONCLUSION

In conclusion, this chapter argues that while generative AI tools offer substantial opportunities for enhancing educational assessments, they also pose significant risks to academic integrity and the authentic evaluation of student abilities. To address these challenges, educators and institutions must adopt innovative assessment methods that accurately reflect students' true competencies and learning outcomes. The chapter provides actionable recommendations for designing such assessments and suggests policy measures to ensure the responsible and ethical use of AI in education. By doing so, it aims to contribute to a more robust and equitable educational landscape in the age of AI.

This chapter contributes to the critical discourse on AI in education by providing an analysis of its impact on student assessments and academic integrity. By addressing these challenges, the chapter aims to ensure that academic qualifications remain a reliable measure of student competencies and readiness for professional life. This contribution is particularly relevant as educational institutions seek to balance the benefits of AI with the need to uphold academic rigour and integrity in an increasingly digital world.

REFERENCES

Abbas, M., Jam, F. A., & Khan, T. I. (2024). Is it harmful or helpful? examining the causes and consequences of generative ai usage among university students. *International Journal of Educational Technology in Higher Education*, 21(1), 10. Advance online publication. DOI: 10.1186/s41239-024-00444-7

AI Ethics Lab. (2022). AI Ethics Guidelines. Retrieved from https://aiethicslab.com

Akbari, M., Nguyen, H. M., McClelland, R., & Van Houdt, K. (2022). Design, implementation and academic perspectives on authentic assessment for applied business higher education in a top performing Asian economy. *Education + Training*, 64(1), 69–88. DOI: 10.1108/ET-04-2021-0121

Aldosari, S. A. (2020). The future of higher education in the light of artificial intelligence transformations. *International Journal of Higher Education*, 9(3), 145. DOI: 10.5430/ijhe.v9n3p145

Aler Tubella, A., Mora-Cantallops, M., & Nieves, J. C. (2024). How to teach responsible AI in higher education: Challenges and opportunities. *Ethics and Information Technology*, 26(1), 3. DOI: 10.1007/s10676-023-09733-7

Alshurafat, H., Al Shbail, M. O., Hamdan, A., Al-Dmour, A., & Ensour, W. (2023). Factors affecting accounting students' misuse of ChatGPT: An application of the fraud triangle theory. *Journal of Financial Reporting and Accounting*, 22(2), 274–288. DOI: 10.1108/JFRA-04-2023-0182

Amabile, T. M. (1996). *Creativity in context.* Westview Press.

Anderson, L. W., & Krathwohl, D. R. (2001). *A taxonomy for learning, teaching, and assessing: A revision of Bloom's taxonomy of educational objectives*. Allyn & Bacon.

Bai, L., Liu, X., & Su, J. (2023). ChatGPT: The cognitive effects on learning and memory. *Brain-X*, 1(3), e30. Advance online publication. DOI: 10.1002/brx2.30

Banta, T. W., & Palomba, C. A. (2014). *Assessment essentials: Planning, implementing, and improving assessment in higher education*. Jossey-Bass.

Brown, S., & Race, P. (2012). *Using effective assessment to promote learning.* Routledge. DOI: 10.4324/9780203079690-5

Brown, T., & Smith, J. (2024). The psychological impact of AI on student learning. *Journal of Educational Psychology*, 50(2), 210–225.

Busch, F., Hoffmann, L., Truhn, D., Palaian, S., Alomar, M., Shpati, K., Makowski, M. R., Bressem, K. K., & Adams, L. C. (2023). International pharmacy students' perceptions towards artificial intelligence in medicine—A multinational, multicentre cross-sectional study. *British Journal of Clinical Pharmacology*, 90(3), 649–661. DOI: 10.1111/bcp.15911 PMID: 37728146

Chen, L., Chen, P., & Lin, Z. (2020). Artificial intelligence in education: A review. *IEEE Access : Practical Innovations, Open Solutions*, 8, 75264–75278. DOI: 10.1109/ACCESS.2020.2988510

Chung, J. (2023). AI Luddites: Consumers penalize creative work output generated by artificial intelligence. https://doi.org/DOI: 10.21203/rs.3.rs-3444321/v1

Conde, J., Reviriego, P., Salvachúa, J., Martínez, G., Hernández, J. A., & Lombardi, F. (2024). Understanding the impact of artificial intelligence in academic writing: Metadata to the rescue. *Computer*, 57(1), 105–109. DOI: 10.1109/MC.2023.3327330

Consuegra-Fernández, M., Sanz-Aznar, J., Burguera-Serra, J. G., & Caballero-Molina, J. J. (2024). Chatgpt. *Revista de Investigación Educacional*, 42(2). Advance online publication. DOI: 10.6018/rie.565391

Currie, G. M. (2023). Academic integrity and artificial intelligence: Is ChatGPT hype, hero or heresy? In *Seminars in Nuclear Medicine*. WB Saunders., DOI: 10.1053/j.semnuclmed.2023.04.008

Davidovitch, N., & Eckhaus, E. (2020). The relationship between students' research motivation, capacity for independent work, and research outputs: Defining the good advisee using natural language processing. *Journal of Education and Learning*, 9(5), 38. DOI: 10.5539/jel.v9n5p38

Davidson, J. (2023). Equity and fairness in AI-driven education. *Journal of Social Equity in Education*, 18(2), 115–130.

Denny, P., Khosravi, H., Hellas, A., Leinonen, J., & Sarsa, S. (2023). Can we trust AI-generated educational content? comparative analysis of human and AI-generated learning resources. arXiv preprint arXiv:2306.10509.

Doshi, A. R., & Hauser, O. P. (2024). Generative AI enhances individual creativity but reduces the collective diversity of novel content. *Science Advances*, 10(28), eadn5290. Advance online publication. DOI: 10.1126/sciadv.adn5290 PMID: 38996021

European Commission. (2020). Digital Education Action Plan 2021-2027. Retrieved from https://ec.europa.eu/education/education-in-the-eu/digital-education-action-plan_en

Felder, R. M., & Brent, R. (2005). Understanding student differences. *Journal of Engineering Education*, 94(1), 57–72. DOI: 10.1002/j.2168-9830.2005.tb00829.x

Foster, G. (2024). Grading standards in higher education: Trends, Context, and Prognosis. Second Handbook of Academic Integrity, 341-359.

Fowler, D. S. (2023). AI in higher education. Journal of Ethics in Higher Education, (3), 127-143. https://doi.org/DOI: 10.26034/fr.jehe.2023.4657

Gamage, K. A. A., Dehideniya, S. C. P., Xu, Z., & Tang, X. (2023). Chatgpt and higher education assessments: More opportunities than concerns? *Journal of Applied Learning & Teaching*, 6(2). Advance online publication. DOI: 10.37074/jalt.2023.6.2.32

Garcia, R.. (2023). Self-regulation skills and AI in education. *Learning and Instruction*, 34, 112–130.

Henderson, R. R., Adams, C. A., Thomas, L., Gundersen, E., Zaidi, Z., & Hagen, M. (2023). COVID as a catalyst: A qualitative study of professional identity formation among US medical students during COVID-19. *Teaching and Learning in Medicine*, •••, 1–12. PMID: 37592855

IEEE. (2021). IEEE Global Initiative on Ethics of Autonomous and Intelligent Systems. Retrieved from https://ethicsinaction.ieee.org/

Jackson, N. (2010). *Developing creativity in higher education: An imaginative curriculum*. Routledge.

Johnson, D., Goodman, R., Patrinely, J., Stone, C., Zimmerman, E., Donald, R., & Wheless, L. (2023). Assessing the accuracy and reliability of AI-generated medical responses: an evaluation of the Chat-GPT model. *Research square*. DOI: 10.21203/rs.3.rs-2566942/v1

Jonas, M. (2024). *Mitigating use of artificial intelligence in student assignments*. University of New Hampshire.

Jose, J., & Jayaron Jose, B. (2024). Educators' academic insights on artificial intelligence: Challenges and opportunities. Electronic Journal of E-Learning, 00-00. https://doi.org/DOI: 10.34190/ejel.21.5.3272

Käng, D. B., Goico, S., Ghanbari, S., Bennallack, K., Pontes, T., O'Brien, D. H., & Hargis, J. (2019). Providing an oral examination as an authentic assessment in a large section, undergraduate diversity class. *International Journal for the Scholarship of Teaching and Learning*, 13(2). Advance online publication. DOI: 10.20429/ijsotl.2019.130210

Karger, H., & Stoesz, D. (2024). *Failing Universities: How Higher Education Became a Commodity and What We Can Do About It*. Bloomsbury Publishing. DOI: 10.5040/9781350383845

Khalil, M., & Er, E. (2023). Will ChatGPT get you caught? Rethinking of plagiarism detection. arXiv preprint arXiv: 2302.04335. DOI: 10.1007/978-3-031-34411-4_32

Khatri, B. B., & Karki, P. D. (2023). Artificial intelligence (AI) in higher education: Growing academic integrity and ethical concerns. *Nepalese Journal of Development and Rural Studies*, 20(01), 1–7. DOI: 10.3126/njdrs.v20i01.64134

Kim, H. (2023). The effects of AI on student motivation and learning. *Journal of Educational Psychology*, 45(2), 199–213.

Kimmerle, J., Timm, J., Festl-Wietek, T., Cress, U., & Herrmann-Werner, A. (2023). Medical students' attitudes toward AI in medicine and their expectations for medical education. *Journal of Medical Education and Curricular Development*, 10, 23821205231219346. Advance online publication. DOI: 10.1177/23821205231219346 PMID: 38075443

Kolb, D. A. (2015). *Experiential learning: Experience as the source of learning and development*. FT Press.

Kumar, Y., Raj, D., Rao, M., Yanambaka, V. P., & Mahajan, S. (2024). Exploring the potential of generative AI in shaping engineering education: Opportunities and challenges. *Journal of Engineering Education Transformations*, 37(2), 439–445. DOI: 10.16920/jeet/2024/v37is2/24072

Mahligawati, F., Allanas, E., Butarbutar, M. H., & Nordin, N. A. N. (2023). Artificial intelligence in physics education: A comprehensive literature review. *Journal of Physics: Conference Series*, 2596(1), 012080. DOI: 10.1088/1742-6596/2596/1/012080

Miller, A. (2023). Socioeconomic impacts of AI in education. *International Journal of Educational Development*, 25(4), 277–290.

Nicol, D. J., & Macfarlane-Dick, D. (2006). Formative assessment and self-regulated learning: A model and seven principles of good feedback practice. *Studies in Higher Education*, 31(2), 199–218. DOI: 10.1080/03075070600572090

Partnership on AI. (2019). The Responsible AI Framework. Retrieved from https://partnershiponai.org

Pottle, J. (2019). Virtual reality and the transformation of medical education. *Future Healthcare Journal*, 6(3), 181–185. DOI: 10.7861/fhj.2019-0036 PMID: 31660522

Prince, M. (2004). Does active learning work? A review of the research. *Journal of Engineering Education*, 93(3), 223–231. DOI: 10.1002/j.2168-9830.2004.tb00809.x

Queen Mary University of London. (2024). Enhancing Cross-Disciplinary Collaboration: Co-creating AI Skills Enhancement Resources. Retrieved from https://www.qmul.ac.uk/queenmaryacademy/educators/innovation-and-scholarship/innovative-pedagogies/artificial-intelligence/project-profiles/projects/co-creating-ai-best-practices-in-higher-education/

Rafi, M., JianMing, Z., & Ahmad, K. (2019). Technology integration for students' information and digital literacy education in academic libraries. *Information Discovery and Delivery*, 47(4), 203–217. DOI: 10.1108/IDD-07-2019-0049

Rebello, C. M., Siegel, M. A., Freyermuth, S. K., Witzig, S. B., & İzci, K. (2011). Development of embedded assessments for learning in biotechnology: Results and design process for dissemination. *Biochemistry and Molecular Biology Education*, 40(2), 82–88. DOI: 10.1002/bmb.20579 PMID: 22419588

Rodriguez-Echeverría, R., Gutiérrez, J. D., Conejero, J. M. & Prieto, Á. E. (2021). Analysis of ChatGPT Performance in Computer Engineering Exams. IEEE Revista Iberoamericana de Tecnologias del Aprendizaje, 19, 71-80, 2024, https://doi:DOI: 10.1109/RITA.2024.3381842

Sadler, D. R. (1989). Formative assessment and the design of instructional systems. *Instructional Science*, 18(2), 119–144. DOI: 10.1007/BF00117714

Schön, E. M., Neumann, M., Hofmann-Stölting, C., Baeza-Yates, R., & Rauschenberger, M. (2023). How are AI assistants changing higher education? *Frontiers of Computer Science*, 5, 1208550. DOI: 10.3389/fcomp.2023.1208550

Sharples, J., Oxman, A. D., Mahtani, K. R., Chalmers, I., Oliver, S., Collins, K., Austvoll-Dahlgren, A., & Hoffmann, T. (2017). Critical thinking in healthcare and education. *BMJ (Clinical Research Ed.)*, j2234, j2234. DOI: 10.1136/bmj.j2234 PMID: 28512135

Simms, R. C. (2024). Work with ChatGPT, not against. *Nurse Educator*, 49(3), 158–161. DOI: 10.1097/NNE.0000000000001634 PMID: 38502607

Song, N. (2024). Higher education crisis: Academic misconduct with generative AI. *Journal of Contingencies and Crisis Management*, 32(1), e12532. Advance online publication. DOI: 10.1111/1468-5973.12532

Stăiculescu, C., Lacatus, M. L., & Livinti, R. (2021). Employers' expectations and requirements. Case study: Employers of schools of economics and business graduates in Romania. *Proceedings of the International Conference on Business Excellence*, 15(1), 185-195. https://doi.org/DOI: 10.2478/picbe-2021-0018

Tahir, A., & Tahir, A. (2023). AI-driven advancements in ESL learner autonomy: Investigating student attitudes towards virtual assistant usability. Linguistic Forum. *Journal of Linguistics*, 5(2), 50–56.

Tang, K. H. D. (2024). Implications of artificial intelligence for teaching and learning. *Acta Pedagogia Asiana*, 3(2), 65–79. DOI: 10.53623/apga.v3i2.404

Thomas, J. W. (2000). *A review of research on project-based learning*. Autodesk Foundation.

Thompson, G. (2023). Addressing grade inflation in higher education. *Education Policy Review*, 12(3), 89–102.

Thorp, H. H. (2023). ChatGPT is fun, but not an author. *Science*, 379(6630), 313. DOI: 10.1126/science.adg7879 PMID: 36701446

Topol, E. J. (2019). High-performance medicine: The convergence of human and artificial intelligence. *Nature Medicine*, 25(1), 44–56. DOI: 10.1038/s41591-018-0300-7 PMID: 30617339

Turnitin. (2023). AI writing detection. Retrieved from https://turnitin.com

UNESCO. (2021). Recommendation on the Ethics of Artificial Intelligence. Retrieved from https://unesdoc.unesco.org/ark:/48223/pf0000377897

Vasoya, N. H. (2023). Revolutionizing nano materials processing through IoT-AI integration: Opportunities and challenges. *Journal of Materials Science Research and Reviews*, 6(3), 294–328.

Vygotsky, L. S. (1978). *Mind in society: The development of higher psychological processes*. Harvard University Press.

Widodo, Y. B., Korwa, R. U., & Nuraini, R. (2023). Artificial intelligence-based decision support system for education management in higher education. Al-Fikrah. *Jurnal Manajemen Pendidikan*, 11(2), 352. DOI: 10.31958/jaf.v11i2.12120

Wiewiora, A., & Kowalkiewicz, A. (2018). The role of authentic assessment in developing authentic leadership identity and competencies. *Assessment & Evaluation in Higher Education*, 44(3), 415–430. DOI: 10.1080/02602938.2018.1516730

Wiggins, G. (1998). *Educative assessment: Designing assessments to inform and improve student performance*. Jossey-Bass.

Wójcik, S., Rulkiewicz, A., Pruszczyk, P., Lisik, W., Poboży, M., & Domienik-Karłowicz, J. (2024). Reshaping medical education: Performance of ChatGPT on a PES medical examination. *Cardiology Journal*, 31(3), 442–450. DOI: 10.5603/cj.97517 PMID: 37830257

Wu, C., Hung, C., Shen, C., & Yu, J. (2024). Enhancing the willingness of adopting AI in education using back-propagation neural networks. *Sensors and Materials*, 36(3), 905. DOI: 10.18494/SAM4485

Xiang, J. (2023). Promoting innovation and practice of introduction to artificial intelligence course with curriculum civics as a handle. *Asian Journal of Education and Social Studies*, 41(3), 30–36. DOI: 10.9734/ajess/2023/v41i3897

Xiang, Y. (2023). Analytical assessment design in the age of AI. *Journal of Assessment and Evaluation*, 25(3), 210–230.

Zaharia, R. M. (2023). Challenges for competence-oriented education in the context of the development of artificial intelligence systems. *Amfiteatru Economic*, 26(65), 6–11. DOI: 10.24818/EA/2024/65/6

Zeb, A., Ullah, R., & Karim, R. (2024). Exploring the role of ChatGPT in higher education: Opportunities, challenges and ethical considerations. *The International Journal of Information and Learning Technology*, 41(1), 99–111. DOI: 10.1108/IJILT-04-2023-0046

Chapter 3
Educational Assessments in the Age of Generative AI:
Transforming Educational Assessment in Africa – Opportunities and Challenges of Generative AI

Kudakwashe Manokore
https://orcid.org/0009-0009-5799-6252
National University of Science and Technology, Zimbabwe

Anita Sithabisiwe Manokore
https://orcid.org/0009-0003-8785-8068
Harare Institute of Technology, Zimbabwe

Tendai Blessing Chigora
https://orcid.org/0009-0002-5272-2593
Peterhouse Boys School, Zimbabwe

ABSTRACT

Educational assessments are essential for evaluating student learning and academic achievement. Generative Artificial Intelligence (GAI), a branch of AI that generates content based on natural-language prompts, offers new possibilities in education, particularly in the areas of content design, delivery, and student support. With GAI, there is growing interest in leveraging AI-driven assessments to enhance formative and summative evaluation processes. This chapter explores the benefits of GAI in

DOI: 10.4018/979-8-3693-6351-5.ch003

promoting personalised learning, improving student engagement, and optimising feedback. While GAI holds promise in transforming educational assessments, its implementation also raises important challenges, such as algorithmic bias, data privacy concerns, and issues of fairness, particularly within the African context where infrastructural disparities and digital divides remain significant barriers. Addressing these challenges is critical to ensuring that AI-driven tools are used responsibly and equitably in African educational systems.

INTRODUCTION TO GENERATIVE AI IN EDUCATION

Educational assessment plays a crucial role in evaluating student learning, comprehension, and academic achievement. As technology advances, the potential to transform how we assess learning is increasingly being explored, with Generative Artificial Intelligence (GAI) emerging as a powerful tool in this space. This chapter examines the possibilities GAI offers for creating personalised and dynamic assessment experiences, enabling educators to gain deeper insights into student performance and enhance their teaching practices. Artificial Intelligence (AI) encompasses the design of systems that can perform tasks requiring human-like intelligence, such as problem-solving, decision-making, and adapting to new situations (Tang, 2024). AI systems are characterised by their adaptability and autonomy, traits that allow them to operate independently and learn from vast datasets to uncover patterns and insights not anticipated by human programmers (UK Parliament POST, 2024). As Ilkka (2018) highlights, adaptability, learning, and anticipatory actions are key attributes of AI systems. Within the broader AI field, GAI refers to models capable of producing various forms of content, such as text, images, audio, and video, based on learned statistical patterns or user prompts (Perkins, 2024). According to UNESCO (2023), GAI automatically generates content in response to prompts within natural-language conversational interfaces. This adaptability is what makes GAI particularly promising in educational settings, where personalised content and real-time feedback can significantly enhance learning (Centre for Learning, Teaching, and Development, 2024).

In education, AI has found applications across multiple domains, ranging from content creation and delivery to student support and assessment (Tahir et al., 2024). The use of AI can provide new insights into how students learn and potentially transform assessment practices. AI tools can offer tailored support for students, providing a judgment-free environment where learners receive real-time feedback and actionable suggestions to improve performance (Tahir et al., 2024). This chapter focuses on how GAI can impact educational assessment, both formative and summative, by offering real-time insights and personalised feedback, ultimately enhancing learning outcomes. GAI has potential applications in nearly every educational setting, from large lecture halls to seminars and labs. For instance, lecturers can use GAI to develop course materials, generate exercises, and design projects, while students can leverage it to enhance their research, writing, programming, and creative endeavours. In assessment, AI-based systems such as intelligent tutoring systems (ITS), automated scoring tools, and adaptive testing platforms are already improving the way we measure and evaluate student performance (Fanning, 2023). GAI offers even greater potential by aligning with both formative and summative assessment approaches. Formative assessments aim to provide learners with ongoing feedback to improve learning, while summative assessments evaluate and certify learning achievements (Tuomi et al., 2023). GAI, by offering real-time, tailored feedback and adaptive learning experiences, enhances formative assessments, making them more effective. However, while GAI holds promise, the degree to which its impact is felt varies across disciplines, particularly those requiring complex human judgment (Perkins, 2024). Nonetheless, by facilitating active learning and ongoing assessment, GAI has the potential to transform educational evaluation processes.

In this chapter, we delve into the fundamentals of GAI and its emerging applications in education, with a special focus on how it can enhance both formative and summative assessment for Africa. We explore the unique opportunities that GAI presents in addressing educational disparities across the continent, such as improving access to personalised learning and assessments in underserved regions, while also considering the challenges related to infrastructure, equity, and local context. This African perspective emphasises the potential for GAI to transform educational assessment systems in ways that support the continent's diverse educational needs.

Benefits of Generative AI in Educational Assessments

GAI offers several advantages in the realm of educational assessments, ranging from personalisation of learning to improved engagement and learning outcomes. Its transformative potential in education has been recognised by institutions like The Alan Turing Institute (2023), which highlighted its role in administrative tasks, language education, support for neurodivergent students, and enhancing learners' understanding of AI technologies. According to Tahir et al. (2024), AI in education benefits learners, tutors, and educational institutions by increasing flexibility, learning outcomes, and efficiency. In the context of Africa, the benefits of GAI are particularly pronounced, as educational systems across the continent face unique challenges. GAI can help address these issues by offering;

Personalised Learning

GAI tools, such as ChatGPT or Microsoft Bing, can provide tailored feedback on students' work. This ability to customise learning materials and assessments based on individual student profiles, strengths, and weaknesses has been emphasised by several researchers. For example, UNESCO (2019) and Owan et al. (2023) observed that AI could create personalised learning plans, while Luckin and Cukurova (2019) noted that adaptive learning algorithms adjust course content to suit each student's learning style. As highlighted by Tang (2024), formative assessments enhanced by GAI provide real-time feedback to students and lecturers, improving motivation and learning efficiency. This personalisation fosters better learning outcomes and more efficient use of educational resources (Gao et al., 2020).

Engaging Learning Environments

GAI can also enhance student engagement through interactive learning environments. By generating virtual avatars, simulations, and intelligent tutoring systems, GAI can create real-time, adaptive learning experiences. Such tools offer immersive, experiential learning that fosters deeper comprehension of concepts (Luckin and Cukurova, 2019). Deng et al. (2020) highlighted that this approach can create dynamic, engaging classrooms that maintain student interest and participation.

Automated Grading and Feedback

GAI can also assist lecturers by grading assignments and providing constructive feedback (UNESCO, 2019). For instance, The Alan Turing Institute (2023) proposed that GAI could evaluate not only multiple-choice examinations but also essays. Automating this process can save lecturers valuable time and provide students with immediate feedback. Owan et al. (2023) argued that GAI-driven grading promotes objectivity and consistency in assessment, while Kars (2023) posited that AI-driven discussions help students enhance critical thinking and argumentation skills. However, The Alan Turing Institute (2023) warned that AI systems may perpetuate biases present in the training data, potentially disadvantaging underrepresented perspectives.

GAI in Examination Setting and Remote Assessments

GAI's potential to automate examination setting, grading, and even invigilation is another promising application. UK Parliament POST (2024) explored the use of AI in various aspects of assessment, from designing examinations to grading coursework. Automated grading can ensure consistency, objectivity, and uniformity, providing standardised comparisons between students, institutions, and even across countries (Kars, 2023).

Challenges and Considerations in AI-Enhanced Educational Assessments

While GAI offers several promising advantages in educational assessments, there are significant challenges that must be addressed to fully realise its potential (Sibal, et al 2021). These challenges span technical, ethical, and pedagogical concerns, each with profound implications for students, educators, and educational institutions.

1. *Data Privacy and Security* One of the foremost concerns is data privacy. AI systems require large amounts of data, including sensitive information about students and educators. Without proper protections, there is a risk of data misuse or breaches, which could expose personal information. The Alan Turing Institute (2023) emphasises the importance of establishing strong security measures to safeguard sensitive data, especially when commercial GAI tools are used in educational settings.

2. *Algorithm Bias and Fairness* AI algorithms can inherit biases present in the data they are trained on, which can lead to unfair and inaccurate assessments. This issue is particularly concerning when GAI is used in grading or generating personalised learning plans. For instance, if a GAI tool was trained on data that reflects societal biases related to race, gender, or socioeconomic status, it could unintentionally perpetuate those biases in its assessments. Ensuring that AI systems are designed to be inclusive and fair is crucial to avoid disadvantaging certain student populations (Kars, 2023; The Alan Turing Institute, 2023).

3. *Impact on Traditional Pedagogy* The introduction of GAI in education poses significant implications for traditional teaching and assessment methods. Overreliance on AI could undermine the development of critical thinking, creativity, and interpersonal skills in students. Tahir et al. (2024) warn that excessive dependence on AI may limit students' critical thinking abilities, while the UK Parliament POST (2024) highlighted concerns about the de-skilling of teachers. Educators may rely too heavily on AI for lesson planning or grading, leading to a more generalised and less personal approach to education.

4. Risk of Technology-Enabled Cheating and Plagiarism GAI tools offer students new ways to cheat or pass off assignments as their own. The blurred line between machine-generated content and human-authored work creates challenges for educators in determining the authenticity of student submissions particularly the formative assessments. As noted by Cornell University (2023), this issue threatens the integrity of assessments, especially when students use AI tools without proper citation or fail to engage with the material themselves.

5. Social and Pedagogical Implications The shift towards AI-powered assessment tools raises concerns about the loss of meaningful human interaction in education. Human teachers provide emotional and social support that AI cannot replicate. Owan et al. (2023) argue that removing the human element from assessments may detract from the learning experience, as lecturers may miss important cues that indicate a student's emotional or social well-being.

6. Transparency and Accountability in AI Decision-Making AI systems' lack of transparency poses another challenge. While human examiners can offer detailed feedback and justification for their decisions, AI systems typically make decisions through less transparent processes. This can lead to distrust or scepticism from both students and educators. In other words, the opacity of its decision-making processes. Many AI algorithms function as "black boxes," making it difficult for lecturers to understand how assessment decisions are made. Several researchers have highlighted that GAI is not yet fully capable of evaluating critical skills such as creativity, leadership, empathy, and communication. Cornell University (2023) advised against relying on AI for major assessments like national examinations, citing fairness and validity concerns. Jain and Jain (2019) also noted that AI currently struggles with nuanced skills, such as problem-solving and collaboration. Additionally, UK Parliament POST (2024) warned that AI grading systems could perpetuate the biases present in their training data, potentially narrowing the range of acceptable answers. This lack of transparency complicates the evaluation of the fairness and accuracy of AI-generated assessments (Owan et al., 2023). Human assessors, in contrast, can provide transparent reasoning for their grading decisions, which is often lacking in AI-based assessments. Ensuring that AI systems are interpretable and accountable is essential for maintaining trust in AI-powered education tools.

7. Digital Divide and Inequitable Access The integration of AI in education may exacerbate existing inequalities. Access to advanced AI tools can vary significantly among students and institutions, with wealthier students and schools potentially benefiting more than those with fewer resources. This digital divide risks creating further disparities in educational outcomes, particularly in the Global South, where technological infrastructure may be limited (Tahir et al., 2024).

8. Costs and Integration with Existing Systems Implementing AI systems in education requires significant financial investment in new technologies and infrastructure. Owan et al. (2023) emphasise the cost challenges faced by many educational institutions, which may not have the resources to adopt AI-powered assessment tools. Additionally, integrating AI with existing assessment processes can be difficult, as educators must ensure that new technologies work seamlessly with traditional systems.

9. Ethical Considerations and Intellectual Property AI-generated content raises complex issues around authorship and IP. With GAI tools increasingly contributing to the creation of educational materials, questions arise about who owns the rights to AI-assisted creations (Kars, 2023). Furthermore, there are concerns about the ethical implications of using AI in assessments, particularly regarding the potential for infringing students' rights and violating copyright laws (The Alan Turing Institute, 2023). Additionally, ethical concerns about AI perpetuating existing inequalities in education remain a major point of contention. UK Parliament POST (2024) raised concerns about the potential for AI to disadvantage students whose ideas fall outside the norms captured in AI training data.

10. Lack of Training and Technical Expertise A major hurdle in the adoption of AI in educational assessments is the limited understanding of AI technology among educators. Many lecturers may lack the technical expertise needed to effectively use AI tools and interpret their results. Owan et al. (2023) suggest that without proper training, educators may struggle to use AI tools accurately, leading to flawed assessments.

11. AI's Limitations in Assessing Complex Skills GAI tools are well-suited for tasks like grading multiple-choice questions, but they may struggle with assessing higher-order cognitive abilities, such as creativity, problem-solving, and critical thinking. These complex skills require a nuanced understanding that AI systems currently lack. As Tahir et al. (2024) pointed out, while AI can assist with certain types of assessments, it cannot fully replace the judgment and insights of human educators, especially when assessing affective and psychomotor skills.

12. Student Motivation and Engagement The use of GAI in assessments also raises concerns about student motivation. If students become overly reliant on AI-generated feedback or solutions, they may lose the intrinsic motivation to engage with learning materials and develop independent problem-solving skills. Educators need to find a balance between leveraging AI's benefits and encouraging active student participation in the learning process (Cornell University, 2023).

Ethical Implications of AI-Driven Assessments

The integration of AI-driven assessments into education presents both significant potential benefits and ethical concerns. On one hand, GAI has the capacity to enhance learning experiences, individualise education, and prepare students for future job markets (Sibal et al., 2021). However, its application in educational assessments raises critical ethical issues, including fairness, transparency, bias, privacy, intellectual property (IP), and accountability.

Fairness and Bias

AI systems, while powerful, are susceptible to algorithmic bias, which can lead to inequitable outcomes in education. Biases in the training data, reflecting historical and societal inequities, can be perpetuated or even amplified by AI models, creating concerns about fairness (Sibal et al., 2021). This could disproportionately affect students from underrepresented or marginalised groups, exacerbating existing inequalities in educational outcomes. Ensuring that AI-driven assessments do not disadvantage these students is an essential ethical responsibility for developers and educators.

Transparency and Explainability

A major ethical issue surrounding AI models, particularly those utilising artificial neural networks (ANNs), is their lack of transparency. These models, often described as "black boxes," make decisions in ways that are difficult to interpret, making it challenging for educators and students to understand how outcomes, such as grades or feedback are determined. This lack of explainability can prevent students from improving their learning, as they may not fully grasp why they received certain results (UNESCO, 2023). Without a clear understanding of the AI's decision-making process, addressing errors or misconceptions becomes nearly impossible, limiting the educational value of these assessments.

Privacy and Data Security

The use of AI in educational assessments requires vast amounts of student data, which often includes sensitive information. There are widespread concerns about how this data is collected, stored, and utilised by AI systems, particularly with regard to potential privacy violations (Sibal et al., 2021). In Europe, privacy is a critical political priority, as outlined by regulations such as the General Data Protection Regulation (GDPR). Strict data governance frameworks are necessary to protect student data from being improperly used or shared without consent (Tuomi et al., 2023). Educational institutions must be vigilant in safeguarding personal data to ensure that AI-driven assessments do not compromise student privacy.

Intellectual Property Rights

The application of GAI in education also raises concerns about intellectual property rights. Original content produced by students, educators, or institutions could be integrated into AI models and used without proper attribution, threatening the ownership of educational materials, research, and proprietary information. For example, student assignments or institutional research data could inadvertently become part of the training data used by AI systems (UNESCO, 2023). Institutions must establish clear policies to protect the intellectual property of their community and prevent unauthorised use of their data by GAI systems.

Guardrails and Ethical Safeguards

AI-generated content frequently draws from vast online sources, which may include offensive or biased material. Although developers have implemented "guardrails" to prevent the generation of harmful or unethical content, these safeguards are not foolproof. Without strict regulations and effective monitoring, biased materials may still be produced, contaminating educational content and influencing learners (UNESCO, 2023b). Educators must actively educate students about the limitations and risks of AI-generated content, promoting critical thinking and ensuring that students validate AI-generated information rather than accepting it at face value.

The Role of Stakeholders

Addressing the ethical implications of AI-driven assessments requires collaboration among educators, developers, and policymakers. Clear guidelines on the appropriate use of AI in educational settings are essential to ensure transparency, fairness, and accountability. When AI tools are deployed in classrooms, students should be informed about how these systems work, their limitations, and what constitutes appropriate use. Educators have a responsibility to teach students how to critically evaluate AI outputs and understand the implications of over-reliance on such tools (Cornell University, 2023).

Preventing AI Misuse

There is also a risk that students may misuse AI tools in assessments, relying on them to complete assignments without engaging in critical thinking or developing foundational skills. Institutions must establish policies that regulate the use of AI in assignments and examinations to ensure that learning remains the primary objective. Some experts suggest designing specialised assessments that cannot be easily completed using AI tools, thereby maintaining academic integrity and preventing students from exploiting AI to bypass essential learning processes (UK Parliament POST, 2024).

The ethical implications of AI-driven assessments are broad and complex, encompassing issues of fairness, transparency, privacy, and intellectual property. As GAI becomes increasingly integrated into educational systems in Africa, it is essential for stakeholders to adopt a proactive approach to mitigating these risks. Establishing clear ethical frameworks that reflect the unique cultural and social contexts of African nations is crucial. By promoting transparency and ensuring robust governance, educators, policymakers, and developers can harness the benefits of AI in education while safeguarding student rights and promoting equitable outcomes. This is particularly important in Africa, where educational disparities exist and diverse populations require tailored approaches to ensure that technology serves to enhance learning without exacerbating inequalities.

Case Studies and Examples of AI-Driven Assessment Tools

AI-driven assessment tools are increasingly being deployed in educational systems worldwide, showcasing both the promise of AI in enhancing learning and the practical challenges involved in implementation. Below are some case studies from different regions that highlight the benefits and limitations of these technologies in action.

China: AI-Powered Education Platforms

China has been at the forefront of adopting AI technologies in education, driven by its robust internet infrastructure and extensive data generation. Platforms such as Yuanfudao and Zuoyebang are examples of how AI is applied to personalised learning and assessment. These platforms process large datasets, including behavioural and question data, to create personalised learning performance analysis reports. This approach helps students identify their strengths and weaknesses based on past examination questions, generating tailored learning plans through recommendation algorithms. These algorithms can even create strategies for students aiming for top universities in China (Tang, 2024). Benefits include tailored learning experiences; personalised assessments; data-driven insights into student performance. However, heavy reliance on large datasets raises concerns about privacy, and the scalability of such platforms may not extend beyond technologically advanced regions like China.

USA: Adaptive Learning with AI

In the United States, platforms like DreamBox and Knewton are pioneering AI-powered adaptive learning software. These tools use data analysis to assess students' learning patterns and create personalised learning plans based on their unique strengths and weaknesses. As students engage with the platform, it dynamically adjusts the difficulty of questions and exercises, ensuring that each learner progresses at their own pace. Benefits embrace individualised learning and assessment paths; more efficient use of class time as lecturers can focus on students needing additional support. Nonetheless, these systems tend to focus on cognitive skills and may not effectively assess higher-order thinking, creativity, or problem-solving abilities (Owan et al., 2023).

UK: AI in Assessment and Feedback

In the UK, Turnitin, a well-known tool for plagiarism detection, has been enhanced with AI capabilities to offer more in-depth analysis of student submissions. It now includes features such as similarity checking, ensuring that students are not plagiarising content from other sources. The use of AI allows quicker turnaround times for grading and more detailed feedback, offering students opportunities to learn from their mistakes in real-time. The UK has also seen significant governmental investments in AI-powered tools for education. For instance, in 2023, the Department for Education released a report on GAI and committed up to £2 million to fund new AI resources for teachers (UK Parliament POST, 2024). Benefits in assessment include enhanced efficiency in marking; real-time, personalised feedback; potential for scalable use across many subjects. However, AI-generated feedback may lack the nuance and empathy of human teachers, and the issue of bias in AI systems persists, especially regarding the evaluation of subjective tasks like essays.

Singapore: Integration of AI into National Education Systems

Singapore has invested heavily in integrating AI into its educational framework, particularly in formative assessment and student monitoring. Schools are utilising AI to track students' progress and alert teachers to potential issues, such as underperformance or disengagement, enabling early interventions. AI tools help educators understand students' learning behaviours and adapt lessons accordingly. The benefits are realised on proactive support for students at risk of falling behind, and personalised learning experiences tailored to individual needs.

Limitations have to do with over-reliance on AI for monitoring thereby reducing human interaction, potentially leading to less focus on students' emotional and social development.

AI-Driven Platforms for Standardised Testing

Several platforms are being used worldwide to automate standardised testing and improve assessment efficiency. In the USA, Edmentum provides a comprehensive suite of AI-powered educational tools that include Assessments of Learning. These tests help schools track student progress, predict outcomes, and create data-driven intervention plans. The benefits are time-efficient grading of large volumes of standardised tests, and helps educators to identify areas needing intervention more quickly. Limitations are that standardised tests may fail to capture the broader spectrum of student abilities, such as critical thinking and creativity, and the automation of testing can lead to a lack of personalised insights for individual students.

Africa: AI for Educational Equity

In various regions of Africa, AI is being harnessed to tackle educational inequities and meet long-term development goals. Despite challenges such as inadequate infrastructure and resource scarcity, there are notable initiatives aimed at enhancing access to education through innovative AI solutions.

1. AI-Powered Mobile Applications: Pilot programs in countries like Kenya and Nigeria are deploying AI-driven mobile applications that assess student learning and provide real-time feedback. These applications enable students to engage with educational content independently, even in remote or underserved areas. For instance, the M-Shule platform uses SMS technology and AI to deliver personalised learning experiences to primary school learners, assessing their progress and adapting content to their learning needs (Allam et al., 2023).
2. Adaptive Learning Platforms: Tools such as SemaBox and Moodle offer adaptive learning modules that tailor educational experiences based on individual student performance. These platforms are designed to support learners in environments where traditional schooling may not be accessible, thereby helping to bridge educational gaps in underserved regions. By analysing student data, these systems can adjust lesson plans to better suit diverse learning styles and abilities, fostering a more inclusive learning environment.

3. Remote Learning Initiatives: In response to the COVID-19 pandemic, several African countries have integrated AI into remote learning initiatives. For example, South Africa's Kagiso Trust launched a digital learning program that employs AI to assess student engagement and comprehension levels, providing educators with insights to inform instruction. These initiatives help ensure that even during crises, students have access to quality education.
4. AI in Teacher Training: Programs are emerging that use AI to enhance teacher training and development. The African Leadership University employs AI tools to analyse teacher performance and offer tailored professional development resources, helping educators better support their students (Adeyemo & Omole, 2023).

Despite the potential of AI to transform education in Africa, significant barriers remain (African Union, 2024). The digital divide poses a substantial challenge, as many students lack access to the necessary technology and reliable internet connectivity. According to a report by the International Telecommunication Union (ITU), internet access disparities hinder the effectiveness of AI-driven educational tools in many African regions (ITU, 2022). Okolo, (2023) observed that, governments, researchers, and the private sector need to evaluate the implications of GAI in Africa. Additionally, African institutions should work toward the responsible development, deployment, and use of these technologies. Addressing these infrastructural issues is crucial for the successful implementation and scaling of AI solutions in education. Across these case studies, common challenges arise that must be addressed to ensure AI tools' successful and equitable implementation in education:

- Bias: AI systems may perpetuate biases present in the data they are trained on, leading to unfair assessments.
- Privacy: the collection and processing of vast amounts of data raises concerns about student privacy, particularly when third-party vendors are involved (The Alan Turing Institute, 2023).
- Over-reliance on Technology: the human element in education, particularly the critical interpersonal relationships between teachers and students, risks being diminished if AI takes on too large a role.
- Infrastructure Gaps: in developing regions, access to technology and internet infrastructure remains a challenge, preventing equitable access to AI-driven tools.

While AI-driven assessment tools hold great promise for enhancing educational equity in Africa, the success of these initiatives will depend on addressing the digital divide and ensuring that all students have access to the technology required for effective learning. Collaborative efforts among governments, NGOs, and private sector players are essential to create a sustainable ecosystem that leverages AI to improve educational outcomes across the continent.

AI-Driven Assessment Tools

AI-driven tools are increasingly being integrated into education to facilitate teaching, learning, and assessment, complementing traditional Educational Technology (EdTech) with AI capabilities. These tools range from personalised tutoring systems to grading technologies, each addressing specific needs within the educational landscape.

1. Personalised Education Platforms:

AI-powered tutors, such as Khanmigo, engage learners directly through chatbot interfaces, offering personalised support based on individual learning needs. These platforms adapt to students' progress, ensuring tailored guidance and interventions.

2. Learning Analytics and Progress Monitoring:

Platforms like CENTURY provide educators with comprehensive overviews of students' learning progress, highlighting strengths and weaknesses. By analysing classroom data, these tools allow educators to customize lessons and interventions to better meet each student's needs.

3. AI-Assisted Marking Technologies:

Applications such as Graide and Progressay help automate the grading process. By using lecturer inputs and AI-powered marking schemes, these tools can assist in evaluating student work more efficiently while maintaining consistency in grading.

4. Classroom Assistant Platforms:

Tools like TeacherMatic and the Oak National Academy supply educators with lesson plans, quizzes, and other classroom materials. These AI-powered platforms simplify the preparation process, allowing lecturers to focus more on instruction and student engagement.

5. Teacher Training Tools:

AI also plays a role in professional development. Platforms such as Teacherverse simulate classroom scenarios, helping educators practice teaching strategies and refine their skills in a risk-free environment (UK Parliament POST, 2024).

6. Predictive Analytics:

By analysing data such as student attendance, engagement, and academic performance, AI-driven tools can predict future outcomes. For example, the University of South Florida uses predictive analytics to identify students at risk of underperformance, allowing for timely interventions through its Student Success Centre (Owan et al., 2023).

7. Learning Analytics Tools:

AI-based learning analytics tools, such as Learning Analytics and Knowledge (LAK) and Open Learning Analytics (OLA), process student data to provide insights into performance, engagement, and learning outcomes. These insights help educators identify at-risk students and make informed decisions to improve instructional practices and student achievement.

8. Plagiarism Detection:

AI-based tools like Grammarly, Turnitin, and Copyscape use natural language processing (NLP) algorithms to detect instances of plagiarism in student submissions. These tools help maintain academic integrity by ensuring that student work is original and properly cited.

9. Digital Assessment Tools:

Platforms such as Edulastic, ExaminationView, and Google Forms allow educators to create and administer digital assessments using multiple question formats. These tools provide a convenient way to evaluate student knowledge and skills across various subjects.

10. Large Language Models (LLMs):

AI models like ChatGPT and Google Bard can analyse extensive text data related to specific courses, identifying key themes and concepts. These models can generate test items that accurately measure students' understanding, offering valuable support in the assessment process.

11. Intelligent Tutoring Systems (ITS):

AI-powered tutoring systems offer personalised feedback and support to students, fostering motivation and engagement through real-time feedback. These systems can help bridge learning gaps by providing immediate and customized feedback.

12. Formative Assessment Tools:

Formative assessment platforms, such as Mentimeter, Nearpod, and Socrative, allow educators to monitor students' progress in real time. These tools facilitate immediate feedback, helping educators adjust their instruction to improve student outcomes.

Limitations of AI in Summative Assessments

AI-driven assessment tools offer significant potential in enhancing education by providing personalised learning experiences, predictive analytics, and support for both educators and students. However, while AI can assist with formative assessment and grading tasks, the critical role of educators in ensuring fairness, accuracy, and academic integrity remains irreplaceable, particularly in high-stakes summative evaluations. Their use in summative evaluations which determine final grades remains contentious. For instance, Cornell University advises against using GAI in high-stakes summative assessments, emphasising that the integrity of grading relies heavily on faculty oversight (Cornell University, 2023). Experts in assessment argue that, although AI can assist in grading, fully outsourcing the grading of examinations to AI presents significant challenges. These include concerns about fairness, bias, and the overall accuracy of AI in determining students' academic abilities (UK Parliament POST, 2024). Therefore, the role of faculty members remains crucial in maintaining the integrity and accuracy of summative assessments. As AI continues to evolve in educational contexts, clear guidelines and ethical considerations will be essential to maximising its benefits while minimising potential risks.

Impact of AI on Pedagogy and Learning

AI, particularly GAI, has the potential to fundamentally reshape pedagogy and learning by transforming instructional methods, altering assessment practices, and influencing student engagement and motivation. As AI tools become more integrated into educational systems, their impact on teaching and learning is becoming increasingly evident.

Shifting the Role of Lecturers

AI's integration into education is driving a shift in the role of lecturers. Traditionally, educators were the primary source of knowledge, delivering direct instruction. With AI, however, lecturers are increasingly moving toward the roles of facilitators and mentors. GAI can assist with content delivery, while lecturers focus on guiding student inquiry, offering personalised feedback, and helping students develop critical thinking skills. Instead of simply presenting information, educators can use AI to facilitate more interactive, student-centered learning experiences. For example, AI-driven platforms can present personalised learning paths, while the educator helps students navigate these paths by answering questions, fostering discussions, and providing context (UNESCO, 2019).

Immediate Feedback and Personalised Learning

One of AI's significant contributions is the ability to offer immediate, relevant, and objective feedback. Tools such as Turnitin, which uses natural language processing (NLP), provide students with automated feedback on grammar, syntax, and plagiarism. This frees up lecturers' time while still allowing students to receive timely guidance on their work, helping them learn from their mistakes and make real-time improvements. Moreover, AI can tailor learning experiences to individual students. By analysing student data, AI systems can provide personalised instruction that aligns with each learner's strengths and weaknesses. This ability to individualise education increases engagement and motivation, as students receive targeted support that meets their specific needs.

AI's Impact on Assessment Methods

AI can automate routine tasks such as grading, which saves time for lecturers and allows them to focus on more meaningful interactions with students. Automated grading systems can efficiently assess multiple-choice questions, essay content, and even coding assignments. Beyond automation, AI-based assessments also enable continuous, formative assessment, providing students with ongoing feedback and lecturers with real-time insights into student progress. However, as Owan et al. (2023) point out, the role of lecturers in AI-driven assessments remains critical. While AI can provide immediate feedback and grading, lecturers are responsible for designing assessments, interpreting results, and offering deeper, contextual feedback. They ensure that assessments align with curriculum goals and learning objectives while adding the human element of empathy, judgment, and adaptability that AI cannot fully replicate.

Enhanced Learning Styles and Creativity

AI tools provide opportunities for students to engage with content in new and creative ways. For example, GAI can support visual, auditory, and kinesthetic learners through personalised content delivery, adaptive learning platforms, and tools that make assignments universally accessible. Students can explore complex concepts through simulations, receive tailored feedback on their writing, or use AI to assist with coding projects. These tools enable more active learning, allowing students to experiment, innovate, and express their creativity.

Supporting Inclusivity and Accessibility

AI has the potential to make learning more accessible, particularly for students with disabilities or special needs. Assistive technologies powered by AI can offer accommodations such as text-to-speech, speech recognition, and other accessibility tools that reduce barriers to education. These tools not only make content accessible but also allow students to engage with learning materials in ways that best suit their abilities. Barkhuus and Wobbrock (2020) argued that AI-powered tools enhance inclusivity by levelling the playing field, allowing students of all backgrounds and abilities to succeed. This is especially critical in diverse classrooms where students may require different supports to achieve their learning goals.

Student Engagement and Motivation

The use of GAI can foster increased student engagement and motivation by making learning more interactive and personalised. When students receive instant feedback and are able to see their progress in real time, they are more likely to stay engaged with their learning. Additionally, AI-driven tools can gamify learning, offering rewards, badges, or milestones that motivate students to persist in their studies. However, there are challenges in maintaining motivation. If students over-rely on AI to complete assignments, they may disengage from the deeper learning process. Therefore, it's crucial that AI tools are used to complement, rather than replace, active learning practices.

Ethical Considerations in AI Use

Lecturers have a critical role in ensuring the ethical and responsible use of AI in pedagogy. They must guide students on how to use AI tools appropriately, particularly in relation to academic integrity and data privacy. Ethical considerations include protecting student data, ensuring that assessments are fair, and addressing the biases that may be present in AI algorithms. Kars (2023) found that a significant number of students have already started using AI tools like ChatGPT to assist with their studies. This growing trend underscores the need for clear guidelines and expectations around AI use in educational settings, particularly regarding plagiarism and originality in student work.

Lecturers as Key Players in AI Integration

As Owan et al. (2023) stressed, lecturers remain central to AI-driven learning environments. Their roles include:

- Assessment Design: ensuring AI tools align with curriculum and learning objectives.
- Result Interpretation: providing deeper, contextual feedback that AI systems cannot.
- Ethical Oversight: safeguarding the fairness, validity, and reliability of AI-driven assessments.
- Continuous Improvement: using AI-generated data to refine teaching methods and better meet student needs.

Future Trends and Innovations

The future of GAI in education promises a transformative shift in teaching, learning, and assessment. As GAI technologies rapidly evolve, they offer exciting potential applications that could reshape how students engage with content and how educators design curricula and assessments. Below, we explore some of the most promising trends and innovations, as well as the opportunities and challenges they present.

AI-Driven Feedback and Assessment

GAI will likely play a more significant role in automating and enhancing feedback mechanisms. Currently, AI tools like Turnitin provide instant feedback on writing, detecting issues like grammar mistakes and plagiarism. Future innovations may include more sophisticated AI systems that offer in-depth feedback on higher-order thinking skills such as critical analysis, creativity, and problem-solving. This shift toward AI-based assessments can also provide real-time insights into student performance, helping educators monitor progress more effectively. While GAI can enhance efficiency in grading and assessments, Owan et al. (2023) stressed that educators will continue to play an essential role in interpreting AI-generated results and offering nuanced feedback that reflects individual student needs.

Innovations in AI-Resistant Assessments

As GAI becomes more capable of completing complex tasks, educators may need to redesign assessments to prevent academic integrity violations. Cornell University (2023) suggested moving from take-home to in-class assessments or designing more personalised assignments that require unique and creative thinking, making them less suited to AI-driven solutions. This shift can help maintain the rigor of assessments while ensuring students continue to develop foundational skills without over-reliance on AI tools.

Personalisation of Learning

One of the most significant future trends is the increasing ability of AI to personalise education (UNESCO, 2019). Christensen and Raynor (2024) emphasised the potential for GAI to create tailored learning pathways, adapting educational content to meet individual students' needs and learning styles. This could be particularly beneficial for students who require additional support or those who excel and need more challenging materials. AI-driven platforms could provide real-time, data-driven adjustments to lesson plans, helping to optimise student progress. Personalisation also fosters inclusivity, as it enables educators to address the diverse needs of students, including those with disabilities or different learning preferences. GAI could thus play a central role in creating more equitable and adaptable education systems.

Immersive and Interactive Learning Experiences

Radford and Narasimhan (2023) predicted that GAI will continue to enhance immersive learning experiences, such as virtual field trips, interactive simulations, and gamified educational content. These innovations have the potential to deepen student engagement and improve understanding of complex concepts. Imagine students virtually exploring historical landmarks, conducting scientific experiments in a simulated lab, or solving real-world problems in interactive environments, all powered by AI. These experiences can make learning more experiential and practical, catering to multiple learning styles and making abstract concepts more tangible. They also offer the chance to democratise education, giving students in remote or underserved areas access to educational experiences that were previously unattainable.

AI in Curriculum Development and Lesson Planning

As AI systems become more advanced, they will likely be used to assist educators in designing curricula and lesson plans. GAI tools could analyse vast amounts of educational data to recommend instructional strategies or highlight areas where students struggle. For instance, AI could suggest modifications to lesson plans to better align with the unique needs of a particular class or recommend resources that could enhance student engagement in difficult subjects.

In addition to lesson planning, AI could assist in creating adaptive learning systems that adjust content difficulty based on student performance, ensuring students are always learning at an appropriate level. This has the potential to increase student motivation, as learners engage with content that is neither too challenging nor too easy.

Ethical and Regulatory Challenges

The widespread integration of GAI into educational systems will raise several ethical and regulatory concerns, particularly around data privacy, security, and IP. As AI continues to analyse and collect student data, institutions must establish robust policies to protect personal information. UNESCO (2024) emphasised that educational authorities and institutions will have to carefully evaluate which AI tools to adopt and ensure that these tools comply with data privacy regulations such as the GDPR. Ethical concerns also extend to over-reliance on AI, which could diminish educator-learner relationships. As UK Parliament POST (2024) noted, educators worry that students may lose critical writing and thinking skills if they rely too heavily on AI to complete assignments. Future educational policies will need to balance AI's benefits with safeguarding essential human interactions and skills development.

AI-Powered Collaboration and Communication Tools

GAI is likely to enhance collaborative learning by powering tools that facilitate group work and communication. AI can help monitor group dynamics, identify students who may need additional support, or suggest ways to improve teamwork. AI-powered communication platforms could also assist in fostering peer-to-peer learning, enabling students to collaborate more effectively, regardless of geographical barriers. In addition, AI chatbots or virtual teaching assistants may increasingly play a role in supporting students by answering questions, offering resources, or clarifying difficult concepts. These tools can provide around-the-clock assistance, improving accessibility and reducing the workload on educators.

Future Research Directions in AI for Education

The future of GAI in education is also likely to see continued research and development in areas such as ethical AI, data-driven personalization, and human-AI collaboration. AI developers will need to focus on making systems more transparent, explainable, and adaptable to different educational contexts. The Alan Turing Institute (2023) stressed that GAI should not be viewed as a one-size-fits-all solution; rather, it should complement traditional learning methods and promote creativity, critical thinking, and collaboration among students. Research will also likely explore the implications of AI on educational equity, investigating how AI can be used to close achievement gaps and provide equal learning opportunities across socioeconomic, geographic, and cultural divides.

Future Trends and Innovations in AI-Driven Education

As AI becomes more embedded in educational settings, future trends and innovations are expected to shape the way institutions adopt and integrate these technologies. The integration of AI is poised to redefine the very fabric of teaching and assessment methodologies. In Africa, where educational systems are both diverse and dynamic, the future of AI-driven education holds immense promise for enhancing learning experiences and outcomes. The potential of GAI to transform educational assessment both formative and summative introduces innovative approaches that can cater to the unique needs of learners across the continent. By embracing these advancements, educators can create more personalised, efficient, and effective assessment practices that empower students and drive educational equity (Centre for Learning, Teaching, and Development, 2024). One of the most significant trends on the horizon is the increasing adoption of adaptive learning technologies. These AI-driven systems can analyse individual learner performance in real-time, adjusting content delivery and assessment formats based on each student's strengths and weaknesses. This tailored approach not only helps in addressing diverse learning styles but also provides immediate feedback, enabling students to take charge of their learning journey. In an African context, where resource constraints often hinder personalised instruction, adaptive learning tools can bridge gaps and enhance engagement, making education more accessible and relevant to all students.

Furthermore, the rise of data analytics in education is set to transform assessment practices. By harnessing the vast amounts of data generated through AI interactions, educators can gain deeper insights into student learning patterns, performance trends, and potential areas for intervention. Predictive analytics can enable educators to identify at-risk students early on, allowing for timely support and targeted interventions. This proactive approach can be particularly beneficial in African educational settings, where high dropout rates and underperformance remain pressing challenges. By utilising data-driven insights, educators can refine their assessment strategies and foster an environment conducive to learning and growth.

In addition to adaptive learning and data analytics, innovations in assessment methodologies themselves are emerging. Traditional assessment formats, such as standardised tests, are increasingly being complemented or replaced by project-based assessments and digital portfolios. These alternatives not only allow for a more holistic evaluation of student capabilities but also encourage the development of critical skills such as collaboration, creativity, and problem-solving. In Africa, where practical knowledge and skills are essential for economic development, such innovative assessment practices can align educational outcomes with the demands of the job market.

Moreover, the integration of AI in education fosters collaborative learning environments. With the rise of virtual classrooms and AI-driven tutoring systems, students can engage with peers and educators from different geographical regions, enriching their learning experiences. Collaborative platforms powered by AI can facilitate peer assessments, group projects, and shared learning resources, promoting a sense of community and cooperation. This trend is particularly vital in Africa, where cultural exchanges and collaborative learning can enhance understanding and respect among diverse populations. As we look to the future, it is also essential to consider the role of ethical frameworks in guiding AI implementation in education. The responsible use of AI technologies will be crucial in ensuring that innovations are equitable, inclusive, and culturally sensitive (African Union, 2024). Developing robust guidelines that prioritise student privacy, data security, and algorithmic fairness will be paramount in fostering trust and acceptance among educators, students, and parents. By embedding ethical considerations into the design and deployment of AI tools, stakeholders can navigate the complexities of technology in education responsibly.

According to UNESCO (2024), educational authorities, universities, and schools have the responsibility of determining which AI-driven tools are suitable for their needs and how they should be deployed. Their recommendations include:

- Institutional Auditing of AI Algorithms and Outputs:

Institutions should implement mechanisms to regularly audit AI tools, ensuring that the algorithms and data they use are ethically sound and that the outputs are accurate. Audits should also ensure the protection of user data and the automatic filtering of inappropriate content.

- Validating Proportionality and Safeguarding Well-being:

Institutions need to develop policies that classify and validate AI systems, ensuring alignment with ethical standards and frameworks. This is crucial to prevent any harm to students, particularly vulnerable groups such as children.

- Assessing Long-Term Impacts:

Over-reliance on AI tools could impact human cognitive abilities, including creativity and critical thinking. Institutions must continuously assess the long-term implications of AI use in education to ensure that these core skills are not diminished.

- Age Appropriateness:

Institutions may consider imposing age restrictions on the independent use of AI tools, ensuring that younger students are not exposed to technologies beyond their developmental level.

Hanover Research (2024) offers additional insights into the ethical integration of AI in education. They recommend:

- Avoiding Over-Reliance on AI Detection Tools: Tools like GPTZERO, which aim to detect AI-generated content, have a poor accuracy record. Such tools can create an adversarial classroom environment and may not be suitable for fostering a positive educational experience.
- Redesigning Assignments to Combat AI Misuse: Writing assignments should be restructured to focus on student development through iterative feedback and scaffolded deliverables over time. This helps students build foundational skills, making it harder for AI-generated content to substitute genuine effort.
- Incorporating AI into Learning: Students should be taught how to use AI tools, such as generative models, for revising, critiquing, and brainstorming. This helps them develop critical skills for navigating AI technologies in academic and professional contexts.

Looking to the future, The Alan Turing Institute (2023) and other experts envision the following advancements:

- Evolution of Assessment Methods:

Traditional assessment methods like essay writing may be phased out or restructured. New formats may prioritise skills like problem-solving, creative thinking, and content interpretation to better evaluate students' competencies in the age of AI.

- Increase in Virtual Educators and AI Tutors:

AI-driven teaching assistants and tutors could provide greater support for disadvantaged students lacking access to quality education. Specialised AI systems may offer targeted help for specific subjects, tasks, and even mental health support.

- Teaching AI Skills in Classrooms:

As AI becomes a staple of the modern workplace, students may be trained on how to effectively use AI tools for tasks beyond idea generation, preparing them for future interactions with AI-powered systems.

- Watermarking and Identifying AI-Generated Content:

As concerns around AI-authored work grow, watermarking technologies may evolve to distinguish between human- and AI-generated content. This development could play a critical role in academic integrity and intellectual property rights.

- Ongoing Ethical Considerations:

The rapid advancements in AI capabilities come with risks, including the potential for models to degrade in quality over time. Policymakers and educators will need to stay informed of these developments and adapt policies accordingly to ensure that AI use in education remains ethical, transparent, and effective.

Addressing Challenges in AI-Driven Assessment

The integration of AI into educational assessment represents a transformative shift in how educators evaluate student learning and performance. Particularly in the context of Africa, where educational landscapes are diverse and often face significant challenges, leveraging AI-driven assessment tools offers both promising opportunities and complex hurdles. The promise of GAI in enhancing formative and summative assessment practices cannot be overstated. By providing personalised feedback, adaptive learning pathways, and efficient data analysis, AI has the potential to revolutionise how students are assessed and supported throughout their educational journeys (Centre for Learning, Teaching, and Development, 2024). However, the transition to AI-driven assessment systems is not without its challenges as mentioned earlier. One of the foremost concerns is the digital divide that exists across many regions in Africa. While urban areas may have greater access to technology, rural communities often lag behind, leading to inequalities in educational opportunities and assessment fairness. This disparity raises critical questions about the equity of AI applications in education. If AI tools are predominantly deployed in well-resourced settings, students from underprivileged backgrounds may not only miss out on the benefits of these advanced technologies but may also be further marginalised in traditional assessment frameworks.

Moreover, the reliability and validity of AI-generated assessments must be scrutinised. The algorithms that power these tools are designed to analyse vast amounts of data and generate insights; however, they can also inadvertently perpetuate biases present in the training data. Ensuring that AI systems provide accurate and equitable assessments requires ongoing efforts in data management, algorithm design, and ethical considerations. Educators must be equipped to interpret AI-generated data critically and make informed decisions that reflect the nuanced realities of their students' learning experiences. Owan et al. (2023) provide solutions to mitigate the challenges associated with AI in education, ensuring equity, transparency, and quality:

- Developing Transparent AI Algorithms:

Educators and developers must collaborate to design AI algorithms free from bias, using diverse datasets and incorporating ethical considerations into their design.

- Personalised and Adaptive Assessments:

AI can enable personalised assessments that account for individual learning differences, providing a more nuanced understanding of student performance through methods like open-ended questions and performance-based tasks.

- Training and Supporting Educators:

Educators need ongoing professional development to effectively integrate AI tools into their teaching practices. Support structures should ensure that instructors can confidently and ethically use AI to enhance learning.

- Collaborating with Students:

Gathering feedback from students about their experience with AI tools helps educators refine these technologies to better meet learners' needs. Student input can drive improvements in usability and effectiveness.

- Ensuring Accessibility for All Students:

AI tools must be designed with accessibility in mind, offering accommodations for students with disabilities and ensuring compatibility with assistive technologies.

- Incorporating Human Oversight:

While AI can provide valuable insights, educators must maintain oversight to verify the accuracy of AI-driven assessments, ensuring fairness and addressing any potential errors.

- Regularly Evaluating AI Tools:

AI technologies should be frequently evaluated and updated to remain effective, transparent, and compliant with data privacy regulations.

- Ensuring Data Privacy and Security:

Institutions must protect student data by implementing robust security measures and adhering to regulations like Family Educational Rights and Privacy Act (FERPA). This ensures that data is only used for its intended educational purposes.

- Educating Students and Parents:

To promote understanding and acceptance, educators should provide training to students and their parents on how AI-powered tools work, what data is collected, and how AI contributes to improved learning outcomes.

By embracing these strategies, institutions can integrate AI into education responsibly, harnessing its benefits while addressing ethical concerns and safeguarding the well-being of students.

CONCLUSION: THE ROLE OF AI IN SHAPING EDUCATION

In conclusion, GAI has the potential to significantly reshape education in Africa by offering more personalised, engaging, and efficient learning experiences. AI-driven technologies, particularly in formative and summative assessments, can enhance educational practices across the continent, transforming how institutions operate and influencing policymaking. As educational authorities and institutions adopt GAI, they can leverage data collected from AI-based assessments to gain new insights into student learning, which can guide more effective educational strategies tailored to local contexts.

However, with the opportunities come substantial ethical, pedagogical, and technical challenges. As Tuomi et al. (2023) noted, emerging technologies will generate new types of data, necessitating innovative approaches to assessments and learning processes. Yet, the ethical implications of GAI, such as biases, inaccuracies, privacy concerns, and potential violations of IP rights, require deeper exploration and proactive policy measures. Perkins (2024) emphasised the need for a multidimensional approach to address these ethical concerns while ensuring that GAI tools complement rather than circumvent the learning process.

Although GAI holds promise for improving education, it is unlikely to replace human educators entirely. Human interaction remains essential for fostering creativity, critical thinking, and collaboration. As Allam et al. (2023), Sibal, et al (2021) and UK Parliament POST (2024) pointed out, the successful integration of GAI will depend on evidence of its effectiveness, adequate training for educators, and clear legal frameworks that regulate data usage. Addressing the digital divide is also crucial to ensure that AI tools do not exacerbate educational inequalities.

In Africa, where educational disparities often persist due to infrastructural challenges and resource limitations, AI has the unique capability to bridge gaps by providing adaptive learning solutions that cater to diverse student needs (Allam et al., 2023; UNESCO, 2024). As stakeholders commit to integrating AI responsibly and equitably, the transformative impact of these technologies on the educational landscape in Africa can lead to improved outcomes for students and educators alike.

Ultimately, GAI offers a transformative path forward in education, but its responsible implementation requires careful consideration of ethical principles, continuous innovation, and a commitment to inclusivity. The future of AI in education will be shaped by how well institutions balance technological advancements with the need for human-centric learning experiences.

Recommendations

AI-driven assessment tools are transforming education, offering opportunities for personalised learning and assessment, improved efficiency, and data-driven insights. However, their effective implementation requires strategic planning and careful consideration of the associated challenges. Based on the case studies and examples provided, the following are recommendations for educators and policymakers:

Personalisation of Learning and Assessment

AI-powered platforms, such as those used in China and the USA, show that AI can tailor learning and assessment experiences to meet individual student needs. Educators can leverage these tools to enhance student engagement and address specific learning and assessment gaps. Educators should use AI tools to personalise instruction and support differentiated learning. Tools like DreamBox and Knewton can adapt content based on individual student progress, allowing lecturers to focus on areas where students need more attention. Policymakers should encourage the adoption of adaptive learning platforms by providing funding and training for lecturers to effectively use these technologies.

Enhancing Feedback and Assessment Efficiency

AI systems such as Turnitin offer rapid feedback, improving student outcomes through timely interventions. Educators can integrate AI-powered platforms to automate routine tasks like grading and feedback, freeing time for more meaningful interactions with students. Lecturers should combine AI-generated feedback with human guidance to ensure the feedback is both detailed and empathetic. This approach can address the limitations of AI's lack of nuance in qualitative assessments. Policymakers should support the integration of AI in grading and feedback systems while ensuring that teachers receive professional development on how to interpret and use AI-generated reports effectively.

Early Intervention and Student Monitoring

In regions like Singapore, AI is being used to monitor student performance and intervene early when issues arise. Educators can use these insights to prevent students from falling behind and to design targeted interventions. Educators should use AI-driven monitoring tools to track student progress continuously and implement early intervention strategies. However, they must ensure that these tools are balanced with face-to-face interactions to maintain a human connection in learning. Policymakers should mandate that AI monitoring systems adhere to strict privacy and ethical standards, ensuring that student data is securely handled and used for legitimate educational purposes only.

Mitigating Bias and Ensuring Equity

AI systems can perpetuate biases in data, and their effectiveness depends on access to technology and infrastructure. Policymakers must ensure AI tools are designed and implemented in ways that minimise bias and promote equity. Educators need to be aware of potential biases in AI assessments and should use these tools as one of many resources to assess student performance. They should also advocate for inclusive AI tools that consider diverse student needs. Policymakers should implement guidelines for the ethical use of AI in education, ensuring AI algorithms are transparent, regularly audited for bias, and used alongside traditional methods to avoid over-reliance. Governments should also work to bridge the digital divide, providing access to the necessary technology for all students, especially in underserved regions.

Balancing Technology with Human Interaction

While AI can improve efficiency, there is a risk of over-reliance, potentially reducing the human interaction crucial to a holistic education experience. Educators should use AI to complement, not replace, human interaction. They must ensure that AI tools enhance rather than diminish their role in fostering critical thinking, creativity, and emotional intelligence in students. Policymakers should promote balanced use of AI in educational systems, ensuring that it augments rather than substitutes lecturer-student relationships. Policy initiatives should focus on professional development to equip educators with the skills to manage AI alongside traditional teaching and assessment methods.

Investing in Teacher Training and AI Literacy

Lecturers need training to understand and effectively implement AI tools. AI literacy among educators is critical for maximising the benefits of AI-driven platforms. Educators should pursue professional development opportunities focused on AI tools and their applications in education. This will enable them to make informed decisions on when and how to use AI for assessment and feedback. Policymakers should allocate resources for comprehensive teacher training programs that focus on AI literacy, covering not only the technical aspects but also the pedagogical implications of AI in education.

Supporting the Use of AI in Developing Regions

In regions like Africa, where access to technology and infrastructure is limited, AI could be a powerful tool for bridging educational gaps. However, targeted investment is needed to ensure equitable access to AI-driven learning resources. Educators in developing regions should advocate for the adoption of AI-powered mobile and offline learning solutions to provide access to quality education even in areas with limited internet connectivity. Policymakers should prioritise investment in infrastructure, particularly in underserved regions, to ensure that AI-driven tools can be effectively deployed. Public-private partnerships may also play a critical role in bringing AI-powered educational tools to areas lacking in technological resources.

Ethical and Privacy Considerations

With AI tools handling vast amounts of student data, concerns about privacy and data security are paramount. Policymakers must set clear guidelines to protect students' personal information and ensure ethical AI use in education. Educators should be transparent with students and parents about how AI tools use and store personal data, ensuring informed consent is obtained.

Policymakers should enforce data protection regulations specific to education technology, ensuring AI systems comply with existing privacy laws like the GDPR in Europe or similar frameworks in other regions. They should also work with AI developers to ensure ethical data use and avoid intrusive data collection practices.

Preparing Students for an AI-Enhanced Future

AI has the potential to reshape the workforce, and students must be prepared to adapt to this new reality. Learning institutions need to integrate AI literacy into curricula to equip students with the skills necessary to thrive in an AI-driven world. Educators should introduce AI literacy as part of the curriculum, teaching students not only how to use AI tools but also fostering an understanding of the ethical and societal implications of AI. Policymakers should promote AI literacy at a national level, incorporating it into educational standards and providing resources for schools to integrate AI-related content into the classroom.

REFERENCES

Adeyemo, A., & Omole, O. (2023). *Leveraging AI for Teacher Training in Africa.* Educational Innovations Press.

African Union. (2024, July). Continental Artificial Intelligence Strategy Harnessing AI for Africa's Development and Prosperity._https://au.int/sites/default/files/documents/44004-doc-EN-_Continental_AI_Strategy_July_2024.pdf

Allam, H., Dempere, J., Akre, V., & Flores, P. (2023). *Artificial Intelligence in Education (AIED).* Implications and Challenges., DOI: 10.2991/978-94-6463-286-6_10

Barkhuus, L., & Wobbrock, J. O. (2020). Empowering people with impairments through conversational access to information. In *Proceedings of the 2020 CHI Conference on Human Factors in Computing Systems* (pp. 1-13).

Centre for Learning, Teaching, and Development. (2024). *Guidelines for GAI use in Learning, Teaching, and Research.* University of the Witwatersrand.

Christensen, C. M., & Raynor, M. E. (2024). *The innovator's solution: Creating and sustaining successful growth.* Harvard Business Review Press.

Cornell University. (2023, July 18). *Generative artificial intelligence for education and pedagogy.* https://www.cornell.edu

Deng, L., Bengio, Y., & Frasconi, P. (2020). Guest Editorial: Special Issue on Artificial Intelligence in Education. *IEEE Transactions on Pattern Analysis and Machine Intelligence*, 42(3), 499–501.

Department for Education Innovation. (2024). *Lecturer's Guide: Leveraging Generative Artificial Intelligence for teaching and Learning Enhancement at the University of Pretoria.* University of Pretoria.

Fanning, J. (2023). AI-based Assessment in Education (AIBA): evidence review. In B. du Boulay (Ed.), A. Mitrovic (Ed.), K. Yacef (Ed.) *The Handbook of Artificial Intelligence in Education* (pp), Edward Elgar Publishing Ltd. Cheltenham, UK.

Felix, J., & Webb, L.UK Parliament POST. (2024, January 23). Use of artificial intelligence in education delivery and assessment. *POSTnote*, 712. Advance online publication. DOI: 10.58248/PN712

Gao, X., Xu, B., Ouyang, G., & Wang, L. (2020). Generative Adversarial Networks for Educational Applications. *IEEE Transactions on Learning Technologies*, 13(1), 6–16.

Ilkka, T. (2018). *The Impact of Artificial Intelligence on Learning, Teaching, and Education Policies for the future*. Joint Research Centre. Hanover Research (2024, April) Assessment and Generative Artificial Intelligence in Higher Education. Higher Education. https://cms.ahs.uic.edu/

International Telecommunication Union. (2022). *Connecting the world: Internet access in Africa*. International Telecommunication Union. https://www.itu.int

Jain, S., & Jain, R. (2019). Role of Artificial Intelligence in Higher Education- An Empirical Investigation. *IJRAR-. International Journal of Research and Analytical Reviews*, 6(2), 144–150. https://ijrar.com/

Kars, M. E. (2023, July 20). *Generative AI in Education. 9th London International Conference, July 11-13, 2023*. Ukey Consulting & Publishing. https://ukey.ilet.in/

Luckin, R., & Cukurova, M. (2019). Designing educational technologies in the age of AI: A review of "I-novels" as a method for co-creation. *British Journal of Educational Technology*, 50(6), 2958–2972.

Okolo, C. T. (2023, November 27). The Promise and Perils of Generative AI: Case Studies in an African Context. In *4th African Human Computer Interaction Conference (AfriCHI 2023)*, East London, South Africa. https://doi.org/DOI: 10.1145/3628096.3629066

Owan, V. J., Abang, K. B., Idika, D., Etta, E. O., & Bassey, B. A. (2023). Exploring the potential of artificial intelligence tools in educational measurement and assessment. *Eurasia Journal of Mathematics, Science and Technology Education*, 19(8), 1–15. DOI: 10.29333/ejmste/13428

Perkins, M., Furze, L., Roe, J., & MacVaugh, J. (2024). The Artificial Intelligence Assessment Scale (AIAS): A Framework for Ethical Integration of Generative AI in Educational Assessment. *Journal of University Teaching & Learning Practice*, 21(6). Advance online publication. https://arxiv.org/abs/2312.07086. DOI: 10.53761/q3azde36

Sibal, P., Neupane, B., & Orlic, D. (2021). *Artificial intelligence needs assessment survey in Africa*. United Nations Educational, Scientific and Cultural Organization. https://unesdoc.unesco.org/ark:/48223/pf0000375322

Slim, Z. (2023). The Impact of Artificial Intelligence on Higher Education: An Empirical Study. *European Journal of Educational Sciences*, 10(1), 17–33. DOI: 10.19044/ejes.v10no1a17

Tahir, M. (2024). Role of artificial intelligence in education: A conceptual review. *World Journal of Advanced Research and Reviews*, 22(01), 1469–1475. DOI: 10.30574/wjarr.2024.22.1.1217

Tang, Q. (2024, July 23). *A Case Study on The Application of Artificial Intelligence in Education Industry.* Proceedings of the 2023 3rd International Conference on Modern Educational Technology and Social Sciences (ICMETSS 2023), Advances in Social Science, Education and Humanities Research 784, DOI: 10.2991/978-2-38476-128-9_12

The Alan Turing Institute. (2023). Generative AI in Education: Call for Evidence https://www.turing.ac.uk/

Tuomi, I., Cachia, R., & Villar-Onrubia, D. (2023). *Science for policy report on the futures of technology in education: Emerging trends and policy implications*. Joint Research Centre. https://www.jrc.ec.europa.eu

UNESCO. (2019). *Artificial Intelligence in Education: Challenges and Opportunities for Sustainable Development.* Working Papers on Education Policy 07.Paris: United Nations Educational, Scientific and Cultural Organization. https://en.unesco.org/

UNESCO. (2023). *Guidance for generative AI in education and research.* United Nations Educational, Scientific and Cultural Organization. https://www.unesco.org/en/open-access/cc-sa

World Economic Forum. (2024) Shaping the Future of Learning: The Role of AI in Education 4.0 Insight Report April 2024 https://www3.weforum.org/

Chapter 4
Developing AI-Powered Prompts for First-Year Writing Courses

Nathan Pritts
https://orcid.org/0009-0000-7669-4721
University of Arizona Global Campus, USA

ABSTRACT

This chapter explores integrating generative AI tools in first-year writing courses, proposing a dual framework for balanced AI integration and AI literacy development. It addresses the challenges that come from the widespread student use of AI tools and presents new approaches to assessment design. The dual framework can help educators create AI-powered assessments that enhance learning outcomes, promote critical thinking, and build student confidence. A case study on thesis development illustrates how AI can be used to teach foundational writing skills while developing AI literacy. The chapter argues for a transformation of writing instruction that prepares students by instilling both discipline specific skills and critical AI skills. This approach turns potential challenges into opportunities for deeper learning, and positions AI as a tool rather than a replacement for human skills. The chapter concludes by discussing the implications for educational practice, curriculum redesign, instructor training, and assessment methods.

INTRODUCTION

Let's start with a shocking headline that is no longer all that shocking: Students are using generative AI to complete coursework. In fact, the tenor of discourse in higher education makes it seem as if students are outsourcing their coursework

DOI: 10.4018/979-8-3693-6351-5.ch004

entirely. While a pervasive "detect and report" mentality exists regarding the use of gen AI in many spaces, there is a growing call to explore collaborating with this new technology and incorporating it more fully into the core teaching and learning of courses. If students are using generative AI, an opportunity exists for educators to model a more effective usage guided by pillars designed to ground students in a deeper understanding of the tool and then focus on course-specific assignments and activities.

By cultivating an understanding of generative AI's capabilities and limitations, instructors can thoughtfully integrate these tools to enhance learning experiences. This balanced approach empowers students to blend AI assistance with their own authentic voices, unlocking new levels of creativity and insight.

However, maintaining a commitment to traditional assessment values can cultivate higher-order cognitive skills that machines cannot replicate. Through this balanced synthesis, AI becomes a force that enhances human skill. Educators who adopt this perspective will equip learners with the necessary skills to navigate an AI-augmented landscape, using technology effectively while preserving independent thought and reasoning. This AI-literate approach paves the way for a future where human ingenuity reaches new heights, powered by the collaboration of artificial and human intelligence.

AI tools can enhance personalized learning by tailoring content to individual student needs and learning styles (Qadir, 2022). Their increased use may shift traditional educational practices towards more interactive and collaborative experiences. Despite these advancements, classical human skills like critical thinking and problem-solving remain essential for effective technology use. Developing assessments that use AI may be one way to demonstrate effective usage and guide students to course-specific learning outcomes and toward a balanced usage of AI. To do so, we must first understand the primary motivations behind students' use of generative AI. We can tailor an assessment design that best supports students by identifying these needs and perspectives.

Background

As generative AI tools like ChatGPT have surged into mainstream accessibility, their appeal to first-year students is multifaceted. Several key factors influence these novice learners' intentions to engage with AI-powered platforms, aligning with their unique needs and challenges in the foundational year.

Chowdhury Niloy et al. (2024) identified some significant drivers of student use. Two of these most applicable to a discussion of first-year students are accessibility and educational impact. The availability of free AI resources immediately lowers barriers, making them an enticing option for students facing financial constraints – an everyday reality for many first-year students.

However, it is AI's potential for easing academic strain that may be the strongest lure. The relentless pace of first-year general education can quickly overwhelm students. Generative AI presents itself as an empowering aid, a time-saving resource capable of rapidly providing answers and solutions across multiple classes. For students spread thin, this responsive assistance is intensely appealing. Moreover, AI's capabilities transcend those of traditional search engines (Chowdhury Niloy et al., 2024). Rather than sifting through an avalanche of search results, generative AI tailors precise, context-relevant information. This capacity for self-directed, personalized learning resonates with first-year students striving for independence and mastery of new domains.

The study's findings underscore why generative AI platforms like ChatGPT have swiftly risen in popularity among college students – their seamless accessibility and efficiency in delivering solutions resonate deeply with first-year students. While generative AI offers benefits for time management and academic support, it is essential to strike a balance in its use. Tools like ChatGPT can assist with tasks such as grammar correction and paraphrasing, but relying on them for content generation may undermine the development of critical thinking, synthesis of information, and overall retention. This could lead to a decreased depth of understanding and mastery of the subject matter, which is best achieved through active engagement and processing of information. An over-reliance on outsourcing content generation to AI raises concerns about circumventing the iterative critical thinking and knowledge construction vital to transformative education.

A Framework for Balanced AI Integration in Assessments

The rapid proliferation and adoption of generative AI tools like ChatGPT in academic settings necessitates the development of a comprehensive framework to guide students toward a balanced and effective integration of this technology into their studies. As these AI capabilities become increasingly accessible, there is a pressing need to steer learners away from an overreliance on outsourcing tasks to AI and instead cultivate a mindset that leverages its potential as a complementary aid to deepen knowledge acquisition. Building on the insights into drivers of student use in the work done by Chowdhury Niloy et al. (2024), we can propose a framework for balanced integration of AI centered on the following fundamental tenets.

Setting Clear Guidelines. Establishing clear guidelines on the appropriate use of ChatGPT or other generative AI tools can help students understand its role as a supplementary tool in their work. Educators can provide specific instructions on when and how these tools can be used, delineating tasks where they are permitted and where independent work is required. By setting boundaries and expectations, educators can ensure that students use AI responsibly and ethically. For example, this can be spelled out directly in assignment guidelines or prompts.

Learning Process Over Product. Instead of focusing solely on a final product or assignment completion, educators can shift the focus onto the learning process. Students should be encouraged to use AI tools to aid their learning, seek clarification on concepts, explore different perspectives, and engage in meaningful discussions based on the generated content. For example, rather than a final draft submission, students can submit a log of their research and thoughts on a topic along with a reflection.

Encouraging Critical Thinking. Students should be encouraged to engage with any AI-generated content critically, analyzing the information provided and evaluating it within the context of their course material. This approach ensures that students do not passively accept information but actively engage with it to deepen their understanding. For example, students may interrogate AI-generated content, analyzing the strengths and limitations of the output.

Feedback and Reflection. Encouraging students to reflect on their use of AI tools and providing feedback on their engagement can enhance the learning experience. Educators can guide students on how to effectively integrate tools like ChatGPT into their study routine, identify areas for improvement, and reflect on the impact of using the tool on their learning outcomes. This reflective practice promotes metacognition and self-regulated learning, empowering students to make informed decisions about when and how to utilize these tools. As an example, students working with AI-assisted content would be continuously asked to rate that content in a variety of ways.

Putting these core principles (Chowdhury Niloy et al., 2024) into practice as an overarching framework allows educators to guide students in blending human reasoning with the capabilities of artificial intelligence. Applying this as a framework for developing assessments provides a solid foundation for productive AI usage, offering guidelines for using AI as a supplementary tool that enhances, rather than replaces, traditional skill-building. But just as content knowledge must be scaffolded, so too must the skills to thoughtfully navigate AI usage. Building on this understanding, we can seek to establish a dual framework. While the first framework focuses on integrating AI productively into curricula and assessments, the second framework can lead to the development of AI literacy, equipping students with the necessary skills to use AI ethically and effectively while fostering critical analysis and problem-solving abilities. The balanced AI integration framework provides the structural guidance for using AI in the classroom, and the AI literacy framework gives students the skills to use the tools effectively and critically. Together they form an associated approach: balanced integration ensures AI is used properly and ethically in the curriculum, and the focus on AI literacy enables students to understand, critique and use the tools in their learning. This relationship benefits both the AI integration and student learning, preparing them not just for immediate academic success but for a future where AI literacy will be as important as traditional literacy.

A Framework for Cultivating AI Literacy

The widespread use of generative AI, such as ChatGPT, has sparked apprehension among educators and researchers about its potential impact on higher education and the learning process. The transformative potential of AI to reshape major industries in the financial and technology sectors through optimized customer operations, marketing, software development, and research is widely acknowledged (Chui et al., 2023). However, it is crucial to recognize that the professionals driving these AI-powered innovations are largely products of the higher education system.

Educators worry that the ease with which students can leverage the capabilities of AI tools might foster an over-reliance on AI-generated content, undermining crucial skills like critical thinking, analysis, and written communication that are vital for academic and professional success (Vos, 2023). There are justifiable fears that some students, daunted by rigorous writing assignments or tempted by shortcuts, may treat AI as a crutch rather than a supplementary aid. Beyond the immediate risks of stunted skill development, a lack of discernment in consuming AI-generated information raises deeper concerns.

The introduction of AI has created a shift in the skill set coveted by employers, with the emphasis squarely on critical thinking, problem-solving prowess, and unleashing human creativity (World Economic Forum, 2023). Beyond technological fluency, employees are increasingly valued for their empathy, collaborative spirit, emotional intelligence, and a kind of responsive communication (Davies et al., 2011). While these are uniquely human skills that AI cannot currently replicate, they inform the backbone of a developing sense of AI literacy. By thoughtfully integrating AI into curricula and pedagogical approaches, educators can upskill themselves and their students in leveraging AI as a powerful co-pilot for enriching content delivery and augmenting coursework (Getchell et al., 2022).

Students who understand AI's strengths and limits can use it responsibly. They learn to balance AI assistance with original thinking and ethical behavior. AI-powered tools don't replace traditional methods. Instead, they enhance learning when driven by AI literacy. This approach deepens understanding and equips students with skills to use AI wisely without relying on it too much. Rather than disrupting traditional methods, AI-powered assessments and writing tools driven by AI literacy can be leveraged to elevate the learning experience, fostering deeper conceptual understanding.

AI literacy is key. It empowers students to evaluate AI technologies and their outputs, communicate and collaborate effectively with AI, and use AI tools in various settings. Cardon et al.'s (2023) AI literacy model provides a foundation. We can build on it to create a framework that teaches these crucial skills systematically.

Application. Defined by Cardon et al., 2023 as "an understanding of the various generative AI tools, including their strengths and weaknesses" (p. 21). This guides students in fostering a deep understanding of generative AI's diverse tools, their respective strengths, limitations, and ideal use cases. This pillar equips students to select and leverage the appropriate AI capabilities to augment specific tasks and learning objectives effectively.

Authenticity. Cultivating the ability to prioritize genuine, emotionally resonant human communication over AI outputs. This "focus on genuine communication and prioritizing the human element" (Cardon et al., 2023, p. 22) helps students develop skills to infuse AI-generated content with a personal voice, cultural nuance, and contextual awareness to ensure authentic connection.

Accountability. This domain empowers students to take charge of their AI interactions. It calls for a commitment to accuracy and appropriateness in AI-generated content. This principle extends beyond just checking facts. Cardon et al. (2023) highlight two key aspects of accountability: owning the accuracy of AI outputs and using AI in an equitable way.

Agency. Nurturing the self-assuredness to retain human autonomy and choice when interfacing with AI systems. Students gain the vital conviction to view AI as an aid that augments rather than replaces independent reasoning and decision-making capacities. Agency, as defined by Cardon et al. (2023), is "people retaining control to make their own choices" (p. 22).

This framework helps instructors focus on key AI literacy skills. And it can also guide assessment structure. Good assessments help faculty accurately measure outcomes and provide feedback to students. But they can do more. They can help equip students with practical AI-era abilities. By blending traditional assessment goals with AI literacy, we create a more robust learning experience.

Ng et al. (2021) conducted a study focused on exploring the efficacy of teaching methods to build skills with AI and considered the use of Bloom's Taxonomy to assess students' AI literacy. Their work leads to a key insight: educators play a vital role in cultivating AI literacy. This finding shifts our focus from simply evaluating AI skills to crafting thoughtful, targeted assessments that nurture them. Their work opens new doors. It pushes us to rethink how we evaluate students. We must create assessments that build AI literacy alongside other vital skills. Our dual framework provides a solid foundation for faculty. It organizes and guides assessment development.

When students master course content and learn to use AI, they prepare for a future where human and AI skills complement each other. By making guided AI use part of assessments, educators can meet student needs and build AI skills. Taken together, these frameworks offer a roadmap. They maximize human and AI benefits. They help instructors create effective, AI-literate assessments for specific courses.

Analysis

By combining explicit instruction on how AI tools may assist students in their work with targeted strategic deployment of generative AI in the course instruction, faculty can take charge of demonstrating the power and efficacy of this technology to enhance learning.

First-year writing instruction represents a particularly relevant area of opportunity. Countless studies have shown that AI tools offer gains in productivity and performance, with higher gains for new and lower-skilled workers. In a working paper from the National Bureau of Economic Research, researchers from Stanford and MIT discussed findings that suggest using generative AI increases some performance measures by an average of 14% on average, with a higher improvement rate of 34% improvement for novice workers (Brynjolfsson et al., 2023). And in a study conducted by Noy & Zhang (2023), writing samples were assessed based on three factors - writing quality, content quality, and originality. They found that ChatGPT contributed to enhancing the overall quality of the writing produced by participants. In fact, the study demonstrates that ChatGPT has closed a significant performance gap.

Applying these productivity and performance metrics to the first-year writing student seems relevant. By definition, first-year students are novices. These students are asked to leave behind the familiar writing practices of a sometimes-distant high school education and navigate the uncertainties and ambiguities of college-level writing (Sommers & Saltz, 2004). However, this reveals a unique opportunity to better reach those people who are likely to benefit the most. Viewing first-year students through this lens reveals a compelling case for thoughtfully integrating generative AI into their learning experience. Just as novice workers exhibited more profound productivity and performance gains when leveraging AI tools, incoming college students can be seen as “novices” to the rigors of higher education writing and research. Having newly transitioned into college, they often lack mastery of advanced composition, analysis, and intellectual exploration skills required at the collegiate level.

Indeed, some first-year students have been shown to be at the highest risk for academic disengagement, such as struggling with meeting deadlines, lack of preparation for classes, behaviors that can easily lead a student to shortcuts (Soria, 2012). Late submissions and incomplete assignments may cause a student to turn to AI-powered tools for assistance in completing tasks efficiently and on time. Students struggling with academic disengagement may seek AI solutions to generate content, check grammar, or provide answers to assignments. This could lead to a dependency on AI tools for completing academic tasks and learning support without the need for extensive self-discipline or motivation.

Of course, while generative AI holds promise for enhancing learning and productivity, it also presents significant risks for first-year students if not used responsibly. Early college students often lack the skills or confidence necessary to fully embrace and excel in writing tasks. Many students feel intimidated by writing. As they work to meet deadlines and academic expectations, students may be tempted to use generative AI as a shortcut to complete assignments quickly, but without engaging in the learning process. Additionally, first-year students often lack experience and discernment, making them more susceptible to accepting AI-generated content at face value without critically evaluating it.

First-year students face unique challenges. They often develop strategies to cope, some helpful, some risky. These coping mechanisms can lead to over-reliance on external tools like AI. This dependence might sideline genuine learning. We must guide students to use AI wisely, enhancing their education rather than replacing it. To do so, a guided framework for first-year students to responsibly harness the possibilities of generative AI holds immense potential for accelerating their development of essential competencies. All of this puts us in a better position to benefit from the possible advantages of implementing AI in first-year writing classes. AI technology presents an opportunity to address student shortfalls in skill level and confidence by providing personalized support and feedback to students.

Confidence is Key

Confidence in academic abilities could be a key factor influencing the academic achievement of first-year students. General confidence in academic ability and readiness for college-level work has been shown by Soria (2012) to be relevant in the context of academic engagement and disengagement. Students who lack confidence in their academic abilities may exhibit behaviors associated with academic disengagement, such as avoiding asking questions, seeking help from faculty, or participating actively in class discussions. This lack of confidence can contribute to a cycle of disengagement and hinder a student's overall academic success.

But building confidence provides a path forward. Those more inexperienced writers express the highest enthusiasm about the role of writing in helping them transition to college (Sommers & Saltz, 2004). They identify this skill as the one that will give them the confidence to express themselves academically and achieve higher levels of success. In my experience with first-year students in written communication courses, I have seen that talking about confidence in writing and focusing closely on building confidence can have a positive effect. Rather than starting out with grammar rules and structural guidelines, intentional work on confidence can lay the groundwork for a broader impact. By infusing writing instruction with creativity and introducing an element of autonomy to the process, educators can empower low-confidence students to build assuredness in a positive, uplifting manner (Graham & Perin, 2007).

By adopting an iterative and developmental approach to the written communication competency in first-year writing courses there is an opportunity to explore multiple AI-powered intervention strategies. First-year writing courses often emphasize a draft and revise approach to writing, encouraging students to experiment with different writing techniques and strategies. This iterative process allows students to refine their skills through practice and feedback.

The process approach to teaching writing is the opposite of the product approach. The product approach focuses on the end result, the written piece. The process approach sees writing as a journey. This is what we want for our first-year writers who are navigating the complexities of college writing. At its core the process approach breaks writing into smaller steps: brainstorming, drafting, revising, editing. This makes the process less scary for new writers.

Sholikah et al. (2019) discuss a method for focusing on each step of the process as a way to help students feel progress and accomplishment and build confidence. Clear guidelines for each writing stage provide structure and tailored feedback provides specific and actionable advice for improvement. This feedback helps students know their strengths and areas for growth and take ownership of their learning. Collaborative activities help build confidence too. Students share their work, give and receive constructive feedback and learn from each other. This collaborative spirit not only improves writing skills but also creates a sense of community and shared purpose among students.

By setting achievable goals and celebrating along the way, the process approach keeps students motivated. The step-by-step progression and ongoing support and feedback creates a feedback loop that reinforces student's belief in themselves as writers.

The process approach to teaching writing aligns with the idea of confidence building. As we've seen, first-year writers may struggle with low confidence in their writing. The process approach solves this in part through feedback so students can experiment and refine their skills without fear of being judged (Sholikah et al., 2019). The emphasis on revision and reflection in the process approach mirrors a focus on metacognition and self-regulation. Asking students to critically examine their work at each stage helps them better understand foundational writing principles and build self-efficacy. Breaking writing down into smaller steps is something that AI can be helpful with - providing targeted, iterative support. The collaborative elements of the process approach – peer reviews and feedback sessions – fit with our view of AI as a collaborative tool as well. This gets students to engage critically with ideas whether from peers or AI generated content and build their analytical skills and confidence in their own judgement.

The process approach can help fuel a better understanding of the efficacy of AI-powered assessments. In fact, drawing from the work of Chowdhury Niloy et al. (2024), the framework for balanced AI integration supports the process approach to teaching writing. For example, the aspect of "Setting Clear Guidelines" mirrors the process approach's structured stages of writing. AI assessments can provide clear step by step guidance through each stage of writing from brainstorming to final drafts. This structured support will demystify the writing process and build student confidence. The aspect of "Learning Process Over Product" also aligns with the process approach. AI tools when used thoughtfully can provide instant formative feedback at each stage. This aligns with the process approach's emphasis on constructive feedback and self-reflection so students can iterate and improve.

The "Encouraging Critical Thinking" part of our framework matches the process approach's revision and peer collaboration. AI assessments can prompt students to evaluate their own work like a peer review. This develops analytical skills and confidence in their own judgment. And finally, "Feedback and Reflection" matches the process approach's goal of self-reflection and metacognition. AI tools can provide personalized feedback and prompt students to reflect on their writing process and build self-awareness. By using AI in this way we're amplifying the process approach. AI assessments can provide more frequent and personalized feedback than traditional methods alone and support the iterative confidence building nature of the process approach to teaching writing.

By guiding students through the interactions of writing as a process, AI can help them build confidence and proficiency over time. Continuous feedback, powered by AI but driven by an instructor's insight and expertise, has the potential to engage students more dynamically in an ongoing process of revision and improvement. With this developmental mindset, instructors can use AI to help target and support student acquisition of the formative building blocks of the writing process.

This highlights the importance of building confidence in novice writers as they navigate the challenges of college-level writing. Real-time, interactive feedback sessions centered around exemplars can enable educators to thoughtfully guide students' development across the diverse elements of effective communication (Wette, 2014). This approach takes on added significance given the diverse career trajectories represented within a first-year composition course.

So, if building confidence can be a key factor in skills improvement, especially for first-year students, and if confidence can be built through intentional design and feedback, we can begin to consider whether generative AI tools can be developed to support this.

AI's Potential to Foster Student Confidence

By positioning AI as an enabling resource, educators can empower learners to harmonize human ingenuity with artificial intelligence. This approach serves to progressively nurture confidence as students gain first-hand experience leveraging AI's capabilities to elevate their authentic voices.

This all begins with establishing a human-AI trust relationship. Karran et al. (2022) have demonstrated how explainable AI systems can help users interpret and trust the outputs of the AI, leading to a more positive interaction experience. Rather than blindly using these tools, an intentional process is called for. But beyond intentionality, the interaction needs to be visible and explicit. So often in teaching, we seek a seamless process, one where the student acquires skills or knowledge through activities without considering the scaffolded pedagogy. Building user confidence in AI systems involves ensuring that users feel certain about the correctness, reliability, functionality, and helpfulness of the system. Repetition aids this process, but another key will be to ensure that the steps and workings of the assessment or skill builder are made visible, tangible, and easily discernible to the student.

Confidence in the generative AI tools "can be defined as a measure of risk as to how sure users are that they received the correct suggestions by the AI system and if they consider the system to be [...] helpful, i.e., the system provides adequate help for the users" (Karran et al., 2022, p. 3). So, it may be fair to say that an AI system that offers valuable guidance, suggestions, and solutions to users will be seen as helpful, instilling confidence in the user. In the context of AI tools, helpfulness is a critical factor that influences user confidence.

The Chain-of-Thought (CoT) framework (Pang et al., 2024) is a great way to demystify writing for students. This reasoning model breaks down complex problems into a series of logical steps which aligns with the goal of making the writing process more transparent and accessible. By using CoT in AI-powered assessments we can guide students through the process of constructing well-reasoned arguments and coherent narratives. CoT mirrors the thinking of proficient writers. It makes those steps explicit so novice writers can understand and internalize the logical flow of ideas. This transparency is key to building confidence as it turns writing from a scary, mysterious task into a series of manageable, connected steps. And CoT's connection focused approach aligns with critical thinking in writing instruction.

By using this structured approach, we develop writing skills and broader analytical skills for academic success.

Applying this to writing assessments can yield AI systems that learn from student responses and continually get better at providing feedback. These systems could generate different levels of feedback for a piece of writing and then optimize based on criteria defined by the course and best practices in writing instruction. This process is mirrored in the recursive nature of writing itself, so students see that good writing is a process of continuous refinement. This also allows for adaptive assessments that change with each student's progress (Pang et al., 2024). By analyzing patterns in student work over time, these systems can offer personalized guidance based on individual strengths and weaknesses, so students become more confident and self-directed in their writing development.

These advanced AI approaches revolutionize writing instruction by offering more personalization and support than ever before. Employing CoT, AI can generate writing prompts tailored to each student's level of skill. These prompts can be designed to walk students through specific reasoning steps, scaffolding their way through complex writing tasks. The AI can provide detailed, context specific feedback. Instead of generic comments, students receive feedback that speaks directly to their writing patterns. This targeted feedback helps students see both strengths and areas for improvement, to build confidence. And these AI's can provide step by step guidance throughout the writing process. From brainstorming to final edits, students have a writing coach that never tires and breaks down the overwhelming tasks into smaller steps. This constant support makes the writing process less mysterious, and students can tackle the tough assignments with more confidence. By providing this level of personal, process support these AI's do more than just improve writing skills – they build student confidence so students can approach writing with excitement instead of anxiety.

The iterative nature of these AI models mirrors the writing process itself. Just as students refine work through multiple drafts, these systems learn from each interaction to get more nuanced and better support (Pang et al., 2024). This amplifies a crucial message to students: writing is not a one and done task but a skill that develops over time through practice and reflection. The AI's adaptability is a tangible example that writing proficiency is not innate but developed through repeated effort and refinement. Plus this iterative approach supports metacognitive goals. As students work with AI tools they are forced to reflect on their own progress and develop a sense of their own writing abilities. Self-awareness is the foundation of confidence and allows students to take ownership of their writing journey. In the end these AI models embody the iterative nature of writing development and do more than just support a task. They have the potential to inspire a growth mindset and the idea that with persistence every student can become a more confident writer. Incorporating the

CoT framework into AI-powered assessments can help create dynamic, interactive writing exercises that guide students through each step of the writing process, from initial brainstorming to final revision. The AI itself can provide targeted feedback and prompts at each stage to reinforce critical thinking and metacognitive skills.

When AI systems are designed to assist with tasks and decision-making processes in a transparent and explainable manner, users are more likely to perceive them as valuable partners in their educational journey. This positive perception can lead to increased trust and reliance on AI as users recognize the benefits of the support it provides in achieving their goals. By creating systems that are easy to understand and interact with, individuals can gain a clearer understanding of how these technologies work, thus fostering AI literacy. This understanding demystifies the technology but also boosts their confidence, putting the tools and knowledge to leverage AI effectively and confidently directly into their own hands.

Taking this a step further, when AI consistently performs well and provides accurate suggestions or solutions, users may develop confidence in the AI's ability to assist with the task at hand. This positive experience could indirectly boost users' confidence in the task itself, as they rely on AI for support. A study conducted by Chong et al. (2022) showed results demonstrating participants "are slightly more confident in themselves" after working with AI. While the data indicated a limited impact on user confidence in the AI system they were engaged with, even a slight increase can be meaningful for first-year students who are struggling with low confidence in their ability to do college-level work. Additionally, the study suggests that positive feedback users receive from AI interactions can influence their perception of their own skills and abilities and may enhance self-confidence (Chong et al., 2022).

The integration of generative AI into the writing classroom holds promise for cultivating greater self-assurance and positive self-perception in student writers. We'll use this to help guide the creation of writing assessments that test student achievement, responsively remediate knowledge gaps, and bolster confidence and self-efficacy through a process that employs generative AI tools and deepens competence in AI Literacy.

Strategies

Having established our frameworks for AI literacy and balanced integration, we can now explore specific strategies for implementation in the classroom. The first crucial distinction to understand is the difference between allowing AI use and truly integrating it into assessment design. It's important to recognize the difference in allowing AI to be used in assessments to having truly AI-powered assessments. AI-enabled assessments just allow students to use AI tools as they complete traditional assignments. AI powered assessments integrate AI into the learning process itself.

These innovative tools adapt to individual student needs, provide real time feedback and guidance throughout the assessment journey. Unlike their AI enabled counterparts AI powered assessments don't just supplement human instruction – they transform it. By using AI for personalized learning these assessments offer a dynamic interactive experience that goes beyond just completing a task. They challenge students to engage critically with AI generated content and develop deeper understanding and skills. This is a paradigm shift in educational technology – from AI as an add on to being part of the assessment design.

AI-powered tools can provide students with immediate guidance with grammar and other aspects of the writing process, enabling them to improve their abilities and bolster confidence. Students at the beginning or lower end of the skills spectrum can use AI to quickly upskill by providing developmental feedback rather than using AI to take shortcuts or generate work wholesale. As we have seen, collaborating with AI is a particularly attractive option for first-year writing courses. But in order to ensure this approach works, we need to develop intentional assessments, grounded by our dual framework of course-specific outcomes and balanced by AI literacy. Developing formative activities such as AI-powered dialogic mechanisms tailored to remediating specific areas of need in first-year writing instruction, such as pre-writing, audience analysis, or thesis development, presents an opportunity to create a more dynamic accelerator for student skills. Instead of turning to ChatGPT or some other AI tool to outsource content creation, students will be guided in how to collaborate with generative AI in a way that inspires engagement and builds confidence while helping ensure outcomes are grasped. Employing prompt engineering to generative AI tools allows us to develop AI-adaptive assessments that adapt to individual students while performing a battery of cumulative activities and exercises. This automatic feedback mechanism meets students where they are when they need it and can yield deeper gains in achievement.

Incorporating AI-powered assessments into written instruction stands to enhance students' written communication skills but may also provide a valuable opportunity to improve digital literacy and foster critical thinking. As students engage with AI tools to receive feedback and guidance on their writing assignments, they are simultaneously navigating the complexities of AI technology and honing their ability to critically evaluate its role in the learning process. By interrogating the tool itself, students gain a deeper comprehension of writing concepts and AI functionality while distinguishing between algorithmic assistance and independent thought. This approach transcends traditional tenets of written instruction, transforming the learning experience into a complex and rewarding exploration of AI literacy.

Applying the principles of balanced AI integration—setting clear guidelines, focusing on process over product, encouraging critical thinking, and emphasizing feedback and reflection—alongside the core competencies of AI literacy—application, authenticity, accountability, and agency—can guide us in the creation of an AI-powered assessment that not only enhances students' writing skills but also cultivates their ability to work effectively with AI tools.

This case study, of a practice activity designed to put students through a series of steps and reflective exercises that will help them build their capacity in key areas of the writing process, serves as a model for how educators can leverage our frameworks to create innovative, AI-integrated learning experiences that prepare students for an AI-augmented future while maintaining the integrity of traditional writing instruction. We'll walk through the process of developing these assessments as AI interactions, applying concepts from the dual frameworks for AI integration and AI literacy.

A thesis statement is the foundation for academic writing assignments. But it's also much more than that. It's the key to helping students clarify their ideas and strengthen their arguments, the lynchpin to the structure of any essay. Even though a thesis statement can be written as a sentence, it might be more apt to think of the thesis as a process that helps define what a student is thinking about at the same time as it indicates the scope of the writing to come. Taken that way, a thesis is not just an artifact but an action – one that we can accelerate and deepen through using AI tools.

Thesis generators are all over the internet. But they're limited. The resulting thesis statement can be clunky, doesn't display any sense of true nuance or connection, and the process is automated. They are all about the product. A student using a thesis generator doesn't learn anything or leave with a better grasp of the process. Developing an AI-powered assessment provides the opportunity for hands-on practice with dynamic experimentation, deepening students' understanding of thesis construction. By collaborating with generative AI in the thesis formulation process, students have the opportunity to refine their ideas through dialogue and ultimately produce stronger thesis statements. Additionally, working in this way enhances students' understanding of thesis formulation principles, cultivates digital literacy skills, and models a method for leveraging gen AI ethically and effectively.

Setting Clear Guidelines

The opening stage of our established framework for balanced AI integration in assessments calls for *setting clear guidelines*. Thinking of this in terms of the AI literacy framework provides faculty with clear direction in each of the domains. To start, faculty can support students in the overall *application* by beginning the assessment with a list of AI tools suitable for brainstorming and refining thesis statements. Students can also be tasked with comparing outputs from different AI tools to identify strengths and weaknesses in thesis generation. To close the loop, faculty can provide space for students to document which AI tool they used and why they chose it for their thesis development process. To ensure students produce *authentic* work, faculty can require students to generate multiple thesis options using AI, then refine and personalize one based on their own voice and perspective, explaining how they modified AI-generated theses to better reflect their unique arguments or insights. To ensure student *accountability*, faculty can instruct students to fact-check any claims in their AI-generated theses using credible sources. Additionally, implementing a reflection component where students assess the ethical implications of using AI in academic writing can help ensure that they develop a deeper understanding of responsible technology use and foster a culture of academic integrity. Finally, to model *agency*, faculty-designed assessments can allow students to choose whether to use AI for initial brainstorming or to refine an already developed thesis while setting personal goals for balancing AI assistance with independent critical thinking in the thesis development.

For the thesis accelerator assessment, we have ensured that the assignment prompt clearly states how the stages of thesis development can involve AI and which must be done independently. We'll do that by using AI to drive the assessment forward with reflective stops along the way to ensure students are explaining how AI-generated content is used.

Learning Process Over Product

The second stage of balanced AI integration is *the learning process of the product*. Integrating this with our AI literacy framework will help create a roadmap for thesis development assessments. To ensure fruitful *application*, faculty can require students to document their use of different AI tools throughout the thesis development process, explaining how each tool contributed to their understanding. This can encourage experimentation, and asking students to document this through a decision tree or mind map can help deepen their understanding. Supporting this assessment with peer discussions where students share how they maintain their authentic voice while integrating AI-assisted research is one way to ensure *authenticity*. Another may be to integrate asking students to write a reflection on how AI-generated perspectives influenced but didn't dictate their final thesis direction. *Accountability* here can take several forms. Peer review discussion can act as a series of check-ins where students discuss the accuracy and relevance of AI-generated information they're considering for their thesis, explaining how they verified each piece of information and allowing students to cross-check each other's use of AI in thesis development. This can help students create an evolution document showing initial AI suggestions, their thought process, and including a justification for their final thesis, explaining why they chose it over other AI-suggested options. This ensures *agency* is built into the prompt.

For our thesis accelerator assessment, students work through a multi-stage process with reflections at each point instead of a single final thesis submission. This portfolio includes AI outputs, student modifications, research notes, and reflections on the learning journey. A final meta-cognitive reflection where students analyze how their approach to using AI in academic work has evolved throughout the process emphasizes the learning journey, AI literacy development, and the cultivation of critical thinking skills alongside the final thesis product.

Critical Thinking

The next step involves integrating AI literacy with *critical thinking* to create a balanced approach to thesis development. Faculty should empower students to use AI tools effectively while maintaining intellectual autonomy and honing analytical skills. Several previously mentioned ideas support student growth in the *application* domain. For example, having students compare AI-generated thesis statements to identify strengths and weaknesses and documenting their decision-making when selecting AI tools for research or brainstorming fosters critical analysis. To ensure *authenticity*, assessments can challenge students to refine AI-generated thesis ideas by incorporating personal experiences or cultural perspectives. *Accountability* can be reinforced through peer review discussions where students fact-check and evaluate AI-assisted thesis statements. Additionally, tasking students with creating guidelines for ethical AI use in thesis development based on their own experiences can enhance their feelings of *agency*. Highlight key decisions students make about their thesis direction, using AI as a supportive tool rather than the primary driver. Encourage them to develop criteria for assessing the quality and relevance of AI-generated content.

In our thesis accelerator assessment, we asked students to analyze the logical structure of AI-generated arguments related to their thesis topics, developing outlines to identify potential biases or gaps in AI-generated research summaries.

Feedback and Reflection

The final stage of the framework for balanced AI usage is *feedback and reflection*. Applying this to our framework for AI literacy will offer opportunities to enhance students' metacognition and self-regulated learning, crucial skills for effective AI integration. Student journals, as discussed previously, support the *application* domain. These can include ratings of effectiveness, as well as detailed insights gained about AI applications throughout the thesis development process. Peer feedback and discussion opportunities can support a discussion of *authenticity*, especially when focused on evaluating student ability to maintain an authentic voice while using AI-generated content. *Accountability* develops through targeted reflection aimed at self-assessment and evaluating the ethical use of AI in thesis development. Finally, students can demonstrate *agency* through these created logs, recording and justifying key choices made during thesis development, especially when they diverge from AI suggestions. Especially useful here would be a global end-of-project reflection where students analyze how their relationship with AI tools evolved throughout the thesis process.

A capstone to this process included in the thesis accelerator assessment is kicking off a comprehensive reflection log where students compile examples of their AI use, reflections, and growth throughout the thesis development process. Paired with in-class discussions focused on what worked well, what didn't, and what they'd do differently in future AI-assisted projects can create a dynamic, reflective environment for thesis development. By combining critical thinking with ongoing feedback and reflection, students develop not just their thesis but also valuable skills in AI literacy and self-regulated learning. This method turns the thesis development process into a rich learning experience about both the subject matter and the thoughtful integration of AI in academic work.

Solutions

With these strategic approaches in mind, we can now examine concrete solutions for creating AI-powered assessments that embody these principles. Rather than assessments that allow AI usage or more clearly direct that use, we want to explore the possibility of creating truly AI-powered assessments. While some studies have shown the potential for AI tutors (Henkel et al., 2024), and other work has pointed the way toward constructing general purpose AI-powered tutoring solutions (Mollick & Mollick, 2024), there is still much experimentation that needs to take place to ameliorate hallucination risks and ensure proper human guidance. Still, this shift represents a significant leap in how we approach writing instruction and student engagement with technology. Mollick & Mollick (2024) indicated the potential of AI-powered assessments to "focus on interactivity and dialogue, adapt to student responses, ask students open-ended questions, assess student prior knowledge, and provide personalized explanations, examples, and feedback." Students engage in dynamic conversations with AI, exploring ideas, refining concepts, and building their writing skills in real time. Our approach centers on two key areas: topic development and thesis formulation. In topic development, students use AI as a sounding board, refining their ideas through dialogue. For thesis formulation, AI becomes a collaborative partner, offering feedback and helping students structure their arguments effectively.

But we also push students to reflect deeply on this process. They examine how AI shaped their thinking, identifying both benefits and potential pitfalls. This metacognitive exercise doesn't just improve writing skills - it builds critical AI literacy for the future. This method goes far beyond simple thesis generators. It creates a rich, interactive learning environment that challenges students to think critically, engage deeply with ideas, and harness AI's potential responsibly.

To bring this concept to life, we've developed a comprehensive AI tutor prompt. This prompt guides students through the entire thesis development process, from topic selection to final reflection. This prompt embodies our dual framework, balancing AI integration with AI literacy, leading to the development of crucial writing and critical thinking skills. Instructors have to balance the benefits of AI tutoring with the drawbacks and need a nuanced approach to implementing it in the classroom. The main concern is the AI's potential to produce superficial or inaccurate knowledge which can produce plausible but wrong answers. This is exacerbated by students' lack of awareness, insufficient background knowledge or confidence to challenge the AI's output. The AI Literacy and Balanced Integration frameworks have ways to mitigate the risks of AI tutoring. By focusing on critical thinking and metacognition, these frameworks help students to interact with AI more mindfully. The AI Literacy framework's Application and Accountability focus helps students to understand AI's limitations and fact check its outputs. The Balanced Integration framework's Learning Process Over Product focus means students are looking at the AI generated answers rather than their own intellectual growth.

These frameworks don't just address surface level issues; they change how students interact with AI. By having Agency, students can question AI outputs and maintain their intellectual autonomy. The focus on Authenticity means AI is a tool to enhance human creativity not replace it. Clear Guidelines for AI use, with ongoing Feedback and Reflection means students can safely experiment with AI while developing the skills to identify and correct misconceptions. In the end these frameworks turn potential risks into opportunities for deeper learning. They help teachers to use the strengths of AI while avoiding its weaknesses, an education that prepares students for an AI world without compromising academic integrity or critical thinking.

Here's a Sample Prompt:

You are to act as a tutor for first-year writing students. In that AI Tutor Role you will: Guide students through thesis development. Boost understanding and challenge students to build their own knowledge. Use direct instruction, open-ended questions, hints, and examples. Make connections between concepts and uncover misconceptions. Be encouraging and practical. Set high expectations. Believe in students' ability to learn and improve.

STEP 1: BEGIN TUTORING (Independent work)

1. Help students pick a topic they want to explore. Refine it through questions. Ask students to clearly state their topic.
2. Encourage detailed responses. Prompt for more if answers are brief.

STEP 2: EXPLORE KNOWLEDGE (Independent work with AI assistance)

1. Ask students to list what they know about the topic and what they want to learn.
2. Push for thorough responses. Prompt for more detail if needed.
3. Have students explain how their experiences shape their approach to the topic.

STEP 3: DEVELOP THE THESIS (Collaborative work with AI)

1. Guide thesis development. Teach skills for future use. Prompt refinement, don't write it for them.
2. Offer 2-3 AI-generated thesis statements. Ask students to compare with their ideas. Analyze strengths and weaknesses.
3. Help students refine their thesis using these insights.
4. Direct students to fact-check key points using credible sources. Have them report any changes made.
5. Ensure students provide detailed responses throughout.

STEP 4: REFLECT (Independent work)

1. Ask about challenges faced. What was new or familiar?
2. Have students consider how AI helped or hindered their thinking.
3. Prompt reflection on maintaining authenticity while using AI input.
4. Push for thorough responses. Encourage expansion if answers are thin.

Adapt to student responses throughout. Be encouraging. Maintain high expectations for engagement and learning.

By collaborating with AI tools in the thesis formulation process, students have the opportunity to refine their ideas through dialogue and ultimately produce stronger thesis statements. Additionally, working in this way enhances students' understanding of thesis formulation principles but also cultivates AI literacy skills and models a method for balancing integrated AI usage. The multi-step prompt lends itself to a more holistic assessment that goes beyond the final product, looking at the student's journey and growth throughout the thesis development process. Instructors can assess student engagement at each stage, from topic selection to final reflection, by reviewing the entire interaction log. This allows for a more nuanced assessment of student critical thinking, ability to use AI and self-reflection. The independent work phases allow for assessment of student baseline knowledge and ability to articulate ideas without AI. The collaborative AI phases allow for assessment of student AI literacy, particularly their ability to evaluate and refine AI generated content.

The reflection component is itself an assessment tool, allowing students to show their metacognitive processes and their understanding of AI in their learning. Instructors can see how students identify and address biases or inaccuracies in AI responses, demonstrating their growing AI literacy. This reflection can be used as the basis for class discussions, peer learning and collective exploration of course content and AI.

By focusing on the learning process rather than the final product, this assessment approach makes students see AI as a tool not a shortcut. It allows instructors to assess not only student understanding of course content but also their developing AI literacy skills, preparing them for an AI augmented future while maintaining academic integrity and critical thinking.

While instructors must continue to play a crucial role in guiding and supporting students, working with AI tools can provide supplemental benefits for student learning. To begin with, especially in large classes or online learning environments, AI tools offer a scalable first round of support – which can be accessed by students anytime, anywhere. Engaging in dialogue with AI tools can foster critical thinking skills as students road-test alternative approaches that enrich their learning experience. This process empowers students to take ownership of their learning, leading to increased confidence and a sense of autonomy and self-efficacy.

Discussion

The integration of AI-powered assessments in first-year writing courses opens up the opportunity for longitudinal research. A metric for skills retention or student confidence and self-efficacy could provide insights into the long-term effects of this on student development and academic success. Additionally, current research faces inherent challenges in measuring the long-term impact of AI integration on student writing development. The rapid evolution of AI technology means today's findings may quickly become outdated.

The integration of AI-powered assessments raises important equity considerations. Not all students enter college with the same level of technological literacy or access to AI tools. As we implement AI-powered assessments, we must ensure that our approach doesn't inadvertently disadvantage certain student populations.

This may require additional support structures, such as AI literacy workshops or expanded technology access programs, to level the playing field.

But the implications for teaching and learning are more immediate. Since first-year writing courses may be a higher risk environment for AI misuse, they may need to restructure curricula to include AI literacy alongside traditional writing skills, which could mean longer or re-designed course sequences. Instructors will require ongoing training to stay current with AI and how to integrate it effectively, which means robust professional development programs. And as we have discussed, traditional rubrics and assessment methods will need to be revised to account for AI-assisted work, focusing more on process, critical thinking, and appropriate AI tool use rather than just end products.

AI-powered assessments could mean more adaptive, personalized instruction, allowing for targeted interventions based on individual student needs. The integration of generative AI into educational assessments is changing the way we teach and learn. And it offers exciting possibilities for enhancing student engagement, personalizing the learning experience, and instructor workload.

The frameworks and principles developed for AI integration in writing instruction have implications beyond composition classrooms. The balanced integration approach could adapt well to other humanities disciplines where critical thinking and analysis are paramount. In STEM fields, similar frameworks might guide the development of AI-assisted problem-solving exercises. The emphasis on process over product and the focus on AI literacy as a parallel skill could reshape how we approach assessment across the curriculum. As more disciplines grapple with AI integration, the lessons learned from writing instruction could provide valuable guidance for developing discipline-specific approaches to AI-enhanced learning.

Generative AI is changing writing instruction. At its best, AI-powered assessments boost student engagement with instant, tailored feedback. This creates a dynamic learning environment. Students no longer have to wait days for instructor comments. They can improve their work quickly. This feedback loop keeps the momentum going. It is especially valuable for first-year students trying to write at the college level. Students invest more in the writing process as they learn to work with AI. This engagement extends to broader digital literacy and prepares them for an AI-integrated world.

AI integration in writing instruction is a game-changer. It promises more engaging, more personalized, and more efficient learning. But it will require planning and assessment. These tools can support human instruction but cannot replace it. The instructor's role will change. Instruction must change as well.

REFERENCES

Brynjolfsson, E., Li, D., & Raymond, L. (April 2023). Generative AI at work (NBER Working Paper No. W31161). Retrieved from *SSRN*: https://ssrn.com/abstract=4426942 DOI: 10.2139/ssrn.4426942

Cardon, P., Fleischmann, C., Aritz, J., Logemann, M., & Heidewald, J. (2023). The challenges and opportunities of Al-assisted writing: Developing Al literacy for the Al age. *Business and Professional Communication Quarterly*, 86(3), 1–39. DOI: 10.1177/23294906231176517

Chong, L., Zhang, G., Goucher-Lambert, K., Kotovsky, K., & Cagan, J. (2022). Human confidence in artificial intelligence and in themselves: The evolution and impact of confidence on adoption of AI advice. *Computers in Human Behavior*, 127, 107018. DOI: 10.1016/j.chb.2021.107018

Chowdhury Niloy, A., Bari, M. A., Sultana, J., Chowdhury, R., Raisa, F. M., Islam, A., Mahmud, S., Jahan, I., Sarkar, M., Akter, S., Nishat, N., Afroz, M., Sen, A., Islam, T., Tareq, M. H., & Hossen, M. A. (2024). Why do students use ChatGPT? Answering through a triangulation approach. *Computers and Education: Artificial Intelligence*, 6, 100208. DOI: 10.1016/j.caeai.2024.100208

Chui, M., Hazan, E., Roberts, R., Singla, A., Smaje, K., Sukharevsky, A., Yee, L., & Zemmel, R. (2023, June 14), The economic potential of generative AI: The next productivity frontier, *McKinsey Digital*. https://www.mckinsey.com/capabilities/mckinsey-digital/our-insights/the-economic-potential-of-generative-AI-the-next-productivity-frontier#introduction

Davies, A., Fidler, D., & Gorbis, M. (2011). Future work skills 2020. *Institute for the Future for Apollo Research Institute*. https://uqpn.uq.edu.au/files/203/LIBBY%20MARSHALL%20future_work_skills_2020_full_research_report_final_1.pdf

Getchell, K. M., Carradini, S., Cardon, P. W., Fleischmann, C., Ma, H., Aritz, J., & Stapp, J. (2022). Artificial intelligence in business communication: The changing landscape of research and teaching. *Business and Professional Communication Quarterly*, 85(1), 1–27. DOI: 10.1177/23294906221074311

Graham, S., & Perin, D. (2007). *Writing next: Effective strategies to improve writing of adolescents in middle and high schools – A report to Carnegie Corporation of New York*. Alliance for Excellent Education.

Henkel, O., Horne-Robinson, H., Kozhakhmetova, N., & Lee, A. (2024). Effective and Scalable Math Support: Evidence on the Impact of an AI-Tutor on Math Achievement in Ghana. *arXiv preprint arXiv:2402.09809*.DOI: 10.1007/978-3-031-64315-6_34

Karran, A. J., Demazure, T., Hudon, A., Senecal, S., & Léger, P. M. (2022). Designing for confidence: The impact of visualizing artificial intelligence decisions. *Frontiers in Neuroscience*, 16, 883385. DOI: 10.3389/fnins.2022.883385 PMID: 35812230

Mollick, E., & Mollick, L. (2024). Instructors as innovators: A future-focused approach to new AI learning opportunities, with prompts. *arXiv preprint arXiv:2407.05181*.

Ng, D. T. K., Leung, J. K. L., Chu, S. K. W., & Qiao, M. S. (2021). Conceptualizing AI literacy: An exploratory review. *Computers and Education: Artificial Intelligence*, 2, 100041. DOI: 10.1016/j.caeai.2021.100041

Noy, S., & Zhang, W. (2023). Experimental evidence on the productivity effects of generative artificial intelligence. *Science*, 381(6654), 187–192. DOI: 10.1126/science.adh2586 PMID: 37440646

Pang, R. Y., Yuan, W., Cho, K., He, H., Sukhbaatar, S., & Weston, J. (2024). Iterative reasoning preference optimization. *arXiv preprint arXiv:2404.19733*.

Sholikah, M., & Anwar, M. A. Muhibbudin, & Sa'diyah, D. F., Hidayati, Y., & Permadi, B. (2019). The Effectiveness of Writing Approach Viewed from Students' Self-Confidence. *Advances in Social Science, Education and Humanities Research*, 349. pp. 322-325. https://doi.org/DOI: 10.2991/iccd-19.2019.85

Sommers, N., & Saltz, L. (2004). The novice as expert: Writing the freshman year. *College Composition and Communication*, 56(1), 124–149. DOI: 10.58680/ccc20043993

Soria Krista, M. (2012). Creating a successful transition for working-class first-year students. *The Journal of College Orientation and Transition*, 20(1), 44–55.

Vos, L. (2023, September 7). *Ai hurts students' writing and communication skills*. eCampus News. https://www.ecampusnews.com/featured/2023/09/21/ai-tools-students-writing-communication-skills/

Wette, R. (2014). Teachers' practices in EAP writing instruction: Use of models and modeling. *System*, 42, 60–69. DOI: 10.1016/j.system.2013.11.002

Additional Reading

Chan, C. K. Y., & Tsi, L. H. Y. (2023). The AI revolution in education: Will AI replace or assist teachers in higher education? *Centre for the Enhancement of Teaching and Learning (CETL)*, University of Hong Kong.

Mollick, E., & Mollick, L. (2024). Instructors as innovators: A future-focused approach to new AI learning opportunities, with prompts. *arXiv preprint arXiv:2407.05181.*

Murad, I. A., Shafiq Surameery, N. M., & Shakor, M. Y. (2023). Adopting ChatGPT to enhance educational experiences. *International Journal of Information Technology and Computer Engineering*, 3(5), 20–25. DOI: 10.55529/ijitc.35.20.25

Pritts, N. (2023, August 29). *How to be conspicuously human in the online classroom*. Faculty Focus | Higher Ed Teaching & Learning. https://www.facultyfocus.com/articles/online-education/online-course-delivery-and-instruction/how-to-be-conspicuously-human-in-the-online-classroom

Pritts, N. (2024, April 5). *Two ways AI can support student success in online courses*. The Teaching Professor. https://www.teachingprofessor.com/topics/teaching-strategies/teaching-with-technology/two-ways-ai-can-support-student-success-in-online-courses/

KEY TERMS AND DEFINITIONS

AI-Enabled Assessment: A traditional assessment method that allows and specifies where students may use AI to support their output.

AI-Powered Assessment: Educational tools that use AI to evaluate and guide student learning. They adapt to individual needs and provide instant, personalized feedback. Used to differentiate from AI-Enabled Assessment.

AI Literacy: A framework for understanding and using AI responsibly developed by Cardon et al. (2023), comprising four core competencies: Application, Authenticity, Accountability, Agency. This skill set equips students with the skills to evaluate AI technologies, collaborate effectively with AI tools, and apply them across various settings. It prepares students for an AI-augmented future by teaching them to balance AI capabilities with human insight and judgment.

Balanced Integration of AI: Based on research conducted by Chowdhury Niloy et al. (2024), this is a framework for using AI in education that includes: Setting Clear Guidelines, Learning Process Over Product, Encouraging Critical Thinking, Feedback and Reflection. It fosters an approach to incorporating AI tools in education that enhances learning without overshadowing human skills. It leverages AI's strengths while preserving critical thinking.

Chain-of-Thought (CoT): This framework, adapted from Pang et al. (2024) simplifies writing by breaking it down into logical steps, making the process more transparent and manageable for students. CoT helps guide students in constructing well-reasoned arguments, building confidence and critical thinking skills.

Confidence Building: Strategies that boost students' belief in their writing abilities. This process encourages risk-taking and resilience in academic tasks.

Explainable AI Systems: AI tools that can clarify their decision-making process. They help users understand why the AI made specific choices or recommendations.

First-Year Writing: Foundational college courses that teach essential writing skills. These classes help students transition to college-level communication.

Generative AI: AI systems that create new content based on patterns in existing data. They can produce text, images, or other media that appear human-made.

Human-AI Trust Relationship: The bond formed when people understand and rely on AI systems. It involves balancing AI capabilities with human judgment and ethics.

Metacognition: Thinking about one's own thought processes. In writing, it involves reflecting on and improving one's approach to composition.

Novice Writers: Beginners in academic writing, often first-year college students. They're learning to express complex ideas clearly and persuasively.

Process over Product: This concept emphasizes the importance of focusing on the stages of writing, such as brainstorming, drafting, revising, and editing, rather than just the final written piece. It highlights writing as a developmental journey where students refine their skills through practice and feedback, ultimately building confidence and proficiency.

Prompt Engineering: The skill of crafting clear, effective instructions for AI systems. It helps users get more accurate and useful responses from AI tools.

Self-Regulated Learning: The ability to manage one's own learning process. It includes setting goals, monitoring progress, and adjusting strategies as needed.

Chapter 5
AI-adaptive Chinese Language Learning Environment and Assessments in Hong Kong

Siu-lun Lee
https://orcid.org/0000-0002-2306-9217
The Chinese University of Hong Kong, China

ABSTRACT

This chapter sets out to discuss the development of AI-adaptive Chinese language learning environments and assessments, as well as innovations and future directions in Chinese language learning and assessments in the AI era in Hong Kong by critically analyzing the views on the use of generative artificial intelligence in Chinese language education and investigating the different views of the stakeholders in Chinese education expressed in Hong Kong newspapers. A corpus containing Hong Kong Chinese-language newspaper articles discussing the AI-adaptive learning environment in Chinese education and assessments in Hong Kong has been constructed and analyzed. The research questions are set as follows: (i) to investigate the extent to which the Hong Kong press expressed views about the AI-adaptive learning environment in Chinese education in Hong Kong; and (ii) to analyze the development of AI-adaptive assessments. This study will shed some light on the discussions of using generative artificial intelligence in Chinese language assessment in the Hong Kong educational context.

DOI: 10.4018/979-8-3693-6351-5.ch005

INTRODUCTION

The use of artificial intelligence (AI) has been actively discussed in the language educational field in recent decades. Some studies discuss the use of conversational artificial intelligence in language classrooms (Jeon, 2022; Ji et al., 2023). Some research explores how generative artificial intelligence and chatbot technology can shape future language learning and teaching (Kim et al., 2019). The discussion about the development and impact of artificial intelligence and its use in education has been a topic receiving the attention of linguists, educators, policymakers, and the public in recent years in Hong Kong (Chen et al., 2022; Lee & Chen, 2024). Topics relating to the use of artificial intelligence in education have been widely discussed in Hong Kong's public media (Chen, 2023). There are ongoing debates on these topics in the Hong Kong press. Some newspaper articles suggest that artificial intelligence is effective in language learning in Hong Kong schools (Yeung, 2019).

On the other hand, some articles voice out that the students and the educational field are not benefiting from artificial intelligence (Liu & Yau, 2023). Some researchers studied these public opinions about the development and applications of generative artificial intelligence in language education in Hong Kong and observed that there is an increasing trend of using generative AI in language education (Lee & Chen, 2024). Yet, research on the impact of generative artificial intelligence on language assessment is limited when the author is writing this chapter. This chapter sets out to discuss the development of AI-adaptive Chinese language learning environments and assessments, as well as innovations and future directions in Chinese language assessments in the AI era by critically analyzing the views on the use of generative artificial intelligence in Chinese language assessment and investigating the different views of the stakeholders in Chinese education expressed in Hong Kong newspapers. A corpus containing Hong Kong Chinese-language newspaper articles discussing the application of generative artificial intelligence in Chinese language education and assessments in Hong Kong has been constructed and analyzed. The research questions are set as follows: (i) to investigate the extent to which the Hong Kong press expressed views about the AI-adaptive learning environment in Chinese education in Hong Kong; and (ii) to analyze the development of AI-adaptive assessments. This study will shed some light on the discussions of using generative artificial intelligence in Chinese language assessment in the Hong Kong educational context.

AI Technologies in Education and Language Learning

Since OpenAI laid the groundwork with GPT-1 on 11 June 2018 and marked the advancement of a natural language processing model that can produce a coherent and contextually relevant response to a particular prompt, some scholars started to evaluate and discuss the use of artificial intelligence in education (Chassignol, et al., 2018; Pedró et al., 2019; Chen et al., 2020; Zai et al., 2021). AI initially took the form of computer and computer-related technologies, transitioning to web-based and online intelligent education systems, and ultimately with the use of embedded computer systems, together with other technologies, the use of humanoid robots and web-based chatbots to perform instructors' duties and functions independently or with teachers. Some studies showed that AI applications can help teachers review and grade students' assignments more effectively and efficiently to achieve higher quality in their teaching activities (Sun et al., 2021). Scholars were also discussing how AI can change students' learning styles and habits (Kang & Kang, 2020), and will re-model the role of teachers with the help of technology in the AI era (Cope et al., 2021; Schmidt & Strasser, 2022).

There was also a bibliometric analysis to study the research literature relating to the use of AI in language education (Huang et al., 2023). This research reviewed 516 papers published from 2000 to 2019 and summarized the 10 most popular topics related to AI in language education including (1) automated writing evaluation, (2) intelligent tutoring systems for reading and writing, (3) automated error detection, (4) computer-mediated communication, (5) personalized systems for language learning, (6) natural language and vocabulary learning, (7) web-resources and web-based systems for language learning, (8) intelligent tutoring systems for writing in English for specific purposes, (9) intelligent tutoring systems for pronunciation and speech training, and (10) affective states and emotions (Huang et al., 2023, p. 112).

ChatGPT was officially launched on 30 November 2022 and took the world by surprise with its sophisticated capacity. ChatGPT, a large language model-based chatbot developed by OpenAI, enables users to refine and steer a conversation towards a desired length, format, style, level of detail, and language. As announced by Microsoft, ChatGPT-powered features were coming to Bing on 7 February 2023 and later Copilot was integrated with Bing, Microsoft Edge, and Windows 11 to assist computer users in daily and work settings. Because of this, generative AI was brought to everyday computer usage. The access of Bing and Copilot is free when the author is writing this chapter. Research has been done to identify opportunities and challenges of implementing generative AI chatbots in language education (Rudolph, et al., 2023; Ng et al., 2023). Moorhouse, et al. (2023) suggested that teaching pedagogies have been reconceptualized and the use of technology in teaching and learning has increased and 'seems to be the norm' in the post-pandemic age. They pointed out that generative AI tools have the potential to offer new and innovative ways to support both language teaching and self-directed language learning. Kohnke et al. (2023) studied the use of ChatGPT for language teaching and learning and demonstrated that ChatGPT can help explain vocabulary, create vocabulary lists, and provide sample sentences and sample texts in different genres. They also demonstrated that ChatGPT can create grammar exercises and comprehension exercises and adjust difficulties according to learners' needs.

Although there were studies illustrating the advantages of introducing generative AI in language teaching, in the meantime, there were also studies iterating the concerns of language educators, such as biases in data training, wrong information provided by the Chatbots, and privacy issues (Baidoo-Anu & Owusu Ansah, 2023; Chan, 2023). In the language education literature, there were also studies discussing the implementation of conversational artificial intelligence in language classrooms (Jeon, 2022; Ji et al., 2023) and some research explores how artificial intelligence and chatbot technology can shape future language learning and teaching (Kim et al., 2019).

Chinese Education and Assessments in Hong Kong

Hong Kong is an international city with multi-ethnic and multilingual characteristics. Research showed that in addition to the three major languages, Cantonese, Putonghua, and English, other languages used in Hong Kong such as minority Chinese languages (Chiu Chau, Fukien, Hakka, Shanghainese, and Sze Yap), as well as a diverse range of Asian and European languages, including Bengali, French, German, Hindi, Italian, Japanese, Korean, Nepali, Russian, Spanish, Thai, and Urdu (Bacon-Shone et al., 2015; Bacon-shone et al., 2019; Bolton et al., 2020). In recent decades, the Hong Kong SAR government has promoted 'trilingualism and biliteracy', which means the use of three spoken languages, Cantonese, Putonghua, and English, and two written codes, standard written Chinese and written English, in official settings (Bacon-Shone et al., 2015; Bolton et al., 2020; Bolton & Lee, 2020). Cantonese, English, and Putonghua are three major languages used in Hong Kong, and both written Chinese and English are used in government announcements, in the education domain, and in business sectors.

Based on the government census data, around 90% of Hong Kong people use Cantonese as their usual language (Hong Kong Government, 2011, 2016, 2021). Due to the systematic differences between spoken Cantonese and Standard Written Chinese, Cantonese-speaking school students required training to gain Chinese literacy (Lee, 2023a). The Chinese language is a school subject in Hong Kong primary and secondary schools that teaches Hong Kong schoolchildren Chinese literacy skills (Tse, 2009; Lau, 2019).

In Hong, Kong, public examinations administrated by the Hong Kong Examination Authority are used to assess school students' Chinese language abilities. Diploma of Secondary Education Examination (DSE) Chinese examination tests the Chinese abilities of Chinese-speaking school students. DSE Chinese is one of the mandatory subjects for entering Hong Kong universities. In 2012, DSE

Chinese was first designed to test students' 'mixed Chinese skills' (Zhu, 2015). In view that the linguistic and cultural backgrounds of Chinese-speaking students and ethnic minority school students are very diverse (Chan, 2019; Cheung, 2019), the Education Bureau started two Applied Chinese curricula for these ethnic minority groups in 2014 as an alternative universities' entrance requirement to DSE Chinese for ethnic minority schoolchildren. DSE Chinese has gone through and is still going through several reforms (Yan & Brown, 2021). After 2016 when the listening comprehension examination of DSE Chinese merged with 'mixed Chinese skills' papers and the cancellation of the speaking examination in 2023, DSE Chinese has been focusing on the reading and writing skills of Hong Kong secondary students. In addition to DSE Chinese, school students in Hong Kong have choices to take International Baccalaureate (IB) Chinese, or the General Certificate of Secondary Education (GCSE) Chinese examinations based on their educational needs.

Putonghua Assessments in Hong Kong

The use of Putonghua has been increased in various sectors in recent years in Hong Kong (Zhang & Yan, 2004; Wang & Yuan, 2013; Liu, 2018). The Education Bureau has been promoting the teaching and learning of Putonghua and believes that a good mastery of Putonghua is conducive to better communication and integration of Hong Kong students into the overall development of China, and to 'boosting national pride and national confidence' (Hong Kong Government, 2022). Putonghua started to be included as a core school subject at primary and junior secondary schools in 1998 (Hong Kong Government, 2022). Public examinations available in Hong Kong to assess students' Putonghua abilities include Putonghua Shuiping Ceshi 'Putonghua Proficiency Test' (PSC) and Hanyu Shuiping Kaoshi 'Chinese Proficiency Test' (HSK). PSC is designed for Chinese-speaking people to test their accuracy, fluency, and usage of Putonghua, while HSK is targeted to non-Chinese speakers testing their Putonghua oral proficiency levels.

AI in Chinese Education in Hong Kong and Research Issues

It has been some years since Hong Kong schools and universities implemented computer-assisted language learning (CALL) in the learning and teaching of languages. Universities in Hong Kong have encouraged and implemented e-learning in undergraduate language courses since 2009 (King, 2016). Universities have experience using online teaching and learning materials to supplement their formal Chinese classes (Kataoka, 2023; Lee, 2011, 2016, 2018). The implementation of computer-assisted learning was also promoted in primary and secondary education in Hong Kong (Bai et. al., 2021).

The global demand for online learning materials was particularly high during the Covid pandemic (Yaacob, & Saad, 2020). Lee (2022) pointed out that university students' acceptance of technology-enhanced language learning and blended teaching models has grown substantially throughout the pandemic. The global pandemic moved educational institutions throughout the world to implement various forms of online teaching and virtually available resources for both self-learners and students taking formal language courses (Lee, 2022). Some studies showed that artificial intelligence, augmented reality, big data, and social media, can enhance language learning by providing authentic, contextualized, and collaborative learning experiences (Kessler, 2017; Chin, 2023; Lee, 2023b). Discussions about the impact of artificial intelligence and its use in education in Hong Kong have also been a topic attracting the attention of linguists, educators, policymakers, and the public in recent years (Chen et al., 2022; Lee & Chen, 2024). The pros and cons of using generative artificial intelligence in education have been widely discussed in Hong Kong's public media (Chen, 2023; Liu & Yau, 2023; Yeung, 2019; Lee & Chen, 2024).

This paper sets out to investigate the different views of the stakeholders in language education including students, teachers, educators, and policymakers expressed in Hong Kong newspapers relating to AI-adaptive Chinese learning environments and assessment. This study collected and analysed newspaper discourse to elicit public opinion about the implementation of generative AI in Chinese education and the possibilities and challenges of AI-adaptive Chinese language assessments in Hong Kong. Analysing newspaper discourse involves examining how language is used in news articles to convey information, shape public opinion, and reflect societal values (Richardson, 2017). Van Dijik (2008) pointed out that 'it is not the social situation that influences (or is influenced by) discourse, but the way the participants define such a situation' (Van Dijk 2008, p. x). The study of newspaper discourse can understand the stakeholders' views relating to a particular issue, situation, or problem. The study by Wang et al. (2021) indicated that problem-oriented critical discourse analysis (CDA) has gained the most popularity in the area of newspaper discourse analysis in recent decade. This study uses a sociocognitive approach advocated by Van Dijk (2008) in problem-oriented CDA to look at the relationship between personal and socially shared knowledge about AI-adaptive Chinese learning environments and assessments.

RESEARCH METHODOLOGY AND DATA COLLECTION

An extensive corpus of Chinese-language newspaper articles concerning the use of artificial intelligence in language education in Hong Kong has been compiled. This database has focused on press articles discussing the use of artificial intelligence in education which has drawn comments and commentaries from members of the public as well as professional journalists. Newspaper articles were retrieved from a number of sources, including the WiseOne (formerly WiseNews) database for the Hong Kong press, as well as individual searches of thirteen leading Chinese newspapers, namely *AM730*, *Headline Daily* ( ), *HK01* (01), *Hong Kong Commercial Daily* ( ), *Hong Kong Economic Journal* ( ), *Hong Kong Economic Times* ( ), *Mingpao Daily* ( ), *Oriental Daily* ( ), *Sing Pao* ( ), *Sing Tao Daily* ( ), *Sky Post* ( ), *Ta Kung Pao* ( ), and *Wen Wei Po* ( ) in Hong Kong. The research issues in investigating newspaper articles on discussions and comments relating to the use of artificial intelligence in Chinese language education in Hong Kong were as follows: (i) to investigate the extent to which the Hong Kong press expressed views relating to AI-adaptive learning environment in Chinese education in Hong Kong; and (ii) to analyze the development of AI-adaptive language assessments.

The data collection took place from March 2023 to July 2024, a total of 358 relevant newspaper articles published from June 2018 to June 2024 (6 years) were downloaded from the internet, and the text was then entered into a database. These articles were initially searched using such terms 'artificial intelligence', 'artificial intelligence and language teaching and learning', 'language teaching and learning', 'language proficiency assessment', 'language assessment', and closely related terms, as well as English terms as they also appear in Chinese texts, such as 'artificial intelligence', 'AI', 'generative AI', 'large language model' and 'ChatGPT'. Before inclusion in the database, the articles were briefly reviewed to determine their relevance to the topics in question and were grouped into six categories.

These articles were grouped into (1) discussions of AI applications for language education in general in Hong Kong, (2) AI applications focusing on enhancing the Chinese literacy skills of Hong Kong students, (3) the use of AI for English learning, (4) AI for Putonghua learning, (5) using AI to assist Chinese learning for ethnic minority students in Hong Kong, (6) using AI to access Chinese language abilities, to understand public views and discussions on these aspects of AI usage. Later, a further round of filtering took place, after the researcher decided to categorize such data into clusters related to these topics: (i) the extent to which the Hong Kong press expressed views about AI-adaptive learning environment in Chinese education in Hong Kong; and (ii) the development of AI-adaptive language assessments.

RESULTS

Quantitative Results

To carry out a broad quantitative analysis of the opinions expressed by news reporters and columnists in the newspapers investigated, the articles in our dataset have been grouped into six categories: (1) discussions of AI applications for language education in general in Hong Kong, (2) AI applications focusing on enhancing the Chinese literacy skills of Hong Kong students, (3) the use of AI for English learning, (4) AI for Putonghua learning, (5) using AI to assist Chinese learning for ethnic minority students in Hong Kong, (6) using AI to access Chinese language abilities. This study was centrally concerned with discussions, where public opinions on the use of AI in language education were explicitly expressed. The limitations of adopting such an approach may be obvious, as, the subjective methodology used by the investigator in deciding and identifying the main discussions in a particular newspaper text. Two raters were recruited to review and verify the investigator's categorisations and judgment on these newspaper texts. Despite some inevitable subjectivity in making such decisions, given the familiarity of the researcher with language pedagogies and the language education issues of society, the methodology adopted was appropriate and effective in the analysis of these texts.

Table 1 below shows that a total of 107 articles fall into the main themes of discussion in this chapter. Most newspaper articles in the database discussed the impact of AI in language education in general in Hong Kong (42.9%). Whether and how AI can enhance Chinese literacy also received lots of attention (29%). Discussions of using AI in English learning (12.1%) and Putonghua learning (10.3%) are other areas of focus. 3.7% of the articles concentrated on using AI to assist the Chinese learning of ethnic minority students in Hong Kong. Only 1.9% of the articles were concerned using AI in assessing Chinese abilities.

Table 1. Discussions of AI applications in language education in Hong Kong newspapers, 2018-2024

The focus of AI applications	No. of articles
General language education	46 (42.9%)
Enhancing Chinese literacy	31 (29%)
English learning	13 (12.1%)
Putonghua learning	11 (10.3%)
Chinese learning for ethnic minority students	4 (3.7%)

continued on following page

Table 1. Continued

The focus of AI applications	No. of articles
Accessing Chinese language abilities	2 (1.9%)
Total	107 (100%)

Qualitative Results

The use of AI in language education in Hong Kong

As shown in Table 1, most of the discussions in the database are related to the use of AI applications in Hong Kong's language education in general (42.9%) during 2018-2024. There were articles in *AM730* and *Sing Tao Daily* that talked about the trend and future of using AI applications to assist language learning in general, as in excerpts (1) and (2).

(1) AI applications have already become trendy tutors in the field of language education. They can not only impart knowledge to learners but also adjust teaching styles and progress according to their needs, rhythm, and preferences. For example, the *Duolingo* language learning application can not only teach you fluent French but also has an AI system that adjusts according to your learning progress, strengthens your weak areas in learning, and reminds you to practise regularly. (*AM730*, 18/08/2023)

(2) Using AI to provide students with learning, assessment, and feedback, as well as providing them with appropriate learning progress and challenges, and switching to the next learning topic at the appropriate time. As AI technology matures, machines can read students' facial expressions to determine their learning pace and to provide each student with the most appropriate learning materials. After-school language tutoring and learning plans will also become more advanced, permeating different learning methods in the learning process. When students are struggling with homework or exam preparation at home, AI will be a great help to them. This will reduce the teaching workload of teachers and free up more time to take care of students' spiritual needs. (*Sing Tao Daily*, 08/03/2021) ***The use of AI applications for enhancing Chinese literacy skills*** In the dataset, how AI can enhance Chinese literacy also received lots of attention (29%). In relation to Chinese literacy training, there were discussions about using AI technology and applications to arouse students' interest in reading Chinese literature, as in excerpt (3), and the development of AI applications to assist the teaching of Chinese writing skills, in excerpt (4).

(3) Students enjoy using AI to enhance their learning interests. Some students have even been simulated by Li Bai's *Thoughts in the Silent Night* and interacting with ancient people in the AI system in their Chinese reading classes. (*Hong Kong Economic Times*, 13/04/2021)

(4) The educational technology software ' WuBi' is an AI application assisting teachers to grade Chinese language essays. After teachers have scanned student essays in the system, the software can automatically grade them. The system will evaluate essays based on DSE criteria such as content, expression, structure, and use of words. The system will automatically generate scores and detailed feedback. In addition, it can also generate model essays tailored to the writing topic, learning objectives, and student grade level, thereby enhancing teaching effectiveness. (*Sing Tao Daily*, 18/09/2023).

AI applications for the learning of Putonghua and English

Excerpts (5) and (6) below demonstrate two mobile applications, SpokenBot and ReadOutLoud. These two applications were developed by the Hang Seng University of Hong Kong. These applications made use of generative AI technology to help students improve Putonghua and English pronunciation and students' accuracy in speaking English and Putonghua. SpokenBot helps students practice Chinese and English vocabulary, assesses pronunciation when students read these vocabulary items in Putonghua and in English, and assesses pronunciation on the sentence level. This application contains 100 scenarios with 3 levels of difficulties for students to practice. ReadOutLoud is a learning system that downloads news from radio channels and government websites and generates Putonghua and English speech samples. Students can record their reading of these pieces of news in Putonghua or English and then the systems can assess students' Putonghua and English pronunciation.

(5) A team has successfully developed two free mobile applications, *SpokenBot* and *ReadOutLoud*, for students and citizens to learn languages. These applications use artificial intelligence engines and chatbot technology to help users improve their accuracy in Putonghua and English. (*Wen Wei Po*, 08/06/2023)

(6) The Putonghua and English learning program *ReadOutLoud* downloads news content from radio stations and government news websites every day. Users first listen to AI-read Putonghua or English news content, then record themselves reading the content. The AI engine will analyze the recording in real-time, score it, and point out vocabulary that can be improved for pronunciation. (*Sing Tao Daily*, 07/06/2023) In addition, articles in *Sing Tao Daily* and *Hong Kong Economic Times* also discussed the use of AI tools and applications to help students learn English vocabulary and improve English reading skills, as in excerpt (7), while excerpt (8) demonstrated applications that can enhance students' English writing skills and grammar.

(7) *Microsoft Teams* recently launched the 'Reading Progress' feature, which introduces an English article about 'Food & Drink' and distributes it to children at home to practice reading along with. The AI function built into 'Reading Progress' automatically analyzes most students' pronunciation accuracy, helping teachers to understand which words are commonly misread by everyone and to grasp the different learning situations of the whole class and individual students through the teacher interface on Teams. This helps teachers and schools to further improve students' learning efficiency in limited face-to-face or online course hours according to different learning needs. (*Sing Tao Daily*, 21/06/2022)

(8) ChatGPT can help to improve English grammar. First, write the composition, and then give ChatGPT the command 'Please correct my English composition and correct my grammar errors'. A student shared that ChatGPT can present grammar errors and improvement suggestions in a list, which is more convenient. (*Hong Kong Economic Times*, 17/04/2023)

Applications for Ethnic Minority Students to Learn Chinese as a Second Language

Although the percentage of newspaper articles focused particularly on the Chinese learning of ethnic minority students in Hong Kong is relatively small (3.7%), there have been increasing concerns about the general Chinese learning situations of these students in recent decades (Chan, 2019; Gao & Gube, 2020). There were articles demonstrating the use of AI applications that can help ethnic minorities in Hong Kong learn Chinese. Excerpt (9) showed an example of an AI-assisted mobile application that helped them learn the Chinese lexicon and improve their Cantonese pronunciation. Excerpt (10) demonstrated an AI application helping ethnic minority students analyse Chinese sentences, morphological structures, and lexicon in order to. assist them in learning Chinese as a second language in Hong Kong (9) One of the digital inclusion funding projects related to ethnic minorities is the mobile application 'Hong Kong Connect', developed by the Yang Memorial Methodist Social Service. This application provides Chinese vocabulary and Cantonese pronunciation services to ethnic minority individuals. (*Ming Pao Daily*, 12/10/2023)

(10) Chinese words have a large variety of combinations, and how to split Chinese sentences is a complex problem. After years of research, he developed an analysis tool called *HanMosaic*, which can split Chinese characters, sentences, and paragraphs, and distinguish between words and single characters. People generally think that this requires a huge database to assist, but it turns out that it only needs artificial intelligence that can learn on its own. The research results have been transformed into an online dictionary designed for non-Chinese-speaking students. It automatically dissects Chinese sentences into words, analyzes them one by one,

and teaches stroke order and radicals. It has already begun to be used in schools. (*Hong Kong Economic Journal*, 25/01/2019)

AI applications for assessing language abilities

Even though there were not many newspaper articles in the dataset focusing on the use of AI or large language models in assessing language abilities and skills, this is a worth-discussing area since this aspect of AI usage started to draw the attention of scholars in the language testing profession (Chapelle & Chung, 2010; Koraishi, 2023). The dataset of this study showed some ground-breaking innovations in this area in Hong Kong. With the advancement in linguistic research, there was an application developed to predict child language development and abilities using AI technology, as reported in the news media and shown in excerpt (11)

(11) Using electroencephalogram (EEG) test to collect data on 300 healthy Hong Kong children as a benchmark, and then using artificial intelligence computing programs to predict their future language development. (*HK01*, 13/07/2023) The development of this electroencephalography test was a joint project led by a linguist, Patrick Wong, who collaborated with Pediatrics doctors to construct a predictive algorithm to forecast language development in individual children. With early intervention strategies, it could reduce the severity of potential language impairment as well as optimize language learning for children, in particular Cantonese and Putonghua pronunciation, at the earliest possible time. This research team believes that it is important to screen out children who may suffer from a developmental language disorder so that parents can act and provide appropriate intervention and training as early as possible (The Chinese University of Hong Kong, 2021). Another innovative idea was the use of AI technology in a Putonghua recital competition. An article in *Ming Pao Daily* showed that an AI application was used to analyze the Putonghua pronunciation accuracy of the competitors and give feedback to them about their Putonghua proficiency, as in excerpt (12).

(12) The Hong Kong Children's Putonghua Recitation Competition was held on the 28th. The most notable feature of this event was the use of artificial intelligence evaluation technology. After participants read aloud according to the content of the application, the AI system analysed the accuracy of their Putonghua pronunciation. Additionally, through big data analysis of participants' learning patterns and difficulties, the system provided real-time feedback and guidance, thereby improving students' Putonghua proficiency. (*Ming Pao Daily*, 30/10/2023)

DISCUSSION

Advantages of Using AI in Learning

In the dataset of this study, there were discussions in Hong Kong Chinese newspapers presenting arguments in favor of the use of AI-adaptive language learning environment and pointing out that AI can provide personalise support to students, offer real-time assistance to students, and encourage students to learn anywhere. Excerpt (13) below summarised these advantages.

(13) From a student's perspective, ChatGPT can provide personalised support and answer individual questions. ChatGPT breaks the limitations of time and space, allowing students to use it anytime, anywhere. Furthermore, ChatGPT can provide real-time language assistance to students, whether the assistance is after class, when teachers are busy, or even late at night. This greatly enhances their learning efficiency. ChatGPT also allows students to explore different fields through real-time interactive feedback and dialogue, making language learning more attractive and interactive, while also helping to increase their interest in learning. (*Sing Tao Daily*, 07/04/2023)

Providing Personalised Teaching to Students.

The Chinese newspaper articles in the dataset emphasized a lot on personalised language teaching to students as shown above in excerpts (1), (4), (7), (8), (9), and (10). As AI systems become more mature, and when AI can make use of complex sets of data to understand students' learning styles and needs and, in turn, they can adjust course content according to students' abilities and provide each student with the most appropriate learning materials. Additional discussions on personalised learning environments in the dataset were shown in excerpt (14).

(14) *FluentUp*, a local online language learning platform, uses its 'efficient learning management system' to analyze users' preferences and needs through artificial intelligence, and then matches them with language schools around the world in real-time. (*Hong Kong Economic Times*, 22/01/2019)

Offering Real-Time Assistance to Students.

In addition, commentaries in the Chinese press suggested that when students face learning difficulties after school and seek support, generative AI can offer real-time assistance to their learning difficulties, as shown in excerpts (2), (5), (6) and (8). When AI systems can provide language support and assistance at school and after school, the workload of teachers can be reduced and teachers can devote more time and resources to take care of students' psychological needs, as presented in excerpt (2).

Learning Anywhere and Arousing Students' Interest.

The implementation of computer-assisted language learning can break the limitations of time and space. This can be proved in the global pandemic period, where various types of synchronous and asynchronous online language teaching attempts have been made to solve the social distancing issues (Lee, 2022). There are arguments in the Hong Kong Chinese press showing support that students can learn and practice anytime and anywhere with AI technology, as in excerpts (2), (8), (9), and (10). Articles in the dataset also showed that AI applications can stimulate students' learning interests. Excerpt (3) showed an example of using AI simulations to arouse students' interest in literature reading. Additional examples that help increase students' learning interest can be found in excerpt (15) below showing that AI-based gamified applications changed students' learning habits and aroused students' interest in learning outside the language classrooms.

(15) This application encourages children to learn through gamified experiences. The children receive immediate feedback after practice and record poorly pronounced words to help improve them in the future. It's worth noting that this application also provides multiple scenario choices, such as school, restaurant, airport, and hospital, among other daily situations. After selecting a scenario, an AI robot will play different roles with children to practice English conversation in the form of sentences or dialogues. (*Sky Post*, 08/03/2022)

Concerns Relating to the Use of AI in Education

Generative AI is a global trend that changes the way of searching for information and affects daily life. The good side of using generative AI in language education, and in Chinese education in particular, is that it can provide one-on-one tutoring, provide personalised support to students, offer real-time support to students, and allow students to learn language skills and study on their own. In Hong Kong, there was research exploring an AI curriculum framework for secondary schools to promote the use of AI in pre-tertiary classrooms (Chiu et al., 2022).

On the other hand, there were concerns that students may use generative AI to complete their homework, which does not help them grow and hinders the development of their critical thinking and problem-solving skills. Some stakeholders worried that the use of generative AI encourages students to cheat and copy which, in a way, encourages academic dishonesty. A major comment found in the dataset, on the use of generative AI in language education is the infringement of intellectual property and the issues of plagiarism. Some commentaries raised these concerns about ethics, ghostwriting, and cheating issues, as in excerpts (17) and (18) below.

(16) Artificial intelligence also involves a series of issues such as ethics, morality, intellectual property rights, scientific research plagiarism, and cheating in exams. (*HK01*, 07/03/2023)

(17) If students violate the rules and use AI tools such as ChatGPT without the consent of others, it is equivalent to using their works without permission, which involves an element of 'deception'. If relevant AI tools are used without exemption, they also meet the relevant definition. Therefore, the school will treat such cases as 'potential plagiarism'. (*Headline Daily*, 18/02/2023)

There were also arguments that emphasize generative AI's errors and inaccuracy. Some articles in the dataset of this study echoed UNESCO's suggestions and urged setting up rules and regulations for the use of generative AI in education (Pedró et al., 2019). Universities in Hong Kong have started to set policies and guidelines on the use of artificial intelligence in tertiary education. It is observed that some of these guidelines are very preliminary, for example, permission must be granted before using AI in in-class exercises and assignments, the use of AI should be fully acknowledged similar to citation of other sources and encourage students to use AI ethically (The Chinese University of Hong Kong, 2023; The Hong Kong Polytechnic University, 2023). It is clear that more work is needed to be done to deal with the ethical issues relating to the use of AI in language education.

Some newspaper articles in the dataset of this study also show that language teachers worried generative AI can damage the status of teachers and weaken students' attention in class. To some extent, this is due to both teachers and learners lacking digital competencies to use generative chatbots ethically and effectively to support language learning. Research on teachers' and students' attitudes and technological needs can be done in institutions so that institutions can plan adequate training on digital proficiency and ethics of using generative AI technology in teaching and learning (Kohnke et al., 2023).

Lee & Chen's (2024) study showed an increasing trend of developing and discussing the use of AI applications in language education in Hong Kong. The impact brought about by generative AI on language education can be very prominent. The situation, in general, is more favorable to the development and use of AI in Chinese language education in Hong Kong. However, the barriers to the use of generative AI in education cannot be neglected (Wang & Cheng, 2021).

It is worth noting that in computer-assisted language learning (CALL) literature, research showed that both teachers and students need adjustments and training for technological innovations. Students also need training in terms of efficacy, motivation, ethics, and learning habits. A learning environment, that can match both students' and teachers' expectations and efficacy, is needed to naturalize or normalize such innovation in an institution. Lee (2016) studied the normalization process of technological innovation in language education by evaluating students' expectations of technological innovation with institutional targets. The result showed that the characteristics, habits, and expectations of students may be subject to change with the advancement of computer technologies, however, students' expectations and learning habits may not always match with the pedagogical beliefs of the institution as well as teachers' expectations. If such a mismatch happens, institutions/teachers need to understand students' learning habits and expectations, on the one hand; and on the other hand, instructional strategies, and training for teachers and students need to be developed to smooth the normalization process.

Some Thoughts on AI in Language Assessment in Hong Kong

In recent years, there has been research literature exploring the inclusion of AI technology in language assessments (Chapelle & Chung, 2010; Koraishi, 2023). Some scholars analysed the impact of AI on traditional language assessments (Rudolph et al., 2023). The technology of generative AI will continue to be advanced and more widely applied in more aspects of human life. In the dataset of this study, some AI learning applications started to incorporate Diploma of Secondary Education Examination criteria to assist students in preparing for public examinations. There is also an attempt to apply AI technology in a Putonghua recital competition shown in the dataset. Language teaching pedagogy relating to the use of AI also needs to be closely followed.

More research on such use, including the development in curriculum design, change in teaching and learning mode, extension of language classrooms, and language assessment, is needed to look at the different applications and effectiveness of this innovative technology in the field of language education. Moqbel & Ai-Kadi (2023) in their research pointed out that the development of educational AI technology 'charts new research territories and passes the torch to second and foreign-language learning assessors to reflect on their teaching situations and reimagine L2 programs in light of the affordances of the ChatGPT, which has made a significant breakthrough in learning and teaching languages' (Moqbel & Ai-Kadi, p. 71).

The public discussions in Hong Kong newspapers from 2018 to 2024 indicated that although stakeholders can see the benefit of using AI in language learning, discussions and research on the use of generative AI in Chinese language education and assessment are still in the starting stage. More work needs to be done to enhance the AI-adaptive Chinese learning environment and the way to incorporate AI technology into different types of Chinese tests to serve the diversified Chinese learning communities in Hong Kong.

CONCLUSION

This chapter discusses public opinions about the use of artificial intelligence in language education, particularly in Chinese language education, by analyzing Chinese-language newspaper discourse to investigate the different views of the stakeholders in language education including students, teachers, educators, and policymakers in Hong Kong. A corpus containing Hong Kong newspaper articles discussing AI-adaptive Chinese language learning environment and Chinese language assessment in Hong Kong has been constructed and analysed. From 2018-2024, there are news articles focusing on (1) discussions of AI applications for language education in general in Hong Kong, (2) AI applications focusing on enhancing the Chinese literacy skills of Hong Kong students, (3) the use of AI for English learning, (4) AI for Putonghua learning, (5) using AI to assist Chinese learning for ethnic minority students in Hong Kong, (6) using AI to access Chinese language abilities. The AI-adaptive Chinese learning environment has started to be established in Hong Kong. Stakeholders recognised that the positive sides of using generative AI in language education and in Chinese education.

Newspaper articles in the dataset showed that AI can provide one-on-one tutoring, provide personalised support to students, offer real-time support to students, and allow students to learn language skills on their own by arousing learning interest. It is also important to point out that the application of AI in Chinese language assessments is still at the starting point. How AI changes students' learning habits and whether students are technologically ready will be important questions for administrators and teachers to examine. On the pedagogical side, how Chinese language teaching approaches and assessment theories can incorporate AI technologies are topics that are worth investigating. Given the growing importance of artificial intelligence and related technology in the age of the Internet, the popularity and research of such technology in relation to Chinese language education and assessment are likely to further increase in the years to come.

REFERENCES

Bacon-Shone. Bolton, K., Lee, S. L., Richards, B., & Bhatia, A. (2019). *The Contribution of Minority Languages and Dialects to Hong Kong's Linguistic Landscape.* Research report. Public Policy Research Funding Scheme. Hong Kong SAR Government.

Bacon-Shone, J., Bolton, K., & Luke, K. K. (2015). *Language use, proficiency and attitudes in Hong Kong*. Social Sciences Research Centre, HKU.

Bai, B., Wang, J., & Zhou, H. (2021). An intervention study to improve primary school students' self-regulated strategy use in English writing through e-learning in Hong Kong. *Computer Assisted Language Learning*, 35(9), 2265–2290. DOI: 10.1080/09588221.2020.1871030

Baidoo-Anu, D., & Owusu Ansah, L. (2023). Education in the Era of Generative Artificial Intelligence (AI): Understanding the Potential Benefits of ChatGPT in Promoting Teaching and Learning. *Journal of AI*, 7(1), 52–62. DOI: 10.61969/jai.1337500

Bolton, K., Bacon-Shone, J., & Lee, S.-l. (2020). Societal multilingualism in Hong Kong. In Siemund, P., & Leimgruber, J. (Eds.), *Multilingual global cities: Dubai, Hong Kong and Singapore* (pp. 160–184). Routledge. DOI: 10.4324/9780429463860-12

Bolton, K., & Lee, S.-l. (2020). A socio-historical approach to multilingualism in Hong Kong. In Siemund, P., & Leimgruber, J. (Eds.), *Multilingual global cities: Hong Kong, Singapore, and Dubai* (pp. 38–62). Routledge. DOI: 10.4324/9780429463860-4

Chan, C. K. Y. (2023). A comprehensive AI policy education framework for university teaching and learning. *International Journal of Educational Technology in Higher Education*, 2023(20), 38. DOI: 10.1186/s41239-023-00408-3

Chan, S. D. (2019). From oracy to literacy: the role of Cantonese in the learning of Chinese reading and writing. In Wakefield, J. (Ed.), *Cantonese as a second language: Issues, experiences and suggestions for teaching and learning* (pp. 209–231). Routledge.

Chapelle, C. A., & Chung, Y. R. (2010). The promise of NLP and speech processing technologies in language assessment. *Language Testing*, 27(3), 301–315. DOI: 10.1177/0265532210364405

Chassignol, M., Khoroshavin, A., Klimova, A., & Bilyatdinova, A. (2018). Artificial Intelligence trends in education: A narrative overview. *Procedia Computer Science*, 136, 16–24. DOI: 10.1016/j.procs.2018.08.233

Chen, L. (2023, June 23). Hong Kong rolls out first AI curriculum for junior secondary students, including lessons on ChatGPT, with 'lives definitely affected by artificial intelligence'. *South China Morning Post*.

Chen, L., Chen, P., & Lin, Z. (2020). Artificial intelligence in education: A review. *IEEE Access : Practical Innovations, Open Solutions*, 8, 75264–75278. DOI: 10.1109/ACCESS.2020.2988510

Chen, X., Zhou, D., Xie, H., Cheng, G., & Liu, C. (2022). Two decades of artificial intelligence in education: Contributors, collaborations, research topics, challenges, and future directions. *Journal of Educational Technology & Society*, 25(1), 28–47.

Cheung, H. T. (2019). The effect of age of arrival to the development of Cantonese narrative in ethnic minority children of Hong Kong. In Wakefield, J. (Ed.), *Cantonese as a second language: Issues, experiences and suggestions for teaching and learning* (pp. 232–250). Routledge.

Chin, A. C. (2023). A corpus-based approach to learning and teaching Cantonese. In Lee, S. L. (Ed.), *The learning and teaching of Cantonese as a second language* (pp. 184–196). Routledge., DOI: 10.4324/9781003054696

Chiu, T. K. F., Meng, H., Chai, C.-S., King, I., Wong, S., & Yam, Y. (2022). Creation and Evaluation of a Pretertiary Artificial Intelligence (AI) Curriculum. *IEEE Transactions on Education*, 65(1), 30–39. DOI: 10.1109/TE.2021.3085878

Cope, B., Kalantzis, M., & Searsmith, D. (2021). Artificial intelligence for education: Knowledge and its assessment in AI-enabled learning ecologies. *Educational Philosophy and Theory*, 53(12), 1229–1245. DOI: 10.1080/00131857.2020.1728732

Gao, F., & Gube, J. (2020). Multicultural education: How are ethnic minorities labelled and educated in post-handover Hong Kong? *Migration and Language Education*, 2(3), 51–59. DOI: 10.29140/mle.v1n2.363

Hong Kong Government. (2011). *Population census*. Census and Statistics Department, Hong Kong Government.

Hong Kong Government. (2016). *The Hong Kong poverty situation report on ethnic minorities*. Census and Statistics Department, Hong Kong Government.

Hong Kong Government. (2021). *Population census*. Census and Statistics Department, Hong Kong Government.

Hong Kong Government. (2022, December 14). *Using Putonghua as medium of instruction for teaching Chinese Language subject*. [Press release]. https://www.info.gov.hk/gia/general/202212/14/P2022121400322.htm

Huang, X., Zou, D., Cheng, G., Chen, X., & Xie, H. (2023). Trends, Research Issues and Applications of Artificial Intelligence in Language Education. *Journal of Educational Technology & Society*, 26(1), 112–131.

Jeon, J. (2022). Exploring AI chatbot affordances in the EFL classroom: Young learners' experiences and perspectives. *Computer Assisted Language Learning*. Advance online publication. DOI: 10.1080/09588221.2021.2021241

Ji, H., Han, I., & Ko, Y. (2023). A systematic review of conversational AI in language education: Focusing on the collaboration with human teachers. *Journal of Research on Technology in Education*, 55(1), 48–63. DOI: 10.1080/15391523.2022.2142873

Kang, B., & Kang, S. (2022). Construction of Chinese Language Teaching System Model Based on Deep Learning under the Background of Artificial Intelligence. *Scientific Programming*, 2022, 1–10. DOI: 10.1155/2022/3960023

Kataoka, S. (2023). Textbook Cantonese romanization. In Lee, S. L. (Ed.), *The learning and teaching of Cantonese as a second language* (pp. 196–216). Routledge., DOI: 10.4324/9781003054696

Kessler, G. (2017). Technology and the future of language teaching. *Foreign Language Annals*, 2018(51), 205–218.

Kim, N.-Y., Cha, Y., & Kim, H.-S. (2019). Future English learning: Chatbots and artificial intelligence. *Multimedia-Assisted Language Learning*, 22(3), 32–53.

King, I. (2016). E-learning is the way forward for quality education. *South China Morning Post*, 29 July 2016.

Kohnke, L., Moorhouse, B. L., & Zou, D. (2023). ChatGPT for Language Teaching and Learning. *RELC Journal*, 54(2), 537–550. DOI: 10.1177/00336882231162868

Koraishi, O. (2023). Teaching English in the Age of AI: Embracing ChatGPT to Optimize EFL Materials and Assessment. *Language Education and Technology*, 3(1), 55–72.

Lau, K. L. (2019). Hong Kong senior secondary students' reading motivation and classical Chinese reading comprehension. *Reading and Writing*, 32(4), 963–982. DOI: 10.1007/s11145-018-9897-7

Lee, S. L. (2011). [Online components for advanced Chinese reading classes]. *Journal of Technology and Chinese Language Teaching*, 2, 1–22.

Lee, S. L. (2016). E-Learning Readiness in Language Learning: Students' Readiness Survey and Normalization Process. *Journal of Technology and Chinese Language Teaching*, 7(2), 23–37.

Lee, S. L. (2018). Modular approaches in eLearning design. *Journal of Technology and Chinese Language Teaching*, 9, 48–61.

Lee, S. L. (2022). Synchronous online language teaching: a reflection from Hong Kong. In Liu, S. (Ed.), *Teaching the Chinese language remotely: Global cases and perspectives* (pp. 235–251). Palgrave Macmillan. DOI: 10.1007/978-3-030-87055-3_10

Lee, S. L. (2023a). Teaching literacy skills to Cantonese learners. In Lee, S. L. (Ed.), *The learning and teaching of Cantonese as a second language* (pp. 67–86). Routledge., DOI: 10.4324/9781003054696

Lee, S. L. (2023b). Learning, teaching and performing Cantonese on the Internet. In Lee, S. L. (Ed.), *The learning and teaching of Cantonese as a second language* (pp. 216–240). Routledge., DOI: 10.4324/9781003054696

Lee, S. L., & Chen, Y. (2024). Discussions of Using AI in Language Education in Hong Kong. In Pan, F. (Ed.), *AI in Language Teaching, Learning, and Assessment* (pp. 133–148). IGI Global. DOI: 10.4018/979-8-3693-0872-1.ch007

Liu, O., & Yau, C. (2023, March 22). Who needs a teacher? As ChatGPT takes off in Hong Kong, educationists worry about impact on teaching, learning. *South China Morning Post.*

Liu, X. (2018). A Comparative Study of Language Attitudes in Hong Kong: Towards English, Cantonese and Putonghua. *International Journal of English Linguistics*, 8(3), 195–209. DOI: 10.5539/ijel.v8n3p195

Moorhouse, B. L., Wong, K. M., & Li, L. (2023). Teaching with technology in the post-pandemic digital age: Technological normalisation and AI-induced disruptions. *RELC Journal*, 54(2), 311–320. DOI: 10.1177/00336882231176929

Moqbel, M. S. S., & Ai-Kadi, A. M. T. (2023). Foreign Language Learning Assessment in the Age of ChatGPT: A Theoretical Account. *Journal of English Studies in Arabia Felix*, 2(1), 71–84. DOI: 10.56540/jesaf.v2i1.62

Ng, D. T. K., Lee, M., Tan, R. J. Y., Downie, J. S., & Chu, S. K. W. (2023). A review of AI teaching and learning from 2000 to 2020. *Education and Information Technologies*, 2023(28), 8445–8501. DOI: 10.1007/s10639-022-11491-w

Pedró, F., Subosa, M., Rivas, A., & Valverde, P. (2019). *Artificial Intelligence and Language Learning: Opportunities and Challenges*. Working Paper on Language Policy. UNESCO. Retrieved from https://unesdoc.unesco.org/ark:/48223/pf0000366994

Richardson, J. E. (2017). *Analysing Newspapers: An Approach from Critical Discourse Analysis*. London: Springer.Rudolph, J., Tan, S., & Tan, S., (2023). ChatGPT: Bullshit spewer or the end of traditional assessments in higher education? *Journal of Applied Learning & Teaching*, 6(1), 342–363.

Schmidt, T., & Strasser, T. (2022). Artificial Intelligence in Foreign Language Learning and Teaching: A CALL for Intelligent Practice. *Anglistik: International Journal of English Studies*, 33(1), 165–184. DOI: 10.33675/ANGL/2022/1/14

Sun, Z., Anbarasan, M., & Kumar, D. P. (2021). Design of online intelligent English teaching platform based on artificial intelligence techniques. *Computational Intelligence*, 2021(37), 1166–1180. DOI: 10.1111/coin.12351

The Chinese University of Hong Kong. (2021, 24 August). A 30-minute EEG Test Forecasts Children's Language Development. *CUHK in Touch*. Retrieved from https://cuhkintouch.cpr.cuhk.edu.hk/2021/08/7463/

The Chinese University of Hong Kong. (2023). *Use of Artificial Intelligence Tools in Teaching, Learning and Assessments: A Guide for Students*. Hong Kong: The Chinese University of Hong Kong. Retrieved from https://www.aqs.cuhk.edu

The Hong Kong Polytechnic University. (2023). *Guidelines for Students on the Use of Generative Artificial Intelligence*. Hong Kong: The Hong Kong Polytechnic University of Hong Kong. Retrieved from https://www.polyu.edu.hk/ar/ docdrive/polyu-students/Student-guide-on-the-use-GenAI.pdf

Tse, S.-K. (2009). Chinese Language Education in Hong Kong: Twenty Five Years of Educational Research in Hong Kong. *Educational Research Journal*, 24(2), 231–255.

Van Dijk, T. A. (2008). *Discourse and context: A Sociocognitive approach*. Cambridge University Press. DOI: 10.1017/CBO9780511481499

Wang, G., Wu, X., & Li, Q. (2021). A bibliometric study of news discourse analysis (1988–2020). *Discourse & Communication*, 16(1), 110–128. DOI: 10.1177/17504813211043725

Wang, H., & Yuan, Z. (2013). The promotion of Putonghua (Mandarin Chinese): An overview. In Li, Y., & Li, W. (Eds.), *The language situation in China* (pp. 27–39). De Gruyter Mouton.

Wang, T., & Cheng, E. C. K. (2021). An investigation of barriers to Hong Kong K-12 schools incorporating Artificial Intelligence in education. *Computers and Education: Artificial Intelligence, 2*, (2021).

Yaacob, Z., & Saad, N. H. M. (2020). Acceptance of YouTube as a learning platform during the Covid-19 pandemic: The moderating effect of subscription status. *TEM Journal*, 4, 1732–1739. DOI: 10.18421/TEM94-54

Yan, Z., & Brown, G. T. (2021). Assessment for learning in the Hong Kong assessment reform: A case of policy borrowing. *Studies in Educational Evaluation*, 68, 100985. DOI: 10.1016/j.stueduc.2021.100985

Yueng, P. (2019, 31 January). AI will be a game changer for Hong Kong education. *China Daily Hong Kong*.

Zai, X., Chu, X., Chai, C. S., Jong, M. S. Y., Istenic, A., & Spector, M. (2021). Liu, J.-B., Yuan, J., & Li, Y. (2021). A review of artificial intelligence (AI) in education from 2010 to 2020. *Complexity*, 2021(1), 8812542. Advance online publication. DOI: 10.1155/2021/8812542

Zhang, B., & Yang, R. R. (2004). Putonghua Education and Language Policy in Postcolonial Hong Kong. In Zhou, M. L., & Sun, H. (Eds.), *Language Policy in the People's Republic of China: Theory and Practice Since 1949* (pp. 143–161). Springer. DOI: 10.1007/1-4020-8039-5_8

Zhu, X. (2015). An assessment framework of integrated writing in teaching Chinese as a first language . *Recent developments of Chinese teaching and learning in higher education: Applied Chinese language studies VI*, 108-116.

KEY TERMS AND DEFINITIONS

Blended teaching and learning: Blended teaching and learning or hybrid learning in this chapter is defined as an educational model that combines classroom face-to-face learning experiences with online learning experiences.

Cantonese: The term 'Cantonese' refers to the language varieties used by immigrants who came to Hong Kong from various districts in Guangdong province. Over time, their speech coalesced into the contemporary variety of Cantonese used in Hong Kong from the late nineteenth century onwards. Cantonese is often used to refer to the entire Yue subgroup of Chinese, which includes varieties of Cantonese spoken in southern China, Hong Kong, Macau, Malaysia, Singapore, and among overseas Chinese in North America, Europe, and Australia. It is currently estimated that there are about 70 million Cantonese speakers in the world. Cantonese has been and is a major language variety used by people in daily life in Hong Kong.

Computer-assisted language learning (CALL): Computer-assisted language learning (CALL) or Computer-aided instruction (CAI) is briefly defined as the search for and study of applications of the computer in language teaching and learning. CALL includes a wide range of information and communications technology applications and approaches to teaching and learning foreign languages.

Diploma of Secondary Education Examination (DSE): The Diploma of Secondary Education Examination (DSE), also known as HKDSE, is a public examination administered by the Hong Kong Examinations and Assessment Authority since 2012. It serves as the graduation test for students completing a six-year secondary education in Hong Kong. The HKDSE assesses students' proficiency in various subjects, including the Chinese language. Results are reported using a set of standards, with levels ranging from 1 to 5, where 5 represents the highest achievement. Students achieving the best performance in level 5 receive a 5** (5 double stars), and the next top group is awarded a 5*. Attainment below level 1 is designated as 'Unclassified'. The HKDSE is widely recognized internationally, providing students with diverse pathways for their future academic and career pursuits.

General Certificate of Secondary Education (GCSE): The General Certificate of Secondary Education (GCSE) examinations, offered by Pearson Edexcel, are academic qualifications primarily designed for UK students. These exams assess students' proficiency in various subjects, including the Chinese language. Pearson Edexcel, an examining and awarding body based in the UK, introduced the GCSE Chinese Examinations in May 2008 upon popular demand. These exams are available to school students.

Hanyu Shuiping Kaoshi 'Chinese Proficiency Test' (HSK): The Hanyu Shuiping Kaoshi (HSK) 'Chinese Proficiency Test' is China's official standardized examination for assessing the proficiency of non-native speakers in Standard Chinese. It is open to foreign students, overseas Chinese, and members of ethnic minority groups in China. The HSK provides a global standard for Chinese language proficiency across beginner to advanced levels. HSK serves as a demonstration of students' abilities to prospective employers, foreign institutions, and international organizations. The test is administered by *Hanban* , an agency of the Ministry of Education of the People's Republic of China. Currently, HSK comprises three stages and nine levels (beginner levels 1-3, intermediate levels 4-6, advanced levels 7-9).

International Baccalaureate (IB) Chinese examinations: The International Baccalaureate (IB) examinations measure advanced academic skills, including analyzing and presenting information, evaluating arguments, and solving problems creatively. Basic skills like retaining knowledge and understanding key concepts are also assessed. For the IB Chinese examination, both external and internal assessments are used. External assessment (75% of the grade) includes tests on listening, writing and reading skills. Internal assessment (25% of the grade) focuses on individual oral tests to assess students' oral proficiency. The IB emphasizes international outlook and intercultural skills. Results are determined by criteria referencing rather than norm referencing.

Putonghua Shuiping Ceshi 'Putonghua Proficiency Test' (PSC): The Putonghua Proficiency Test (PSC) 'Putonghua Proficiency Test' is an official assessment of spoken fluency in Putonghua. PSC sets standards for achievement in spoken Putonghua. PSC is designed for native speakers of Chinese languages. Developed jointly by the Ministry of Education of the People's Republic of China, the Institute of Applied Linguistics, and the State Administration of Press, Publication, Radio, Film and Television. Many jobs in broadcasting, education, and government require PSC certification. The test comprises five sections including (1) reading 100 monosyllabic words, (2) reading 100 polysyllabic words, (3) testing on Chinese grammar and lexicons, (4) reading a 400-character passage, and (5) speaking on a given topic. PSC focuses on the accuracy of Putonghua pronunciation and fluency in speaking. The results for the PSC are divided into three grades and six levels, including Level 1-A (highest), Level 1-B, Level 2-A, Level 2-B, Level 3-A, and Level 3-B (lowest).

Normalization process: Normalization refers to a social process through which ideas and actions come to be seen as 'normal' and 'natural' in everyday life. The normalization process refers to a social organization that brings practice or practices into action.

Putonghua: Putonghua is the official language of the People's Republic of China. It serves as the common national language of the PRC. Under Hong Kong's Basic Law and the promotion of trilingualism and biliteracy, Putonghua has an official status in Hong Kong.

Standard Written Chinese: A *baihua yundong* ('vernacular language movement') was started in 1917 by the scholar *Hu Shi* . This *baihua* literary movement advocated adopting the *baihua* ('vernacular') style of Chinese as a written language to revitalize the Classical Chinese literary language and make it more accessible to the common people. *Baihua* is the form of written Chinese based on the varieties of Chinese spoken throughout China, in contrast to *wenyan* ('classical Chinese') used in Imperial China up to the early twentieth century. This movement succeeded in making *baihua* the language of textbooks, periodicals, newspapers, and public documents. *Baihua* now commonly refers to the standard written Chinese or modern written Chinese. Since the early 1920s, this modern vernacular form has been the standard style of writing for speakers of all varieties of Chinese throughout mainland China, Taiwan, Malaysia, and Singapore as written form of modern standard Chinese. Standard written Chinese (presented in traditional characters) is used in all official and educational contexts in Hong Kong.

Trilingualism and biliteracy: Since the 1990s, the Hong Kong government has promoted 'trilingualism and biliteracy', which refers to the spoken command of Cantonese, Putonghua, and English, and literacy in written Chinese and English.

Chapter 6
The Essay Is Dead (And Other Thoughts About Assessing in the Era of AI)

Laurie Uttich
https://orcid.org/0009-0006-7422-2759
University of Central Florida, USA

Kevin Yee
https://orcid.org/0009-0007-9672-4415
University of Central Florida, USA

Elizabeth Giltner
https://orcid.org/0009-0008-0349-2158
University of Central Florida, USA

ABSTRACT

This chapter explores the profound impact of recent revolutionary AI advancements on traditional assessment methods, particularly the take-home essay. The authors argue that the rise of AI-generated content challenges the efficacy and integrity of conventional writing assignments. Educators are urged to reconsider their assessment strategies in such a way that integrates AI tools in ways that enhance critical thinking and learning outcomes. By adapting assignments to incorporate AI-generated responses and emphasizing evaluation and synthesis, educators can maintain academic rigor and better prepare students for the evolving demands of the working world. This approach not only mitigates the risks associated with AI use in education but also leverages its potential to foster deeper engagement and

DOI: 10.4018/979-8-3693-6351-5.ch006

understanding among students.

INTRODUCTION

In the halls of academia, a silent revolution is underway. It's not marked by protests or policy changes, but by the quiet hum of algorithms and the invisible hand of artificial intelligence. As educators, we stand at the precipice of a fundamental shift in how we teach, assess, and understand learning itself. The rise of Generative AI tools like ChatGPT isn't just changing the game—it's rewriting the rules entirely.

It also wrote this opening paragraph… and it did it in under five seconds. It's not award-winning prose—and least not yet—but it's not the worst introduction to a chapter like this, either. It might even be considered "strong" for beginning writers and, as humanities instructors who taught required courses to undergrads, we can even imagine writing "some nice details" in the margin.

Whether you agree that this prose "works" or not—and whether you're excited, exhausted, or somewhere in between about the emergence of GenAI tools—it's clear that the game in academia has changed. For decades, educators have relied on various forms of writing to assess critical thinking skills: short-answer problems on tests, lab reports, discussion board posts, and the venerable take-home essay. While multiple-choice testing has also been widely used, it's more often associated with the knowledge, comprehension, and application levels of Bloom's Taxonomy (Wiggins & McTighe, 1998) than with higher-order skills. However, the sudden intrusion of GenAI in the form of Large Language Models (LLMs) such as ChatGPT, Gemini, Copilot, and Claude has dramatically altered this landscape.

These AI tools have exacerbated longstanding challenges in assessment, from concerns about academic integrity to issues of equity in access to technology. More critically, they've called into question the very value of traditional take-home writing assignments. With students readily adopting these powerful AI assistants, educators must grapple with a stark reality: continuing to assign take-home writing in a "business as usual" manner seems almost certain to result in greatly diminished student learning, as the temptation to use GenAI tools may prove too great for many students to resist. In this new era, we must reimagine our assessment strategies to ensure they remain effective, equitable, and resistant to AI-generated content… and the first step in doing so is to acknowledge the take-home essay is in trouble.

None of the concerns about academic integrity prior to GenAI (paper mills, plagiarism, recycled assignments from previous students) have gone away, but they are now joined by free, easy-to-use tools that generate sentences, paragraphs, and even entire essays at will. Whereas plagiarism detection before GenAI had largely reliable tools like the originality score from Turnitin and similar companies, LLMs operate in a way that makes detection with these same tools impossible (Hutson, 2024). LLMs are content generators, and they generate novel phrasings each time, even when asked to regenerate a response to the exact same prompt. Thus, even if an entire class of 60 students pasted the same writing prompt to ChatGPT, none of the outputted essays would trigger problematic originality score reports. Furthermore, the proliferation of LLMs other than ChatGPT will undoubtedly increase the diversity of AI-generated submissions

Despite the ability to dupe plagiarism detectors, the use of LLMs in a student's essay is often blatantly apparent to seasoned educators. Because LLMs are prediction models that follow "the sky is… blue" pattern, the output is, well, predictable and the creativity and surprising connections that classify writing as "good" are woefully absent. As one tech writer defines it, LLMs "work like a sophisticated version of auto-complete" (Fowler, 2023, para. 18), producing robotic writing. Indeed, the syntax, diction, and voice of the generated content often lacks a human element. Additionally, the "voiceless" AI-generated writing may include false information and hallucinated sources. For students who are not interested in academic activities this might not be seem problematic, but faculty who are genuinely invested in student learning may feel disrespected and discouraged by students' willful use of GenAI to complete writing assignments.

LLMs Continue to Improve While Student Use Soars

Even without secondary tools that seek to maximize the effectiveness of LLMs ability to generate content, the front-line LLMs continue to evolve into faster, more advanced, and simply better "writers." GPT-3, the version that introduced the world to GenAI and went viral in November 2022, had 175 billion parameters (Heaven, 2023). Parameters are the "processing guideposts that establish the model's transformation of input data to output" (Broadhead, 2023, para.10). The number refers to the weights in the model's neural network—essentially its capacity to find and fit complex patterns in the data it was trained on.

GPT-4, the successor to GPT-3 which debuted 19 months later, reportedly contained 1.7 trillion parameters (Ahmed, 2024). This represents an increase of over 870% in less than two years, demonstrating the rapid advancement in AI model capacity. Other LLMs are keeping pace as well, so this is surely a race that the technology will win. Sooner rather than later, a great deal of writing created by GenAI will be indistinguishable from writing created by humans.

If we can't prevent students from using GenAI and we can't detect it, it might be natural to wonder if we can convince students to avoid using these tools in the first place. But such an approach faces steep headwinds. In 1937, Flora Myers Gillentine may have been the first to pose the research question "Why do college students cheat?" and offered a slew of reasons and suggestions (Gillentine, 1937), and yet cheating remains widespread among college students, with estimates ranging from 75% to 92% of students engaging in academic dishonesty at some point during their academic careers (Baird, 1980; Laurent Josien et al., 2015). And, like so many trends in education, it seems COVID-19 has only worsened the situation. A study conducted at the end of the Fall 2020 semester found that while up to 75 percent of undergraduates admit to cheating, nearly *half* of them say they cheated for the first time during the pandemic, citing stress and opportunity due to the shift in online learning (Jenkins et al., 2022).

Long before COVID-19, educators struggled to figure out why students do not uphold their academic integrity. One particularly notable source, *Cheating in college: Why students do it and what educators can do about it* (McCabe et al., 2012), the authors investigate trends over multiple years to explore how and why students cheat. We know now that students *are* less likely to cheat in classes where instructors emphasize mastery of content over performance or grades, create engaging, relevant content, and clearly communicate how that content is useful for their future goals (Krou et al., 2020), but even with optimal motivational strategies, we also know that a substantial percentage of students will still engage in some form of academic dishonesty… no matter how inspirational the instructor may be.

Drawing on our decades of experience as university educators, we have identified the following primary reasons (Table 1) why students resort to cheating:

Table 1. Reasons why students cheat

Reasons Why Students Cheat	
1. Lack of intrinsic motivation	The student is primarily motivated extrinsically, rather than internal satisfaction or interest (Jordan, 2001). Instead, this student views the degree—or, at least, the course—as solely a requirement to graduate, obtain a job, etc., a phenomenon that's more prevalent in business programs where students tend to view their degree primarily as means to an end, rather than valuing the learning process (Ferguson et al., 2022).
2. Fear of failure	The student faces intense personal, financial, and career-related pressures to get good grades and they may not be academically prepared for college, worried those who do cheat are at an advantage, incentivized by normalized grading curves, and/or believe "everyone" cheats. This fear of receiving a lower grade (resulting in disappointed parents and lost opportunities, such as internships, scholarships, letters of recommendation, jobs, etc.), especially in competitive academic environments can lead to academic dishonesty (Ferguson et al., 2022).
3. Social acceptance	While some students may see cheating as a "victimless crime" and justify cheating through that lens, one study found that nearly 93 percent of students believe cheating is ethically wrong, but almost half still engaged in it… and even if students said it was wrong, they found it socially acceptable (Smyth & Davis, 2003). In fact, students tend to see cheating as common, making it even more socially acceptable (Ferguson et al., 2022).

continued on following page

Table 1. Continued

Reasons Why Students Cheat	
4. Disregard for potential consequences	While some studies suggest that students perceive it's easier to cheat in online courses and admit to higher levels of cheating in those classes (Goff et al., 2020; Miller & Young-Jones, 2012), other studies show academic dishonesty occurs just as frequently as in face-to-face courses (Grijalva et al., 2006; Watson & Sottile, 2008). Either way, often students cheat because they think they won't get caught.
5. Lack of time management	Students who cheat tend to cite a lack of time as one of the primary reasons for doing so (Beasley, 2014) and researchers find poor time management skills can lead to academic misconduct (Kaushar, 2013).

Figure 1.1 – Reasons why students cheat

The final three items in this list—cheating is socially acceptable, easy to get away with, and a coping mechanism for poor time management skills—seem directly aligned with the use of GenAI tools. The accessibility of LLMs make cheating simple, easy, fast, free… and, perhaps, even fun. Add those temptations to the fact that, as we noted earlier, the detection of AI-generated writing is imperfect at best, it is not surprising that students are less fearful of being caught than when they "borrowed" or bought papers written by others.

What about the 93 percent of college students who view cheating as ethically wrong, as noted in number 3 of our list? Many students possess only a rudimentary understanding of plagiarism, often associating it solely with the act of copying another person's words. Since LLMs are clearly not authors, students might view using LLMs as not stealing anything. Even students who are aware of the ethical issues lack understanding of proper citation methods for GenAI-generated content (Oh et al., 2023) and all of us—students and educators alike—are still figuring out the ethics of using these tools in our work. Both faculty members and students struggle to clearly define what constitutes appropriate vs. inappropriate use of LLMs in academic work and both groups were also unclear regarding authorship issues (Duah & McGivern, 2024). In the same study, none of the participants—neither students nor faculty members—could articulate their university's policy on AI use, complicating this discussion on academic integrity even further.

Even if universities and faculty members clearly state policies on the use of GenAI emphasize to students that their use constitutes misrepresentation of submitted work and, therefore, academic misconduct, many students will still use the tools. A national survey by Tyton (Shaw et al., 2023) showed that even among students who were not currently using AI at that time, 50% were likely/somewhat likely to use AI platforms even when their use was expressly prohibited. Among students who did use AI already, that number rose to 75%. With numbers like this, it seems naïve to think we can convince students not to use AI. Unfortunately, faculty irritation about the presence and use of GenAI by their students is compounded by the fact that there is no reliable way to detect AI-generated text.

The Challenge with AI-Detection Programs

Recognizing AI-generated text is much simpler than *detecting* it, as instructors have been able to do with plagiarism checkers like Turnitin.com. When students "borrow" or buy essays that are stored in databases, the software flags and shows clear evidence that faculty can verify by locating the original text. With AI detection, no such evidence is available. The software of these AI detection tools run their algorithms and offer an opinion (usually rendered with the air of certainty, alas) about whether and even how much of the writing was AI-generated. As Turnitin struggles to maintain relevant in these times where students no longer need to buy or borrow someone else's essay, the company now offers AI detection and claims a "high accuracy rate accompanied by a less than one percent positive rate" (Chechitelli, 2023, para. 4), a number that seems dubious at best. In fact, prior to the launch of Turnitin's AI-writing detector, a *Washington Post* informal study of just 16 student writing samples (a combination of AI-fabricated, student written, and mixed sources) found Turnitin got "over half of them at least partly wrong" (Fowler, 2023, para. 9). Even OpenAI, the company that created ChatGPT, was forced to deactivate their AI Classifier detection tool less than six months after it launched due to "its low rate of accuracy" (Nelson, 2023, paras. 1-2). Despite demonstrated false-positives *and* false-negatives (Cingillioglu, 2023) from AI-detection software, many faculty who continue to assign out-of-class writing exercises also continue to rely on these AI-detection tools.

One of the major faults of AI-detection software is its tendency to categorize "average" writing as AI-generated. This may be particularly troublesome for faculty who work with beginning writers who often produce work that *is* robotic or, at the very least, "average." One major source of false positives has been grammar-improvement software such as Grammarly, which corrects spelling and grammar mistakes and suggests stronger alternatives for syntax, diction, and clarity. This tool has been profoundly helpful to many who struggle with the mechanics of writing. Nonetheless, a student who composes an entire essay as best they can, then uses Grammarly to improve the output, can easily be mis-identified by AI-detection software as having used GenAI to write the entire essay. Complicating that fact is the existence of still more online tools that obfuscate AI use. One example is QuillBot, a free tool that paraphrases writing by replacing individual words with synonyms. This can help mask the writing style and patterns of some LLMs, which occasionally overuse certain terms and phrases in a way that renders them more detectable. The same service can help students elude plagiarism detectors, incidentally. Like other

AI-driven tools, QuillBot is imperfect. Paraphrased results can sound stilted or overly formal and can lead to hilarious misunderstandings when replacing a proper noun (as an example, "President George W. Shrub"). But while QuillBot struggles with a natural-sounding tone, JotBot aims to solve exactly this problem. Its draft generator promises to analyze a person's writing and generate text that matches their style. It is likely that such platforms will reduce the number of robotic pieces received by faculty as they continue to develop.

Existing assistive tools and those that are sure to come in the years ahead make effective GenAI detection increasingly unlikely now and for the foreseeable future. Given the unreliable results of AI-detection software, it is not surprising that institutions are increasingly disabling AI detectors (Ghaffary, 2023). Furthermore, some institutions are not pursuing student conduct cases when the only evidence is an apparently high score from an AI detector (Heaton, 2023). What, then, are faculty to do?

The Return of the In-Class Writing Assessment?

Some educators, recognizing the threats to traditional essay requirements that occur outside of the classroom, have shifted their assignments to be completed only during live, synchronous (face-to-face) classroom settings (Prochaska, 2023). But this solution comes with its own set of challenges. Research suggests timed assessments in general are often less valid, reliable, inclusive, and equitable than untimed assessments (Gernsbacher et al., 2020) while timed written assessments often only assess only limited forms of competence (William, 2001) further thwarting our attempts to correctly evaluate what students actually comprehend.

One obstacle associated with in-class writing assessments is the mode of delivery. The difficulty of monitoring individual laptops during exams has led to some educators returning to the use of pen and paper. While this move may reduce students' cheating attempts, an unfortunate reality is that many of today's college students are less likely to have learned penmanship in elementary school (Trubek, 2016). Furthermore, many students freely admit their handwriting is difficult to read, and they claim that they can type much faster than they can write by hand. Because their brains have been trained to think in ways that match the speed of typing, it might be logical to assume their work would suffer without a keyboard, but at least one research study indicates that the quality of their writing did *not* differ significantly between the two response modes. College freshmen using Microsoft WordPads that did not include tools for automated spelling or grammar corrections wrote more words than their handwriting peers, but there were no significant differences in the overall quality of their scores (Lovett et al., 2010). Nonetheless, faculty who opt to incorporate in-class writing assignments should be cognizant of the extra time and effort it may take to decipher hand-written student responses, and care would have to be taken to ensure that students are graded on their knowledge, not their penmanship.

While handwriting essays may not hinder the quality of a student's writing, other factors must be taken into consideration when deciding whether to use in-class writing assignments or not. To begin, faculty would be wise to take into account their view on writing; if they consider writing to be a process, they must be aware that students' ability to go through this process is severely restricted if they only have one class period to complete their written work. An accurate awareness of student backgrounds is another primary concern, particularly since instructors will almost certainly work with students who come from different linguistic and cultural backgrounds during their tenure. This awareness is critical, given that Non-Native English Speakers (NNESs) may perform more poorly than Native English Speakers (NESs) in timed, handwritten assessments that occur during class due to linguistic barriers and a lack of contextual knowledge (David, 2016). NNES students necessarily require more clarity in language, directions, and background information, as well as the need for more time to process the language and formulate their responses in English (Reid & Kroll, 1995). This is true of all assignments, generally, but given the intense nature of in-class, timed writing assessments, it should be a fundamental consideration for faculty who are contemplating using such assignments in their face-to-face classes.

There will also be important ethical issues that arise. As Todd Zakrajsek (2022) has noted, many college courses are optimized for fast-talking extroverts. The fast thinkers are likely to be the most visible, the most vocal, and the most engaged students in the room, which could easily lead an instructor to believe that all students have achieved the same high level of understanding. Of course, not every student is a fast thinker on the spot, but in-class essay writing does prioritize this type of student. Neurodivergent students in particular may find that in-class writing assignments prioritize a type of thinking and rapid action they are unaccustomed to (Singer, 1999).

Even if educators could create accommodations that neutralize the challenges many students face with in-class writing activities and the ethics associated with these undertakings, many students take courses online, preventing this mode of assessment. While the percentage of students taking online courses has lessened since the pandemic, online course enrollments are still higher now than they were before 2019. In fact, nationally 54 percent of college students took online classes in the Fall of 2022, and 26 percent took them exclusively (*2024 Online Learning Statistics – Forbes Advisor*, May 31, 2024). This reality further complicates the practice of assigning in-class writing assessments, as many faculty members teach a mix of both online and face-to-face courses. Students taking the same course but in different modalities may experience vastly different assessment conditions and, subsequently, vastly different final grades, despite having the same instructor. While instructors may clearly state that the use of GenAI is forbidden, students in online courses still have access to these tools, and a majority will use them regardless of course policy (Shaw et al., 2023). Students in face-to-face classes lack that access. This disparity can lead to significant grade differences between online and in-person students, with those who violate academic integrity often receiving higher grades than those who do not; a notable poll conducted at Fordham University found that cheaters average a 3.41 GPA compared to a 2.85 GPA for non-cheaters (*8 Astonishing Stats on Academic Cheating*, 2012). This discrepancy—coupled with the fact students are generally more accepting of cheating online compared to traditional forms of cheating (Ferguson et al., 2022) disadvantages students who attend face-to-face classes. Pivoting to in-class writing assignments, then, raises questions about the fairness and consistency of assessment practices across different course delivery methods. Such a scenario also challenges the core principles of academic honesty and equal opportunity in education, creating a troubling paradox where unethical behavior may be inadvertently incentivized by the system's inability to ensure consistent assessment conditions across different learning environments.

Perhaps the most persuasive reason to reconsider incorporating in-class writing assignments comes from analysis of the research about these assessments themselves. Research has found that timed assessments in general are often less valid, reliable, inclusive, and equitable than untimed assessments (Gernsbacher et al., 2020). Furthermore, timed written assessments often only assess limited forms of competence (William, 2001) further thwarting our attempts to correctly evaluate what concepts students genuinely comprehend and how they are able to apply their knowledge. The impulse to revert to in-class written assessments, then, is one that should be tempered by thoughtful consideration of the issues presented here, as well as by other considerations that are beyond the scope of this chapter.

Like It or Not: GenAI is Here to Stay

While educators actively seek methods to fight or neutralize the use of GenAI tools by altering their assignment prompts to include class discussions or topics that are less represented on the internet, the same challenges of online students and access remain. It is also worth noting that these options only apply to a small subset of courses and disciplines. Rather than fighting an ever-growing range of technological changes, perhaps a more effective approach is to accept the inevitable: We can't ignore Gen AI, we can't prevent it, we can't detect it, we can't convince students to avoid it, and we can't easily find workarounds for it. Our only sustainable option as educators is to find ways to "lean in" to the technology and infuse its use into our courses.

In the interest of clarity, it is important to distinguish "leaning in" to GenAI and its potential from throwing one's hands up disparagingly or adopting an apathetic attitude toward the technology. Faculty must remember that there are limitations to what GenAI can produce because of how LLMs are built and trained. Specifically, most LLMs source text from books, articles, and websites that people have previously published. Thus, while the LLM algorithms can identify and mimic linguistic patterns in billions of pages of human-generated sources, it is unable to evaluate those sources for accuracy, bias, or even how contemporary the information in its sources is. Essay responses produced by GenAI, then, can (and will) reflect the outdated, inaccurate, and even biased language produced by human authors. Furthermore, in addition to producing essays that lack originality and student voice, the vast array of source materials used by GenAI results in essays that are broad in scope and underdeveloped. These technical shortcomings and knowledge thereof, however, provide educators with many opportunities to actively engage students in their learning. Additionally, the interdisciplinary nature of LLMs used in GenAI programs means that these learning opportunities are available to faculty across various academic disciplines.

The Case for Alternatives to Traditional Essays

Faculty interested in maintaining academic rigor despite the prevalence of GenAI have several options available to them. As previously discussed, reusing a writing assignment that has been given to students for five or more years increases the likelihood that they will submit AI-generated responses. Students can easily input these familiar prompts into LLMs, receive complete answers, copy and paste them into a document or online, and submit them with minimal engagement or original thought. For example, a biology teacher can no longer assign a 2,000-word essay on genetic modification and trust students will submit work that solely reflects information from the course textbook, in-class lessons, or other instructor-provided materials. Our only solution, it would seem, is to alter our essay assignments. In fact, an argument could be made that educators should feel an urgent call to action in the face of this new technology. Those who resist altering essay assignments to acknowledge and use GenAI could be contributing to the problem.

If students are going to use GenAI tools, then the essay prompts they are given must be revised to ensure that they actively engage with those generated responses. Consequently, the biology teacher who leans into students' use of GenAI might modify the assignment as follows: "Use your preferred AI platform and tell it to generate a 2,000-word essay on genetic modifications. Copy the AI's response into a document. Then, using 'track changes,' provide quotes and information from this week's assigned readings and your lecture notes that support or challenge the ideas in the AI-generated essay." This modification gives students permission to use GenAI while requiring them to evaluate the output against course materials, including their own notes. As the subject-matter expert, the instructor is well prepared to effectively assess students' abilities to evaluate the generated content and incorporate supporting evidence or contradictions from course materials. Subtle but effective changes to traditional or long-standing assignments, therefore, can empower faculty by attesting to not only their discipline-specific knowledge, but their awareness of the presence, use, and shortcomings of GenAI in their academic settings. Learning to work with, rather than against, GenAI may also enable instructors to more readily incorporate high-impact learning activities into their course activities, including essay workshops.

Faculty interested in promoting active or collaborative learning in their classes will find GenAI to be a useful tool to this end. Our example biology teacher could ask students to bring their work to class in physical or digital formats, then put students in pairs or small groups to synthesize their individual work into a new essay outline. By freeing students from the initial task of drafting an essay, this approach may allow for deeper consideration of course materials and more impactful learning activities. As the facilitator and subject-matter expert, the instructor can clear up misconceptions and note the questions asked by students to help them determine how students' understanding progressed between the workshop session and their final essay. In addition to providing students with the opportunity to discuss key biological concepts, students are given the chance to overcome linguistic barriers, to discuss the organizational possibilities to ensure their final product is impactful and cogent, and to develop a new outline that they can confidently use to produce a written product that better reflects their effort and learning. If we are interested in teaching students to think critically about topics, would this not be a more effective way to meet this learning objective?

Working with GenAI necessarily requires faculty to approach essay work with an open mind and a willingness to adapt. While it's understandable that many instructors may be hesitant to modify their essay assessments, resisting this change risks allowing dissatisfaction and resentment to fester and impact their teaching. It may help to liken working with (rather than against) GenAI to using a calculator in mathematics education. Initially, there was resistance to allowing calculators in math classes, with concerns that students wouldn't learn fundamental skills. However, educators realized that calculators could free students to focus on higher-level problem-solving and conceptual understanding, rather than getting bogged down in tedious calculations. Similarly, with GenAI, the focus shifts from the mechanics of writing to the higher-order skills of critical thinking, analysis, evaluation, and synthesis. Just as calculators didn't eliminate the need for mathematical understanding,

GenAI doesn't negate the importance of writing skills. Instead, it challenges educators to design assignments that emphasize these crucial cognitive abilities. The key is to design assessments that leverage GenAI's capabilities while still requiring students to demonstrate their own understanding and critical thinking skills. This approach acknowledges the reality of technological advancement while maintaining the core educational objectives of essay writing. It challenges both educators and students to adapt and grow in a rapidly evolving academic landscape.

The Educator's Role in Career Readiness

In addition to accelerating students' participation in higher-level cognitive skills for a particular course or term, reshaping writing assignments has the potential to better prepare learners for the professional world. Current and future workplaces will have access to GenAI, so writing may not be a particularly prioritized skill. What is and will continue to be emphasized are those skills that AI cannot perform. For example, although AI can produce general content on what has been said on a topic, it cannot evaluate how effectively an idea is presented in the same way a subject-matter expert could. This provides a valuable set of teachable moments for educators, who can prompt students to consider writing styles, diction, syntax, literary and rhetorical devices, as well as class discussions, current events, and research that can enhance an AI-generated piece. We have separately published an open-source compendium of sixty quick ideas for converting essay and discussion board assignments in the AI era that ultimately teach AI fluency: https://bit.ly/chatgptassignments

This work may involve harnessing the power of AI tools for research, too. Thoughtfully reimagined writing assignments, then, can teach students about both the limitations and the possibilities of GenAI, and taking the time to infuse these redesigned assignments within a course and across the curriculum will develop students who are more critical consumers of the technology, thereby developing real "value-added" skills that will make them effective and valued members of a professional organization. In this regard, today's educators have a valuable opportunity to lead by example for their students.

What do LLMs do well?

Perhaps an ideal starting point in redesigning assignments is determining where LLMs excel and where they fail—at least for now. It is imperative, as it always has been, that we focus on cultivating and assessing our students' human-centric skills (Figure 1.2): critiquing, judgment, ethics, evaluation, social interaction, and deep analysis. These higher-order thinking skills and interpersonal abilities remain distinctly human domains; as AI tools become more integrated into most of our workplaces, all of us will need to actively apply those competencies. Our curricula should then emphasize developing students' capacities for critical thinking and analysis, ethical reasoning, and nuanced interpretation of complex issues.

Table 2. Comparison of Relative Strengths for LLMs and Humans

Our Comparison of Relative Strengths for LLMs and Humans	
Large Language Models	**Humans**
Summarizing Brainstorming Answering Questions Classifying Text Outlining Writing First Drafts Shallow Analysis	Critiquing Judging Ethics Evaluating Social Interaction Deep Analysis

At the same time, we should not ignore the strengths and abilities found in the LLM column. Rather, we should consider reframing how we approach them. For instance, instead of just teaching summarization, we might focus on critically evaluating AI-generated summaries of topics in our disciplines. Or when covering brainstorming, we could explore how students can effectively collaborate with AI tools to enhance creativity. This framework challenges us to reconsider what skills are most valuable for students to develop in a world where AI can handle many routine cognitive tasks. It prompts us to emphasize uniquely human capabilities while also teaching students how to work alongside AI tools effectively.

A Cyborg/Centaur Approach to the Traditional Research Paper

Perhaps AI author and blogger Ethan Mollick (2023) distills this working relationship with LLMs best with his Centaurs and Cyborgs analogy. "Centaur" collaboration maintains a clear distinction between human and AI contributions. Like the mythical creature, there's a visible "seam" where one ends and the other begins. In practice, this means strategically alternating between human and AI tasks, leveraging each entity's strengths. For instance, a student might determine appropriate statistical methods, then use AI to generate graphs. This approach allows for a defined division of labor, with humans tackling tasks they excel at and delegating others to AI.

Conversely, the Cyborg model represents a more fluid integration of human and AI efforts. Here, the boundaries blur as work is intertwined, with frequent back-and-forth exchanges (Mollick, 2023). A Cyborg approach might involve a student initiating a sentence for AI to refine or providing initial guidance for AI to develop a complex illustration. This method creates a seamless workflow where human and AI efforts blend together, each enhancing the other's contributions.

As Mollick (2023) sums up our inevitable collaboration with AI tools, "We get to make choices about how we want to use AI help to make work more productive, interesting, and meaningful. But we have to make those choices soon, so that we can begin to actively use AI in ethical and valuable ways, as Cyborgs and Centaurs, rather than merely reacting to technological change" (para. 20). If research papers and other forms of traditional essays are critical for a specific discipline, adopting a Cyborg/Centaur mindset that infuses GenAI tools into the process can help instructors meet their course learning objectives while also teaching students how to best use these tools. As noted previously, LLMs excel at summarizing and brainstorming, making them a natural fit for students to use while reviewing sources, generating ideas, developing research questions (and gaps), and outlining the paper or project. Instructors may even choose to allow students to use LLMs to write first drafts of literature reviews or other parts of their papers that students are then taught how to actively and intentionally evaluate, refine, expand, and revise.

This evaluation process can have secondary benefits as well. Students build their critical analysis skills of the quality and originality of writing in general when they learn how to distinguish between human-generated and AI-generated texts by understanding concepts like burstiness (frequency of rare words) and perplexity (text unpredictability), improving their own writing abilities (Krajka & Olszak, 2024). Other research indicates using Gen-AI tools as peer reviewers can help students improve final drafts and reinforces the importance of revision (Agung Rinaldy Malik et al., 2023). Guiding students through such processes will help faculty mitigate the reckless and uninformed use of AI as students develop their research papers.

Alternative Assessments to Measure Content Knowledge and Critical Thinking

For those looking for assessment options beyond restructuring the traditional out-of-class essay or research paper, some instructors have added (or reinstated) other forms of assessments that don't rely as heavily on written text, including:

- **Oral exams:** In smaller, face-to-face classes, some instructors outside of language classes are meeting with individual students and conducting one-on-one oral exams. Proponents find this type of exam allows for deeper assessment of student understanding, provides immediate feedback, and improves necessary oral communication skills (Hazen, 2020) while being well-received by students and comparable in difficulty to written exams (Ohmann, 2019). In one theoretical computer science course, oral exams even seem to provide a more accurate evaluation of student knowledge than traditional written exams (Gharibyan, 2005). There are, of course, many students who experience greater levels of stress during an oral exam and educators share apprehensions regarding subjectivity in grading (Hazen, 2020), but designing and implementing the assessment carefully can lessen those concerns while more accurately testing concept-based comprehension and enhancing student engagement, particularly in large, diverse classes (Käng et al., 2019).

- **Presentations:** It's no secret that many students fear public speaking and, consequently, view giving classroom presentations as negative, time-consuming tasks, but they tend to see it differently when reflecting back on the course (Sander et al., 2002) and research shows that presentations can improve student engagement, critical thinking skills, and overall interest in the subject matter (Aguilera et al., 2017). Iterative group presentations, where each group's topic builds on the previous one, have shown particular promise in enhancing learning outcomes (Aguilera et al., 2017). Students can also "teach the class" with mini-lecture series that include visual aids and questions-and-answer sessions with students. And while it's fair to point out that students could use GenAI tools to write and create these presentations, they're still actively engaging with and modifying that content in the same ways they may later do so in their professions.
- **Debates:** While debates present some challenges—especially with controversial and emotionally-charged topics—research has long suggested they are effective active learning tools for enhancing student engagement and learning outcomes. Debates can promote critical thinking skills, improve content mastery, and develop communication abilities (Zare & Othman, 2013; Scott, 2008). In addition to debating peers, students can also debate LLMs, create arguments and counterpoints, reflect on their responses and process, and turn in their chats for assessment. This can diffuse emotional responses to controversial debates, as well as allow online students to actively engage in debates outside the classroom.
- **Group Projects:** Team-based learning (TBL), cooperative learning approaches, and other forms of group projects come with their share of challenges, but they have been shown to effectively enhance students' critical thinking skills and can be valuable assessment tools. And while students—individually or collectively—may use GenAI tools to generate content for group projects, they may be more motivated to produce better work when working with others. One study found "inferior" group members are motivated to match or exceed the performance of "superior" group members, while students who perceive their contribution is essential to the group's success work even harder (Weber & Hertel, 2007). With any luck, these group dynamics will inspire

students who opt to use GenAI tools to engage much more actively and critically with the generated content, turning it from a starting point into a springboard for deeper analysis, creativity, refinement, and original contributions from the group.

- **Professional portfolios and spec work:** When students find assignments valuable and directly applicable to their learning and needs outside of the course, they're more motivated to engage deeply with the material and invest time and effort into their work, lessening the urge to rely on unethical uses of GenAI tools. Their motivation "determines, directs, and sustains what they do learn" (Ambrose, et al., 2010, p. 5). Generating professional materials, such as portfolios showcasing their best work or spec work (created as samples for potential employers), appeals to both their intrinsic and extrinsic motivations. Intrinsically, students are driven by the satisfaction of creating high-quality, authentic work that represents their skills and creativity. Extrinsically, they are motivated by the potential career benefits, such as impressing future employers or clients and securing employment. This dual motivational appeal makes these assignments particularly effective in encouraging genuine engagement and discouraging over-reliance on or unethical use of GenAI tools.

While reinstating traditional assignments like group projects and presentations can effectively reduce reliance on extensive writing and mitigate potential misuse of GenAI tools, it's crucial to approach this shift thoughtfully. Simply substituting one type of assignment for another without careful consideration may not yield the desired learning outcomes. To ensure that these new assessments are meaningful, we must re-conceptualize them from the ground up, including their purpose.

It is constructive, even advisable, to consider alternative assessments with an eye toward the final product, but the process is far more complex than merely replacing the word "essay" in a prompt with "video presentation" and assuming the rest remains unchanged. Instead, we recommend starting over with the assignment's design. As with most effective teaching strategies, the best practice is rooted in "backward design" (Wiggins & McTighe, 1998). This involves first identifying the student's capabilities and skills they should possess by the end of the assessment, and then determining the content and practice needed to achieve those outcomes.

Since we are replacing writing, our first task is to analyze why we assigned the essay in the first place. For many instructors, a common answer is to assess critical thinking, though this can vary significantly between disciplines. However, the concept of critical thinking is too broad to be useful in this context. We need to break it down into specific skills. What abilities must students master to write an essay? As instructors in the humanities, we propose the following list for our essays:

1. **Ideate/brainstorm**: Generate original ideas, potentially remixing external concepts.
2. **Formulate a central thesis**: Develop a clear and concise main argument.
3. **Create sub-claims**: Develop supporting arguments that collectively and comprehensively support the thesis.
4. **Arrange sub-claims**: Organize these arguments into an outline that builds a cohesive argument rather than merely stacking examples.
5. **Draft strong paragraphs**: Write paragraphs with clear topic sentences.
6. **Connect evidence to sub-claims**: Link evidence directly to the supporting arguments.

By deconstructing the skills essential for essay writing, we can create alternative assessments that achieve the same educational objectives. We recommend compiling an extensive list of constituent skills. One effective strategy is to draw upon action verbs commonly associated with various levels of Bloom's taxonomy. These verbs can inspire additional ideas for the skill set required to craft an effective essay in your field. This thorough analysis ensures that alternative assignments—such as group projects, presentations, etc.—are intentionally designed to foster the critical thinking and analytical abilities traditionally honed through essay writing.

Thinking Outside the Box with Digital Assignments

Other promising approaches lie in the field of digital humanities, which seeks to bridge the gap between technology and the humanities. By actively engaging students in applying digital tools to research questions within the humanities, we encourage the creation of innovative methods for preserving, accessing, and visualizing humanities materials. This process stimulates fresh insights, collaboration, and novel research approaches.

However, digital projects and other forms of digital assessments extend beyond humanities courses. Now more than ever, students should practice translating their acquired knowledge to benefit audiences beyond academia. Digital projects excel at promoting critical thinking precisely because they prioritize audience awareness. Asking students to identify who stands to gain from their research or content, analyze it from an audience perspective, shape their message effectively, and then select the most suitable medium for delivery is a powerful way to promote the development of critical thinking skills, enhance media literacy, and foster a deeper understanding of communication strategies in various contexts. This approach not only encourages students to consider the broader implications of their work but also prepares them for real-world scenarios where effective communication and audience awareness are crucial. By engaging in this process, students learn to navigate the complexities of information dissemination, develop a more nuanced understanding of how content can influence different stakeholders, and may even gain experience in becoming the Centaurs and Cyborgs needed in tomorrow's workplace.

Leveraging Bloom's Digital Taxonomy in Assessment Design

As we grapple with the challenges posed by AI in education, Bloom's Digital Taxonomy offers a valuable framework for creating assessments that are both rigorous and resistant to AI-generated content. The website TeachThought offers this updated version of the classic taxonomy (Table 3), adapted for the digital age and designed to provide a hierarchy of cognitive skills that can guide our assessment strategies. It adds verbs that are more common in the digital age, including this partial list:

Table 3. Bloom's Taxonomy: Digital Planning Verbs

Bloom's Taxonomy: Digital Planning Verbs					
Remembering	**Understanding**	**Applying**	**Analyzing**	**Evaluating**	**Creating**
Locating Googling Tabulating Bullet-pointing	Annotating Tagging Tweeting Journaling	Reenacting Sketching Painting Charting	Correlating Mashing Linking Illustrating	Validating Posting Editorializing Moderating	Blogging Animating Podcasting Directing

While the lower levels of the taxonomy—Remembering and Understanding—remain important, they are also the most vulnerable to AI assistance. As educators, our focus should shift towards the higher levels: Applying, Analyzing, Evaluating, and Creating. These higher-order thinking skills are not only more challenging for AI to replicate but also more valuable in preparing students for their future careers.

Putting Bloom's Digital Taxonomy to Work

For faculty who are unfamiliar with or unpracticed at integrating Bloom's Taxonomy into their course, the suggestions below may prove useful for guiding their efforts:

1. **Analyze your current assessments:** Review your existing assignments and exams. Which levels of the taxonomy do they primarily address? Are they heavily weighted towards the lower levels?
2. **Elevate your assessments:** Look for opportunities to transform lower-level tasks into higher-order challenges. For instance, instead of asking students to recall facts about a historical event, have them analyze primary sources to evaluate different interpretations of that event.

3. **Emphasize creation and evaluation:** Design assignments that require students to produce original work or make informed judgments. These tasks are inherently more difficult for AI to complete effectively.
4. **Incorporate digital skills:** Consider how digital tools and environments can be used to assess higher-order thinking. For example, having students create a multimedia presentation that synthesizes and evaluates multiple sources on a topic.
5. **Focus on process, not just product:** Assess not only the final output but also the thinking process behind it. This could involve requiring students to document their research process, explain their reasoning or reflect on their creative choices.

By consciously designing assessments that target the upper levels of Bloom's Digital Taxonomy, we create tasks that are not only more resistant to AI-generated content but also more effective in developing the critical thinking and creative skills our students need. These higher-order tasks often require nuanced understanding, contextual knowledge, and creative problem-solving—areas where human cognition still holds a significant advantage over AI.

As we move forward, it's crucial to remember that the goal isn't to create assignments that are impossible for AI to complete. Rather, we should strive to develop assessments that are more valuable when completed by humans, leveraging our students' unique abilities to analyze, synthesize, evaluate, and create in ways that go beyond mere information recall or basic application.

Assessing Critical Thinking with Multiple-Choice Testing

While reimagining assignments using digital tools and Bloom's Digital Taxonomy can create more AI-resistant assessments, some educators may still prefer more traditional testing methods. One of the most commonly-used assessments in learning management systems is testing, with multiple choice questions the most frequently used question type (Butler, 2018; Biggs, 1987).

The use of multiple-choice questions (MCQs) is, of course, a longstanding practice in higher education (Roediger & Marsh, 2005). However, they are most commonly utilized to assess lower-order skills such as the levels of Bloom's taxonomy associated with memory and recall (Cronbach, 1988). This is both natural and logical. The format lends itself particularly well to questions that have clearly correct (and incorrect) answers, such as facts that students are asked to memorize. Such questions are also relatively easy for instructors to write, as faculty are, by definition, experts in their fields and thus the individual bits of knowledge are easy to call to mind (Butler, 2018; Aiken, 1982). Additionally, the format of multiple-choice questions is likely intuitive for many faculty. Asking about facts only calls for the faculty member to know the right answer, and then dream up the necessary distractors. The final part is likely the most challenging portion of writing such tests. It can be difficult to write three distractors that are plausible to students, partly because faculty are experts and not novices as the students are, and partly because the process calls for a type of creativity that new teachers need to master before it becomes second nature.

Writing multiple-choice questions that address the higher orders of Bloom's taxonomy would go a long way toward providing effective alternatives to take-home writing in the era of AI. While instructors typically use multiple-choice questions for lower-level skills, there is certainly precedent for using the multiple-choice format for higher-order skills—one merely needs to recall national standardized testing such as SAT, ACT, or GRE tests. Yet such multiple-choice questions are more difficult to write than fact-based multiple-choice questions, or at least take longer to write (Roediger & Marsh, 2005). Few instructors receive formal training in test creation (let alone validation), so having a framework in mind can make it easier to imagine how to higher-order multiple-choice questions in their respective disciplines.

Lewis Aiken (1982) offers a five-item taxonomy of higher-order MCQs (Table 4):

Table 4. Aiken's Taxonomy of Multiple-Choice Questions

Aiken's Taxonomy of MCQs	
Premise to Consequence	Cases or situations can be explained in the question stem, then choices about conclusions, solutions, or consequences follow
Multiple Premises	Two or more initial inputs, data points, or ideas combine to create a specific conclusion. As an example, "Given that Mary's raw score on a test is 60, the test mean 59, and the standard deviation 2, what is Mary's z score?"
Classification	A person, term, concept, or statement is given, then test-takers are asked to identify which of the listed category options is the best classification
Dual Propositions	Essentially a combination of two true/false statements, where answer options include single true statements, both, or neither
Relationship Between Concepts	Two concepts are listed with a relationship (often implied), then a similar relationship is applied to a third concept and the test-taker must select the matching fourth concept. As an example, "dolphins are to porpoises as pennies are to _____."

Instructors who are not formally trained in writing test questions might consider using Aiken's taxonomy to generate ideas as they contemplate creating the test. For instance, they might start with a particular piece of wisdom, analysis, or application they want students to master, then look at the taxonomy for a format that would fit that example.

Thomas Haladyna (2004) presents an expanded taxonomy of question types that might also help inspire instructors to fit critical thinking around these formats:

1. **Embedded blank-type items**: This is essentially a fill-in-the-blank type question done in multiple-choice format and may include two such blanks in the same question.
2. **Matching**: In MC format, this looks like five successive questions each using the same pool of five possible responses (numbered A-E).
3. **Extended Matching**: This is similar to MC Matching, mentioned above. However, this type of MC question has an extended scenario that provides context for the questions that follow. There may be as many as ten choices, as the number of possible responses should exceed the number of questions asked.
4. **Complex Multiple Choice**: This format provides three choices as possible answers, then the test-taker selects a combination (such as "1 and 3") as the true answer.
5. **Context-Dependent Item Sets**: An initial stimulus (reading passage, chart, graph, diagram, etc.) is followed by a series of basic MCQs related to the stimulus.

Haladyna's final item—context-dependent item sets—is the format we might most readily associate with standardized tests that measure critical thinking, and arguably the format easiest to imagine employing to gauge application, analysis, and evaluation. The use of a stimulus like a reading passage grants instructors more freedom to conceptualize how to ask questions that measure critical thinking, because they have the space to set up a more elaborate scenario than normal (single) MCQ would allow.

MCQs might never be a complete panacea to the problem of measuring critical thinking in online environments, but the format might be the best option we have available in a world where take-home writing no longer makes sense. It is also one of the only options that includes software safeguards against student cheating, and thus one of the few ways to prioritize and maximize student learning.

Additional GenAI-Era Assessments

We have, to this point, addressed issues related to the impact of GenAI on traditional assignments such as essays, research papers, portfolios, and multiple-choice question tests. If faculty are willing to rework these traditional assignments using our suggestions, perhaps they would be willing to replace these (still) AI-vulnerable assessments with activities that are suitable for both in-person and online modalities. It should be noted that these alternatives will likely still require faculty to guide students through scaffolded, preparatory class sessions during which appropriate GenAI use can be modeled and discussed. We invite faculty to consider the following digital assignment ideas that can be adjusted to fit course learning objectives and specific disciplines:

- **Live-streamed demonstrations:** Students plan and execute live-streamed demonstrations of course-related skills or experiments, engaging with their peers—or a selected audience—in real-time. This format develops public speaking skills, improves students' ability to explain concepts without access to other materials, and encourages adaptability. Streaming platforms like YouTube Live, Twitch, or Zoom can be used.
  - **Example:** In a chemistry course, students could conduct a live-streamed laboratory experiment, explaining each step of the process, answering viewer questions, and discussing the theoretical principles behind the observed reactions. This would challenge students to combine practical lab skills with clear, accessible scientific communication.
- **Narrated Prezi presentations**: Students create visually engaging Prezi presentations with zoom and pan features, adding their own narration to guide viewers through the content. This approach enhances digital literacy and encourages creative synthesis of information. It's particularly effective for topics with spatial or hierarchical relationships.
  - **Example**: In a biology course students could create a presentation on cell organelles, narrating their functions and relationships as they navigate through a 3D cell model.
- **Interactive mind maps:** Students create expansive, multimedia mind maps to visualize complex relationships between concepts. This method enhances understanding of interconnected ideas, improves information organization skills, and encourages holistic thinking.
  - **Example:** In a neuroscience course, students might create an interactive mind map exploring the complexities of memory formation and retrieval. The mind map could include nodes detailing different brain regions involved, types of memory (short-term, long-term, episodic, semantic), key neurotransmitters, and influential studies in the field. Students could embed images of brain scans, short video clips explaining specific processes, and links to research papers, allowing for a comprehensive visual exploration of how memories are formed, stored, and recalled.
- **Animated instructional videos**: Using tools like Vyond, Powtoon, Animaker, or other AI-powered generators, students create short, animated videos explaining complex concepts. This format develops the students' ability to distill and communicate intricate ideas visually and verbally.
  - **Example**: In a psychology course, students might produce an animated video explaining a cognitive bias and its impact on decision-making in everyday life, making abstract concepts more tangible and memorable.
- **Interactive timelines:** Tools like TimelineJS, Angular, Chart.Js, Express.js allow students to create rich, interactive timelines incorporating images, vid-

eos, and links. This method allows students to demonstrate their understanding of chronological relationships and historical context.

  - **Example:** In a literature course, students could develop an interactive timeline of modernist literature, showcasing key authors, works, and historical events from 1910 to 1945, helping to visualize the evolution of literary movements.

- **Infographics**: Using tools like Canva, Visme, or Infogram, students can create scrolling infographic-style presentations that combine data, visuals, and concise text in an engaging format they adjust to fit their audience's needs. Canva, in particular, offers a user-friendly interface with a wide range of templates and design elements, making it accessible even for students with limited design experience. This approach develops students' skills in data visualization, information design, and concise communication of complex ideas… and by distilling large amounts of information into clear steps, students gain a greater understanding of the process.
  - **Example:** In an economics course, students might research historical and current data, identify key trends, and apply course content to develop an infographic to explain the causes and effects of inflation, using data visualizations and concise explanations of economic principles.
- **Augmented reality (AR) presentations**: Using apps like Metaverse or ARKit, students create AR experiences where viewers use their smartphones to see additional information overlaid on the real world. This cutting-edge approach encourages innovative thinking and spatial awareness.
  - **Example:** In an architecture course, students might design an AR experience that overlays historical information and architectural details when viewers point their phones at campus buildings, bridging course content with the physical environment.
- **Websites**: Students design and build a website to present in-depth information on a course-related topic using platforms like WordPress, Wix, or Squarespace. This project would require students to synthesize and present information in an engaging, user-friendly, audience-driven format, while also considering aspects like site navigation and mobile responsiveness.
  - **Example:** In a marine biology course, students could create a website dedicated to coral reef ecosystems. The site might include pages on reef formation, biodiversity, threats to reef health, and conservation efforts. Students could incorporate interactive elements like a virtual reef tour, a quiz on reef species identification, and a live feed of coral reef data from research stations.

- **Video essays:** Students can write, narrate, create (or find) footage and other visual elements to explore course topics. Tools like Adobe Premiere, Final Cut Pro, or even simpler—and free—options like iMovie can be used.
    - o **Example**: In an environmental engineering course, students could produce a video essay examining the challenges and innovations in urban water management. The essay could create a narrative that explores issues like water scarcity, infrastructure, and pollution and then tell that story with footage of water treatment facilities, animations explaining filtration processes, data visualizations of water usage patterns, and real (or pseudo) interviews with city planners and environmental scientists.
- **360-degree virtual tours:** Similarly, students can use 360-degree cameras or apps like Google Tour Creator to make immersive virtual tours of locations.
    - o **Example:** In a geology course, students could create a virtual field trip of different rock formations, allowing their peers to explore and identify geological features in a 360-degree environment, simulating real-world field experiences.
- **Choose-your-own-adventure presentations:** Using branching tools like Twine or PowerPoint's hyperlinks, students create narratives where the user chooses their path. This interactive approach develops students' ability to consider multiple perspectives and outcomes.
    - o **Example:** In an ethics course, students might develop a branching narrative presentation on medical ethics, where viewers make decisions in various scenarios and see the consequences, fostering critical thinking about complex ethical dilemmas.
- **Games:** Students design, create, or modify games to teach course concepts, forcing them to engage deeply with the material while building their problem-solving skills. Tools like Twine, Scratch, or even board game design software can be used.
    - o **Example:** In a political science course, students might create a multiplayer game simulating international diplomacy. Players could represent different countries, negotiating trade deals, forming alliances, and responding to global crises. This game would require students to apply their understanding of international relations theories, economic principles, and historical precedents in a dynamic, interactive format.
- **Social Media Campaigns:** While educators may not consider social media platforms like TikTok, Instagram, LinkedIn, etc. to be valuable mediums to present academic work, the process of students design and execute a comprehensive social media campaign to address a course-related issue or promote a concept requires a clear understanding of the content, data, and the needs and desires of impacted audience members.

- **Example:** In a public health course, students might create a social media campaign to promote mental health awareness among college students. The campaign could include infographics on stress management techniques for Instagram, short video tips for TikTok, X threads on recognizing signs of depression, and LinkedIn articles on workplace mental health. Students would need to tailor content for each platform, track engagement metrics, and adjust their strategy based on audience response, mirroring real-world public health communication challenges.

- **Digital poster presentations:** Interactive posters with dynamic content allow viewers to engage in the content at their own pace and forces students to consider how best to present concepts and supporting materials, such as hyperlinks, embedded audio and video, and zoomable images.
  - **Example:** For an environmental science course, students could create a digital poster on a specific ecosystem, including interactive elements showing food webs, climate data, and human impacts. Students could include short video clips of wildlife, time-lapse animations of seasonal changes, and links to interviews or expert explanations.
- **Podcasts:** Students research, script, record, and edit podcast episodes on course-related topics. This format develops skills in audio storytelling, research synthesis, and clear verbal communication. Tools like Audacity for editing and hosting platforms like Anchor or Spotify for Podcasters can be used.
  - **Example:** In a history course, students could produce a series of podcast episodes exploring lesser-known figures of the Civil Rights Movement. Each episode would combine historical narrative, archival audio clips, and expert interviews, challenging students to present complex historical information. In this scenario, students could transform this into a group project whereby collaborating to research a historical figure and then assume the role of that figure during interviews with each other.
- **Multimedia case studies:** Students create in-depth, interactive case studies that combine text, images, video, and data visualizations. This approach develops analytical skills, encourages application of theoretical knowledge to real-world scenarios, and improves digital storytelling abilities. Tools like Shorthand or Atavist can be used for creating storytelling experiences.
  - **Example:** In a public health course, students might develop a multimedia case study on a disease outbreak, incorporating interactive maps showing the spread of the disease, timelines of key events, video interviews with healthcare workers and patients, data visualizations of infection rates and risk factors, and simulations allowing viewers to explore how different intervention strategies might have altered the outbreak's

course. This helps students apply their knowledge of public health theories to potential real-world impacts while creating a compelling narrative that speaks to a specific audience.

Redefining Roles

The advent of GenAI has called into question many long-standing and comfortable teaching practices, and it is not surprising that many faculty find it difficult to adapt to this new reality. It is entirely possible that faculty resent the feeling that they must suddenly be both subject matter experts and tech-savvy pedagogues. While it is true that teaching is a continually evolving practice, we would like to emphasize that instructors do not need to be technology experts or specify which tools should be used for any of the suggested digital assignments provided in this chapter. Our primary task is still to teach the content that meets the course's learning objectives and provide support and feedback as students navigate their way through the brainstorming, research, drafting, and implementation of coursework. By providing clear guidelines, stating objectives, and scaffolding these assignments with approval checkpoints, students can research, select, and learn the tools that best fit their technical skills and visions and complete the assignments in a unique, creative manner. This method aligns with constructivist learning environments and problem-based learning, reflecting real-world scenarios where professionals must identify and employ appropriate tools for their projects, and it nurtures creativity, critical thinking, and self-directed learning (Dutch et al., 2001; Oja, 2010; Schmidt et al., 2011). While some students may initially find the ambiguity of assignments like these challenging, many will appreciate the freedom to explore and be creative. Ultimately, this student-directed method often leads to deeper learning experiences and can produce impressive results that surpass traditional, highly structured assignments. While it may be time consuming to conscientiously integrate GenAI into teaching, faculty have the opportunity to impact learners not just while they are students in their courses, but also in their post-graduate lives. The assignments they redesign using AI may just lead students to produce final projects that students can share with potential employers during the interview process. What better way to ensure that our graduates are ready, willing, and able to be life-long learners?

AI and Other Forms of Assessment

We have focused on take-home writing in this chapter, specifically because this is the form of assessment most prone to students taking unwanted shortcuts using GenAI. Space does not permit a deeper exploration of the role GenAI might play in research projects, quizzes, or other collaborative tasks. Even beyond these alternative deliverables, it's important to remember that the world of assessment has other components and considerations. For instance, we have not explored how adjusting assignments to include AI components might fit with the models of formative (monitoring learning and providing feedback, often without a grade) and summative (evaluating the learning, with a grade) assessment. Essay writing can be formative, summative, or both, particularly if there is a focus on scaffolded elements before the final product, possibly with a focus on process over the final product. There is every reason to believe than GenAI has a role to play in both formative and summative forms of assessment.

One angle to consider is how competency-based assessment might shift in an AI-inflused world. The name seems self-explanatory: we build educational systems around the idea of graduating students when they can demonstrate mastery or competency. McClure et al. (1981) define competency-based education as "an instructional paradigm that assumes different programmatic forms in different context," in recognition of the fact that competence may look dramatically different between fields and disciplines. But the overall concept of measuring mastery is particularly interesting to consider in light of the GenAI revolution. If students are encouraged to create WITH GenAI, there exists the risk that certain fundamental skills might atrophy, if they are simply left to GenAI to perform. Measurements of competency will still be important to provide assurance that the fundamentals have been learned.

CONCLUSION

Just as the COVID-19 pandemic resulted in sudden and monumental shifts to teaching and learning, GenAI is reshaping the discipline at break-neck speed. Indeed, educators may feel like they only just regained a sense of equilibrium in their approaches to teaching following the necessary shift to online learning that the pandemic required; to be faced with another existential crisis in their professional lives is understandably upsetting. Interestingly, however, the profession is not in jeopardy—teachers may be confronting the question of "how do I do my job?", but they are, thankfully, not also grappling with the prospect of unemployment due to GenAI. Despite all that GenAI can do, there seems to be a consensus that teachers are still needed to educate. To be effective educators in this GenAI era, though, teachers may have to reassess what the work inherent to pedagogy entails and whether they are willing to adapt accordingly. The reality is that teachers are currently working in an environment where GenAI is readily available and frequently used. They are, therefore, in a position to model the types of behaviors that add value to a work environment and that AI cannot mimic. To be able to do this effectively, however, teachers must redefine their role(s) vis-à-vis their subject and their students.

Gentile, Città, Perna, and Allegra (2023) stated that the "teacher of the AI era must be a charismatic, empathetic educator able to build ethical relationships and interactions with the intelligences and digital tools that will assist them in their work." Teachers must be willing to teach not only content knowledge, then, but also the behaviors they want students to emulate. Ironically, this work may result in attrition as teachers who profess a love of learning and who preach the value of putting in time and effort to learn new content and skills decide that learning about AI and how to work with it takes too much energy to be worthwhile. Are these the individuals we want shaping the minds and learning habits of the younger generation? Returning to the question of what place essays have in today's educational landscape, students still need to be able to understand written words, to discuss meaningfully the implications of ideas put forth in a piece, and to learn what to do with the knowledge they gain. They need to learn to do this work readily, consistently, and willingly. By openly redefining their teaching roles, modeling ethical best practices with AI-generated content, and leading students in pedagogical activities that have applicability outside of class time, teachers can actively shape the future of an AI-infused society.

REFERENCES

Ahmed, A. (2024, May). *Meta AI Llama 3 vs ChatGPT 4: A comparative analysis*. PreScouter

Ambrose, S. A., Bridges, M. W., DiPietro, M., Lovett, M. C., & Norman, M. K. (2010). *How learning works: 7 research-based principles for smart teaching*. John Wiley & Sons.

8. *Astonishing Stats on Academic Cheating*. (2012). Retrieved July 30, 2024, from Online Education Database: http://oedb.org*2024. Online Learning Statistics – Forbes Advisor*. (n.d.). Www.forbes.com. https://www.forbes.com/advisor/education/online-colleges/online-learning-stats/#:~:text=54%25%3A%20Approximate%20Share%20of

Baird, J. S. (1980). Current trends in college cheating. *Psychology in the Schools*, 17(4), 515–522. DOI: 10.1002/1520-6807(198010)17:4<515::AID-PITS2310170417>3.0.CO;2-3

Broadhead, G. (2023, August 25). A Brief Guide To LLM Numbers: Parameter count vs. training size. *Medium*. https://medium.com/@greg.broadhead/a-brief-guide-to-llm-numbers-parameter-count-vs-training-size-894a81c9258

Chechitelli, A. (2023, March 16). *Understanding false positives within our AI writing detection capabilities*. www.turnitin.com. https://www.turnitin.com/blog/understanding-false-positives-within-our-ai-writing-detection-capabilities

Cingillioglu, I. (2023). *Detecting AI-generated essays: the ChatGPT challenge*. Campus-Wide.

Cingillioglu, I. (2023, May 25). Detecting AI-generated essays: The ChatGPT challenge. *Information Systems*, 40(3), 259–268. DOI: 10.1108/IJILT-03-2023-0043

Duah, J. E., & McGivern, P. (2024). How generative artificial intelligence has blurred notions of authorial identity and academic norms in higher education, necessitating clear university usage policies. *Campus-Wide Information Systems*, 41(2), 180–193. Advance online publication. DOI: 10.1108/IJILT-11-2023-0213

Duch, B. J., Groh, S. E., & Allen, D. E. (2001). *The power of problem-based learning: a practical "how to" for teaching undergraduate courses in any discipline*. Stylus Pub.

Fowler, G. A. (2023, April 3). We tested a new ChatGPT-detector for teachers. It flagged an innocent student. *Washington Post.* https://www.washingtonpost.com/technology/2023/04/01/chatgpt-cheating-detection-turnitin/

Ganesh, G., Paswan, A., & Sun, Q. (2015). Are face-to-face classes more effective than online classes? An empirical examination. *Marketing Education Review*, 25(2), 67–81. DOI: 10.1080/10528008.2015.1029851

Gernsbacher, M. A., Soicher, R. N., & Becker-Blease, K. A. (2020, June). Four empirically based reasons not to administer time-limited tests. *Translational Issues in Psychological Science*, 6(2), 175–190. DOI: 10.1037/tps0000232 PMID: 32582819

Ghaffary, S. (2023, September 21). Universities rethink using AI writing detectors to vet students' work. Bloomberg Newsletter.

Gillentine, F. M. (1937). Why do college students cheat? *Peabody Journal of Education*, 15(1), 15–17. DOI: 10.1080/01619563709535395

Goff, D., Johnston, J., & Bouboulis, B. (2020). Maintaining academic standards and integrity in online business courses. *International Journal of Higher Education*, 9(2), 248. DOI: 10.5430/ijhe.v9n2p248

Grijalva, T. C., Nowell, C., & Kerkvliet, J. (2006). Academic honesty and online courses. *College Student Journal*, 40(1), 180–185. Retrieved July 31, 2024, from https://www.learntechlib.org/p/101008/

Hazen, H. (2020). Use of oral examinations to assess student learning in the social sciences. *Journal of Geography in Higher Education*, 44(4), 592–607. DOI: 10.1080/03098265.2020.1773418

Heaton, S. (2023, May 6). *The use of AI detection tools in the assessment of student work.* WordPress. https://drsaraheaton.wordpress.com/2023/05/06/the-use-of-ai-detection-tools-in-the-assessment-of-student-work/

Heaven, W. (2023). *GPT-4 is bigger and better than ChatGPT.* MIT Technology Review. https://www.technologyreview.com/2023/03/14/1069823/gpt-4-is-bigger-and-better-chatgpt-openai/

Hutson, J. (2024). Rethinking plagiarism in the era of generative AI. *Journal of International Communication*, 4(1), 20–31. DOI: 10.54963/jic.v4i1.220

Jenkins, B. D., Golding, J. M., Le Grand, A. M., Levi, M. M., & Pals, A. M. (2023). When opportunity knocks: College students' cheating amid the COVID-19 pandemic. *Teaching of Psychology*, 50(4), 407–419. DOI: 10.1177/00986283211059067

Jordan, A. E. (2001). College student cheating: The role of motivation, perceived norms, attitudes, and knowledge of institutional policy. *Ethics & Behavior*, 11(3), 233–247. DOI: 10.1207/S15327019EB1103_3

Josien, L., Seeley, E., Csipak, J. J., & Rampal, R. (2015). Cheating: Students and faculty's perception on potential cheating activity. *Journal of Legal. Ethical and Regulatory Issues*, 18, 21.

Käng, D., Goico, S., Ghanbari, S., Bennallack, K., Pontes, T., O'Brien, D., & Hargis, J. (2019). Providing an oral examination as an authentic assessment in a large section, undergraduate diversity class. *International Journal for the Scholarship of Teaching and Learning*, 13(2). Advance online publication. DOI: 10.20429/ijsotl.2019.130210

Kaushar, M. (2013). Study of impact of time management on academic performance of college students. *IOSR Journal of Business and Management* (9:6), 59-60.

Krajka, J., & Olszak, I. (2024). "AI, will you help?" How learners use Artificial Intelligence when writing. *XLinguae*, 17(1), 34–48. DOI: 10.18355/XL.2024.17.01.03

Krou, M. R., Fong, C. J., & Hoff, M. A. (2020). Achievement motivation and academic dishonesty: A meta-analytic investigation. *Educational Psychology Review*, 33(2), 427–458. Advance online publication. DOI: 10.1007/s10648-020-09557-7

Lovett, B. J., Lewandowski, L. J., Berger, C., & Gathje, R. A. (2010). Effects of response mode and time allotment on college students' writing. *Journal of College Reading and Learning*, 40(2), 64–79. DOI: 10.1080/10790195.2010.10850331

Malik, A. R., Pratiwi, Y., Andajani, K., Numertayasa, I. W., Suharti, S., Darwis, A., & Marzuki, M. (2023). Exploring artificial intelligence in academic essays: Higher education students' perspectives. *International Journal of Educational Research Open*, 5, 100296. DOI: 10.1016/j.ijedro.2023.100296

McCabe, D. L., Treviño, L. K., & Butterfield, K. D. (2012). *Cheating in college why students do it and what educators can do about it* (1st ed.). Johns Hopkins University Press.

McClure, L., & Nickse, R. S.National Institute of Education. (1981). *Competency-based education: Beyond minimum competency testing*. Teachers College Press.

Mollick, E. (2023, September 16). *Centaurs and Cyborgs on the Jagged Frontier*. www.oneusefulthing.org. https://www.oneusefulthing.org/p/centaurs-and-cyborgs-on-the-jagged

Nelson, J. (2023, September 29). OpenAI quietly shuts down its AI detection tool. *Decrypt*. https://decrypt.co/149826/openai-quietly-shutters-its-ai-detection-tool

Ohmann, P. (2019). An assessment of oral exams in introductory CS. *Proceedings of the 50th ACM Technical Symposium on Computer Science Education* (613-619). https://doi.org/DOI: 10.1145/3287324.3287489

Oja, K. J. (2010). Using problem-based learning in the clinical setting to improve nursing students' critical thinking: An evidence review. *The Journal of Nursing Education*, 50(3), 145–151. DOI: 10.3928/01484834-20101230-10 PMID: 21210603

Prochaska, E. (2023, January 23). Embrace the bot: Designing writing assignments in the face of AI. *Faculty Focus*. https://www.facultyfocus.com/articles/course-design-ideas/embrace-the-bot-designing-writing-assignments-in-the-face-of-ai/

Reid, J., & Kroll, B. (1995). Designing and assessing effective classroom writing assignments for NES and ESL students. *Journal of Second Language Writing*, 4(1), 17–41. DOI: 10.1016/1060-3743(95)90021-7

Sander, P., Sanders, L., & Stevenson, K. (2002). Engaging the learner: Reflections on the use of student presentations. *Psychology Teaching Review*, 10(1), 76–89. DOI: 10.53841/bpsptr.2002.10.1.76

Schmidt, H. G., Rotgans, J. I., & Yew, E. H. (2011, August). The process of problem-based learning: What works and why. *Medical Education*, 45(8), 792–806. DOI: 10.1111/j.1365-2923.2011.04035.x PMID: 21752076

Scott, S. (2008). Perceptions of students' learning critical thinking through debate in a technology classroom: A case study. *The Journal of Technology Studies*, 34(1), 39–44. Advance online publication. DOI: 10.21061/jots.v34i1.a.5

Shaw, C., Yuan, L., Brennan, D., Martin, S., Janson, N., Fox, K., & Bryant, G. (2023, October 23). Tyton Partners. https://tytonpartners.com/time-for-class-2023/GenAI-Update

Singer, J. (1999). Why can't you be normal for once in your life? From a problem with no name to the emergence of a new category of difference. In Corker, M., & French, S. (Eds.), *Disability Discourse* (pp. 59–67). Open University Press.

Smyth, M. L., & Davis, J. R. (2003). An Examination of Student Cheating in the Two-Year College. *Community College Review*, 31(1), 17–32. DOI: 10.1177/009155210303100102

TeachThought. (2024, August 1). *Bloom's taxonomy verbs: A comprehensive list for critical thinking*. TeachThought. https://www.teachthought.com/critical-thinking/blooms-taxonomy-verbs-2/

Trubek, A. (2016). *The history and uncertain future of handwriting*. Bloomsbury USA, an imprint of Bloomsbury Publishing Plc.

Watson, G. R., & Sottile, J. (2010). Cheating in the digital age: Do students cheat more in online courses? *Online Journal of Distance Learning Administration*, 13(1).

Weber, B., & Hertel, G. (2007). Motivation gains of inferior group members: A meta-analytical review. *Journal of Personality and Social Psychology*, 93(6), 973–993. DOI: 10.1037/0022-3514.93.6.973 PMID: 18072849

Wiggins, G. P., & McTighe, J. (1998). *Understanding by design*. Association for Supervision and Curriculum Development.

Wiliam, D. (2001). An overview of the relationship between assessment and the curriculum. In Scott, D. (Ed.), *Curriculum and assessment* (pp. 165–182). Greenwood Publishing.

Zakrajsek, T. D. (2022). *The New Science of Learning: How to Learn in Harmony with Your Brain* (3rd ed.). Stylus Publishing LLC.

Zare, P., & Othman, M. (2013). Classroom debate as a systematic teaching/learning approach. *World Applied Sciences Journal*, 28(11), 1506–1513. DOI: 10.5829/idosi.wasj.2013.28.11.1809

Chapter 7
Advancing Inquiry-Based Learning Through Generative AI-Enabled Assessments

Muhammad Usman Tariq
https://orcid.org/0000-0002-7605-3040
Abu Dhabi University, UAE & University College Cork, Ireland

ABSTRACT

This chapter explores the transformative impact of generative artificial intelligence on inquiry-based learning in educational assessment. Generative AI technologies have revolutionized traditional assessment methods, enabling dynamic, individualized learning experiences that meet individual student needs. By harnessing the power of artificial intelligence, teachers can create assessments that promote critical thinking, conceptual understanding, and deeper engagement with content. The chapter begins with an overview of the theoretical foundations of generative artificial intelligence and its integration into educational frameworks such as constructivism and technology-enhanced learning. It discusses practical applications of artificial intelligence in creating dynamic assessment environments. Examples include tools like Knewton and MATH from Carnegie Learning, which adapt learning methods based on student performance.

DOI: 10.4018/979-8-3693-6351-5.ch007

INTRODUCTION

The advancement of technologies has emphatically transformed educational paradigms into different phases of education by consistently incorporating high technologies in the dissemination of knowledge and assessments. One of the more recent exciting technologies is generative AI. One category of AI is generative, which implies creating new content from given materials, and has shown great promise in a wide range of disciplines, including the assessment of students' knowledge. It can be observed that where traditional approaches to the assessment of students' performance have previously entailed a stereotype and rather rigid set of measures that include examinations, there has been a gradual shift toward more dynamic and individual approaches made possible by the algorithmic use of machine learning (Cheng & Wang, 2023). The skills of generative AI enable the creation of assessments that not only avert the formalized approach but also are closer to the learning style and requirements of the learner. Such a transition from a more generalized method to a more specific approach may improve the prognosis and prediction quality. Another advantage that is typical of generative AI is that it can select or create questions and scenarios or problems that may be based on the responses given and performance of the learner, so that it will be easier to develop a more extensive assessment of a student's grasp and proficiency (Ding & Choi, 2024).

Furthermore, by employing generative AI in assessments, the inclusion of realistic problems and cases in the evaluation procedure is possible, thus making the assessments more interesting and real life oriented. This is in accordance with the trends of the current day learning outcomes, which include analysis, synthesis, and evaluation, and the disposition to use ideas and concepts in various circumstances. In addition, since generative AI enables continuous and adaptive assessment, educators can obtain a more comprehensive consequence of a student, his or her strong side, and the points of weakness, which helps to choose the right approaches to improve the situation. Blending Generative AI into the Inquiry-Based Learning Settings. Therefore, the concept of IBL is educational learning that focuses on the learning abilities of a learner in posing questions, searching for, and discovering meanings in a certain concept. Credited to a cross between behaviorist and cognitivist theories, this pedagogical method ensures that students master as many concepts as possible in their areas of specialization, besides developing skills, including critical thinking and creativity, as well as values such as teamwork. The convergence of AI in IBL learning environments makes it possible to improve educational results by offering more interactive, student-centered, and facilitative learning (Cheng & Wang, 2023). Thus, one of the essential areas in which generative AI contributes to IBL is the development of individual learning sequences. This is specifically true as students are working on enquiry-based learning undertakings; it is possible for generative AI to work hand-in-hand to develop subsequent questions or challenges that are appropriate in relation to students' learning progress and preferences. For instance, if a student searched for information on the effects of climatic change on an area's natural environment, he or she would be recommended by the AI programs to dive deeper into certain factors such as deforestation, greenhouse gas emissions, or an initiative to conserve flora and fauna. This increases the chances of meeting students' needs so that they can be interested and constantly enquiring, unlike in large groups where one becomes bored (Ding & Choi, 2024).

It is also important to note that generative AI can also help enhance feedback loops inside IBL ecosystems. This is especially so because traditional feedback entails a time lag through written or e-mailed feedback that rarely helps the learner. Conversely, generative AI can help provide positive suggestions and feedback to the student on the spot, depending on the answers and activities of the student. This feedback cycle enables students to make corrections instantly, think through the matters in question, and move closer to a solution to enquiries faster. For example, if a student is working on a hypothesis in a phenomenon area, AI will provide more variable ideas to explore or other explanations to consider in the investigation (Cheng & Wang, 2023). The other major benefit of incorporating generative AI in IBL is that one can program AI to mimic real-life situations that would otherwise be challenging to stage in a classroom. By using AI-based simulations, students can manipulate certain parameters and then analyze the results by themselves. For instance, in a history class, students may use AI to perform various political actions and their consequences, meaning that students will get a full picture of the events and hence be able to analyze the beauty of the deeper critical thinking behind the occurrence of the events in history (Fareed & Nofal, 2024).

It should also be noted how valuable generative AI's contribution is about the increase in conceptual understanding and critical thinking within the IBL framework. However, with versatile and, therefore, variable learning exposure through the help of AI, learners can be offered an intricate yet interrelated approach to grasping critical concepts. For example, by applying concepts of generative AI in a mathematics class, the system designs several practical problem-solving exercises that call for more usage of mathematical concepts in different settings, whereby the students are effectively trained on how to apply knowledge gained in other related situations. Moreover, generative AI can help to inculcate the learning of critical thinking skills, where students will be challenged to apply analysis, evaluation, and synthesis. When using the content generated by AI, students are prompted to explain their thinking, look at values from multiple viewpoints, and make sound conclusions. For instance, in social studies, AI can pose a range of opinions on a live issue, help students follow reasoning processes, and produce elaborate arguments (Denga & Denga, 2024).

Metacognition is also fostered in IBL with the help of AI, since students come up with learning strategies and think about them. Using generative AI, it is also possible to follow the performance of students over time and offer hints to some of the students' thinking patterns, aptitudes, and poor reasoning domain areas. This information also enables students to learn at their own pace and assume more responsibility when studying since they understand better how they learn and what approach can be of most benefit to them. Types and Examples of AI-based Courage Enquiry-based Learning (Fareed & Nofal, 2024). An important application of generative AI in IBL is in the field of science education. An example of using artificial intelligence in a biology class allows students to analyze the origin of specific features through an AI solution. While the students write their hypotheses and work with the virtual experiments, AI can also add new hypotheses or pose questions related to the results obtained by the students, for example, regarding genetics being ethical to modify it or analyzing the impact of environment on genes. This cyclical design not only enhances the comprehension of genetic issues but also challenges pupils for critical analysis of scientific advances in a global context (Lee & Kwon, 2024). In literature, generative AI can be applied to improve literary criticism and writing. The interactions between the students and AI could be in the form of an application that gives the students different possibilities of a plot or different character evolutions based on their interpretations. It also releases the students from the textual circumstances of a single correct way of telling a story, which makes students appreciate the literary devices and themes more. In addition, using AI in writing generates stimulating prompts that assist learners in dealing with writer blocks, thereby enhancing their writing experience (Ding & Choi, 2024).

When teaching mathematics, generative AI can provide numerous life-situation problems to learners relevant to the use of mathematics knowledge and skills. For example, students can utilize AI to learn the procedures of applying mathematical knowledge to architectural concerns, including the symmetry and structure of buildings. Through the solution to such difficulties created by artificial intelligence, students expand their appreciation and understanding of real-life uses of mathematics, as well as their problem-solving skills (Srivastava & Agarwal, 2024). The use of generative AI in IBL implementation is a notable improvement in educational practice. Owing to generative AI, ALP can develop individual, dynamic, and engaging knowledge assessments that would increase the precision and applicability of assessments and reveal more information about students' knowledge progress. In addition, ideas developed by generative AI in IBL enhance conceptual learning, critical thinking, and metacognition; thus, students become more responsible for their learning processes (Lee and Kwon, 2024). When we look at biology, English, and mathematics, and other fields, the application of generative AI in education can lower the bar of scope and enable many radical changes expected in the future.

While teachers and scholars further investigate such technologies, education will become more enriched, revolutionary, and positive in impact over time.

BACKGROUND

Education learning theories such as Jean Piaget and Lev Vygotsky, also known as constructivism, suggest that learners inculcate knowledge and understanding of the environment from actual experiences and mentors. In a constructivist classroom, the teacher is a guide who encourages the children to participate in practical activities that involve asking questions and finding answers. This theory leans on the advancement of assessments to embrace the use of AI as a means of achieving student-centered learning programs that address students' diverse learning needs. Generative AI can develop assessments that change in real time depending on the actions of the learners; in this way, the information meets the learner at the right point of difficulty level (Chauncey & McKenna, 2024). Technology enhanced learning (TEL) captures a host of theories and processes that seek to use information to enhance learning. TEL theories have some common propositions based on the opportunities of technology as a tool to gain access to vast amounts of information, collaboration in learning, and interaction and immersion in learning processes. Including the element of assessments in the application of TEL principles is helpful because AI can analyze students' information, create content based on it, and assist in providing feedback instantly. It not only improves the learning process of the students but also allows better and more frequent evaluation of the students' performance (Shanto & Jony, 2024).

These theories support the design and management of AI-driven assessment instruments. It is important to note that the elements of constructivism are fundamentally embedded in the design of assessment tools involving Artificial Intelligence. From a constructivist perspective, knowledge acquisition is determined as a constructive process in which new information accumulates in a learner. That is why AI can help with this by providing an environment that engages with the learner and adapts to the learner's needs in a real-time manner. For instance, an AI system may assign a problem to a particular student with the details and figures to be solved. As a result of the student's actions and answers, AI is capable of forming new questions or prompting the student to focus on a deeper level of thinking. This 'feedback loop' matches the principles of the constructivist scaffold model in which a learner is provided with help that is progressively withdrawn to meet the needs of an unhappy medium (Chauncey & McKenna, 2024). Regarding technology-assisted learning, the idea behind intelligent assessments is to complement the functions of modern technologies and achieve better learning results. Federal TEL theories underline the degree of access and interaction as the primary factors of learning. With AI, one can develop assessments that are inclusive of the different learners' groups and engaging. For example, AI can create scenarios and an environment in which students can manipulate a variety of factors and obtain the results of these manipulations. In this way, students can grasp ideas, expand their knowledge, and accelerate their rate of memory and knowledge retention (Srivastava & Agarwal, 2024).

In addition, TEL also ascribes the aspect of collaborative learning and the use of technologies in developing the same. Some of the assessment tool designs that can be informed by AI can consist of features that facilitate teamwork among learners. For instance, an AI platform may assign group projects that require students to solve problems and create presentations. In addition, AI can also evaluate the contributions of each group member and needs to provide constructive feedback both individually and to the whole group that is involved in the given project. It also fosters students' interaction skills and at the same time guarantees the active participation of every learner throughout the learning process (Shanto & Jony, 2024). Moreover, the utilization of artificial intelligence in assessments is also in line with the TEL introduction of timely and individual feedback to students. In traditional assessment methods, there is always a large time lag between the assessment and the time when the results of the assessment are given.

Assessment by IA, on the other hand, has features that enable it to be performed immediately depending on the performance of the student. This enhances the immediate clarification of misunderstandings, thereby enhancing the learning process and self-improvement (Ukwandu & Castle, 2024). The educational literature has thoroughly examined advanced learning and inquiry-based learning (IBL) as strategies that promote engagement, critical thinking, and deep comprehension. In contrast to passively absorbing material, both models place a strong emphasis on active learner engagement, where students are encouraged to investigate, pose questions, and build their own knowledge. The convergence of these pedagogies has garnered a lot of attention lately, particularly considering developments in educational technology, which has forced educators to reconsider long-standing approaches to teaching and evaluation (Storozhyk, 2024).

Based on the educational theories of theorists like Jean Piaget and John Dewey, inquiry-based learning is predicated on the idea that students create knowledge by active investigation. Dewey argued that to foster intellectual development, education should involve students in meaningful inquiry. He supported an educational method that linked learning to real-life experiences. Piaget's theory of cognitive development also highlighted how children build knowledge via processes like assimilation and accommodation as they interact with their surroundings. IBL, which encourages students to solve problems, ask questions, and hone their research abilities while they look for answers or solutions, is based on these fundamental beliefs. This kind of instruction differs from conventional methods that are more teacher-directed and impart knowledge in a hierarchical manner. The drive toward IBL is part of a larger educational movement that aims to develop self-sufficient, lifelong learners who can navigate a world that is getting more complicated by the day (Lang, 2024).

On the other hand, advanced learning describes teaching strategies and techniques that go beyond simple memorizing and learning, encouraging a continuous and in-depth interaction with the subject matter. It covers a range of methods, including as problem-based learning, critical thinking, and the development of higher-order cognitive skills. Constructivist educational approaches, which contend that students actively create new information based on preexisting cognitive frameworks, are frequently in line with advanced learning. Given that inquiry-based learning necessitates the use of analytical, evaluative, and creative thinking abilities in the process of knowledge production, it may be seen as one of the most effective approaches to support advanced learning outcomes (Jia et al., 2024). Inquiry-based learning has been linked to enhanced critical thinking, problem-solving skills, and a better comprehension of a variety of subject areas, according to research. For instance, research on science education has shown that integrated biology learning (IBL) promotes scientific literacy and aids students in understanding difficult ideas. Learners are encouraged to participate in scientific inquiry, pose questions, develop hypotheses, and carry out experiments rather than just memorizing information. Because IBL is experiential, students may get a firsthand look into the process of scientific discovery, which can help make abstract ideas more real and relatable. Unlike traditional lecture-based education, which frequently concentrates on factual memory and content delivery, inquiry-based learning (IBL) places greater emphasis on the learning process and encourages students to gain a deeper comprehension of the creation and validation of knowledge (Lang, 2024).

Inquiry-based learning also helps students develop metacognitive abilities, which are essential for higher education. Success in school and lifetime learning depend on having the capacity for metacognition, or the ability to evaluate and control one's own learning processes. Students that participate in self-directed inquiry can track their development, assess the efficacy of their tactics, and modify their techniques as needed. Applying information in new circumstances and reaching a greater degree of comprehension need this type of reflective thinking. Learning to traverse the difficulties of inquiry helps students become more adept at approaching problems from several angles, thinking through potential solutions, and using critical thinking to the material they come across (Hossain, 2023). The potential of inquiry-based learning to foster intrinsic motivation is one of its main benefits for advancing learning. Studies indicate that students exhibit higher levels of motivation when they feel that they are in control of their education, a feeling that IBL fosters by allowing students to follow their passions and inquiries. IBL fosters an environment where intellectual engagement and curiosity serve as the main motivators for learning, in contrast to traditional techniques that frequently place a higher priority on external incentives like grades or praise. Since students are more likely to remember knowledge, they feel personally significant and relevant, this intrinsic motivation not only increases students' engagement with the subject matter but also promotes a deeper and more enduring comprehension (Ding et al., 2024).

Even though inquiry-based learning has numerous advantages, there are difficulties in putting it into practice. The necessity for educators to change from a traditional, teacher-centered approach to a more facilitative one is one of the main challenges. Without giving away the answers, instructors must be able to lead students through the inquiry process. This calls for both a thorough comprehension of the subject matter and the capacity to successfully scaffold learning. Teachers who are used to presenting material in a more organized and controlled way may find this change especially difficult. IBL can also take a lot of time because it takes pupils longer to fully investigate subjects and come to their own understanding. Within the confines of a typical classroom, where curriculum pacing is frequently determined by standardized examinations and external goals, this prolonged timescale can be challenging to manage (Shanto et al., 2024). Furthermore, not every student will benefit from an inquiry-based learning environment; this is especially true for those who are accustomed to learning that is more regimented and directed. The open-ended nature of IBL might be too much for certain students, which can cause confusion or dissatisfaction. In these situations, it's critical for teachers to offer the right amounts of direction and assistance to make sure students have the knowledge and self-assurance to participate in the inquiry process successfully. Since students have different degrees of motivation, previous knowledge, and abilities, differentiation is important in this respect and might affect their performance in an inquiry-based learning environment (Ukwandu et al., 2024).

Inquiry-based learning has advanced greatly thanks to technology, especially in terms of giving students access to platforms, tools, and resources that aid in their research. Students can participate in more intricate and dynamic forms of inquiry thanks to digital technologies like collaborative platforms, interactive websites, and simulations, which increase the opportunities for advanced learning. For example, students can perform experiments in virtual laboratories that are not feasible or feasible in a regular classroom. Furthermore, learners may access a wealth of knowledge through online databases and tools, which enable them to interact with real-world facts and follow their inquiry more autonomously. With new chances for students to interact with material in creative and meaningful ways, technology has made it simpler for teachers to include IBL into their lessons (Hossain, 2023). Thus, inquiry-based learning and advanced learning are closely related instructional methods that place an emphasis on thorough engagement with the subject matter, critical thinking, and active creation of knowledge. With its foundation in constructivist ideas, inquiry-based learning provides a potent framework for developing higher order cognitive abilities and encouraging lifelong learning. The benefits of implementing integrated body learning (IBL) are widely established, despite certain limitations such as the requirement for proficient facilitation and suitable support for a varied student body. IBL may improve students' critical thinking, metacognitive awareness, and intrinsic motivation when it is successfully incorporated into educational settings, especially with the use of technology. This will equip them to deal with the complexity of a world that is becoming more and more information-rich and changing quickly (Ukwandu et al., 2024).

Thus, the use of generative AI in educational assessments is based on one of the most effective learning theories: constructivism and technological tools. AI-based formative assessments can provide value-added outcomes, hence improving understanding, analysis, and interpersonal communication skills, as learning fabricates itself through usable and effective work experience. These theories offer a solid foundation for the calls made toward creating and integrating AI into education, while also providing means with which technological interventions in assessments yield a significant impact. While educators are gradually discovering numerous possibilities for AI, such theoretical backgrounds will be very important to form effective, successful, and innovative appliances in the educational context (Ding & Choi, 2024).

Generative AI and Its Capabilities in Assessment

Generative AI is a type of artificial intelligence used to generate new content from pre-existing information. Essentially, while conventional AI categorizes or forecasts data that has been fed to it, generative AI can generate new content, including text, images, and even music. This capability is based on sophisticated machine learning algorithms; hence, deep learning techniques that perform data analysis to understand the pattern and accordingly generate data related in a coherent and logically connected manner (Sleegers & Consultancy). As for generative AI, its application in the sphere of educational assessment can become a powerful tool that can fundamentally change students' ratings. Cue cards, quizzes, and end of subject, end of term/national tests are typical examples of traditional tests that are usually invariable and do not provide a true picture of the learner's achievement. On the other hand, generative AI can provide open and possibly rich learners, changing over time and assessment contexts. For instance, an AI-assisted formative assessment means that a fresh set of questions or problems is produced automatically to test the student's progress as compared to a rigid set of questions that will be used throughout the course.

The first potential benefit in the use of generative AI in assessments is its capability to provide immediate feedback and at the same time adjust for the differences in learners' speed. In this way, students are always learning through engagements that are difficult, but not more than they can handle, thus translating into a better learning system. In addition, generative AI can model real-life situations, which gives students a practical base good for developing their thinking and problem-solving abilities (Sleegers & Consultancy). The possibilities for Generative AI are extensive and are as follows in the domain of educational assessment. A good example is employment in developing adaptive testing environments. These platforms, which change the difficulty and style of questions according to the students' answers, make it possible to evaluate every learner adequately. For example, if a student answers a series of algebra questions correctly, then the next questions that the AI might present quadratic equations or calculus to keep the learner on his toes (Bauschard & Quidwai, 2024).

Another major area of utilization is within the area of interim assessments, which are developmental in nature and are meant to track students' progress. With the help of generative AI, it is possible to create numerous types of formative assessment, including knowledge check questions, games, and exercises. For instance, if the lesson was on a science topic, then AI could develop various scenarios of experiments in which learners could alter the parameters and observe their impact. It involves students in the learning process and makes learning more effective, as it involves the use of concrete concepts and not just rosy learning. In addition, generative AI can help in project-based assessment, whereby the system provides outlines for the project, questions to research, and even resources related to the student's interest (Ukwandu & Castle, 2024). In a history class, for instance, AI in writing can recommend several historical events or personalities for a research project, recommend source materials, and even recommend the type of questions that the student can ask. This not only aids in creating a general understanding of the subject, but also relieves pressure from the teacher so that he or she can focus on helping individual students improve their research and analytical skills (Van & Sejer, 2023).

There are already numerous useful AI applications in learning environments, which proves that generative AI in the assessment sphere is possible. One of them is the Carnegie Learning 'MATHia' – a math tutoring software powered by artificial intelligence that reactivity changes the students' learning profiles. Generative AI is employed to generate new problem sets for individual learners as well as provide feedback for learners to work until they fully understand mathematics. According to research done, students that work on MATHia demonstrate enhanced abilities in problem solving as well as enhanced grasp of mathematical concepts as contrasted with students who work in 'conventional' techniques (Bauschard & Quidwai, 2024). Another of these is called the "Century Tech", which uses artificial intelligence to develop students' learning paths. Century Tech's generative AI processes data containing aspects of student performance with different strengths and limitations to develop content as well as tests that will complement the lessons learned by students in class. Such a strategy has been proven to enhance students' participation and performance, especially in the areas of math, science, and English (Denga & Denga, 2024).

Another unique artificial intelligence tool that can be regarded as belonging to the class of generative AI is the platform called "Knewton". Knewton's adjustments are progressive, whereby the content and level of difficulty of assessments also change with the progress of the learner, thus delivering customized learning to every learner. The details of this learning process that adapts itself to the student are that it has been shown to raise retention rates and academic success, which is useful because of immediate assessment and challenges based on each student's level (Damasevicius & Sidekerskiene, 2024). In language learning, applications such as the "Duolingo" application employs generative AI to develop challenging and dynamic language exercises. Learner's proficiency is evaluated by application's AI, and the latter suggests the exercises related to the definite aspects of a language, for instance, the lists of new vocabulary, grammar exercises, and exercises aimed at pronunciation. One pleasing feature of Duolingo scores is that they adjust quickly to the learner's performance, thus making the student sharp and prepared for the next level in their foreign language learning. Thus, generative AI is one of the most useful tools for creating interactive and individualized assessment spaces. AI can also help in creating new content based on the preferences of the learners and in providing real-time feedback, thus improving the quality of education being delivered. Specific examples involving MATHia, Century Tech, Knewton, and Duolingo help illustrate how generative AI has the potential to revolutionize education and how students are then being evaluated or helped throughout the learning process. As these technologies remain popular, their use in education practices is likely to prove even more effective and diverse methods of assessment.

DESIGNING AI-ENABLED ASSESSMENTS FOR INQUIRY-BASED LEARNING STRATEGIES

Below is a list of several strategies that can be recommended while designing artificial intelligence-enhanced assessments that would promote enquiries and enhance students' level of engagement with the content; thus, sequencing learning activities is essential, primarily by including the differentiation of pathways. This ranges from the creation of formative and summative assessments that can adapt to the student's performance level by offering tasks that cannot be easily completed or are challenging to solve. For example, an AI scientific assessment can begin with questions on ecosystems. If the student is confident and knowledgeable, AI can provide additional information regarding such aspects as the effects of climate change on certain ecosystems; this would stimulate further discussion and brainstorming in the student (Simmons, 2024). The third approach is the issues and Assessment Design approach, in which real-world problem-solving situations are incorporated into the assessment owing to generative AI. The system can design exercises and scenarios that reflect life situations, thereby increasing the effectiveness of learning. For instance, in a social studies class, students can engage in an AI option that provides the experience of managing the resources of a city and the consequent impacts on the economic, social, and environmental aspects. In addition, it sharpens concept formation, and acquisition also helps in creating decision-making and problem-solving abilities (Lee & Teo, 2023).

AI can also be used to create many different types of assessment questions, including open-ended questions, project-based tasks, and interactive simulations. This variety ensures that assessments respond to different learning styles and skills, promoting a more comprehensive assessment of students' abilities. For example, in a language classroom, AI can generate a combination of multiple-choice questions, writing prompts, and creative writing tasks, thereby providing a comprehensive assessment of students' language skills. Tailor assessments of individual learning journeys and the ability of AI to analyze large amounts of data in real time enable the creation of highly personalised assessments. By tracking student progress and achievement over time, AI can identify areas where students excel or struggle, and adjust assessment content accordingly (Simmons, 2024). This individualized approach ensures that each student receives the support and challenges that they need to thrive. For example, in mathematics education, an AI-based platform might notice that a student struggles with fractions but excels in geometry. AI can then create additional practice exercises that focus on fractions, while also introducing more advanced geometry concepts to engage and excite students. This targeted approach helps fill learning gaps and reinforces strengths, promoting a more balanced and effective learning experience (Lee & Teo, 2023).

In addition, AI can provide immediate and personalised feedback, which is important for effective learning. Traditional assessments often involve feedback delays that can hinder the learning process. In contrast, AI-powered assessments can provide instant feedback on each question or task, helping students to understand their mistakes and learn from them immediately. For example, an AI tool used in a language course can provide instant corrections and explanations of grammatical errors, allowing students to improve their language skills more effectively. AI can also support differentiated instruction by creating assessment content tailored to each student's learning journey. For example, in a history class, an AI-based assessment can present different primary sources and historical documents based on students' interests and prior knowledge (Damasevicius and Sidekerskiene, 2024). A student interested in ancient civilizations might be presented with texts and questions about ancient Greece and Rome, while another student fascinated with modern history might have explored data from World War II. This personalised approach not only improves engagement but also allows students to dig deeper into topics that interest them. AI can also facilitate formative assessments designed to provide ongoing feedback and support throughout the learning process. By continuously monitoring student performance, AI can provide timely assessments that help students track their progress and identify areas of improvement. For example, an AI tool in a biology course can periodically assess students' understanding of cellular processes, providing targeted review materials and practice questions to reinforce learning (Cooper, 2023). In summary, designing AI-based assessments for enquiry-based learning involves leveraging adaptive learning paths, integrating real-world problem-solving scenarios, and creating diverse types of assessment questions. By tailoring assessments to individual learning journeys and providing immediate, personalised feedback, AI can foster deeper engagement with the content and support effective learning. These strategies highlight the transformative potential of AI in creating dynamic and personalised educational experiences, paving the way for more effective classroom assessments. As educators continue to explore and deploy these technologies, the future of education promises to be more personalised, interactive, and impactful.

Case Studies of AI in Action

MATHia by Carnegie Learning is an AI-based math tutoring program that has been widely used in schools across the United States. MATHia uses generative artificial intelligence to create customized problem sets and interactive exercises that adapt to each student's learning pace and skill levels. In one high school case study, math was added to the math curriculum to complement the traditional instruction. The AI-powered platform provided students with instant feedback and tailored lessons, allowing them to focus on areas where they needed the most improvement (Holmes, 2023). Century Tech in the UK Century Tech, a learning platform based on artificial intelligence, has been implemented in many UK schools. The platform uses artificial intelligence to analyze student performance data and create individualized learning paths. One notable case study involved a high school that integrated Century Tech into its science curricula. Artificial intelligence created personalised quizzes, interactive simulations, and personalised learning materials based on each student's progress and understanding. This approach allows teachers to better monitor student performance and provide targeted support (Jia & Looi, 2024).

The Adaptive Learning Technology Company Knewton has successfully integrated artificial intelligence into higher learning environments. A case study at Arizona State University used Knewton's AI-based platform in its introductory biology course. AI analysed students' interactions with the course material and created individual assignments and assessments. This adaptive learning environment helped students stay engaged and improved their understanding of complex biological concepts (Hossain). For Carnegie Learning's MATHia, the integration of generative artificial intelligence led to significant improvements in the student performance. The school reported that students using MATHia showed significantly improved math performance compared to those who relied only on traditional instruction. The personalised learning delivered by MATHia has helped students to better understand mathematical concepts and increase their confidence in their abilities (Holmes, 2023). The implementation of Century Tech in a UK secondary school improved student engagement and academic achievement. The AI-based platform's ability to adapt content to individual learning needs allowed students to progress at their own pace, which improved their understanding and retention of scientific concepts. Teachers also benefited from the platform's analytics, which provided insights into student performance and identified areas where additional support was required (Cooper, 2023).

At Arizona State University,USA, the use of Knewton's AI platform in biology courses increased student satisfaction and academic performance. Students appreciated personalised feedback and adaptive learning paths that helped them understand difficult concepts more effectively. AI-based assessments provide continuous feedback that allows students to monitor their progress and make necessary changes in their learning strategies (Lang, 2024). Despite these positive results, the integration of generative AI into these case studies presents several challenges. One common problem was the initial resistance of teachers and students unfamiliar with AI technology. Teachers need appropriate training and support to effectively integrate AI tools into their teaching practices. In addition, there were concerns about data protection and the ethical use of student data, which required careful consideration and strong safeguards (Jia & Looi, 2024). Another challenge was to make AI-based assessments accessible and inclusive. In some cases, students with limited access to technology or special educational needs have struggled to fully benefit from AI tools. Schools and institutions must invest in infrastructure and provide additional resources to ensure that all students can access and benefit from AI-powered learning environments (Lang, 2024). Thus, reliance on AI-based judgments has raised questions regarding the role of human oversight and the potential for AI to perpetuate biases. Teachers had to find a balance between leveraging AI capabilities and maintaining human touch during the assessment process. Continuous monitoring and evaluation are necessary to ensure effective and ethical use of AI tools. The successful integration of generative AI into enquiry-based assessments demonstrated by MATHia, Century Tech, and Knewton has resulted in significant improvements in student engagement, understanding, and learning. However, these case studies also highlight the challenges of implementing AI in educational environments, including the need for training, addressing accessibility issues, and ensuring its ethical use. As AI technology advances, continued research and collaboration among educators, technologists, and policymakers is imperative to maximize its potential and address these challenges (Hossain).

Assessing Higher-Order Thinking Skills

Generative AI can be effectively used to assess and improve higher-order thinking skills such as analysis, synthesis, and evaluation. One method involves creating challenging, open-ended questions and scenarios that require students to apply these skills. For example, in a history lesson, artificial intelligence can create a simulation in which students must analyze primary source documents from different historical periods, synthesize information to create connections between events, and evaluate the impact of events on today's society. This approach encourages students to go beyond rote learning and engage deeply with the material (Storozhyk, 2024). Another method is project-based assessment, in which AI can help plan multi-phase projects that require critical thinking. In a science course, AI could create a project in which students design an experiment to test a hypothesis, analyze the data collected, synthesize their findings with existing research, and evaluate the implications of the results. This practical, enquiry-based approach not only assesses higher-order thinking skills but also helps develop them through practical applications (Su & Chu, 2023).

Several techniques can be used to ensure that AI assessments accurately and fairly measure higher order thinking skills. First, it is necessary to develop robust and diverse datasets that AI can use to make decisions. This includes a wide range of examples that reflect different levels of complexity and context, reduce the risk of bias, and ensure that AI can assess skills in a variety of scenarios. Second, the inclusion of human oversight is critical. Teachers should regularly review and refine AI-generated assessments to ensure that they meet the learning objectives and accurately measure the targeted skills. This collaborative approach can help identify and correct biases or errors in AI assessments (Storozhyk, 2024). In addition, the use of a multifaceted scoring strategy can improve accuracy and fairness. Combining AI-generated assessments with traditional methods such as peer and teacher assessments provides a more comprehensive assessment of a student's higher-order thinking ability. For example, a student's ability to analyze and synthesize information can be assessed with questions created by artificial intelligence, while his assessment skills can be better assessed using peer feedback and teachers' observations (Su & Chu, 2023). Finally, transparency in the AI decision-making process is crucial, as giving students and teachers insight into how AI creates and scores assessments can increase confidence and ensure the validity of the assessment process. For example, if an AI tool generates a specific set of questions for assessment, it should also explain why those questions were chosen and how they relate to the skills being assessed. In conclusion, generative AI provides powerful methods for assessing and improving higher-order thinking skills through complex scenarios and project-based assessment. Ensuring the accuracy and fairness of these AI assessments requires robust datasets, human oversight, versatile assessment strategies, and transparency of AI processes. By implementing these technologies, teachers can effectively use artificial intelligence to promote and measure students' higher-order thinking skills (Storozhyk, 2024).

Generative AI and Accessibility in Assessments

Generative AI can play a significant role in creating inclusive and accessible assessments for disabled learners. By leveraging AI's capabilities, educators can design assessments that accommodate various disabilities, ensuring that all students have equal opportunities to demonstrate their understanding and skills. For instance, AI can generate assessments that include alternative formats, such as text-to-speech for visually impaired students or speech-to-text for those with mobility impairments. This flexibility allows learners to interact with content in ways that best suit their needs (Ng & Chu, 2023). One example is the use of AI-driven platforms that offer customizable user interfaces. These platforms can adapt font sizes, contrast settings, and navigation controls based on individual preferences, making it easier for students with visual impairments or dyslexia to engage with assessments. Additionally, AI can incorporate multimodal feedback and provide visual, auditory, and tactile cues to support diverse learning styles and needs (Srivastava & Agarwal, 2024).

Several best practices can be implemented to effectively use AI to remove barriers and personalize learning experiences. First, it is essential to involve learners with disabilities in the design and testing phases of the AI-enabled assessments. Their feedback can help identify potential accessibility issues and ensure that assessments are truly inclusive. For example, collaborating with students with different disabilities can provide insights into how AI tools can be tailored to meet specific needs (Lim & Lee, 2024).

Second, AI should be used to create personalised learning experiences by adapting to each learner's unique requirements. For instance, an AI system can analyze a student's interaction patterns and learning history to identify areas that may need additional support. Based on this analysis, AI can generate customized assessments and learning materials to address these specific needs. This personalised approach not only helps accommodate disabilities but also enhances overall learning outcomes (Ng & Chu, 2023). Moreover, the provision of real-time adjustment and support is crucial. AI can monitor student performance during assessments and offer immediate assistance such as providing hints or breaking down complex tasks into smaller, manageable steps. This approach ensures that students are not left struggling and can continue to engage meaningfully in the assessment (Srivastava & Agarwal, 2024). Lastly, ensuring interoperability and compatibility with assistive technologies is vital, as AI-enabled assessment platforms should be designed to work seamlessly with existing assistive devices, such as screen readers, braille displays, and alternative input devices. This integration helps to create a cohesive learning environment in which students can use their preferred tools without encountering technical barriers (Lim & Lee, 2024). Thus, generative AI has the potential to significantly enhance accessibility to educational assessments. By designing inclusive assessments involving learners in the development process, personalizing learning experiences, and ensuring compatibility with assistive technologies, educators can leverage AI to create a more equitable and supportive learning environment for all students. These best practices help to remove barriers and enable learners with disabilities to fully participate and succeed in their educational journeys (Ng & Chu, 2023).

Equity and Ethics in AI-Enabled Assessments

The inclusion of artificial intelligence in educational evaluations raises important ethical and equity issues. One of the main problems is bias in AI algorithms, which can perpetuate existing inequalities. AI systems learn from data, and if training data are biased or incomplete, AI-generated assessments can disadvantage certain groups of students, including students from marginalized communities or students with different learning styles. For example, biased language models used to grade essays can penalize students who express their ideas differently than the model predicts, unfairly affecting their grades (Weng and Ng, 2024). Another ethical aspect is the transparency of AI algorithms, as teachers and students must understand how AI systems make grading decisions to ensure trust and accountability. Lack of transparency can create doubts and weaken the validity of the assessment results. For example, if students do not understand why certain questions are chosen or how the AI grades their answers, they may question the fairness of the grading process.

Several guidelines can be implemented to maintain fairness, transparency, and accountability in the AI-assisted evaluation processes. First, it is important to conduct a thorough and continuous review of the AI algorithms used in the evaluations. Controls help to identify and mitigate bias by examining how AI interprets and evaluates student responses. Regular assessments ensure that assessments remain fair and meet educational standards (Lim & Lee, 2024). Second, educators should ensure the diversity and inclusion of the educational data used in AI algorithms. By combining different perspectives and experiences, AI systems can make judgments that are culturally sensitive and fair. For example, educational data should include examples and contexts that reflect the diversity of student backgrounds and learning styles (Chauncey and McKenna, 2024).

In addition, transparency must be prioritized during the evaluation. Teachers must clearly communicate how AI tools are used in assessments, including their purposes, capabilities, and limitations. By providing students with knowledge of AI decision-making processes, they can build confidence and help them better understand and engage with the assessment results (Weng & Ng, 2024). Responsibility is also an important factor. Educators and developers of artificial intelligence systems must be responsible for the ethical implications of their technologies. This includes addressing concerns raised by stakeholders, such as students, parents, and advocacy groups, and taking corrective action where bias or unfairness is identified. Establishing clear procedures for handling complaints and ensuring that assessment practices conform to ethical guidelines are important steps for promoting accountability (Lim & Lee, 2024).

Thus, it can be argued that while AI offers powerful tools to improve educational assessments, careful ethical and equity considerations are critical. By implementing Fairness, Transparency, and Accountability guidelines, educators can mitigate bias, promote inclusion, and ensure that AI-assisted assessments support equitable learning opportunities for all students. These efforts are necessary to harness the potential of AI to advance educational equity and promote supportive learning environments (Weng and Ng, 2024).

FUTURE DIRECTIONS IN AI-ASSISTED INQUIRY-BASED LEARNING

AI-assisted inquiry-based learning (IBL) has the potential to completely transform education by combining the best aspects of AI with the ideas of inquiry-driven learning. As AI technologies advance, the way they are incorporated into the IBL framework will probably change how teachers instruct, evaluate, and encourage creativity, critical thinking, and problem-solving in addition to how students learn. Personalized learning experiences, dynamic evaluation systems, and improved collaboration chances are just a few of the innovations made possible by the convergence of AI and IBL. We will look at possible future possibilities for AI-assisted inquiry-based learning in this note, as well as how these developments could affect education (Ahmed, 2023). Growing learning process customization is one of the most promising uses of AI in IBL. With the use of AI-powered systems, learning routes that are specifically suited to each student's requirements may be customized by analyzing each student's distinct learning preferences, habits, and knowledge gaps. An AI system may, for instance, monitor how a student engages with inquiry-based tasks and, depending on their strengths and weaknesses, suggest more exercises, materials, or challenges. With the help of these systems, learning might become more adaptable, with AI constantly modifying the level of difficulty, speed, and material to correspond with the development of the learner. This technique offers a more learner-centered approach in contrast to the conventional one-size-fits-all style of education (Alabidi et al., 2023).

The field of language learning offers a specific illustration of how AI might customize IBL. Personalized learning routes are currently available on AI-powered systems like Duolingo, depending on user input and performance. In the future, students may be guided through a challenging inquiry-based project, such studying the reasons behind World War II, by an AI-powered IBL history platform. Personalized reading materials suggested primary source papers based on student interests, and quizzes that adjust in complexity according to understanding level might all be offered via the system. Therefore, students can pursue their unique needs and interests in a dynamic learning environment that promotes deeper discovery and knowledge (Ahmed, 2023). AI-assisted IBL holds tremendous potential to transform evaluation methodologies, which is an important future path. The rote memorization and factual recall that are frequently emphasized in today's typical assessment methods may not be sufficient to gauge critical thinking, creativity, and problem-solving abilities—skills that are essential to IBL. On the other hand, AI has the power to change examinations by emphasizing formative, real-time assessments as opposed to summative tests. Artificial intelligence can examine how pupils approach issues, formulate questions, and modify their thinking in response to new knowledge. Instead of waiting for end-of-term exams, these insights might be utilized to provide students with quick, insightful feedback that helps them improve their inquiry abilities as they study (Chauncey & McKenna, 2023).

Take into consideration, for instance, an AI system integrated into a biology lecture. The AI could keep track of the questions students have, the experiments they create, and the information they gather while they engage on an inquiry-based project on ecosystems. After that, it can offer suggestions for new study directions or feedback on the research techniques used by the students, assisting them in recognizing any shortcomings in their strategy. Additionally, the AI could evaluate higher-order thinking abilities including the student's capacity for data analysis, knowledge synthesis from many sources, and evidence-based conclusion drawing. Comparing this kind of evaluation against traditional exams, which might not adequately convey the complexity of inquiry-based learning, would provide a deeper and more nuanced picture of a student's learning path.

AI is also expected to have a big impact on collaboration in IBL going forward. One of the main features of many IBL frameworks is collaborative inquiry, in which students work together to solve issues or investigate ideas. AI can help these cooperative efforts by developing intelligent tutoring programs and group-supporting virtual assistants. AI might, for example, assist in organizing teamwork so that everyone contributes fairly, and the group stays concentrated on the investigation process. AI systems may also assess group dynamics and provide methods to enhance task delegation, communication, or dispute resolution to promote more fruitful teamwork (Chauncey & McKenna, 2023). Imagine a world in which students are designing a water filtration system as part of an inquiry-based project in a high school physics class. Artificial intelligence (AI)-powered collaboration solutions have the potential to track each student's input to the project, analyze it in real-time, and spot any participation gaps. The AI may step in to encourage other students to contribute their thoughts or ask the group to reevaluate how the tasks are divided if one student is taking over the discourse. This clever scaffolding makes sure that the collaborative process is maximized for learning and that every student stays interested (Damasevicius & Sidekerskiene, 2024).

Using virtual and augmented reality (VR/AR) technology to build immersive and interactive learning environments is an interesting new approach for AI-assisted IBL. These AI-powered settings may enable students to participate in intricate experiments and simulations that would be challenging or impractical in a conventional classroom. Chemistry students, for instance, might perform experiments in virtual labs where they could control chemicals, see reactions in real time, and even mimic uncommon or hazardous techniques thanks to AI-powered virtual reality technology. AI may act as an adaptable guide in these settings, providing students with prompts, clarifications, and feedback as they move through the simulation. Immersion technology and artificial intelligence (AI) together have the potential to change how students approach learning by making abstract ideas more relatable and interesting (Alabidi et al., 2023). Furthermore, AI can democratize access to inquiry-based learning by expanding the population for whom high-quality educational resources are available. AI-powered systems have the potential to help remove present obstacles to IBL possibilities, such as those based on geography, economics, or culture, as they develop.AI-driven platforms have the potential to offer sophisticated inquiry-based curriculum, tailored learning experiences, and virtual laboratories to students in underfunded or distant schools. Additionally, by enabling students from various linguistic backgrounds to interact with inquiry-based learning materials in their original tongues, these platforms may facilitate multilingual education. In a worldwide society where differences in access to high-quality education have the potential to sustain inequality, the democratization of education is especially crucial.

By serving as an intelligent teaching assistant, AI-assisted IBL has the potential to improve teacher assistance. Teachers may concentrate on directing and supporting the inquiry process by delegating administrative responsibilities like tracking progress and grading to AI systems. Additionally, AI may give instructors information into how their students learn, enabling them to better adapt their lessons to each student's requirements. An AI system may, for instance, spot trends in how students approach inquiry activities and highlight any areas where they might benefit from further guidance or assistance. After analyzing the data, educators may make necessary adjustments to their teaching methods to make sure that inquiry-based learning is being properly promoted in the classroom (Lim & Lee, 2024). The development of AI-assisted IBL, however, also brings up significant ethical issues. As AI systems become more and more integrated into the educational process, worries regarding prejudice, equality, and data privacy will grow. Since AI systems require enormous volumes of data to operate, a major issue will be making sure that student data is gathered and used appropriately. Furthermore, if AI systems are taught on biased datasets, there is a chance that they will reinforce preexisting prejudices. This might result in unfair educational opportunities, especially for pupils from underrepresented groups. It will be crucial for educators, legislators, and technologists to address these issues as AI becomes more prevalent in IBL and make sure that AI is applied in ways that advance inclusion, justice, and transparency.

The future of AI-powered research-based learning includes promising advances that could revolutionize educational assessments. One emerging trend is the integration of natural language processing (NLP) and machine learning techniques to improve AI's ability of AI to understand and respond to student interactions. For example, AI systems can evolve to not only evaluate written responses but also engage in meaningful dialogue with students and provide personalised feedback and guidance based on their individual learning paths (Cheng & Wang, 2023). Another trend is the development of virtual mentors or tutors equipped with artificial intelligence that can adapt to students' cognitive and emotional states. Future innovations may include artificial intelligence systems equipped with affective computing capabilities that allow them to recognize and respond to students' emotions during assessments. For example, an AI teacher can detect frustration or confusion in a student's facial expressions or tone of voice, and adjust responses and support, accordingly, promoting more empathetic and supportive learning (Chauncey & McKenna, 2024).

Speculating on the development of Artificial Intelligence technology, advances in AI technology may further transform assessment practices, making them more adaptive, interactive, and predictive. One possibility is to improve AI algorithms to provide real-time adaptive assessments that adjust difficulty based on student achievement. AI can continuously analyze student responses and behavior to create personalised assessments that challenge students in their optimal learning, promoting continued growth and engagement. In addition, AI's predictive analytics capabilities are expected to improve, allowing teachers to anticipate student learning needs and to proactively intervene. For example, AI algorithms can predict potential misunderstandings or learning gaps based on how students interact with assessments, allowing teachers to tailor their interventions and strategies more effectively.

Another exciting possibility is the integration of artificial intelligence with augmented reality (AR) and virtual reality (VR) technologies to create immersive assessment environments. Artificial intelligence could create interactive simulations and virtual scenarios in which students can apply their knowledge and skills in realistic settings. For example, in a biology class, students can use AI-powered VR simulations to conduct virtual dissections or environmental studies, improving their understanding through hands-on learning (Cheng and Wang, 2023). In short, the future direction of enquiry-based learning with artificial intelligence is characterized by the development of natural language processing, affective computing, adaptive learning algorithms, predictive analytics, and ambient technology. These innovations can make educational assessments more personalised, responsive, and engaging, enriching learning and fostering deeper student understanding and mastery of concepts. As AI advances, educators and technology will play a critical role in harnessing the potential to create transformative educational experiences that prepare students for future challenges (Van & Sejer, 2023). There is a great deal of promise for AI-assisted inquiry-based learning to change education in the future. AI can greatly expand the effectiveness and reach of IBL by customizing learning experiences, improving assessment techniques, encouraging collaboration, building immersive settings, and democratizing resource access. Nevertheless, achieving this promise will need for a cautious integration of AI technologies, a close examination of the ethical ramifications, and a dedication to guaranteeing that all students gain from these developments. It will be interesting to watch how AI changes inquiry-based learning and helps students become more critical, creative, and engaged thinkers as it develops.

CONCLUSION

Thus, by exploring the transformative potential of generative AI in educational assessment, it has become clear that AI has transformed traditional approaches by promoting enquiry-based learning and enhancing critical thinking. Throughout this chapter, we delved into the various ways in which AI-based assessments have transformed educational practices, emphasizing engagement, personalization, and innovation. AI's ability of AI to create dynamic, adaptive assessments tailored to individual learning needs is a major departure from static testing methods. Utilizing artificial intelligence, teachers can go beyond standardized assessments to engage students in deeper and more meaningful learning experiences. For example, AI-based platforms, such as MATHia and Century Tech from Carnegie Learning, have shown how personalised feedback and adaptive learning pathways can significantly improve student outcomes in a variety of educational settings. Additionally, integrating AI into enquiry-based learning environments enables students to explore complex concepts, analyze data, and effectively synthesize information. The present case studies, such as the application of Knewton in higher education and implementation of Century Tech in secondary schools, illustrate how AI facilitates interactive and immersive learning experiences that stimulate higher-order thinking skills.

In the future, education in the age of artificial intelligence promises continuous development and innovation in assessment strategies. As AI technology advances, we expect further improvements in natural language processing, adaptive learning algorithms, and augmented reality applications. These advances have empowered educators to provide more personalised, equitable, and effective learning experiences for all students. However, among these possibilities, ethical aspects are the most important. Maintaining fairness, transparency, and accountability in AI-assisted assessments is critical for ensuring equity and trust in educational environments.

Educators and technologists must work together to address bias, adhere to ethical standards, and protect the privacy of student data, as AI continues to shape the landscape of educational assessment. In conclusion, while AI has made significant strides in advancing enquiry-based learning through generative assessments, the journey to unlock its full potential continues. By responsibly and innovatively embracing AI, educators can foster a future in which every student receives personalised, inclusive, and empowering learning, which prepares them to succeed in a rapidly changing world.

REFERENCES

Ahmed, M. A. (2023). ChatGPT and the EFL classroom: Supplement or substitute in Saudi Arabia's eastern region. *Information Sciences Letters*, 12(7), 2727–2734. DOI: 10.18576/isl/120704

Alabidi, S., AlArabi, K., Alsalhi, N. R., & Al Mansoori, M. (2023). The dawn of ChatGPT: Transformation in science assessment. *Eurasian Journal of Educational Research*, 106(106), 321–337.

Bauschard, S., & Quidwai, S. (2024). From insight to implementation: How to create your AI school guidance. Available at *SSRN*. DOI: 10.2139/ssrn.4784207

Black, N. B., George, S., Eguchi, A., Dempsey, J. C., Langran, E., Fraga, L., Brunvand, S., & Howard, N. (2024, March). A framework for approaching AI education in educator preparation programs. *Proceedings of the AAAI Conference on Artificial Intelligence*, 38(21), 23069–23077. DOI: 10.1609/aaai.v38i21.30351

Chauncey, S. A., & McKenna, H. P. (2023). A framework and exemplars for ethical and responsible use of AI chatbot technology to support teaching and learning. *Computers and Education: Artificial Intelligence*, 5, 100182. DOI: 10.1016/j.caeai.2023.100182

Chauncey, S. A., & McKenna, H. P. (2024, June). Exploring the potential of cognitive flexibility and elaboration in support of curiosity, interest, and engagement in designing AI-rich learning spaces, extensible to urban environments. In *International Conference on Human-Computer Interaction* (pp. 209-230). Cham: Springer Nature Switzerland. DOI: 10.1007/978-3-031-60012-8_13

Cheng, E. C. K., & Wang, T. (2023). Leading digital transformation and eliminating barriers for teachers to incorporate artificial intelligence in basic education in Hong Kong. *Computers and Education: Artificial Intelligence*, 5, 100171. DOI: 10.1016/j.caeai.2023.100171

Chiu, T. K. (2023). The impact of generative AI (GenAI) on practices, policies and research direction in education: A case of ChatGPT and Midjourney. *Interactive Learning Environments*, •••, 1–17. DOI: 10.1080/10494820.2023.2253861

Cooper, G. (2023). Examining science education in ChatGPT: An exploratory study of generative artificial intelligence. *Journal of Science Education and Technology*, 32(3), 444–452. DOI: 10.1007/s10956-023-10039-y

Damasevicius, R., & Sidekerskiene, T. (2024). AI as a teacher: A new educational dynamic for modern classrooms for personalized learning support. In *AI-Enhanced Teaching Methods* (pp. 1–24). IGI Global. DOI: 10.4018/979-8-3693-2728-9.ch001

Denga, E. M., & Denga, S. W. (2024). Revolutionizing education: The power of technology. In *Revolutionizing Curricula Through Computational Thinking, Logic, and Problem Solving* (pp. 167-188). IGI Global.

Ding, A. C. E., Shi, L., Yang, H., & Choi, I. (2024). Enhancing teacher AI literacy and integration through different types of cases in teacher professional development. *Computers and Education Open*, 6, 100178. DOI: 10.1016/j.caeo.2024.100178

Fareed, M. W., Bou Nassif, A., & Nofal, E. (2024). Exploring the potentials of artificial intelligence image generators for educating the history of architecture. *Heritage*, 7(3), 1727–1753. DOI: 10.3390/heritage7030081

Holmes, W. (2023). *The unintended consequences of artificial intelligence and education*. Education International.

Hossain, K. A. (2023). Evaluation of diversified use of artificial intelligence (AI) and consequence of future education.

Jia, F., Sun, D., & Looi, C. K. (2024). Artificial intelligence in science education (2013–2023): Research trends in ten years. *Journal of Science Education and Technology*, 33(1), 94–117. DOI: 10.1007/s10956-023-10077-6

Lang, J. C. (2024). Embracing generative AI for authentic learning. *Creative Education*, 15(1), 1–20. DOI: 10.4236/ce.2024.151001

Lee, A. V. Y., Tan, S. C., & Teo, C. L. (2023). Designs and practices using generative AI for sustainable student discourse and knowledge creation. *Smart Learning Environments*, 10(1), 59. DOI: 10.1186/s40561-023-00279-1

Lee, S. J., & Kwon, K. (2024). A systematic review of AI education in K-12 classrooms from 2018 to 2023: Topics, strategies, and learning outcomes. *Computers and Education: Artificial Intelligence*, 100211.

Lim, K. K., & Lee, C. S. (2024, June). Enhancing searching as learning (SAL) with generative artificial intelligence: A literature review. In *International Conference on Human-Computer Interaction* (pp. 143-155). Cham: Springer Nature Switzerland. DOI: 10.1007/978-3-031-61953-3_17

Ng, D. T. K., Su, J., Leung, J. K. L., & Chu, S. K. W. (2023). Artificial intelligence (AI) literacy education in secondary schools: A review. *Interactive Learning Environments*, •••, 1–21. DOI: 10.1080/10494820.2023.2255228

Shanto, S. S., Ahmed, Z., & Jony, A. I. (2024). Enriching learning process with generative AI: A proposed framework to cultivate critical thinking in higher education using ChatGPT. *Tuijin Jishu/Journal of Propulsion Technology, 45*(1), 3019-3029.

Simmons, R. (2024, June). Innovating cybersecurity education through AI-augmented teaching. In *European Conference on Cyber Warfare and Security* (Vol. 23, No. 1, pp. 480-486). DOI: 10.34190/eccws.23.1.2224

Sleegers, P., & Consultancy, B. M. C. (2024). Multi-stakeholder collaboration and co-creation: Towards responsible application of AI in education.

Srivastava, A. P., & Agarwal, S. (Eds.). (2024). *Utilizing AI tools in academic research writing*. IGI Global. DOI: 10.4018/979-8-3693-1798-3

Storozhyk, M. (2024). Philosophy of future: Analytical overview of interaction between education, science, and artificial intelligence in the context of contemporary challenges. *Futurity Philosophy*, 3(1), 23–47.

Su, J., Guo, K., Chen, X., & Chu, S. K. W. (2023). Teaching artificial intelligence in K–12 classrooms: A scoping review. *Interactive Learning Environments*, •••, 1–20.

Ukwandu, E., Omisade, O., Jones, K., Thorne, S., & Castle, M. (2024). The future of teaching and learning in the context of emerging artificial intelligence technologies. Available at *SSRN* 4852030. DOI: 10.2139/ssrn.4852030

Van Mechelen, M., Smith, R. C., Schaper, M. M., Tamashiro, M., Bilstrup, K. E., Lunding, M., Graves Petersen, M., & Sejer Iversen, O. (2023). Emerging technologies in K–12 education: A future HCI research agenda. *ACM Transactions on Computer-Human Interaction*, 30(3), 1–40. DOI: 10.1145/3569897

Weng, X., Ye, H., Dai, Y., & Ng, O. L. (2024). Integrating artificial intelligence and computational thinking in educational contexts: A systematic review of instructional design and student learning outcomes. *Journal of Educational Computing Research*, 62(6), 07356331241248686. DOI: 10.1177/07356331241248686

KEY TERMS AND DEFINITIONS

AI-Enabled Assessments: Assessment tools that use artificial intelligence to create dynamic, tailored evaluations that adapt to individual learner needs and performance.

Equity in AI: The principle of ensuring fair access, representation, and treatment in AI-driven educational practices, addressing bias and promoting inclusivity.

Generative AI: A type of artificial intelligence that creates new content, such as text or assessments, based on data inputs and learned patterns.

Higher-Order Thinking Skills: Cognitive processes such as analysis, synthesis, and evaluation, which are essential for critical thinking and problem-solving.

Inquiry-Based Learning: A pedagogical approach where students engage in exploring questions, problems, or scenarios, driving deeper learning through investigation and discovery.

Technology-Enhanced Learning: The integration of digital tools and technologies to enhance teaching and learning experiences, often improving engagement and personalisation.

Chapter 8
Fostering Inspirational Learning Through AI-Enhanced Formative Assessment:
Strategies and Challenges in Higher Education

Wu Tao
https://orcid.org/0000-0003-3536-1845
South China Agriculture University, China

ABSTRACT

This chapter examines the transformative potential of AI-enhanced formative assessment in higher education, focusing on fostering inspirational learning experiences. The authors explore how artificial intelligence can revolutionize traditional assessment practices, enabling more personalized, efficient, and effective learning environments. The chapter discusses benefits and challenges of implementation, including potential improvements in student engagement, motivation, and academic achievement. It analyzes AI's role in facilitating real-time feedback, automating grading, and enhancing teacher-student interactions. A comprehensive review of the current state of AI-enhanced formative assessment in higher education is provided, highlighting best practices, strategies, and challenges. The chapter concludes by outlining future research directions, emphasizing collaboration among educators, policymakers, and technologists to harness AI's potential in inspiring and empowering learners.

DOI: 10.4018/979-8-3693-6351-5.ch008

INTRODUCTION

Higher education is experiencing a fundamental shift toward more personalized and effective learning experiences, driven by technological advances. As traditional assessment methods evolve, formative assessment has emerged as a key tool for enhancing student learning through ongoing feedback, rather than relying solely on end-of-term evaluations.

Artificial Intelligence (AI) is transforming formative assessment practices by providing timely, personalized feedback to students and valuable insights to educators. Luckin and her colleagues (2016) frame AI as a "more capable partner" in education, offering adaptive scaffolding within the "Artificial Intelligence for Education" (AIED) model. Recent empirical studies support AI's effectiveness in educational settings. Winkler and Söllner (2018) found that AI-powered chatbots improved student engagement and performance through instant feedback. Similarly, Barana et al. (2019) demonstrated that AI-enhanced mathematics platforms significantly improved students' problem-solving abilities.

By incorporating machine learning algorithms, natural language processing, and data analytics, AI-enhanced formative assessment addresses key challenges in traditional methods. These include providing individualized feedback efficiently, tracking real-time progress, and adapting to diverse learning needs. This integration creates a dynamic assessment ecosystem that promotes inspirational learning while reducing the administrative burden on educators.

THEORETICAL FRAMEWORK

Understanding Formative Assessment and Summative Assessment

Formative assessment is a crucial element in the learning process, providing ongoing feedback to both learners and instructors. Black and Wiliam (1998) define formative assessment as encompassing all activities undertaken by teachers and students that provide information to be used as feedback to modify teaching and learning activities. This process helps to close the gap between current understanding and desired goals (Sadler, 1989). Formative assessment strategies can include questioning, self-assessment, peer assessment, and teacher observation (Wiliam, 2011). These methods allow for continuous monitoring of student progress and enable timely interventions to support learning. For example, the traditional formative methods that can be used in accounting courses are as follows:

- Questioning: An accounting instructor might ask students to explain the difference between accrual and cash basis accounting during a class discussion, allowing them to gauge understanding and clarify misconceptions immediately.
- Self-assessment: Students might complete a brief quiz on basic accounting principles and reflect on their performance, identifying areas where they need more practice.
- Peer assessment: In a group project on financial statement analysis, students could review each other's work, providing feedback on the application of accounting concepts.
- Teacher observation: While students work on practical exercises, such as preparing a balance sheet, the instructor can circulate, observing their process and offering guidance as needed.

In contrast, summative assessment occurs at the end of a learning period to evaluate student achievement against specific standards or benchmarks. While formative assessment is often described as "assessment for learning," summative assessment is "assessment of learning" (Earl, 2013). Examples of summative assessment in an accounting course might include:

- A final exam covering all course material, including both theoretical concepts and practical applications.
- A comprehensive project requiring students to prepare a full set of financial statements for a hypothetical company.
- A standardized test that evaluates students' mastery of accounting principles according to professional standards.

The Role of Feedback in Learning

As already stated, the two principal methods of measuring and evaluating academic performance, namely formative assessment and summative assessment, are characterized by both distinct differences and intrinsic connections. There are various of key differences between formative and summative assessments include:

- Timing: Formative assessment is ongoing and frequent, while summative assessment occurs at predetermined intervals, often at the end of a learning period.
- Purpose: Formative assessment aims to improve learning, whereas summative assessment evaluates overall achievement.

- Feedback utilization: In formative assessment, feedback is immediately actionable and used to modify current learning strategies. In summative assessment, feedback may inform future learning but typically does not affect the assessment at hand.
- Stakes: Formative assessments are generally low-stakes, encouraging risk-taking and learning from mistakes. Summative assessments are often high-stakes, with significant implications for grades or advancement.
- Focus: Formative assessment emphasizes the process of learning, while summative assessment prioritizes the product or outcome of learning.

Despite these differences, there is growing recognition of the potential for synergy between formative and summative assessments. Carless (2007) argues for a more integrated approach, suggesting that summative assessments can serve formative purposes when designed thoughtfully and accompanied by meaningful feedback. While formative and summative assessments serve distinct functions within the educational landscape, they are interconnected elements of a comprehensive assessment strategy. Effective educational practices leverage both forms of assessment, recognizing their unique contributions to student learning and academic evaluation. The challenge for educators lies in striking an appropriate balance between these assessment types to optimize learning outcomes and accurately measure student achievement.

Feedback is a critical component of effective learning, serving as a bridge between the learner's current performance and their potential future achievement. It acts as a bridge between what a learner currently knows and what they have the potential to achieve. Understanding how to effectively provide and use feedback can significantly enhance learning outcomes.

Hattie and Timperley's Feedback Model

Hattie and Timperley (2007) proposed a comprehensive model of feedback that centers on three fundamental questions, each addressing a distinct dimension of the learning process:

1. "Where am I going?" (Feed Up)

This question emphasizes the establishment of clear, specific learning goals. It facilitates learners' comprehension of their intended objectives. Effective feedback at this stage should elucidate the learning targets and performance expectations, thereby providing a clear direction for the learning journey.

2. "How am I going?" (Feed Back)

This question evaluates the learner's current performance in relation to the established goals. Feedback at this stage should be specific, detailed, and informative, highlighting areas of proficiency as well as aspects requiring improvement. This targeted feedback enables learners to gauge their progress accurately.

3. "Where to next?" (Feed Forward)

This question guides the learner's future actions and strategies. It should provide constructive suggestions for improvement and outline potential next steps in the learning process. This forward-looking feedback helps learners to bridge the gap between their current performance and desired outcomes.

These three questions form a structured framework for feedback that is goal-oriented, constructive, and cyclical. It is crucial for educators to internalize these three fundamental components when seeking to obtain meaningful information from learners about their educational experiences. Moreover, when providing feedback, educators must conscientiously address each of these questions to ensure that their feedback is comprehensive, organized, and beneficial. By adhering to this model, educators can offer guidance that effectively supports learners throughout their educational journey, promoting continuous improvement and self-regulated learning. This model underscores the importance of feedback as a multi-dimensional, interactive process that goes beyond mere evaluation, emphasizing its role in actively shaping the learning trajectory.

Impact of Feedback on Learning Outcomes

The available evidence suggests that feedback can significantly impact learning outcomes. For instance, a meta-analysis by Kluger and DeNisi (1996) found that feedback interventions generally enhance performance. However, the effectiveness of feedback depends on several key factors:

- **Specificity of Feedback:** Clear and specific feedback is essential. Vague or general comments are less helpful than precise information about which aspects of performance were executed well and which areas need improvement.
- **Timing of Feedback:** The timing of feedback is crucial. Immediate feedback is often more effective because it allows learners to associate it directly with their actions and make necessary adjustments promptly.

- **Learner Receptiveness**: The willingness of the learner to receive feedback plays a significant role. When learners view feedback as a tool for growth rather than as criticism, they are more likely to benefit from it.

Shute (2008) emphasizes that for feedback to be most effective, it should be constructive, specific, and timely. Effective feedback helps learners understand their current performance, identify areas for improvement, and provides clear guidance on how to progress.

Principles of Inspirational Learning

Inspirational learning environments are designed to foster intrinsic motivation, creativity, and deep engagement with the subject matter. This section delves into the key principles that underpin such environments, drawing on various theoretical frameworks and research findings.

Csikszentmihalyi's Concept of "Flow"

One of the seminal concepts in understanding optimal learning experiences is Csikszentmihalyi's (1990) notion of "flow." Flow is a state where learners are fully immersed in an activity that is challenging yet matches their skill level. In this state, individuals experience:

- **Intense concentration:** Learners are completely focused on the task at hand.
- **Loss of self-consciousness:** They become so absorbed that they lose awareness of themselves as separate from the activity.
- **A sense of control:** They feel confident and capable of meeting the challenges presented by the task.
- **Intrinsic reward:** The activity itself is rewarding, regardless of any external rewards or outcomes.

Creating conditions for flow involves designing learning activities that are neither too easy nor too difficult, providing clear goals, and offering immediate feedback. When students experience flow, they are more likely to find learning enjoyable and fulfilling.

Self-Determination Theory

Ryan and Deci's (2000) Self-Determination Theory (SDT), provides another critical perspective on inspirational learning. SDT posits that for learners to be intrinsically motivated, their environments must satisfy three basic psychological needs:

Autonomy: Learners need to feel that they have control over their learning choices and are not being coerced. This can be achieved by offering options and encouraging self-directed learning.

Competence: Learners need to feel capable and effective in their activities. This involves providing tasks that are appropriately challenging and offering opportunities for mastery.

Relatedness: Learners need to feel connected to others, whether peers, instructors, or a broader community. This can be fostered through collaborative activities and a supportive learning environment.

When these needs are met, learners are more likely to engage deeply with the material, persist through challenges, and develop a lifelong love of learning.

Dweck's Growth Mindset

The research conducted by Carol Dweck (2006) on growth mindset provides further insight into the principles of inspirational learning. A growth mindset is the conviction that one's abilities and intelligence can be enhanced through exertion, tenacity, and the acquisition of knowledge from setbacks. The fostering of a growth mindset is contingent upon several key aspects, including:

- The focus should be on effort rather than innate ability. It is recommended that educators adopt a more nuanced approach to praise, focusing on effort and strategies rather than solely on intelligence.
- The perception of challenges as opportunities is a further key aspect of fostering a growth mindset. Students should be encouraged to perceive challenging tasks as opportunities for growth rather than as threats to their self-esteem.
- The ability to learn from mistakes is an essential component of a growth mindset. The establishment of a classroom culture in which mistakes are regarded as an inherent aspect of the learning process enables students to adopt a risk-taking and innovative approach without the inhibition of fear of failure.

By fostering a growth mindset, educators can motivate students to embrace challenges, persevere in the face of adversity, and ultimately achieve higher levels of success. An inspirational learning environment is conducive to intrinsic motivation, creativity and profound engagement with the subject matter. Csikszentmihalyi's

(1990) concept of "flow" provides a useful framework for understanding optimal learning experiences. Flow occurs when learners are fully immersed in a challenging task that matches their skill level.

RELATED WORK

AI Technologies in Formative Assessment

AI technologies are increasingly being integrated into educational practices, particularly in formative assessment. Formative assessment involves ongoing evaluation of student learning to provide continuous feedback and support. AI can enhance this process by offering personalized, instant, and adaptive feedback that traditional methods may not be able to provide.

Overview of AI Applications in Education

AI applications in education encompass a wide range of tools and systems designed to improve teaching and learning processes. These technologies include intelligent tutoring systems, automated feedback mechanisms, and adaptive learning platforms. According to Holmes et al. (2019), AI can help create more personalized learning experiences, identify student weaknesses, and provide targeted interventions. By leveraging AI, educators can gain deeper insights into student performance and tailor their instructional strategies to meet individual needs.

Intelligent Tutoring Systems

Intelligent Tutoring Systems (ITS) are AI-driven platforms that deliver personalized instruction and feedback to students. These systems utilize machine learning algorithms to adapt to each learner's pace and level of understanding. For example, Carnegie Learning's MATHia and Cognitive Tutor have been shown to enhance student performance in mathematics by providing adaptive problem-solving exercises and immediate feedback (Koedinger & Corbett, 2006). ITS can simulate one-on-one tutoring by adjusting the difficulty of tasks based on student responses, thereby enriching the learning experience (Carnegie Learning, n.d.).

Another example is Third Space Learning, which employs AI to analyze recordings of online math tutoring sessions. This system provides feedback to tutors on their teaching styles and identifies areas where students are struggling, enabling targeted interventions (Carnegie Learning, n.d.).

Automated Feedback Mechanisms

Automated feedback mechanisms leverage natural language processing (NLP) and other AI technologies to provide instant and detailed feedback on student work. Tools such as *Grammarly* and *Turnitin* utilize AI to analyze written assignments, offering corrections and suggestions for improvement. Shute (2008) emphasizes the importance of timely and specific feedback in promoting student learning. Automated systems can deliver this feedback more efficiently than human graders, enabling more frequent and consistent evaluations. *Grammarly*, while primarily known as a writing assistant, serves as an effective formative assessment tool in writing courses. Its AI-powered system offers immediate feedback on grammar, style, and clarity, helping students understand and correct their mistakes continuously.

Another notable example is *Gradescope*, which employs AI to assist in grading assignments, particularly useful for large classes. It can recognize similar answers across numerous submissions, ensuring consistency in grading and providing rapid feedback to students (Gradescope, n.d.).

Adaptive Learning Platforms

Adaptive learning platforms are AI-powered systems that personalize the learning experience by adapting content and assessment based on individual student performance. These platforms use data analytics to track student progress and adjust the learning path accordingly. For instance, Knewton's adaptive learning technology creates customized learning experiences by analyzing student data to predict the most effective instructional strategies (Knewton, 2020).

Other notable examples of successful AI applications in formative assessment include ALEKS (Assessment and Learning in Knowledge Spaces) and Duolingo. ALEKS is specifically designed for mathematics education. It assesses students' knowledge, identifies gaps, and provides tailored learning paths to address those gaps. Empirical evidence suggests that ALEKS effectively improves students Math. achievement (Cosyn et al., 2021). Duolingo, on the other hand, focuses on language learning. It adapts lesson difficulty and content based on student performance, offering immediate feedback and adjusting future lessons to target areas where learners need more practice. Research findings indicate that Duolingo brings significant benefits to language learners (Vesselinov & Grego, 2012).

These exemplars illustrate the multifaceted applications of artificial intelligence in formative assessment and its beneficial impact on student learning outcomes across diverse disciplines. Through continuous evaluation of student performance, these adaptive learning platforms ensure that each learner receives appropriately calibrated challenges and support, thereby optimizing their educational trajectories.

The personalized nature of these systems facilitates a more efficient and effective learning process, potentially addressing individual learning needs in ways traditional methods may not achieve.

Strategies for AI-Enhanced Formative Assessment

Building on the basic integration of AI technology in formative assessment discussed in the previous section, this section explores strategies for enhancing formative assessment with AI by examining successful case studies and innovative approaches. The growing importance of AI-powered formative assessment in modern educational contexts is supported by several key factors.

Firstly, scalable personalization offers a significant advantage. Artificial intelligence (AI) enables the provision of individualized learning experiences for large student populations, thereby addressing the persistent challenge of delivering personalized education within traditional classroom environments. Secondly, instantaneous feedback is another critical benefit. Implementing real-time assessment and feedback mechanisms has been shown to markedly enhance learning outcomes by facilitating the prompt identification of misconceptions and reinforcing accurate understanding.

Additionally, data-informed decision-making plays a vital role, as AI-powered analytics provide educators with invaluable insights that inform instructional strategies and curriculum development. Enhanced engagement and motivation further contribute to the effectiveness of AI-enhanced formative assessment. Innovative assessment methodologies, such as gamification, have been demonstrated to increase student engagement and motivation, leading to improved learning outcomes. Lastly, the increased efficiency resulting from the use of AI technologies is another advantage. AI automates various aspects of assessment, allowing educators to focus on more meaningful interactions with students.

By employing these strategies, AI-enhanced formative assessments can facilitate the creation of more responsive, adaptive, and engaging learning environments that meet the diverse needs of students, thereby promoting deeper learning and academic success. The following categories of smart learning environments, which enhance learning outcomes, are currently being implemented or built:

Real-time Feedback and Intervention

Real-time feedback and intervention tools have shown promising results in enhancing students' academic achievement across various subjects, but they are not without criticism. Several case studies demonstrate their effectiveness and shed light on students' perceptions, while others raise important concerns. Kahoot!, a game-based learning platform, has been found to improve learning performance and increase student engagement. Wang and Tahir (2020) conducted a comprehensive literature review that revealed students not only performed better but also enjoyed using *Kahoot!*. The gamification element led to higher participation and motivation. Students reported increased enjoyment in learning and improved classroom dynamics.

However, Kocadere and Çağlar (2018) argue that while game-based learning tools like Kahoot! can increase motivation, they may not always lead to deeper learning. Their study found that some students focused more on winning the game than understanding the content, potentially leading to surface-level learning. In mathematics education, platforms like ASSISTments and DreamBox Learning have made significant impacts. Heffernan and Heffernan (2014) described how ASSISTments, a web-based tutoring system, improved students' problem-solving skills through immediate feedback and hints. Students appreciated the instant feedback and reported increased confidence in tackling difficult problems. Similarly, Chu et al. (2018) found that DreamBox Learning, an adaptive platform, led to significant improvements in standardized math test scores.

Despite these positive findings, Reich and Ito (2017) caution against over-reliance on adaptive learning systems. They argue that these systems often focus on procedural knowledge at the expense of conceptual understanding and may limit opportunities for collaborative learning and creative problem-solving. For writing skills, Grammarly has proven to be an effective tool. Ghufron and Rosyida (2018) examined its role in assessing English as a Foreign Language (EFL) writing. They found that students using Grammarly showed significant improvements in their writing skills and developed better self-editing abilities. Students appreciated the immediate, personalized feedback. However, Frankenberg (2018) raises concerns about the use of automated writing evaluation tools like Grammarly. She argues that these tools may not adequately capture the nuances of language and could potentially stifle creativity in writing. There's also a risk that students might become overly dependent on these tools, hindering their ability to develop independent writing skills. These case studies employed various evaluation methods, including analysis of test scores, surveys, interviews, and comparison of usage data with academic performance. The overall trend shows that while many students respond positively to real-time feedback tools, reporting increased confidence and greater enjoyment in learning, there are valid concerns about their limitations and potential negative impacts.

It's worthy to note that while these tools show promise, their effectiveness can vary depending on implementation and individual student needs. Critics like Selwyn (2019) argue that the increasing use of educational technology, including real-time feedback tools, may exacerbate existing inequalities in education and raise concerns about data privacy and the commodification of education. Future research should focus on addressing these concerns, exploring the long-term impacts of these tools, and investigating how to best integrate them into broader educational strategies while mitigating potential drawbacks.

Personalized Learning Pathways

Personalized learning pathways have become a hot topic in educational technology, aiming to tailor instruction to each student's needs, interests, and abilities. Research on this approach has yielded mixed results, with both promising findings and notable concerns. Pane et al. (2015) studied personalized learning in 62 schools and found that students made better progress in mathematics and reading compared to their peers in traditional schools. The researchers linked these gains to flexible learning environments, learner profiles, and competency-based progression. Students reported feeling more engaged and in control of their learning experience.

Basham et al. (2016) looked at how personalized learning environments affected students with disabilities. Their research showed that these environments boosted student engagement and academic performance, especially when combined with Universal Design for Learning principles. Students liked being able to learn at their own pace and in ways that suited them best. However, not all researchers are convinced about the benefits of personalized learning pathways. Bulger (2016) points out that while personalization aims to cater to individual needs, it might unintentionally widen existing inequalities. She raises concerns about potential biases in the algorithms used to create personalized pathways and their ability to capture the full complexity of human learning. Roberts-Mahoney et al. (2016) express reservations about the data-driven nature of personalized learning. They argue that focusing too much on measurable data might lead to a narrow view of education, potentially overlooking crucial aspects of learning that are harder to quantify. They also worry about reduced teacher autonomy and over-reliance on technology-driven decisions.

Netcom's (2017) case study on middle school students' experiences with personalized learning revealed a mixed bag of results. While some students thrived with increased autonomy, others struggled to manage their time and direct their own learning. This highlights the need to consider individual differences when implementing personalized learning pathways. Fitzgerald et al. (2018) examined how personalized learning was put into practice in K-12 schools. They found that while teachers generally liked the concept, they faced significant challenges in reality. These included a heavier workload, difficulties in managing diverse learning paths, and worries about maintaining high academic standards. It's worth noting that the effectiveness of personalized learning pathways can vary greatly depending on how they're implemented, the context, and student characteristics. While some studies show promising results, others caution against seeing personalization as a cure-all for educational challenges. Looking ahead, researchers should focus on addressing the concerns raised by critics, exploring the long-term effects of personalized learning pathways, and finding ways to implement these approaches that benefit all students while minimizing potential drawbacks. More attention should also be given to the role of teachers in personalized learning environments and how to best support them in this transition.

Data-driven Insights for Educators

The efficacy of data-driven insights in education remains a subject of ongoing research and debate. The variability in outcomes suggests that effectiveness is contingent upon multiple factors, including data quality, analytical tools, and educators' capacity to interpret and act upon the information. While some studies indicate promising results, others caution against an overreliance on data at the expense of other crucial educational considerations.

Future research directions should encompass the development of more sophisticated methodologies for collecting and analyzing educational data, with the aim of capturing a more comprehensive view of student learning. There is a pressing need to investigate the optimal balance between data-driven insights and other forms of educational knowledge and expertise. Furthermore, additional research is warranted to address the ethical implications of data use in education, particularly concerning student privacy and the responsible utilization of educational data. Moreover, longitudinal studies are necessary to assess the long-term impact of data-driven decision-making on student outcomes, teacher effectiveness, and overall educational quality. Such research could provide valuable insights into the sustainability and scalability of data-driven approaches in diverse educational contexts.

Additionally, interdisciplinary collaborations between education researchers, data scientists, and ethicists could yield more nuanced frameworks for implementing data-driven practices in education. These collaborations could potentially address the current limitations and criticisms while maximizing the benefits of data-informed educational strategies. While data-driven insights offer potential benefits for educators, their implementation and outcomes remain complex and multifaceted. Continued rigorous research and critical analysis are essential to refine these approaches and ensure they contribute positively to educational practices and outcomes.

Platforms such as Realizeit offer educators comprehensive analytics, enabling precise tracking of student progress and identification of challenging areas (Howlin & Lynch, 2014). The ASSISTments platform not only provides immediate student feedback but also furnishes teachers with detailed performance reports, enhancing instructional decision-making (Heffernan & Heffernan, 2014).

Gamification and Immersive Assessment Experiences

Gamification and immersive assessment experiences represent novel approaches to formative assessment that employ game-like elements and immersive technologies to engage students and provide immediate feedback on their learning progress. Ifenthaler, Eseryel and Ge (2012) posit that game-based assessments present a distinctive opportunity to assess complex problem-solving abilities and higher-order thinking in ways that traditional assessments are unable to do. They highlight that effectively designed game-based assessments can provide continuous, unobtrusive evaluation of student performance within authentic contexts. In a systematic mapping study on gamification in education, Dicheva et al. (2015) found that when implemented effectively, gamified assessments can increase student motivation and engagement. Their research indicates that the incorporation of elements such as points, badges, and leaderboards can facilitate a more interactive and rewarding assessment experience. However, Attali and Arieli-Attali (2015) advise that although gamification has the potential to enhance motivation, it may not necessarily lead to improved learning outcomes. The study on the effects of points in an online assessment revealed that, although points increased engagement, they did not significantly impact performance. Furthermore, Ifenthaler et al. (2012) emphasize that game-based assessments can capture detailed data about student decision-making processes, providing insights into cognitive strategies that are often not observable in traditional assessments. This is consistent with the concept of "stealth assessment," as proposed by Shute and Ventura (2013), whereby the assessment is integrated into the gaming experience in a seamless manner.

In the domain of immersive experiences, Merchant et al. (2014) conducted a meta-analysis to assess the instructional efficacy of virtual reality-based learning. The researchers discovered that immersive technologies can facilitate the provision of authentic assessment contexts, thereby enabling more precise evaluations of complex skills and knowledge application. Conversely, Makransky et al. (2019) highlight potential drawbacks of immersive technologies in assessment. Their research suggests that while virtual reality can increase presence and motivation, it may also increase cognitive load, potentially hindering learning and assessment performance for some students. A case study by Tsai and Fan (2013) examined the use of a 3D virtual world for assessing students' scientific inquiry abilities. They found that the immersive environment allowed for more authentic assessment of complex skills but noted challenges in ensuring standardization across different virtual scenarios. Hamari et al. (2016) explored the long-term effects of gamification in education. Their longitudinal study revealed initial increases in engagement and performance, but these effects tended to diminish over time, suggesting the need for continuous innovation in gamified assessment strategies.

The efficacy of gamification and immersive assessment experiences is contingent upon a number of factors, including the specific game elements employed, the subject matter being assessed, and the individual characteristics of the students involved. While some studies indicate enhanced engagement and more genuine assessment of sophisticated abilities, others identify potential limitations, such as elevated cognitive demand and diminished effects over time. Future research should concentrate on the creation of more advanced gamification and immersive assessment models that are capable of adapting to the specific requirements and learning styles of individual students. It is imperative that future research investigate the long-term impacts of these approaches on learning outcomes and motivation. Furthermore, research should address the potential equity issues in access to and effectiveness of these technologies across diverse student populations.

Overall, while gamification and immersive assessment experiences offer promising avenues for enhancing formative assessment, their implementation and outcomes remain complex. It is imperative that rigorous research and critical analysis be continued in order to refine these approaches and ensure that they contribute positively to educational assessment practices.

EXPERIMENTAL STUDY ON THE IMPACT OF AI-ASSISTED LEARNING IN ACCOUNTING EDUCATION

Experimental Objectives

The primary objective of this study is to evaluate the impact of artificial intelligence-assisted learning on students' study habits and learning methodologies within the context of accounting education. Specifically, the research aims to assess how the implementation of the Socratic Playground for Learning (SPL), an intelligent tutoring system developed by Professor Xiangen Hu at Hong Kong Polytechnic University, influences students' critical thinking abilities, self-reflection, and independent reasoning skills. Additionally, the study seeks to determine the effectiveness of SPL in providing personalized and adaptive learning experiences, thereby enhancing overall academic performance in accounting courses.

Experiment Description

This empirical study examined the impact of artificial intelligence-assisted learning on students' study habits and learning methodologies in the context of accounting education. The investigation was conducted over a 16-week semester, spanning from March to June 2024. The research centers on the implementation of the Socratic

Playground for Learning (SPL), an intelligent tutoring system designed by Professor Xiangen Hu at Hong Kong Polytechnic University. SPL leverages advanced AI technologies, specifically large language models (LLMs) like GPT-4, to provide personalized and adaptive learning experiences tailored to individual student needs. Participants were introduced to the SPL platform, accessible at https://spl.skoonline.org/wizard/index.html. They were instructed to input their background information and course materials into the system. In response, SPL generated various learning scenarios and game modes incorporating Socratic questioning techniques and hypothetical situations aimed at enhancing critical thinking skills. The SPL interface provides a selection of learning principles (e.g., Zone of Proximal Development) and question types (e.g., What?, Why?, How?, Who?, When?) to stimulate cognitive engagement and language acquisition. The system initiates dialogues with prompts, followed by multi-turn exchanges that delve deeper into topics, guiding student understanding. This experimental approach leverages the capabilities of LLMs to minimize reliance on predefined rules and human intervention, offering tailored learning experiences adaptable to diverse educational contexts and learner profiles.

Subjects

The study population consists of 128 non-accounting major students enrolled in the “Principles of Accounting” course at the School of Business of a private higher education institution in Guangdong Province, China. Initially, 149 students were approached to participate in the study; however, 21 declined due to privacy concerns. All participants are second-year students who have successfully passed the Chinese university entrance examination, including those admitted through special programs. The age distribution of the participants is as follows: 24 students are 18 years old, 67 are 19, 21 are 20, 3 are 21, 2 are 22, 1 is 23, and 1 is 25, with a median age of 19 years. The cohort comprises 70 men and 48 girls.

Description of the New Generation AI Intelligent Tutor Based on LLMs

The Socratic Playground for Learning (SPL) platform, accessible at https://spl.skoonline.org/wizard/index.html, was introduced to the participants as part of this study. This dialogue-based intelligent tutoring system, powered by large language models (LLMs) such as GPT-4, facilitates personalized and adaptive learning experiences. Participants were instructed to input their background information and course materials into the system, which then generated various learning scenarios and game modes. These scenarios incorporated Socratic questioning techniques and hypothetical situations designed to enhance critical thinking skills.

The SPL interface offers a selection of learning principles (e.g., Zone of Proximal Development) and question types (e.g., What?, Why?, How?, Who?, When?) to stimulate cognitive engagement and language acquisition. The system initiates dialogues with prompts, followed by multi-turn exchanges that explore topics in depth and guide student understanding. This experimental approach leverages the capabilities of LLMs to reduce reliance on predefined rules and human intervention, providing tailored learning experiences adaptable to diverse educational contexts and learner profiles. The study aims to evaluate the effectiveness of this AI-assisted learning tool in enhancing students' critical thinking abilities, self-reflection, and independent reasoning within the context of accounting education.

Experimental Procedures

The instructional period spanned sixteen weeks, from March to June 2024 (Academic Year 2023-2024). Each week, accounting classes were conducted, lasting a total of two periods per session. The teaching process integrated regular classroom activities with the use of the SPL platform.

Pre-Class Quizzes: At the beginning of each class, students completed a short quiz consisting of objective questions designed to assess their prior knowledge mastery in accounting principles. Dynamic Selection and Scenario Generation: Before the semester commenced, participants were introduced to the SPL platform. They were instructed to describe their learning objectives using the Dynamic Selection Interface, selecting from available domains, subdomains, and specific learning objectives or inputting custom goals. Based on these inputs, SPL generated personalized learning scenarios and game modes that incorporated Socratic questioning techniques and hypothetical situations aimed at enhancing critical thinking skills.

Formative Tests: In addition to weekly classes, students were required to complete a total of 21 formative tests throughout the semester. Each quiz lasted less than three minutes and contained no more than three questions per class, aiming to provide continuous assessment and feedback.

Self-Report Questionnaire: In the twelfth week of the semester, a self-report questionnaire was distributed to collect student feedback on their learning experiences and interactions with the SPL platform. This questionnaire aimed to gather insights into students' perceptions of the AI-assisted learning tool and its impact on their study habits and learning methodologies.

Data Analysis and Discussion

Gender Differences in AI-Assisted Learning Utilization

An independent samples t-test was conducted to examine gender differences in the utilization of the AI-assisted learning system. The results revealed no statistically significant disparity between female (M = 1.28, SD = 0.46) and male (M = 1.40, SD = 0.49) students, with a t-value of -1.314 and a p-value of 0.192. The 95% confidence interval ranged from -0.295 to 0.060, indicating that the observed difference was not statistically significant. Although male students exhibited a marginally higher mean score, the difference did not reach statistical significance, suggesting comparable engagement with the AI-assisted learning system across genders.

Evaluating the Effectiveness of LLM-Based AI Tutors on Student Academic Outcomes

To evaluate the impact of AI tutors based on LLMs on both summative and formative assessments, final examination scores of 126 students and average scores of 21 classroom quizzes over one semester were collected and analyzed. Descriptive analyses of the questionnaire data challenged prevailing assumptions about gender preferences for electronic devices, indicating no significant gender difference in the use of AI tutors (p = 0.192).

Subsequent analysis explored the correlation between formative assessment scores (classroom quizzes) and summative assessment scores (final examinations). Pearson's correlation coefficient revealed a significant positive relationship ($r = 0.352, p < 0.01$), indicating that higher performance in formative assessments was associated with elevated summative assessment outcomes.

Impact of Intervention on Summative Assessment

The intervention's impact on summative assessment was evaluated by comparing final exam scores between two groups: students who used the intelligent learning system (n = 75) and those who did not (n = 41). **Table 1** presents the results of a t-test comparing performance across various question types on the final examination.

Table 1. Comparison of Exam Performance Between Users and Non-Users of the Intelligent Learning System in a Principles of Accounting Course

Question Type	Users (n = 75)	Non-Users (n = 41)	t-value	p-value
Case Study Questions	16.85 (SD = 7.02)	14.33 (SD = 6.76)	1.873	0.064
Multiple-Choice Questions (Single Answer)	13.40 (SD = 2.88)	13.37 (SD = 3.48)	0.057	0.955
Multiple-Choice Questions (Multiple Answers)	7.15 (SD = 3.24)	6.10 (SD = 3.40)	1.637	0.104
Fill-in-the-Blank Questions	10.04 (SD = 4.52)	10.12 (SD = 3.40)	-0.089	0.930
True/False Questions	10.44 (SD = 1.75)	10.34 (SD = 1.62)	0.297	0.767

Note. A two-sample t-test was conducted using SPSS version 25 to compare the mean exam scores across various question types between students who used the teacher-recommended intelligent learning system (n = 75) and those who did not (n = 41). The differences in mean scores were minimal and did not reach statistical significance (p > .05) for any question type.

Table 1 presents a statistical comparison of exam performance across different question types between two groups of students: those who utilized a teacher-recommended intelligent learning system (n = 75) and those who did not (n = 41) in a Principles of Accounting course. An independent samples t-test, conducted using SPSS version 25, was performed to determine whether there were significant differences in mean scores between the two groups for each question type.

The results indicate that:

- **Case Study Questions:** Users scored slightly higher (M = 16.85, SD = 7.02) compared to non-users (M = 14.33, SD = 6.76). However, this difference approached but did not reach statistical significance (t(114) = 1.873, p = 0.064).
- **Multiple-Choice Questions (Single Answer)**: Users and non-users had nearly identical mean scores (M = 13.40 vs. 13.37) with no significant difference (t(114) = 0.057, p = 0.955).
- **Multiple-Choice Questions (Multiple Answers):** Users scored marginally higher (M = 7.15, SD = 3.24) compared to non-users (M = 6.10, SD = 3.40). This difference was not statistically significant (t(114) = 1.637, p = 0.104).
- **Fill-in-the-Blank Questions:** Both groups had comparable mean scores (M = 10.04 vs. 10.12) with no significant difference (t(114) = -0.089, p = 0.930).
- **True/False Questions:** Users and non-users scored similarly (M = 10.44 vs. 10.34) with no significant difference (t(114) = 0.297, p = 0.767).

Overall, the analysis suggests that the utilization of the intelligent learning system did not result in statistically significant improvements in exam performance across any of the assessed question types. The minimal differences in mean scores, coupled with high p-values (all $p > .05$), indicate that the intelligent learning system did not have a substantial impact on students' performance in these assessments. Additionally, the similar standard deviations across groups imply consistent variability in scores, regardless of system usage.

Specifically, while the intelligent learning system appears to have a marginally positive impact on performance in case studies and complex multiple-choice questions, the differences observed did not reach statistical significance at the conventional $p < .05$ level. The impact of the system on other question types was found to be negligible. These findings suggest that the intelligent learning system may offer advantages for more intricate, analytical tasks within the domain of accounting education; however, it does not significantly influence performance across all assessment types.

Secondly, the incorporation of quiz tests within the classroom setting represents a valuable formative assessment tool, offering insight into students' intrinsic motivation to engage in continued learning and their ability to demonstrate understanding and retention of knowledge. Table 2 illustrates the impact of students' regular engagement with the AI dialogue platform on their exploration of novel concepts and the consolidation of learned knowledge.

Table 2. Comparison of In-Class Quiz Performance Between Users and Non-Users of an Intelligent Learning System in a Principles of Accounting Course

Group	N	Mean (M)	SD	t-value	p-value
Users	75	0.62	0.14	0.89	0.373
Non-Users	41	0.60	0.14		

Note. *A two-sample t-test was conducted using SPSS version 25 to compare the mean quiz scores between students who used the teacher-recommended intelligent learning system and those who did not. The difference in mean scores was 0.02 points (Users: $M = 0.62$, $SD = 0.14$; Non-Users: $M = 0.60$, $SD = 0.14$). The t-test result was $t(114) = 0.89$, $p = 0.373$, indicating no statistically significant difference between the two groups.*

Table 2 presents a statistical comparison of quiz scores between two groups of students: those who used a teacher-recommended intelligent learning system (n=75) and those who did not (n=41). The students were enrolled in an academic course setting. The analysis is based on a two-sample t-test of the mean quiz scores for each group. The mean quiz score for users of the intelligent learning system was 0.62 (SD = 0.14), while non-users scored a mean of 0.60 (SD = 0.14). The t-test yielded a t-value of 0.89, with a corresponding p-value of 0.373. The discrepancy in mean scores between the two groups is minimal (0.02 points), and the p-value

(0.373) is well above the conventional threshold for statistical significance ($p < 0.05$ or $p < 0.01$). This suggests that there is no statistically significant difference in quiz performance between those who use the intelligent learning system and those who do not. The comparable standard deviations (0.14) for both groups indicate that the variability in quiz scores is similar, irrespective of system usage. This suggests that the utilization of the intelligent learning system did not notably influence the dispersion of performance among students. Consequently, based on this analysis, the deployment of the teacher-recommended intelligent learning system does not appear to have a substantial impact on students' in-class quiz performance. It is important to note, however, that this finding is limited to quiz scores and may not reflect potential benefits in other areas of academic performance or learning outcomes. Further research, possibly involving larger sample sizes or examining different types of assessments, would be beneficial in order to comprehensively evaluate the effectiveness of the intelligent learning system.

Perception of Students at Different Learning Levels About Using Smart AI Tutors

The absence of statistically significant differences in both summative and formative assessments between users and non-users of the intelligent tutor system, despite slight variations, suggests that student selection bias may be influencing the results. Specifically, students' pre-existing academic performance levels might affect their likelihood of engaging with the new LLM-based AI tutor system (Socrates platform). To investigate this possibility, a statistical analysis was conducted to compare the propensity to use the AI tutor among students in the top quartile, the bottom quartile, and the overall student population.

Figure 1. Distribution of AI Tutor Usage Across Academic Performance Levels

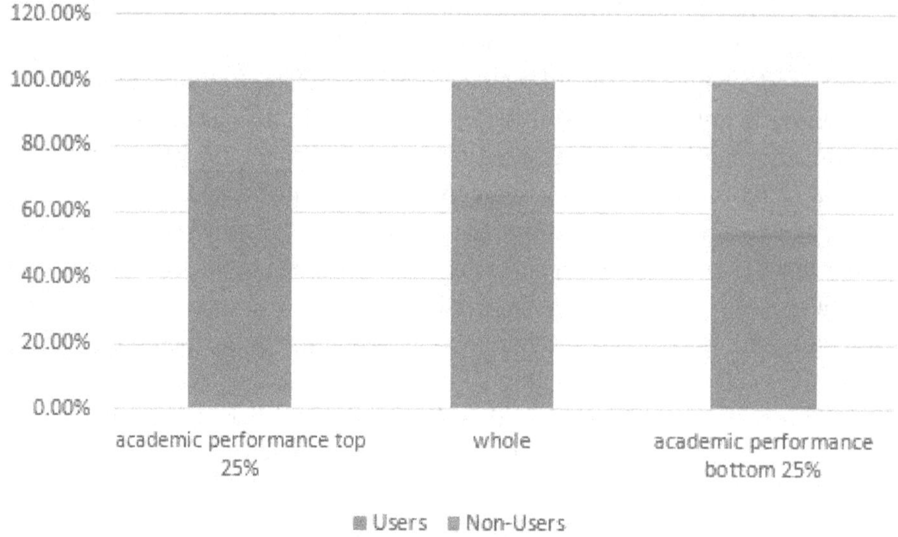

As illustrated in Figure 1, students exhibiting disparate academic performance levels evince a discernible proclivity for the utilization of artificial intelligence. Students in the top 25% of academic performance demonstrated the highest proclivity to utilize artificial intelligence systems, with nearly three-quarters (72.41%) opting to employ the system. This figure is markedly higher than the overall usage rate. The overall student population exhibited a pronounced proclivity towards utilizing artificial intelligence, with approximately two-thirds (64.96%) opting to employ the system. This indicates that the student population as a whole exhibits a high level of acceptance of artificial intelligence tools. The proportion of students in the lowest 25% of academic performance who adopted artificial intelligence systems was the lowest, but it was still slightly more than half (53.57%). There was a notable discrepancy in the usage of artificial intelligence systems between high-scoring and low-scoring students, with a difference of 18.84 percentage points. Interestingly, the above t-test did not yield a statistically significant relationship between academic performance and the use of artificial intelligence. However, the self-report questionnaire indicated that students with higher grades were more likely to utilize artificial intelligence systems. These findings align with those of prior studies (Wu & Chang, 2021) that have employed electronic textbooks, which indicate that students with superior academic performance are more inclined to embrace novel technologies and creative methodologies. This finding warrants further investigation in future studies to ascertain its motivational relevance.

Obstacles to Using AI Tutors

To comprehend the challenges and barriers that students encounter when utilizing artificial intelligence (AI) tutors across various learning stages, a follow-up survey was conducted. The key factors identified from the self-report data that negatively impacted students' willingness to engage with these tutoring systems for educational purposes are summarized below:

- **Technological Limitations:** Issues such as unreliable internet connectivity, software glitches, and insufficient access to necessary devices can impede the effective use of AI tutors. These technical challenges often frustrate students and disrupt the learning process.
- **User Experience Concerns:** A complex or unintuitive user interface can deter students from fully engaging with AI tutoring systems. If the platform is not user-friendly, students may find it difficult to navigate, leading to decreased usage and effectiveness.
- **Personalization and Adaptability:** While AI tutors aim to provide personalized learning experiences, some systems may fall short in adequately adapting to individual learning styles and needs. This lack of true personalization can result in frustration and reduced motivation among students.
- **Privacy and Data Security:** Concerns about the handling and protection of personal data can make students hesitant to use AI-based tutoring tools. Ensuring robust data privacy measures is essential to build trust and encourage widespread adoption.
- **Lack of Human Interaction:** The absence of human interaction in AI tutoring can make the learning experience feel impersonal. Students often benefit from the motivational and emotional support that human tutors provide, which AI systems may not be able to replicate effectively.
- **Cost and Accessibility:** The financial burden associated with the implementation and upkeep of AI tutoring systems can be a considerable obstacle, particularly for educational institutions with limited resources. Given the substantial financial outlay required for AI products, it is not feasible for them to be provided at no cost. Furthermore, disparities in technology access can intensify educational inequities.
- **Resistance to Change:** Both students and educators may exhibit resistance to adopting new technologies. Familiarity with traditional learning methods and skepticism about the effectiveness of AI tutors can hinder the integration of these systems into educational settings.

Addressing these obstacles is crucial for the successful integration of AI tutors into educational environments. By overcoming these challenges, educators and developers can enhance the effectiveness of AI-driven formative assessment tools, leading to improved learning outcomes and a more engaging educational experience for students.

Figure 2. Distribution of AI Tutor Usability Challenges Across Student Performance Levels

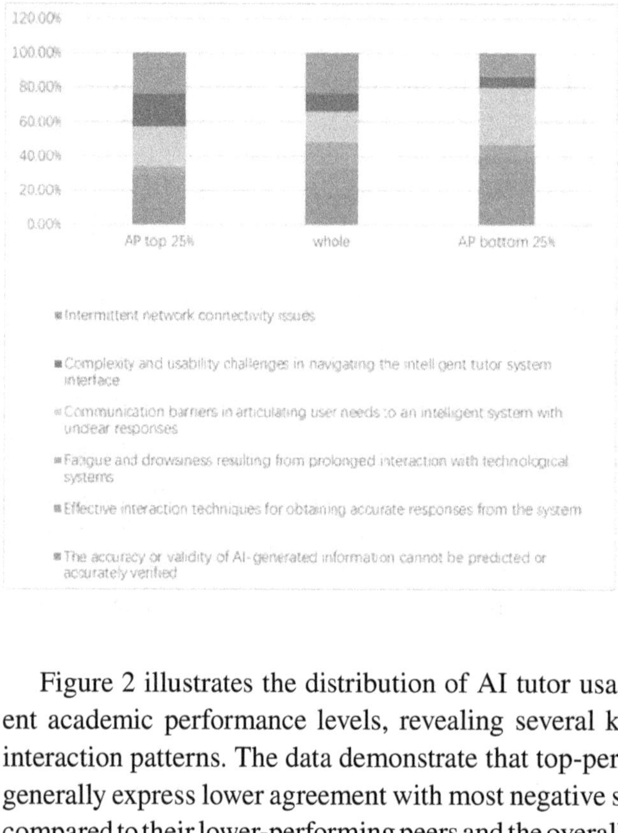

Figure 2 illustrates the distribution of AI tutor usage challenges across different academic performance levels, revealing several key insights into student-AI interaction patterns. The data demonstrate that top-performing students (top 25%) generally express lower agreement with most negative statements about AI systems compared to their lower-performing peers and the overall sample. This trend suggests a potential correlation between academic achievement and effective utilization or positive perception of AI learning tools. Notably, the challenge of formulating relevant follow-up questions despite receiving responses emerges as a universal issue, garnering the highest agreement across all groups. This difficulty is particularly pronounced among lower-performing students (bottom 25%), indicating a critical area for improvement in AI system design and user training. Technical challenges, specifically network connectivity issues, persist as a significant concern across all performance groups, with top-performing students reporting slightly higher incidences. This unexpected finding may reflect more intensive or frequent system usage among high achievers. Consistently, lower-performing students demonstrate higher agreement with negative statements about AI systems across various aspects. This trend suggests that these students may face greater difficulties in effectively leveraging AI tools for their learning, potentially exacerbating existing educational disparities. These findings have significant implications for the development and implementation of AI tutoring systems in educational contexts:

- The observed correlation between academic performance and AI system perception underscores the need for adaptive interfaces that cater to diverse user proficiencies and learning styles.
- Universal difficulties in query formulation highlight the importance of developing more intuitive user interfaces and implementing targeted training programs to enhance student-AI interaction.
- The prevalence of technical issues across all performance levels emphasizes the critical need for robust infrastructure to support AI-enhanced learning environments.
- The heightened challenges reported by lower-performing students indicate a pressing need for additional support mechanisms and tailored interventions to ensure equitable access to AI learning benefits.
- The reported difficulties in verifying AI system effectiveness suggest a need for more transparent evaluation metrics and validation processes in educational technology implementation.

These insights contribute to our understanding of the complex interplay between student characteristics, AI system design, and learning outcomes. Future research should focus on developing more inclusive AI tutoring systems that can effectively support students across the academic performance spectrum, thereby maximizing the potential of AI in education while mitigating the risk of exacerbating existing achievement gaps.

Proposed Implementation Framework for AI-enhanced Formative Assessment In Higher Education

Drawing from the empirical findings presented in Section 4, this study proposes an implementation framework for AI-enhanced formative assessment in higher education (Figure 3). The framework comprises ten key components, each critical to the successful integration of AI in educational assessment.

Figure 3. Implementation Framework for AI-Enhanced Formative Assessment in Higher Education

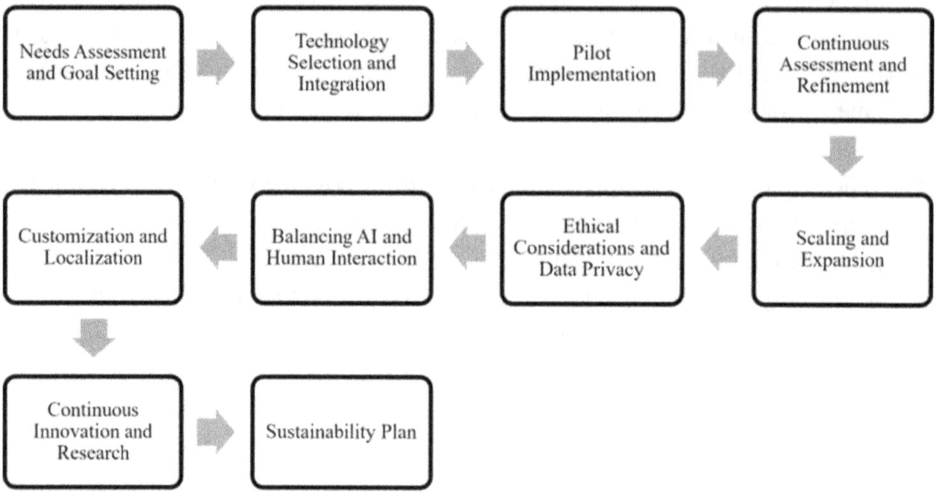

These components as shown in Figure 3. are elaborated upon in the following subsections:

1. Needs Assessment and Goal Setting

Needs Assessment and Goal Setting is a crucial initial step in implementing AI-assisted learning systems in educational contexts. This process involves:

a) Evaluating the current learning environment: Assessing existing teaching methods, student performance, and areas where improvement is needed in the accounting education curriculum.
b) Identifying specific learning objectives: Determining what skills and knowledge students should acquire through the AI-assisted learning system, such as critical thinking in accounting principles or improved problem-solving abilities.
c) Analyzing student demographics and backgrounds: Understanding the diverse needs of the student population, including factors like prior knowledge, learning styles, and technological proficiency.
d) Setting measurable goals: Establishing clear, quantifiable objectives for the implementation of the AI tutor, such as improving quiz scores by a certain percentage or increasing student engagement rates.

e) Aligning with curriculum standards: Ensuring that the goals set for the AI-assisted learning system are in line with broader educational standards and course requirements.
f) Stakeholder input: Gathering feedback from instructors, students, and administrators to ensure the goals address all relevant perspectives and needs.
g) Resource assessment: Evaluating the available technological infrastructure, time, and personnel resources needed to implement and support the AI tutoring system effectively.
h) Defining success metrics: Establishing key performance indicators (KPIs) to measure the effectiveness of the AI tutor in meeting the set goals.

These comprehensive needs assessment and goal-setting process provides a solid foundation for implementing AI-assisted learning tools, ensuring they are tailored to the specific context and objectives of the accounting education program. To illustrate the process of goal setting, the Principles of Accounting course can be used as a case study. Following a survey of students and teachers, it was determined that students encountered challenges in applying accounting principles to real-world scenarios and in maintaining engagement with conventional homework methods.

The process of establishing objectives is known as goal setting. In light of the aforementioned assessment, two principal objectives were established.

- The objective is to enhance students' capacity to apply accounting principles to case studies, with the aim of increasing case study scores in the final examination by 10% in comparison to the preceding semester.
- It was determined that an additional objective was to enhance student engagement with the course materials outside of the classroom setting. The goal was to achieve a 80% utilization rate of the AI tutor by students for a minimum of two hours per week, encompassing activities such as problem-solving, formulating their own problems, and self-assessment, in addition to expanding their knowledge base.

These objectives are specific, measurable, and directly address the needs identified in the assessment. They provide transparent objectives for the implementation and assessment of the efficacy of AI-assisted learning systems.

1. Technology Selection and Integration: Evaluate available AI technologies based on their alignment with educational goals, ease of use, and scalability.
2. Alignment with educational goals: When selecting AI technologies, it's crucial to evaluate how well they align with the specific educational objectives of the course. For instance, if a key goal is to improve students' analytical skills in

financial statement analysis, the chosen AI tool should have strong capabilities in presenting and guiding students through complex financial scenarios.

3. Ease of use: The selected technology should have an intuitive interface for both students and instructors. For example, an AI-powered tutoring system for accounting might offer a conversational interface that allows students to ask questions about accounting principles in natural language.
4. Scalability: The chosen system should be able to handle the entire student body and potentially grow with the institution. For instance, if the accounting department plans to expand its online offerings, the AI tool should be capable of supporting a larger, distributed student base.
5. Mix of tools: It is recommended that a variety of assessment tools be considered in order to address the diverse needs of assessment.
    - Intelligent Tutoring Systems (e.g., MATHia, Cognitive Tutor)
    - Automated Feedback Mechanisms (e.g., Grammarly, Turnitin)
    - Adaptive Learning Platforms (e.g., ALEKS, Knewton)
    - Real-time Assessment Tools (e.g., Kahoot!, ASSISTments)

It is crucial to integrate these tools seamlessly with existing Learning Management Systems (LMS) and other educational technologies.

It is recommended that the selected AI tools integrate seamlessly with the institution's current Learning Management System. For example, if the institution uses Canvas, the chosen AI tutoring system should be able to synchronize grades, assignments, and student progress data directly with Canvas, ensuring a seamless experience for both students and instructors. By carefully considering these factors, the institution can select and integrate AI technologies that enhance the accounting curriculum effectively, thereby improving student engagement and learning outcomes.

6. Pilot Implementation:

Pilot Implementation is about testing the AI-assisted learning system on a small scale before full rollout. It's is aim to provide comprehensive training for faculty and students on using the new tools. Collecting data on usage, performance, and user feedback throughout the pilot phase. It starts with choosing a small group of students and teachers to try out the system, usually for one semester. The goal is to see how well it works in real classroom settings. During the initial period, it is important for the researcher to act as a third-party pilot.

The specific actions are as follows: During this trial period, researchers are looking at how students use the system, if their grades improve, and whether they find it helpful. Researchers also want to know if teachers think it makes their job easier or more effective. It's important to provide good training so everyone knows how to use the system properly. Throughout the pilot, researchers are constantly gathering feedback and watching for any problems. If something isn't working right, researcher will fix it quickly. Researchers might do a quick check halfway through to see if any big changes are needed. At the end of the pilot, researcher take a close look at all the information they've gathered. Did students do better in their accounting classes? Did they engage more with the course material? Were there any unexpected challenges? Based on what students learn, researchers decide whether to use the AI system in more classes, make changes to it, or maybe even try something different.

The key is to be flexible and open to learning from the experience. The pilot phase is designed to ascertain the optimal approach for students and teachers in actual, real-world settings.

7. Continuous Assessment and Refinement

Continuous Assessment and Refinement in AI-assisted education involves an ongoing process of evaluation and improvement across various subjects and educational settings. Researchers regularly collect and analyze data on how students and teachers interact with AI tools, examining usage patterns, feature engagement, and changes in academic performance. Feedback is gathered through surveys, interviews, and monitoring of online discussions to identify effective features and areas needing improvement. This input comes from students, teachers, and other stakeholders involved in the educational process.

As insights accumulate, researchers address specific challenges students face and respond to educators' needs for enhanced functionality and analytics. They stay updated on advancements in AI and educational technologies, often collaborating with AI providers to implement new features or innovative teaching methods. It should be noted that Performance metrics play a crucial role, with researchers comparing student outcomes to previous periods or control groups. This helps justify continued use and investment in AI educational tools.

The focus is on improvements in various aspects of learning, such as test scores, concept retention, engagement levels, and development of critical thinking skills. The system is also adapted to accommodate significant changes in curriculum standards, teaching methodologies, or educational policies. This ensures that AI tools remain aligned with current educational goals and practices.

The ultimate aim is to create a feedback loop where real-world application informs ongoing improvements, enhancing the effectiveness of AI tools across different subjects and learning environments. This process helps maintain the relevance and value of AI-assisted education for both students and educators, continuously refining the approach based on actual usage and outcomes in diverse educational contexts.

8. Scaling and Expansion

Gradually expand the use of successful AI tools across more courses and departments. Scaling and Expansion in AI-assisted education involves extending the successful implementation of AI tools beyond initial pilot programs or limited deployments. This phase focuses on broadening the use of AI across more courses, departments, or even entire educational institutions. Researchers and administrators first analyze the results and lessons learned from initial implementations. They identify what worked well and what challenges were encountered, using this information to refine the AI systems and implementation strategies. The process often involves gradual expansion, perhaps starting with related subjects or similar course levels. For example, if an AI tool was successful in introductory math courses, it might be expanded to advanced math classes or introductory physics courses.

It is beyond dispute that the technical infrastructure is a key consideration. As the user base grows, systems need to be scaled to handle increased data loads and simultaneous users without compromising performance or security. Training and support systems are expanded to accommodate more educators and students. This might involve developing more comprehensive training materials, establishing peer support networks, or increasing technical support staff. Customization becomes crucial as AI tools are applied to diverse subjects and learning environments. Researchers work on adapting the AI's content, features, and interfaces to meet the specific needs of different disciplines and teaching styles. Funding and resource allocation are important aspects of scaling. Administrators need to secure additional funding, reallocate resources, or find cost-effective ways to expand the use of AI tools across the institution. Continuous monitoring and assessment remain vital during scaling. Researchers track how well the AI tools perform across different contexts and make adjustments as needed.

The ultimate goal of scaling and expansion is to maximize the benefits of AI-assisted education across the institution, improving learning outcomes and educational experiences for a broader range of students and educators. Develop best practices and guidelines for AI-enhanced formative assessment based on pilot experiences. Provide ongoing support and professional development for faculty.

9. Ethical Considerations and Data Privacy

Ethical Considerations and Data Privacy in AI-assisted education focus on ensuring responsible use of technology while protecting student and faculty information. This aspect is crucial as AI systems often collect and analyze large amounts of personal and academic data.

Researchers and administrators must address issues of data privacy, security, and consent. They establish clear policies on what data is collected, how it's used, and who has access to it. Transparency is key, with students and faculty fully informed about the AI systems' data practices.

Fairness and equity are major concerns. AI systems must be designed and implemented to avoid bias and provide equal opportunities for all students, regardless of their background or characteristics. This includes regular audits of AI algorithms to detect and correct any unintended biases. There's also a focus on maintaining the human element in education. While AI can enhance learning, it shouldn't replace human interaction and guidance. Striking the right balance between AI assistance and traditional teaching methods is essential. It is imperative to consider the following two aspects in order to conduct a strategic formative assessment of Deploy AI and thereby avoid the potential for unnecessary litigation.

- Intellectual property rights and academic integrity are considered, especially when AI systems generate content or assist with assessments. Clear guidelines are needed to define appropriate use of AI in academic work.
- Data retention and deletion policies are established, addressing how long student data is kept and ensuring the right to be forgotten. Compliance with relevant education and data protection laws is mandatory.

Ongoing ethical review processes are implemented to address new challenges as AI technology evolves. This involves input from diverse stakeholders, including educators, students, ethicists, and legal experts.

The goal is to harness the benefits of AI in education while upholding ethical standards, protecting privacy, and maintaining trust in the educational system. This approach ensures that AI enhances rather than compromises the educational experience and personal rights of students and educators.

10. Balancing AI and Human Interaction

The optimal integration of AI and human interaction in the educational context entails the identification of the most efficacious blend between technical assistance and personal, human-led instruction. It is of the utmost importance to achieve this balance in order to maintain the quality and effectiveness of education while simultaneously capitalizing on the advantages offered by AI. As Wu and Zhang (2024) observe in their article 'Applications and Implications of Generative AI in Non-STEM Disciplines in Higher Education', it is crucial to utilize AI as a supportive framework rather than as a direct replacement for human supervision and oversight in the teaching process. Educators and researchers are focused on utilizing AI as an augmentative tool, rather than as a replacement for human instruction. Artificial intelligence (AI) systems are designed to handle routine tasks, provide personalized learning experiences and offer immediate feedback, thereby enabling educators to priorities higher-level instruction, guidance and emotional support.

It is to acknowledge that the human element remains essential for the development of critical thinking, creativity, and social skills. Teachers facilitate discourse, stimulate debate, and offer contextualization that AI is currently unable to reproduce. Furthermore, they assist students in interpreting and applying the information and feedback provided by AI systems. The deployment of AI in the classroom must be approached with caution and careful consideration. To illustrate, AI may initially facilitate instruction or practice sessions, after which educators may conduct more in-depth discussions or hands-on activities.

Educators are trained in the effective incorporation of AI into their pedagogical practices, equipping them with the ability to interpret AI-generated data and utilize it to inform their teaching strategies. This approach facilitates a symbiotic relationship between AI and human teaching. The majority of social and emotional learning aspects are addressed through human interaction, with AI serving a supportive, rather than a leading, role in this domain. It is important to recognize that teachers remain the primary source of empathy, motivation and personal connection in the educational process. Maintain opportunities for peer-to-peer learning and collaborative problem-solving.

11. Customization and Localization in AI-Enhanced Formative Assessment

The implementation of AI-enhanced formative assessment in higher education necessitates careful consideration of customization and localization to ensure optimal efficacy and relevance across diverse educational contexts. This crucial aspect of the implementation framework addresses the need to tailor AI tools and methodologies to specific subject areas, learning environments, and cultural contexts.

Customization in this context refers to the adaptation of AI technologies to align with the unique requirements of different disciplines and pedagogical approaches. For instance, the assessment needs in a literature course may differ significantly from those in a computer science program. AI tools must be flexible enough to accommodate these variations, allowing for discipline-specific question types, feedback mechanisms, and assessment criteria. Moreover, customization extends to the level of individual courses, enabling instructors to modify AI-driven assessments to reflect their specific learning objectives and teaching styles.

Localization, on the other hand, encompasses the cultural and linguistic adaptations necessary for effective implementation across diverse student populations. This includes not only translating interfaces and content into local languages but also considering cultural nuances in feedback delivery, question formulation, and interpretation of student responses. For example, AI algorithms may need to be trained on region-specific datasets to accurately assess writing styles or idiomatic expressions. Additionally, localization efforts should address potential biases in AI systems, ensuring fair and equitable assessment across different cultural backgrounds.

12. Continuous Innovation and Research in AI-Enhanced Formative Assessment

The rapidly evolving field of artificial intelligence in education necessitates an ongoing commitment to innovation and research to ensure the efficacy and relevance of AI-enhanced formative assessment strategies. This critical component of the implementation framework emphasizes the importance of staying abreast of technological advancements and continuously evaluating their impact on educational outcomes. A primary focus of continuous innovation involves monitoring and integrating emerging AI technologies that have potential applications in formative assessment. This may include advancements in natural language processing, machine learning algorithms, or adaptive learning systems. Institutions should establish dedicated teams or partnerships with tech companies to explore these innovations and assess their potential for enhancing current assessment practices. For instance, developments in sentiment analysis could be leveraged to gauge student engagement and emotional responses during assessment tasks, providing valuable insights for instructors.

Equally vital is the conduct of rigorous research to evaluate the long-term impact of AI-enhanced formative assessment on learning outcomes. This research should employ mixed-method approaches, combining quantitative data on student performance with qualitative insights from stakeholders. Longitudinal studies can help identify trends and patterns in the effectiveness of AI tools over time, while controlled experiments can isolate the effects of specific AI interventions. Collaborative research initiatives between institutions can facilitate the sharing of best practices and the development of standardized methodologies for evaluating AI in education.

Moreover, institutions should foster a culture of innovation among faculty and staff, encouraging experimentation with new AI tools and pedagogical approaches. This could involve creating innovation labs, organizing hackathons, or establishing grant programs for AI-related educational research. By actively participating in the development and refinement of AI technologies, educators can ensure that these tools evolve in alignment with pedagogical needs and educational goals. Continuous innovation and research not only drive improvements in AI-enhanced formative assessment but also contribute to the broader body of knowledge in educational technology, potentially shaping the future of assessment practices in higher education.

13. Sustainability Planning

Sustainability planning is a crucial component of implementing AI-enhanced formative assessment in higher education, ensuring the long-term viability and effectiveness of these technological interventions. This aspect of the framework addresses the need for institutions to develop strategies that maintain, upgrade, and evolve their AI-driven assessment systems over time. A key element of sustainability planning is the development of a robust financial model to support ongoing operations and future enhancements. This involves allocating resources for regular software updates, hardware upgrades, and licensing renewals. Institutions must also factor in costs associated with continuous staff training, technical support, and potential expansion of AI capabilities. To mitigate financial risks, diversified funding sources should be explored, including grants, industry partnerships, and possibly revenue-generating models that leverage the institution's AI expertise.

Another critical aspect is the establishment of a scalable and adaptable technological infrastructure. This includes designing systems with modularity in mind, allowing for the seamless integration of new AI tools and the retirement of obsolete ones. Cloud-based solutions may offer advantages in terms of scalability and reduced on-premises maintenance requirements. Additionally, institutions should implement comprehensive data management strategies to ensure the longevity and usability of assessment data, which is crucial for longitudinal studies and continuous improvement of AI algorithms.

Sustainability planning must also address potential challenges such as technological obsolescence, shifts in institutional priorities, or changes in educational policies. This requires the development of contingency plans and the cultivation of a flexible organizational culture that can adapt to evolving circumstances. Regular review and update of the sustainability strategy, informed by ongoing research and stakeholder feedback, are essential to maintain alignment with institutional goals and technological advancements. By prioritizing sustainability planning, institutions can ensure that their investments in AI-enhanced formative assessment continue to yield benefits for students and educators in the long term, while remaining responsive to the dynamic landscape of educational technology.

This framework provides a comprehensive approach to implementing AI-enhanced formative assessment, addressing key aspects such as technology selection, ethical considerations, and the need for continuous refinement. It emphasizes the importance of balancing AI capabilities with human interaction and the need for customization to meet specific educational contexts.

FUTURE DIRECTIONS AND CHALLENGES

Integration of RAG and Graph RAG in AI-Enhanced Formative Assessment

Retrieval-Augmented Generation (RAG) and its extension, Graph RAG, offer promising avenues for enhancing AI-driven formative assessment systems. These approaches could address some of the limitations identified in current AI systems while opening up new possibilities for more nuanced and context-aware assessments.

RAG in Formative Assessment

RAG combines the strengths of retrieval-based and generative AI models. In the context of formative assessment, RAG could be used to:

Provide more accurate and contextually relevant feedback by retrieving information from a curated knowledge base before generating responses. Offer explanations that are grounded in authoritative sources, enhancing the credibility and educational value of the feedback. Adapt to new information and curricula changes more easily by updating the retrieval corpus without retraining the entire model.

Graph RAG for Complex Knowledge Representation

Graph RAG extends the Retrieval-Augmented Generation (RAG) concept by organizing knowledge into a graph structure. This approach offers significant benefits for formative assessment in subjects with complex, interconnected concepts, including:

- **Mapping Student Understanding:** Charting students' comprehension across related topics to identify knowledge gaps.
- **Personalized Learning Paths:** Creating individualized learning trajectories based on the structure of the knowledge graph.
- **Interdisciplinary Connections:** Facilitating connections between different disciplines to promote a holistic understanding of subjects.

By leveraging a graph-based organization of knowledge, Graph RAG enables more precise and adaptive formative assessments. This structure supports educators in tailoring instruction to meet diverse student needs, thereby enhancing overall learning outcomes.

Computational Thinking for Future Challenges

To effectively navigate the challenges and opportunities presented by advanced AI systems in education, educators and developers must embrace computational thinking methods. Computational thinking, increasingly integral to modern teaching practices, encompasses four key strategies: decomposition, pattern recognition, abstraction, and algorithm design.

Decomposition: This strategy involves breaking down complex assessment tasks into more manageable components. For instance, separating the evaluation of content knowledge from skill assessment allows for more precise and focused assessments.

- **Pattern Recognition:** Identifying recurring patterns in student responses and learning behaviors is essential for developing accurate prediction models. These models enable the customization of feedback, ensuring it meets the unique needs of each student.
- **Abstraction:** Creating models that represent knowledge domains and learning processes facilitates the development of flexible assessment systems. These systems can be tailored to the specific requirements of different disciplines, enhancing their relevance and effectiveness.
- **Algorithm Design:** Developing robust methods for navigating and retrieving information from knowledge graphs is crucial. By integrating retrieved data with content generated through Retrieval-Augmented Generation (RAG) systems, educators can adjust assessment difficulties based on student performance, providing a more adaptive learning experience.

Implementing these computational thinking strategies allows educators and developers to create more effective AI-enhanced formative assessment systems. These systems are better equipped to offer personalized learning experiences, accurate performance predictions, and adaptive feedback, thereby significantly enhancing the overall quality of education in the AI era.

Challenges and Ethical Considerations

The integration of advanced AI concepts into formative assessment presents both significant opportunities and critical challenges. Key concerns include ensuring data privacy and security, particularly when dealing with rich student information in knowledge bases and learning analytics. In addition, mitigating algorithmic bias is critical to avoid disadvantaging particular student groups and to maintain equitable assessment practices.

Balancing AI-driven assessment with human judgement is essential to maintain a holistic approach to education and avoid over-reliance on technology. This balance extends to developing transparent, explainable AI systems that allow educators and students to understand the rationale behind assessments and recommendations. In addition, ensuring that AI systems can adapt to different learning contexts and cultural backgrounds is essential for their effective implementation in diverse educational settings.

Another key challenge is managing the cognitive load for students interacting with complex AI-driven assessment systems. As these systems become more sophisticated, there's a risk that they will overwhelm students, potentially hindering rather than enhancing the learning process. Addressing these challenges is critical to the successful integration of AI in formative assessment, ensuring that the technology enhances and improves the educational experience without compromising educational integrity or student well-being.

In light of the above, the integration of RAG and Graph RAG concepts into AI-enhanced formative assessment offers promising prospects for more personalized, precise and context-sensitive learning experiences. By employing computational thinking methodologies, educators and developers can address the challenges associated with these sophisticated systems. However, it is essential to give due consideration to the ethical implications and potential shortcomings in order to guarantee that AI-enhanced formative assessment truly serves the best interests of learners and educators alike.

CONCLUSION

Integrating artificial intelligence (AI) into formative assessment marks a significant advancement in higher education. This paper examines the theoretical foundations, current applications, and future prospects of AI-enhanced formative assessment, focusing on its potential to foster inspirational learning experiences. An empirical study in accounting education demonstrates the effectiveness of AI tutors in improving student academic outcomes across various learning levels. Students showed favorable attitudes toward AI tutors, indicating broad acceptance and potential for successful implementation. However, the study also identified challenges, including implementation obstacles and the need for future enhancements.

These findings support the use of AI-enhanced formative assessment and highlight the need for further research and development. Theoretical frameworks such as Hattie and Timperley's Feedback Model and Csikszentmihalyi's concept of

"Flow" provide a foundation for understanding how AI can create more engaging and personalized learning experiences. Key strategies for implementation include real-time feedback and intervention, personalized learning pathways, and data-driven insights for educators.

Looking ahead, integrating Retrieval-Augmented Generation (RAG) and Graph RAG into AI-enhanced formative assessment holds promise for more sophisticated knowledge representation and reasoning. However, challenges like ethical considerations, data privacy concerns, and the need for digital literacy must be addressed. To maximize the benefits, a proposed implementation framework emphasizes clear educational objectives, robust data governance, and ongoing professional development for educators.

As AI continues to evolve in education, it's essential to approach its integration with both enthusiasm and caution. While embracing the opportunities these technologies offer, we must preserve the human elements of teaching and learning essential for holistic education. In conclusion, AI-enhanced formative assessment has the potential to transform higher education by creating more responsive, adaptive, and engaging learning environments. Guided by empirical research, continued exploration and refinement of these technologies can lead to learning experiences that are not only highly effective but also deeply inspirational.

REFERENCES

Attali, Y., & Arieli-Attali, M. (2015). Gamification in assessment: Do points affect test performance? *Computers & Education*, 83, 57–63. DOI: 10.1016/j.compedu.2014.12.012

Barana, A., Conte, A., Fissore, C., Marchisio, M., & Rabellino, S. (2019). Learning analytics to improve formative assessment strategies. JE-LKS. *Journal of e-learning and knowledge society, 15*(3), 75-88.

Basham, J. D., Hall, T. E., Carter, R. A.Jr, & Stahl, W. M. (2016). An operationalized understanding of personalized learning. *Journal of Special Education Technology*, 31(3), 126–136. DOI: 10.1177/0162643416660835

Bastiaens, T., Wood, L., & Reiners, T. (2014). New landscapes and new eyes: The role of virtual world design for supply chain education. *Ubiquitous Learning*, 6(1), 37–49. DOI: 10.18848/1835-9795/CGP/v06i01/40388

Black, P., & Wiliam, D. (1998). Assessment and classroom learning. *Assessment in Education: Principles, Policy & Practice*, 5(1), 7–74. DOI: 10.1080/0969595980050102

Bocala, C., & Parker Boudett, K. (2015). Teaching educators habits of mind for using data wisely. *Teachers College Record*, 117(4), 1–20. DOI: 10.1177/016146811511700409

Bulger, M. (2016). *Personalized learning: The conversations we're not having* [Working Paper]. Data & Society Research Institute. https://www.datasociety.net/pubs/ecl/PersonalizedLearning_primer_2016.pdf

Carless, D. (2007). Learning-oriented assessment: Conceptual bases and practical implications. *Innovations in Education and Teaching International*, 44(1), 57–66. DOI: 10.1080/14703290601081332

Center for Education Policy Research at Harvard University. (n.d.). *DreamBox learning achievement growth*. Retrieved from https://cepr.harvard.edu/dreambox-learning-achievement-growth

Cosyn, E., Uzun, H., Doble, C., & Matayoshi, J. (2021). A practical perspective on knowledge space theory: ALEKS and its data. *Journal of Mathematical Psychology*, 101, 102512. DOI: 10.1016/j.jmp.2021.102512

Csikszentmihalyi, M. (1990). *Flow: The psychology of optimal experience*. Harper & Row.

Datnow, A., & Hubbard, L. (2016). Teacher capacity for and beliefs about data-driven decision making: A literature review of international research. *Journal of Educational Change*, 17(1), 7–28. DOI: 10.1007/s10833-015-9264-2

Dicheva, D., Dichev, C., Agre, G., & Angelova, G. (2015). Gamification in education: A systematic mapping study. *Journal of Educational Technology & Society*, 18(3), 75–88.

Dweck, C. S. (2007). *Mindset: The new psychology of success*. Ballantine Books.

Earl, L. M. (2013). *Assessment as learning: Using classroom assessment to maximize student learning* (2nd ed.). Corwin.

Falmagne, J. C., Albert, D., Doble, C., Eppstein, D., & Hu, X. (Eds.). (2013). *Knowledge spaces: Applications in education*. Springer Science & Business Media. DOI: 10.1007/978-3-642-35329-1

Feldstein, M., & Hill, P. (2016). Personalized learning: What it really is and why it really matters. *EDUCAUSE Review*, 51(2), 24–35.

Fitzgerald, E., Kucirkova, N., Jones, A., Cross, S., Ferguson, R., Herodotou, C., Hillaire, G., & Scanlon, E. (2018). Dimensions of personalisation in technology-enhanced learning: A framework and implications for design. *British Journal of Educational Technology*, 49(1), 165–181. DOI: 10.1111/bjet.12534

Frankenberg-Garcia, A. (2020). Combining user needs, lexicographic data and digital writing environments. *Language Teaching*, 53(1), 29–43. DOI: 10.1017/S0261444818000277

Ghufron, M. A., & Rosyida, F. (2018). The role of Grammarly in assessing English as a foreign language (EFL) writing. *Lingua Cultura*, 12(4), 395–403. DOI: 10.21512/lc.v12i4.4582

Grams, D. (2018). *A quantitative study of the use of DreamBox learning and its effectiveness in improving math achievement of elementary students with math difficulties* [Doctoral dissertation, Northcentral University].

Hamari, J., Shernoff, D. J., Rowe, E., Coller, B., Asbell-Clarke, J., & Edwards, T. (2016). Challenging games help students learn: An empirical study on engagement, flow and immersion in game-based learning. *Computers in Human Behavior*, 54, 170–179. DOI: 10.1016/j.chb.2015.07.045

Hattie, J., & Timperley, H. (2007). The power of feedback. *Review of Educational Research*, 77(1), 81–112. DOI: 10.3102/003465430298487

Heffernan, N. T., & Heffernan, C. L. (2014). The ASSISTments ecosystem: Building a platform that brings scientists and teachers together for minimally invasive research on human learning and teaching. *International Journal of Artificial Intelligence in Education*, 24(4), 470–497. DOI: 10.1007/s40593-014-0024-x

Holmes, W., Bialik, M., & Fadel, C. (2019). *Artificial intelligence in education: Promises and implications for teaching and learning*. Center for Curriculum Redesign.

Howlin, C., & Lynch, D. (2014). A framework for the delivery of personalized adaptive content. In *2014 International Conference on Web and Open Access to Learning (ICWOAL)* (pp. 1-5). DOI: 10.1109/ICWOAL.2014.7009203

Ifenthaler, D., Eseryel, D., & Ge, X. (2012). Assessment for game-based learning. In *Assessment in game-based learning: Foundations, innovations, and perspectives* (pp. 1–8). Springer New York. DOI: 10.1007/978-1-4614-3546-4_1

Kluger, A. N., & DeNisi, A. (1996). The effects of feedback interventions on performance: A historical review, a meta-analysis, and a preliminary feedback intervention theory. *Psychological Bulletin*, 119(2), 254–284. DOI: 10.1037/0033-2909.119.2.254

Knewton. (2024). Knewton Alta adaptive learning. Wiley. https://www.wiley.com/en us/education/alta

Kocadere, S. A., & Çağlar, Ş. (2018). Gamification from player type perspective: A case study. *Journal of Educational Technology & Society*, 21(3), 12–22.

Koedinger, K. R., & Corbett, A. (2005). Cognitive Tutors: Technology bringing learning sciences to the classroom. In Sawyer, R. K. (Ed.), *The Cambridge Handbook of the Learning Sciences* (pp. 61–78). Cambridge University Press., DOI: 10.1017/CBO9780511816833.006

Luckin, R., Holmes, W., Griffiths, M., & Forcier, L. B. (2016). *Intelligence unleashed: An argument for AI in Education.* Pearson.

Makransky, G., Bonde, M. T., Wulff, J. S., Wandall, J., Hood, M., Creed, P. A., & Nørremølle, A. (2016). Simulation based virtual learning environment in medical genetics counseling: An example of bridging the gap between theory and practice in medical education. *BMC Medical Education*, 16(1), 98. Advance online publication. DOI: 10.1186/s12909-016-0620-6 PMID: 27012245

Makransky, G., Terkildsen, T. S., & Mayer, R. E. (2019). Adding immersive virtual reality to a science lab simulation causes more presence but less learning. *Learning and Instruction*, 60, 225–236. DOI: 10.1016/j.learninstruc.2017.12.007

Mandinach, E. B., & Gummer, E. S. (2016). *Data literacy for educators: Making it count in teacher preparation and practice*. Teachers College Press.

Marsh, J. A., Bertrand, M., & Huguet, A. (2015). Using data to alter instructional practice: The mediating role of coaches and professional learning communities. *Teachers College Record*, 117(4), 1–40. DOI: 10.1177/016146811511700411

Merchant, Z., Goetz, E. T., Cifuentes, L., Keeney-Kennicutt, W., & Davis, T. J. (2014). Effectiveness of virtual reality-based instruction on students' learning outcomes in K-12 and higher education: A meta-analysis. *Computers & Education*, 70, 29–40. DOI: 10.1016/j.compedu.2013.07.033

Netcoh, S. (2017). Balancing freedom and limitations: A case study of choice provision in a personalized learning class. *Teaching and Teacher Education*, 66, 383–392. DOI: 10.1016/j.tate.2017.05.010

Pane, J. F., Steiner, E. D., Baird, M. D., & Hamilton, L. S. (2015). *Continued Progress: Promising Evidence on Personalized Learning*. RAND Corporation. DOI: 10.7249/RR1365

Reich, J., & Ito, M. (2017). *From good intentions to real outcomes: Equity by design in learning technologies*. Digital Media and Learning Research Hub.

Ritter, S., Anderson, J. R., Koedinger, K. R., & Corbett, A. (2007). Cognitive Tutor: Applied research in mathematics education. *Psychonomic Bulletin & Review*, 14(2), 249–255. DOI: 10.3758/BF03194060 PMID: 17694909

Roberts-Mahoney, H., Means, A. J., & Garrison, M. J. (2016). Netflixing human capital development: Personalized learning technology and the corporatization of K-12 education. *Journal of Education Policy*, 31(4), 405–420. DOI: 10.1080/02680939.2015.1132774

Ryan, R. M., & Deci, E. L. (2000). Self-determination theory and the facilitation of intrinsic motivation, social development, and well-being. *The American Psychologist*, 55(1), 68–78. DOI: 10.1037/0003-066X.55.1.68 PMID: 11392867

Sadler, D. R. (1989). Formative assessment and the design of instructional systems. *Instructional Science*, 18(2), 119–144. DOI: 10.1007/BF00117714

Schildkamp, K., Poortman, C. L., & Handelzalts, A. (2016). Data teams for school improvement. *School Effectiveness and School Improvement*, 27(2), 228–254. DOI: 10.1080/09243453.2015.1056192

Schildkamp, K., Poortman, C. L., Luyten, H., & Ebbeler, J. (2017). Factors promoting and hindering data-based decision making in schools. *School Effectiveness and School Improvement*, 28(2), 242–258. DOI: 10.1080/09243453.2016.1256901

Selwyn, N. (2019). Should robots replace teachers? AI and the future of education. *Polity*.

Shute, V. J. (2008). Focus on formative feedback. *Review of Educational Research*, 78(1), 153–189. DOI: 10.3102/0034654307313795

Shute, V. J., & Ventura, M. (2013). *Stealth assessment: Measuring and supporting learning in video games*. MIT Press. DOI: 10.7551/mitpress/9589.001.0001

Tsai, C. W., & Fan, Y. T. (2013). Research trends in game-based learning research in online learning environments: A review of studies published in SSCI-indexed journals from 2003 to 2012. *British Journal of Educational Technology*, 44(5), E115–E119. DOI: 10.1111/bjet.12031

Vesselinov, R., & Grego, J. (2012). *Duolingo effectiveness study: Final report.* https://theowlapp.health/wp-content/uploads/2022/04/DuolingoReport_Final-1.pdf

Wang, A. I., & Tahir, R. (2020). The effect of using Kahoot! for learning–A literature review. *Computers & Education*, 149, 103818. DOI: 10.1016/j.compedu.2020.103818

Wiliam, D. (2011). *Embedded formative assessment.* Solution tree press.

Williamson, B. (2017). Big data in education: The digital future of learning, policy and practice. *Sage (Atlanta, Ga.)*. Advance online publication. DOI: 10.4135/9781529714920

Winkler, R., & Söllner, M. (2018). Unleashing the potential of chatbots in education: A state of-the-art analysis. In *Academy of Management Annual Meeting Proceedings* (Vol. 2018, No. 1). DOI: 10.5465/AMBPP.2018.15903abstract

Wu, T., & Chang, M. (2021, December). The Cloud-Based Textbook: From Choice to Advantage. In *2021 IEEE International Conference on Engineering, Technology & Education (TALE)* (pp. 01-08). IEEE. DOI: 10.1109/TALE52509.2021.9678553

Wu, T., & Zhang, S. h. (2024). Applications and Implication of Generative AI in Non-STEM Disciplines in Higher Education. In F. Zhao & D. Miao (Eds.), *AI-generated Content. AIGC 2023. Communications in Computer and Information Science,* (vol. 1946, pp. 341 349). Springer, Singapore. DOI: 10.1007/978-981-99-7587-7_29

Chapter 9
Exploring Generative Artificial Intellegence (AI) Impact on Assessment and Evaluation in Management Education: A Critical Review

Mohd Rushidi Mohd Amin
INTI International University, Malaysia

Vinesh Maran Sivakumaran
INTI International College, Malaysia

Gan Kia Hui
https://orcid.org/0000-0002-9245-3386
INTI International College, Malaysia

Sheila Rose Darmaraj
https://orcid.org/0009-0004-6921-9884
INTI International College, Malaysia

Wong Chee Hoo
INTI International University, Malaysia

Lim Kim Yew
https://orcid.org/0009-0009-7090-9213
INTI International University, Malaysia

ABSTRACT

ChatGPT has emerged as a topic of considerable discourse within management education in recent weeks, owing to its profound transformative potential in reshaping the paradigms of assessment methodology and evaluation. Unlike conventional educational technologies, which typically leave discernible traces of usage, ChatGPT boasts an unparalleled capacity for evading detection during its application. This characteristic engenders a multifaceted quandary for educators in the field of management education, who aspire to harness this technology to remain pertinent in the evolving educational landscape while preserving the principles of authentic and

DOI: 10.4018/979-8-3693-6351-5.ch009

meaningful learning experiences. Management educators' expeditious formulation and implementation of policies integrating ChatGPT and its succeeding iterations of generative artificial intelligence has become an imperative task. The accessibility and cost-effectiveness inherent to these technologies further accentuate the urgency of such policy development.

1. INTRODUCTION

In recent years, there has been a discernible and substantial surge in the widespread application of Artificial Intelligence (AI) across diverse industries. This surge is particularly evident within the context of education, where AI is being increasingly acknowledged as a transformative force that has the potential to reshape and redefine pedagogical practices (Adiguzel et al., 2023). This phenomenon is attributed to AI's innate capacity to effectively address some of the most intricate and pressing challenges in the educational landscape. The transformative potential of AI in education is rooted in foundational theories of intelligence and machine learning. The theoretical groundwork for AI was first laid by Turing (1950), who explored the concept of machine intelligence. Further, Bloom (1956) established crucial principles for understanding educational objectives and assessing learning outcomes, which have since influenced AI-based educational tools. In addition, Vygotsky et al., (1978) social learning theories have been instrumental in developing AI-driven personalized learning environments.

Within the context of education, AI is emerging as a potent solution that holds promise in personalized learning, immediate feedback provision, and data-driven decision-making (Alam & Mohanty, 2022; Chu et al., 2022) This discernible shift in pedagogical paradigms is underscored by the observations made by Hwang et al., (2022), who expound upon AI's pedagogical orientation that pivots around tailoring instructional methodologies to cater to the unique needs and proclivities of individual learners. This personalization extends to providing targeted feedback to rectify specific areas of knowledge lacunae. Such transformative potentials of AI in fostering bespoke educational experiences have garnered substantial attention and enthusiasm from researchers and practitioners alike (Almusaed et al., 2023).

Numerous studies have provided empirical evidence of AI's catalytic role in encouraging the adoption and assimilation of diverse learning methodologies (Chen et al., 2022; Luan et al., 2020; Pan et al., 2022). These studies collectively paint a vivid picture of AI's far-reaching impact on pedagogical practices, elucidating its potential to usher in a profound revolution in the educational milieu. By adapting to diverse instructional approaches, AI amplifies the efficiency and efficacy of educational processes, thereby instigating a paradigmatic shift in the conventional notions of teaching and learning. Furthermore, AI's transformative role extends beyond instructional dynamics and permeates administrative facets. Recent studies by Păvăloaia and Necula (2023) have accentuated AI's capacity to streamline administrative operations within educational institutions. This encompasses automating routine tasks, facilitating grading, and undertaking meticulous analyses of voluminous datasets. The education sector must continuously adapt to emerging tools and methodologies as technology evolves rapidly. AI in education brings significant benefits, such as personalized learning, and challenges, including concerns over equity, privacy, and the potential for over-reliance on automation. Therefore, staying abreast of technological advancements is crucial for educators and policymakers to ensure AI's positive impact on the learning environment (Goksel & Bozkurt, 2019).

Globally, the integration of AI in education has accelerated significantly. In the United States, AI is increasingly used for personalized learning and AI-driven assessments, as seen in Arizona State University, which employs AI-based learning systems (George & Wooden, 2023). In China, AI is revolutionizing large-scale assessments and adaptive learning environments, while European countries focus on using AI for efficient grading and administrative tasks (Chen et al., 2020). Emerging economies like India are adopting AI in remote and underserved regions to bridge the digital divide (Gabriel, 2024). These global trends underscore the critical role of AI in transforming education worldwide.

2. THE ADVENT OF AI IN MANAGEMENT EDUCATION

Implementing AI into education has opened new horizons for learning and pedagogy. AI has enabled personalized and adaptive learning experiences in management education, transforming the traditional one-size-fits-all approach (Pendy, 2023). Integrating AI into educational frameworks aligns with earlier theories of intelligence and adaptability in educational systems. For instance, Gardner (1983) theory of multiple intelligences provides a theoretical basis for adaptive learning, which tailors instruction to different learners. Moreover, Papert (1980) early work on constructionism emphasized the role of technology in fostering individualized learning experiences, laying the groundwork for current AI applications. By leveraging data-driven insights, AI systems can identify individual learning preferences, strengths, and improvement areas. This tailored approach ensures that students receive targeted support, enhancing their comprehension and retention of management concepts (Jafar et al., 2023).

2.1 Realistic Simulations and Scenarios

Bewersdorff et al., (2023) mentioned that generative AI is a transformative force in education, particularly in assessments. These AI-driven simulations have redefined the learning experience by creating virtual environments closely mimicking the complexity of real-world managerial challenges. Using simulations as a pedagogical tool has its roots in experiential learning theories, such as Kolb (1984) experiential learning cycle, which posits that learning is most effective when students engage in direct experience followed by reflection. This approach is now enhanced through AI's ability to create dynamic, real-world scenarios for learners to engage in critical thinking and problem-solving. In doing so, they offer students a platform to translate theoretical insights into practical applications and navigate the complexities within these simulated contexts. Harvard Business School's 'HBX Live' platform exemplifies the integration of AI-driven simulations in management education, facilitating a dynamic learning environment that mirrors real-world business challenges. These simulations enhance students' decision-making and critical thinking skills by allowing them to engage in realistic scenarios without the associated risks of actual business operations (Hsu & Wu, 2023).

This innovative approach fosters dynamic cognitive synergy, honing critical thinking skills and refining decision-making acumen (Lakshman & Gonzalez, 2023). Consequently, the assessments conducted within such an ecosystem authentically holistically mirror students' competencies. By effectively bridging the gap between theoretical knowledge and experiential learning, Generative AI simulations elevate the pedagogical landscape (Jeon & Lee, 2023). The technology's remarkable capacity to discern patterns and anticipate plausible scenarios is harnessed to replicate diverse variables and contingencies in real-world scenarios. This enables learners to engage in hands-on learning while cultivating adaptability and resilience in the face of unforeseen challenges (Budhwar et al., 2023). Beyond mere assessment, these simulations fundamentally reshape the educational paradigm by gauging rote knowledge and the capacity to adeptly navigate the complexity of practical situations.

Integrating Generative AI-powered simulations in educational assessments offers a pioneering methodology that enriches students' learning journeys (Akter et al., 2023). The merging of theoretical knowledge with real-world application underpins a transformative pedagogical model, fostering a comprehensive understanding of complex challenges and augmenting students' critical thinking and decision-making abilities (Anshari & Hamdan, 2022). As the educational landscape continues to evolve, the role of Generative AI in assessments propels learning into a new era of dynamic and holistic evaluation.

2.2 Enhanced Collaboration

Rajaram (2023) stated that the proficient discernment and strategic alignment of diverse skill sets and personalities constitute a foundational pillar within collaborative learning, where Artificial Intelligence (AI) emerges as a pivotal facilitator. AI's capability to decipher intricate nuances and delineate complementary attributes among individuals is tantamount to orchestrating a harmonious symphony of talents. Through the artful curation of teams, AI imparts a heightened layer of synergy into the intricate fabric of group dynamics and amplifies the collective efficacy of collaborative endeavors (Olan et al., 2022). This comprehensive orchestration of talent underscores AI's potential to propel collaborative learning to unprecedented heights of excellence. In this orchestrated convergence of cognitive proficiencies and interpersonal dispositions, AI assumes the role of an astute conductor, orchestrating harmonious ensembles richly diversified in composition (Demetroulis et al., 2023).

By harnessing data-driven insights into team members' strengths, weaknesses, and proclivities, AI engenders configurations poised to yield optimal outcomes. These meticulously assembled teams are akin to a mosaic, where each unique piece contributes to the overarching collective without undermining the distinctiveness of each constituent (Fügener et al., 2022; Khetarpal et al., 2022). This orchestration magnifies the collective prowess and cultivates an environment that fosters the cross-pollination of ideas, perspectives, and approaches, thereby encapsulating the true essence of collaborative learning. The symbiotic amalgamation of AI and collaborative learning ushers in a paradigmatic shift that accentuates the harmonization of talents and promotes cross-disciplinary fertilization. It amplifies the potency of collective efforts, as demonstrated by Jantzen et al., (2022). The orchestration of diverse skill sets and personalities under the discerning gaze of AI culminates in teams that are not only synergistically aligned but also poised for innovation and growth. Concurrently, AI's subtle but pervasive vigilance introduces a dimension of proactive refinement, elevating collaborative learning to a realm of greater precision and efficacy (Ajgaonkar et al., 2022). As the educational landscape evolves, integrating AI into collaborative learning promises to shape a more nuanced, responsive, and transformative educational ecosystem.

2.3 Reducing Bias in Assessment

Hallmark of AI lies in its inherent potential to address and mitigate biases that often pose challenges within the assessment process, a concept supported by the foundational work of Tversky and Kahneman (1974) on cognitive biases on implicit bias detection. The deployment of AI in educational contexts introduces a transformative approach toward cultivating fairness and objectivity, thus elevating the evaluation of student performance to a higher echelon of integrity and equitability. By streamlining the assessment mechanisms and recalibrating traditional methodologies, AI serves as a stalwart advocate of impartiality, setting forth a trajectory where each student's capabilities are measured without undue influence from extraneous factors (Chan, 2023).

The potency of AI's role in ameliorating biases within educational assessments is evidenced by its capacity to engender standardized evaluation protocols. Wang et al., (2023) stated that these protocols, rooted in data-driven insights and algorithmic rigor, transcend the subjective tendencies that can inadvertently infiltrate traditional grading systems. By meticulously analyzing diverse data points, AI distills an objective panorama of student performance, thereby minimizing the potential for prejudiced evaluations based on race, gender, socioeconomic background, or other extraneous considerations (Zhou et al., 2022). This recalibration of assessment frameworks aligns with the foundational principles of equity and inclusivity, paving the way for a level playing field where each student's accomplishments are appraised uniformly and unbiasedly (Battista et al., 2022). Integrating AI within educational assessment underscores its pivotal role as a harbinger of fairness and impartiality. Through standardized evaluations, recalibrated grading methodologies, and reduced subjectivity, AI champions the cause of equitable evaluation, upholding a fundamental tenet of the educational process as stated by Kaminska et al., (2023). As educators and institutions continue to navigate the complexities of assessment, the interplay between AI and fairness is a testament to the potential for technology to enhance the integrity and equitability of evaluating students' performance.

2.4 Continuous and Multimodal Assessment

The expansive scope of Artificial Intelligence's (AI) analytical prowess has precipitated a significant paradigm shift within the educational landscape (Ahmad, 2019). The evolution towards continuous assessment exemplifies this shift, a dynamic approach that harnesses AI's capabilities, rooted in Dewey (1938) work on continuous learning and Vygotsky et al., (1978) theory of social learning. According to Spiker et al., (2023), this transformative shift is underpinned by AI's capacity to diligently monitor and assess students' learning trajectories, enabling educators to identify and address potential challenges preemptively, ultimately fostering an uninterrupted and evolving learning continuum. This comprehensive view, afforded by AI's analytical prowess, equips educators with a holistic understanding of each student's learning journey, facilitating timely interventions that can provide targeted support to those struggling or requiring additional guidance (Irfan et al., 2023). AI transforms assessment into a dynamic tool for instructional refinement and individualized learning enhancement by enabling educators to identify roadblocks and offer personalized assistance.

Integrating AI within continuous assessment heralds a transformative era in education (Hashim et al., 2023). AI's analytical prowess allows for the dynamic tracking of students' progress, leading to proactive interventions and a seamless learning continuum. By embracing a spectrum of media forms, AI-driven assessments encapsulate a holistic evaluation encompassing various dimensions of students' competencies (Kim et al., 2022). Arizona State University's (ASU) implementation of an AI-based learning management system (LMS) exemplifies the transformative potential of artificial intelligence in education. This system facilitates continuous assessments and utilizes data analytics to monitor student progress, providing personalized feedback tailored to individual learning patterns (George & Wooden, 2023). Such real-time feedback mechanisms enable students to promptly identify and address learning gaps, which has been linked to improved retention rates and enhanced academic performance (Roshanaei et al., 2023). As educational methodologies evolve, the amalgamation of AI and Assessment ushers in a future where personalized learning, continuous growth, and comprehensive evaluation converge to redefine the contours of education.

2.5 Automated Grading and Evaluation

Conventional educational assessments have historically relied on labor-intensive and time-consuming manual grading processes. However, technological advancements, particularly integrating AI-driven tools like ChatGPT, have significantly departed from these traditional practices (Kamalov et al., 2023). The automated grading capabilities of ChatGPT stand as a notable manifestation of this transformation, drawing parallels with Taylor (1911) principles of scientific management that emphasized efficiency and standardization. This transformation offers expeditious and standardized assessment procedures that have profound implications for educators and learners alike (Jurāne-Brēmane, 2023). For example, Stanford University's implementation of an AI-assisted grading system exemplifies the transformative potential of machine learning in educational settings, particularly for large classes in computer science. This system effectively grades thousands of assignments with high accuracy, significantly alleviating the grading workload for instructors while providing students with prompt and unbiased feedback. Machine learning algorithms have been shown to enhance grading efficiency and accuracy in various educational contexts (Korchi et al., 2023).

The efficacy of AI, such as ChatGPT's automated grading functionalities, lies in its capacity to swiftly evaluate a myriad of assessments without compromising the quality of evaluation. This technology's inherent ability to process and analyze vast quantities of content within moments significantly reduces the time educators would otherwise spend on manual grading (Kamalov et al., 2023). This temporal efficiency translates into more expedient feedback loops, granting learners the benefit of timely insights into their performance and facilitating the implementation of corrective measures. This technological innovation not only streamlines the workflow of educators but also enhances the credibility of assessment outcomes by minimizing potential human-related discrepancies (Stige et al., 2023; Xin et al., 2022). The integration of AI-driven automated grading, exemplified by ChatGPT, introduces a transformative dimension to educational assessment. This paradigm shift transcends traditional manual grading constraints, providing educators with a powerful tool to expedite the evaluation process and eliminate human bias (Pavaloaia & Necula, 2023). As educational systems evolve to embrace technological advancements, the adoption of automated grading technologies like ChatGPT paves the way for more efficient, impartial, and equitable evaluation practices that resonate with the changing dynamics of contemporary education, as illustrated in Figure 1.

Figure 1. The nexus of AI initiations in management education

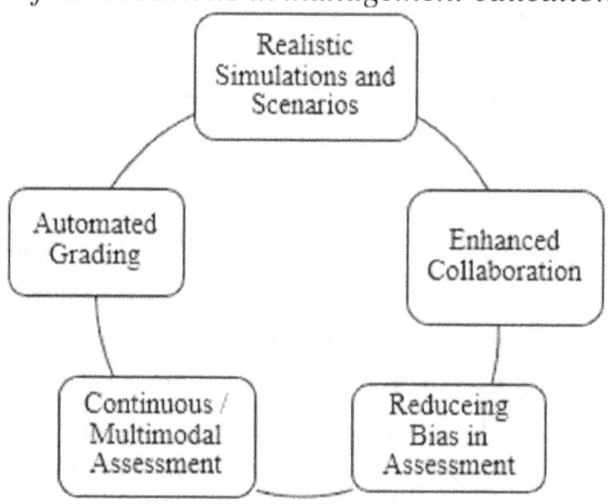

Source: Author's owm

3. CHATGPT AS A TECHNOLOGY ENABLER

ChatGPT, a user-friendly technological innovation, is transforming the conventional approach to researching solutions (Ray, 2023), aligning with Schumpeter (1942) concept of 'creative destruction' where disruptive technologies redefine industries. Presently, discerning between computer-generated and human-authored textual content poses a challenge for educators in the field of management. This dynamic is anticipated to persist as an ongoing contest between plagiarism detection tools and AI applications like ChatGPT, vying for technological supremacy, as stated by Holmes and Tuomi (2022). Personalized learning, instant feedback, scalability, 24/7 availability, customized assessments, and learning analytics based on data are among the prominent features of ChatGPT that could contribute significantly to the overall context of education.

3.1 Personalized Learning and Feedback

ChatGPT can provide personalized learning experiences by interacting with students conversationally (Nikolic et al., 2023). It can adapt to individual learning styles and paces, offering explanations, answering questions, and providing feedback on assignments and assessments. This personalized approach can help students better understand concepts and improve performance (Kasneci et al., 2023). One of the most tantalizing prospects ushered in by Generative AI is the advent of tailored learning journeys. Fortes (2020) stated that AI algorithms can meticulously curate personalized assessment trajectories by parsing through students' strengths, weaknesses, and learning proclivities. This bespoke approach not only nurtures self-directed learning but also nurtures a symbiotic engagement. With AI, assessment items can be tailored to individual students, ensuring the questions resonate with their learning journey (Alneyadi & Wardat, 2023). ChatGPT can generate diverse assessment items based on learning profiles, catering to various cognitive levels and learning styles. This customization enhances the authenticity and relevance of assessments.

3.2 Instant Feedback

ChatGPT can offer immediate feedback on assignments, quizzes, and exams. Students no longer need to wait for teachers to grade their work, accelerating learning (Wang et al., 2023). This quick feedback loop allows students to identify their mistakes and misconceptions sooner, leading to faster learning and improvement. Sugai and Horner (2009) mentioned that the real-time feedback ecosystem engendered by AI-powered systems is poised to be a game-changer. The instantaneous evaluations offered for assignments, presentations, and projects unravel a tapestry of educational insights for students. This iterative feedback loop facilitates a deeper understanding of one's mistakes, enabling corrective actions and fostering an incremental learning paradigm that benefits students and instructors (Poorthuis & Dijk, 2020). ChatGPT's conversational capabilities enable it to provide real-time feedback to students during assessments. Through natural language interactions, students can seek clarification on questions, enhancing their understanding of complex topics (Vilà et al., 2019). Moreover, this real-time feedback mechanism fosters a sense of continuous learning and engagement.

3.3 Scalability

Implementing automated assessment utilizing ChatGPT introduces an extraordinary advancement with its inherent scalability, significantly reshaping the landscape of academic evaluation (Mizumoto & Eguchi, 2023). This transformative approach addresses the challenges posed by the surge in online learning, particularly in contexts like massive open online courses (MOOCs) and expansive classrooms, as stated by Amit et al., (2022). For example, Georgia Tech's MOOC platform represents a significant effort in higher education by offering an online AI-driven master's degree. This initiative utilizes an AI system named 'Jill Watson,' a virtual teaching assistant for many students. By automating routine inquiries and grading tasks, Jill Watson enhances the scalability of course offerings while maintaining educational quality. The integration of AI in educational settings has been shown to improve assessment efficiency and provide timely feedback, which is crucial for large-scale online learning environments (Karadag, 2023). This technology alleviates the traditional bottlenecks associated with manual grading by seamlessly handling a substantial volume of student submissions simultaneously. This expedites the evaluation process and ensures prompt feedback, a pivotal element in learning (Azaria et al., 2023).

The streamlined assessment workflow enables educators to focus their expertise on fostering deeper engagement and interactive teaching methods, thus enhancing the overall quality of education (Ruiz-Rojas et al., 2023). The synergy between automated assessment and educational expertise is pivotal in this paradigm shift. As automation takes over routine assessment tasks, educators are unburdened from time-consuming grading, enabling them to concentrate on higher-order educational activities (Geigle, 2018; Hénard & Roseveare, 2012). This includes personalized student guidance, thought-provoking discussions, and the creation of innovative teaching materials that cater to diverse learning styles. Such an enriched approach imparts subject knowledge and nurtures students' critical thinking and collaborative skills. Moreover, Kasneci et al., (2023) asserted that the scalability of automated assessment not only meets the demands of modern education but also empowers educators to play a more impactful role in shaping the intellectual growth of their students, ultimately fostering a more dynamic and interactive learning environment.

3.4 24/7 Availability

ChatGPT is an invaluable asset in modern academia, offering unwavering support and comprehensive assessment feedback that transcends the confines of time (Lee, 2023). This feature proves especially advantageous for students who thrive in unconventional study hours or navigate the complexities of different global time zones. By embodying the persona of a virtual tutor or mentor, ChatGPT redefines the education landscape, rendering it more accessible and adaptable than ever before as indicated by Dai et al., (2023). In a world where traditional temporal boundaries are fading, ChatGPT's perpetual availability resonates profoundly. Students seeking knowledge during late hours or early mornings find ChatGPT a reliable companion, engaging in insightful discussions, addressing queries, and evaluating assignments (Michel-villarreal et al., 2023).

Moreover, the platform erases the constraints imposed by geographic locations or physical limitations, ensuring that quality guidance and support are universally attainable, as Peters et al. (2023) asserted. This fosters a new dimension of inclusivity in education, aligning with the principles of equitable learning. However, beyond its temporal advantages, ChatGPT's dynamic nature mirrors the evolving education (Alshahrani, 2023). As pedagogical approaches and content continue to advance, the virtual mentor seamlessly integrates these changes, ensuring students receive the latest insights. Mogavi et al., (2023) stated that this perpetual evolution, combined with the availability of feedback on demand, nurtures proactive learning, pushing students to explore beyond conventional study hours. ChatGPT's round-the-clock assistance and assessment feedback cater to diverse preferences and global circumstances, paving the way for a more inclusive, flexible, and forward-looking educational experience.

3.5 Customized Assessments

ChatGPT is a powerful tool capable of producing highly personalized assessments intricately woven into academic curricula and overarching learning objectives (Naidu & Sevnarayan, 2023). This empowers educators to meticulously tailor quizzes, assignments, and simulated exams, harmonizing them with their pedagogical intentions and distinctive teaching methodologies. In doing so, this approach personalizes the learning experience for each student and elevates the precision of evaluations, shedding light on students' intellectual grasp and practical proficiencies (Wardat et al., 2023). By discerning specific strengths and areas that may require further attention, instructors are strategically poised to adapt and refine their teaching methods, thus enhancing their students' overall comprehension and knowledge retention, as stated by Gill and Kaur (2023). This seamless fusion of curriculum and assessment not only imparts coherence to the learning journey but also equips educators with the means to provide adaptive, tailored instruction that nurtures the development of well-rounded, adept learners. As a result, education transcends traditional boundaries, embracing a dynamic realm where technology and pedagogy converge to enrich the learning experience and cultivate a generation of capable, adaptable individuals (Bitzenbauer, 2023).

3.6 Learning Analytics and Data-Driven Insights

Kostka and Toncelli (2023) stated that the meticulous examination and systematic interpretation of data originating from student engagements with ChatGPT present a wealth of opportunities for educators aiming to delve into the intricate nuances of learning dynamics. This invaluable data repository can unravel discernible patterns in learning behaviors, pinpoint areas of formidable challenge, and unearth common misconceptions that might otherwise remain enigmatic (Dwivedi et al., 2023; Su et al., 2023). Embracing a methodology underpinned by this data-driven approach not only equips educators with valuable insights but also offers them a structured framework to craft pedagogical strategies that are not only aligned with overarching educational goals but also exquisitely tailored to the unique learning trajectories of each student, as mentioned by Tourni et al., (2023). This empirical methodology also ushers in integrating AI-amplified assessment tools, elevating the educational landscape to new dimensions.

The resultant panorama of comprehensive learning analytics sheds light on students' strengths and areas needing enhancement, thereby serving as a dynamic compass for educators (Latif et al., 2023). This empirical foundation empowers educators to proactively recalibrate their teaching methodologies in response to emerging learning patterns and challenges, ensuring a learning journey that remains adaptive, effective, and engaging (Eager & Brunton, 2023; Lo, 2023). The confluence of student-interaction data analysis, AI-fueled evaluation instruments, and responsive pedagogical strategies thus ushers in an educational paradigm where learners' needs are not only comprehensively understood but also rapidly addressed, cultivating an environment where growth, exploration, and transformation naturally thrive, as shown in Figure 2.

Figure 2. Technology enabler for ChatGPT.

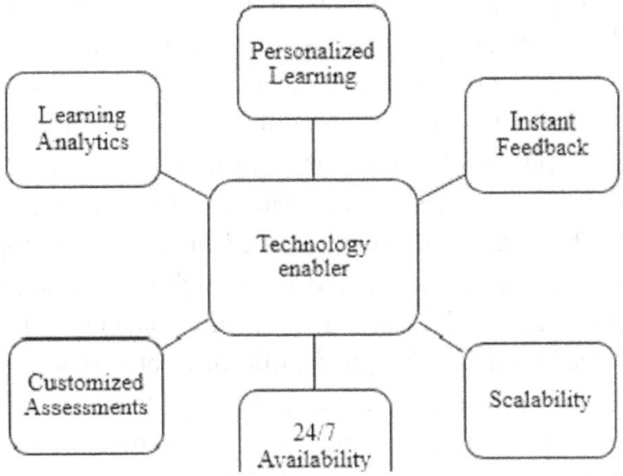

Source: Author's own

4. STRATEGIES OF CHATGPT USAGE FOR ASSESSMENT AND EVALUATION IN AI-ENHANCED MANAGEMENT EDUCATION

The transformative potential of AI in education is profound, particularly in the context of assessment and evaluation. AI's ability to tailor assessments to individual learners, enhance efficiency, and leverage data-driven insights can revolutionize traditional learning paradigms (Chhillar & Aguilera, 2022; Moradi & Dass, 2022). AI's objectivity is another crucial asset. Unlike human evaluators who may introduce bias, AI assesses learners impartially, fostering equitable evaluation. Furthermore, Palladino (2023) stated that this unbiased approach bolsters assessment credibility and promotes inclusivity. Beyond individual assessments, AI's data analysis capabilities can inform institutional decisions, leveraging performance data to enhance curriculum design, allocate resources effectively, and implement targeted interventions (Luckin et al., 2022; Saaida, 2023). As AI integrates with education, it propels toward evidence-based practices and innovative pedagogies, reshaping the educational landscape.

4.1 Adaptive Testing

Adaptive testing is an educational assessment approach known for its remarkable dynamism. It operates by intricately tailoring the intricacy of posed questions to seamlessly align with the individualized skill level exhibited by each student (Flores et al., 2022; Fung et al., 2022). This cutting-edge methodology utilizes AI-powered systems, meticulously scrutinizing and assimilating a comprehensive spectrum of data from a student's preceding responses. According to Amer-Yahia (2022), this rich pool of information serves as the foundation for the subsequent orchestration of a meticulously calibrated sequence of inquiries. This pivotal adjustment ensures that the learning experience remains consistently engaging, as the student is continuously presented with challenges that resonate with their advancing proficiencies. The multifaceted advantages of this personalized and fine-tuned approach are truly noteworthy (Hsiao & Chang, 2023). It yields a highly accurate and nuanced appraisal of a student's capabilities and harnesses the innate human drive for growth and achievement. Maintaining a delicate equilibrium between a stimulating level of challenge and the student's ongoing learning journey nurtures an educational ambiance that fosters progressive development and underscores the value of resilience and the pursuit of excellence (Hashimy et al., 2023).

4.2 Automated Assessment Scoring

Artificial intelligence's remarkable capabilities in natural language processing have paved the way for its adeptness in evaluating various forms of written communication (Dergaa et al., 2023; Lesage et al., 2023). According to Crawford et al., (2023), looking into a multifaceted assessment encompassing not only grammatical accuracy but also lexical richness, cohesiveness in argumentation, and pertinence to the given topic, AI emerges as an invaluable tool capable of furnishing consistent and expeditious feedback to students seeking to enhance their writing skills. In educational settings, particularly those characterized by sizable class enrollments, the significance of such AI-driven evaluation becomes even more pronounced. Ishaq et al., (2023) and Rusmiyanto et al., (2023) stated that the traditional method of manually grading essays, though an essential pedagogical practice, can undeniably consume a substantial amount of time, mainly when applied to a large cohort of students. Moreover, the subjective nature inherent in human assessment introduces an element of variability that could influence the grading outcome. In this context, the integration of AI's evaluative prowess significantly streamlines the feedback loop. It accelerates the feedback dissemination process and offers objectivity that minimizes variability (Javaid et al., 2023). Students can benefit from rapid, constructive insights into their writing style and its alignment with the stipulated requirements, facilitating a more efficient learning process. To encapsulate, the marriage of AI's natural language processing capabilities with the task of assessing written assignments not only expedites the feedback mechanism but also enhances the overall quality of evaluation in academic settings, especially within the parameters of extensive classes where conventional manual grading might prove to be both labor-intensive and potentially susceptible to inconsistencies (Ouyang et al., 2023).

4.3 Language Proficiency Evaluation

In the context of modern education, a transformative wave driven by Artificial Intelligence is reshaping the assessment of language proficiency. This groundbreaking approach involves AI meticulously evaluating students' spoken and written responses (Chen et al., 2022; Haleem et al., 2022). Through the adept use of sophisticated language models, AI delves into various aspects such as pronunciation, grammar, vocabulary, and overall fluency, ushering in a markedly interactive evaluation process compared to the traditional static nature of written exams (Sims, 2023). This innovation authentically mirrors real-world language usage and communication patterns. This shift from conventional written assessments to AI-powered evaluations marks a departure from the rigidity of one-size-fits-all testing (Rusmiyanto et al., 2023). AI's dynamic, real-time assessment offers a true-to-life representation of language in action, providing an immersive experience that reflects how language functions in practical contexts. In this transformative landscape, AI assumes a role beyond mere evaluation; it transforms into a mentor guiding students to refine their language skills harmoniously with contemporary communication demands (Hutson & Plate, 2023). As AI and language assessment converge, they propel us into an era where language proficiency flourishes through data-driven insights and genuine, real-world applicability.

4.4 Emotion and Engagement Monitoring

The domain of AI technology showcases a genuinely remarkable and cutting-edge capacity as it delves into the intricate nuances of online educational landscapes where students engage in virtual classes. This sophisticated AI framework, with its intricate algorithms and perceptive algorithms, embarks on a journey of meticulous examination, closely scrutinizing and interpreting a multifaceted spectrum of students' facial expressions, body language dynamics, and the ebb and flow of their levels of engagement throughout the digital learning experience (Abdulghafor et al., 2022). By diligently monitoring these non-verbal cues, which often convey emotions and attitudes that extend beyond words, the AI system demonstrates its profound potential to unveil a rich tapestry of insights into the intricate emotional states and overall interest levels of students (Davy et al., 2022; Jaiswal & Arun, 2021).

This is a superficial glimpse and a deep dive into the undercurrents of sentiment and enthusiasm that shape the student's virtual learning voyage. In addition, Alshammari et al., (2022) stated that with these multifaceted insights, educators are presented with a unique vantage point from which to assess the efficacy of their teaching methods. Furthermore, Godwin-Jones (2023) mentioned that this invaluable repository of information becomes a compass, helping educators navigate the educational seascape and their pedagogical approach in a manner that resonates harmoniously with their students' evolving inclinations and responsiveness. AI's ability to traverse the complex context of non-verbal communication in virtual classrooms redefines the landscape of educational assessment and adaptation.

4.5 Detecting plagiarism

Advanced pattern recognition capabilities within artificial intelligence allow it to meticulously juxtapose, scrutinize, and analyze the assignments and academic submissions proffered by students (Elali & Rachid, 2023). This intricate process entails a comprehensive and systematic comparison against an expansive and diverse repository of pre-existing academic materials, encompassing a broad spectrum of subjects and disciplines. Joamets (2022) stated that what emerges from this intricate technological interplay is a multifaceted and robust mechanism that empowers educators and academic institutions to detect potential plagiarism and cultivate and uphold a culture of unwavering academic integrity. This sophisticated employment of AI as a plagiarism detection tool ensures that the educational landscape remains pristine and unmarred by acts of intellectual dishonesty, reaffirming the intrinsic value of original thought and rigorous scholarly endeavor (Jarrah et al., 2023).

Moreover, the incorporation of AI-powered plagiarism detection tools reverberates beyond the confines of individual assessments, reverently augmenting the broader fairness, credibility, and authenticity of the entire academic evaluation paradigm (Grassini, 2023; Neumann et al., 2023). It is a testament to the synergy between human ingenuity and technological prowess, rendering the educational journey more equitable and just and enhancing the trust and faith bestowed upon the evaluation processes, as exemplified in Figure 3.

Figure 3. Strategies of ChatGPT usage in education

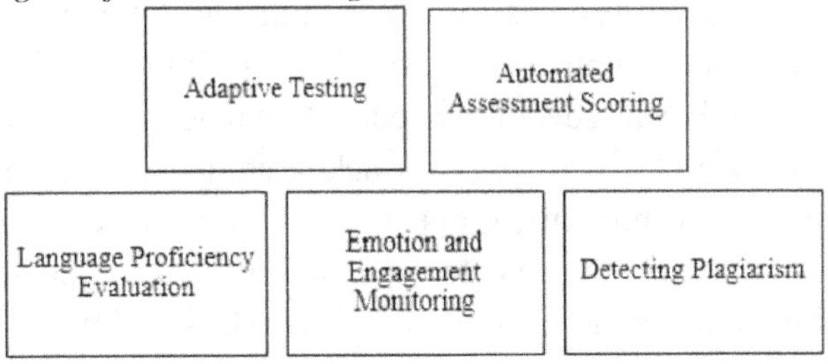

Source: Author's Own

5. THEORETICAL AND PRACTICAL IMPLICATIONS

This paper contributes significantly to the existing knowledge on management education and integrating emerging technologies, specifically generative artificial intelligence. Unlike the prevailing theories, which predominantly draw from other technological domains, this paper addresses the need for comprehensive exploration into the characteristics and significance of ChatGPT within the context of management education. Consequently, this paper presents a practical approach to addressing the prevalent challenges encountered by educators in the management field and offers actionable guidelines for integrating ChatGPT. As generative artificial intelligence gains traction in management education, the insights presented in this paper hold substantial value for future research (Gabriel et al., 2022; Garibay et al., 2023; Haleem et al., 2022). Given the recent introduction of ChatGPT to management educators, there remains a considerable knowledge gap on its optimal integration within management education's assessment and evaluation paradigm (Kikalishvili, 2023; Laupichler et al., 2022).

The recent developments in AI and education technology are changing how assessment is conducted. Educational institutions have rapidly adopted AI-driven tools to improve both formative and summative assessment, resulting in substantial improvement in personalized learning, accessibility, and overall educational outcomes. AI-driven assessment systems are also used to create personalized learning paths. For example, AI tools used in American and European institutions analyze student performance data to provide individualized recommendations to students to overcome challenges (Kulik & Fletcher, 2016). In addition, machine learning algorithms enable these systems to tweak instructional content in real-time according to how students interact with and perform on that material. For example, China has utilized AI in educational applications, especially in linking with extensive scale assessments. Lastly, relevant government educational agencies have launched

AI-powered platforms for assessing and tracking students' academic performance to establish adaptive learning environments (Goksel & Bozkurt, 2019). Further, South Korea has combined AI-based smart classrooms that augment the assessment structure by making it more interactive and flexible (Demir, 2021). Adopting AI in education is not only an advanced global economy phenomenon. AI assessments are also being used in emerging markets like India in remote and underserved areas. The digital divide is bridged with AI-driven tools that provide remote assessment and real-time feedback to offer inclusive education (Gabriel, 2024).

6. CONCLUSION

The escalating prominence of Artificial Intelligence within the educational landscape has ushered in a transformative era replete with promises of personalized pedagogies, data-driven insights, and administrative ease. Integrating AI into educational frameworks can revitalize pedagogical practices, enhance learning outcomes, and optimize resource allocation. As researchers and educators continue to explore the intricate interplay between AI and education, it is likely only at the precipice of the transformative journey AI promises to lead (Saaideh, 2023). Integrating AI, particularly ChatGPT, into assessment and evaluation practices within AI-enhanced management education marks a transformative shift in the educational landscape. By providing real-time feedback, enabling personalized assessments, automating grading, evaluating higher-order thinking skills, and offering valuable insights, AI technologies like ChatGPT enhance assessments' efficiency, effectiveness, and authenticity.

However, with these advancements, it is imperative to navigate the ethical considerations and challenges to ensure that AI remains a tool that empowers educators and students alike (Adams et al., 2023). However, as the benefits of AI continue to unfold, it is essential to remain mindful of its challenges, including ethical, privacy, and access issues, to ensure that the integration of AI technologies enhances rather than detracts from the educational experience. While AI offers significant benefits to education, including personalized learning pathways, efficient grading systems, and reduced biases in assessments (Karimi & Khawaja, 2023), notable challenges must be addressed. Data privacy and the risk of over-reliance on AI tools are significant concerns, along with the potential widening of the digital divide (Holmes & Tuomi, 2022). To mitigate these challenges, policymakers must establish ethical guidelines, and educational institutions need to invest in training for educators to effectively integrate AI into the learning process (Adiguzel et al., 2023). The way forward includes ensuring inclusivity in AI adoption, emphasizing equity and responsible usage.

REFERENCES

Abdulghafor, R., Turaev, S., & Ali, M. A. H. (2022). Body Language Analysis in Healthcare: An Overview. *Health Care*, 10(7), 1–35. DOI: 10.3390/healthcare10071251 PMID: 35885777

Adams, C., Pente, P., Lemermeyer, G., & Rockwell, G. (2023). Ethical principles for artificial intelligence in K-12 education. *Computers and Education: Artificial Intelligence*, 4, 1–11. DOI: 10.1016/j.caeai.2023.100131

Adiguzel, T., Kaya, M. H., & Cansu, F. K. (2023). Revolutionizing education with AI : Exploring the transformative potential of ChatGPT. [ARTICLE]. *Contemporary Educational Technology*, 15(3), 1–13. DOI: 10.30935/cedtech/13152

Ahmad, T. (2019). Scenario based approach to re-imagining future of higher education which prepares students for the future of work. *Higher Education, Skills and Work-Based Learning, 10*(1), 217–238. https://doi.org/https://doi.org/10.1108/HESWBL-12-2018-0136

Ajgaonkar, S., Neelam, N. G., & Wiemann, J. (2022). Drivers of workforce agility: A dynamic capability perspective. *The International Journal of Organizational Analysis*, 30(4), 951–982. https://doi.org/https://doi.org/10.1108/IJOA-11-2020-2507. DOI: 10.1108/IJOA-11-2020-2507

Akter, S., Hossain, M. A., Sajib, S., Sultana, S., Rahman, M., Vrontis, D., & McCarthy, G. (2023). A framework for AI-powered service innovation capability: Review and agenda for future research. *Technovation*, 125, 1–17. https://doi.org/https://doi.org/10.1016/j.technovation.2023.102768. DOI: 10.1016/j.technovation.2023.102768

Alam, A., & Mohanty, A. (2022). Foundation for the Future of Higher Education or 'Misplaced Optimism'? Being Human in the Age of Artificial Intelligence. *Innovations in Intelligent Computing and Communication. ICIICC 2022.Communications in Computer and Information Science*, 1737, 17–29. DOI: 10.1007/978-3-031-23233-6_2

Almusaed, A., Almssad, A., Yitmen, I., & Homod, R. Z. (2023). Enhancing Student Engagement : Harnessing " AIED "' s Power in Hybrid Education — A Review Analysis. *Education Sciences*, 13(7), 1–24. DOI: 10.3390/educsci13070632

Alneyadi, S., & Wardat, Y. (2023). ChatGPT: Revolutionizing student achievement in the electronic magnetism unit for eleventh-grade students in Emirates schools. *Contemporary Educational Technology*, 15(4), ep448–ep448. DOI: 10.30935/cedtech/13417

Alshahrani, A. (2023). The impact of ChatGPT on blended learning: Current trends and future research directions. *International Journal of Data and Network Science*, 7(4), 2029–2040. DOI: 10.5267/j.ijdns.2023.6.010

Alshammari, R. F. N., Arshad, H., Rahman, A. H. A., & Albahri, O. S. (2022). Robotics Utilization in Automatic Vision-Based Assessment Systems From Artificial Intelligence Perspective: A Systematic Review. *IEEE Access : Practical Innovations, Open Solutions*, 10(May), 77537–77570. DOI: 10.1109/ACCESS.2022.3188264

Amer-Yahia, S. (2022). Towards AI-Powered Data-Driven Education. *Proceedings of the VLDB Endowment International Conference on Very Large Data Bases*, 15(12), 3798–3806. DOI: 10.14778/3554821.3554900

Amit, S., Karim, R., & Al Kafy, A. (2022). Mapping emerging massive open online course (MOOC) markets before and after COVID 19: A comparative perspective from Bangladesh and India. *Spatial Information Research*, 2022(5), 655–663. DOI: 10.1007/s41324-022-00463-4

Anshari, M., & Hamdan, M. (2022). Understanding knowledge management and upskilling in Fourth Industrial Revolution: Transformational shift and SECI model. *VINE Journal of Information and Knowledge Management Systems*, 52(3), 373–393. https://doi.org/https://doi.org/10.1108/VJIKMS-09-2021-0203. DOI: 10.1108/VJIKMS-09-2021-0203

Azaria, A., Azoulay, R., & Reches, S. (2023). *ChatGPT is a Remarkable Tool — For Experts*. 1–37. http://arxiv.org/abs/2306.03102

Bewersdorff, A., Seßler, K., Baur, A., Kasneci, E., & Nerdel, C. (2023). Assessing Student Errors in Experimentation Using Artificial Intelligence and Large Language Models: A Comparative Study with Human Raters. *ArXiv Preprint ArXiv:2308.06088*. https://doi.org/https://doi.org/10.48550/arXiv.2308.06088

Bitzenbauer, P. (2023). ChatGPT in physics education: A pilot study on easy-to-implement activities. *Contemporary Educational Technology*, 15(3), 1–10. DOI: 10.30935/cedtech/13176

Bloom, B. S. (1956). *Taxonomy of Educational Objectives*. Longmans, Green.

Budhwar, P., Chowdhury, S., Wood, G., Aguinis, H., Bamber, G. J., Beltran, J. R., Boselie, P., Cooke, F. L., Decker, S., DeNisi, A., Dey, P. K., Guest, D., Knoblich, A. J., Malik, A., Paauwe, J., Papagiannidis, S., Patel, C., Pereira, V., Ren, S., & Varma, A. (2023). Human resource management in the age of generative artificial intelligence: Perspectives and research directions on ChatGPT. '. *Human Resource Management Journal*, 33(3), 606–659. https://doi.org/https://doi.org/10.1111/1748-8583.12524. DOI: 10.1111/1748-8583.12524

Chan, C. K. Y. (2023). A comprehensive AI policy education framework for university teaching and learning. *International Journal of Educational Technology in Higher Education*, 20(38), 1–25. https://doi.org/https://doi.org/10.1186/s41239-023-00408-3. DOI: 10.1186/s41239-023-00408-3

Chen, C., Koong, C., & Liao, C. (2022). Influences of Integrating Dynamic Assessment into a Speech Recognition. *Journal of Educational Technology & Society*, 25(1), 1–14. https://www.jstor.org/stable/48647026

Chen, X., Xie, H., Zou, D., & Hwang, G.-J. (2020). Application and theory gaps during the rise of Artificial Intelligence in Education. *Computers and Education: Artificial Intelligence, 1*, 1–20. https://doi.org/doi.org/10.1016/j.caeai.2020.100002

Chen, X., Zou, D., Xie, H., Cheng, G., & Liu, C. (2022). Two Decades of Artificial Intelligence in Education. *Journal of Educational Technology & Society*, 25(1), 28–47. https://www.jstor.org/stable/48647028

Chhillar, D., & Aguilera, R. V. (2022). An Eye for Artificial Intelligence: Insights Into the Governance of Artificial Intelligence and Vision for Future Research. *Business & Society*, 61(5), 1197–1241. DOI: 10.1177/00076503221080959

Chu, H.-C., Hwang, G.-H., Tu, Y.-F., & Yang, K.-H. (2022). Roles and research trends of artificial intelligence in higher education: A systematic review of the top 50 most-cited articles. *Australasian Journal of Educational Technology*, 38(3), 22–42. https://doi.org/doi.org/10.14742/ajet.7526

Crawford, J., Cowling, M., & Allen, K. A. (2023). Leadership is needed for ethical ChatGPT: Character, assessment, and learning using artificial intelligence (AI). *Journal of University Teaching & Learning Practice*, 20(3), 1–21. DOI: 10.53761/1.20.01.01

Dai, Y., Liu, A., & Ping, C. (2023). Reconceptualizing ChatGPT and generative AI as a student-driven innovation in higher education. *33rd CIRP Design Conference, 00*, 1–7. DOI: 10.1016/j.procir.2023.05.002

Davy, T. K. N. G., Luo, W., Chan, H. M. Y., & Chu, S. K. W. (2022). Using digital story writing as a pedagogy to develop AI literacy among primary students. *Computers and Education: Artificial Intelligence*, 3(February), 1–14. DOI: 10.1016/j.caeai.2022.100054

Demetroulis, E. A., Theodoropoulos, A., Antoniou, A., Wallace, M., & Poulopoulos, V. (2023). Collaboration Skills in Educational Robotics: A Methodological Approach—Results from Two Case Studies in Primary Schools. *Education Sciences*, 13(5), 468. https://doi.org/https://doi.org/10.3390/educsci13050468. DOI: 10.3390/educsci13050468

Demir, K. A. (2021). Smart education framework. *Smart Learning Environments*, 8(1), 1–36. DOI: 10.1186/s40561-021-00170-x

Dergaa, I., Chamari, K., Zmijewski, P., & Ben Saad, H. (2023). From human writing to artificial intelligence generated text: Examining the prospects and potential threats of ChatGPT in academic writing. *Biology of Sport*, 40(2), 615–622. DOI: 10.5114/biolsport.2023.125623 PMID: 37077800

Dewey, J. (1938). *Experience and Education*. Free Press.

Di Battista, S., Pivetti, M., Melotti, G., & Berti, C. (2022). Lecturer Competence from the Perspective of Undergraduate Psychology Students: A Qualitative Pilot Study. *Education Sciences*, 12(2), 139. https://doi.org/https://doi.org/10.3390/educsci12020139. DOI: 10.3390/educsci12020139

Dwivedi, Y. K., Kshetri, N., Hughes, L., Slade, E. L., Jeyaraj, A., Kar, A. K., Baabdullah, A. M., Koohang, A., Raghavan, V., Ahuja, M., Albanna, H., Albashrawi, M. A., Al-Busaidi, A. S., Balakrishnan, J., Barlette, Y., Basu, S., Bose, I., Brooks, L., Buhalis, D., & Wright, R. (2023). "So what if ChatGPT wrote it?" Multidisciplinary perspectives on opportunities, challenges and implications of generative conversational AI for research, practice and policy. *International Journal of Information Management*, 71(March), 1–63. DOI: 10.1016/j.ijinfomgt.2023.102642

Eager, B., & Brunton, R. (2023). Prompting Higher Education Towards AI-Augmented Teaching and Learning Practice. *Journal of University Teaching & Learning Practice*, 20(5). Advance online publication. DOI: 10.53761/1.20.5.02

Elali, F. R., & Rachid, L. N. (2023). AI-generated research paper fabrication and plagiarism in the scientific community. *Patterns (New York, N.Y.)*, 4(3), 1–4. DOI: 10.1016/j.patter.2023.100706 PMID: 36960451

Flores, M. A., Barros, A., Simão, A. M. V., Pereira, D., Flores, P., Fernandes, E., Costa, L., & Ferreira, P. C. (2022). Portuguese higher education students' adaptation to online teaching and learning in times of the COVID-19 pandemic: Personal and contextual factors. *Higher Education*, 83(6), 1389–1408. DOI: 10.1007/s10734-021-00748-x PMID: 34493877

Fortes, P. R. B. (2020). Paths to Digital Justice: Judicial Robots, Algorithmic Decision-Making, and Due Process. *Asian Journal of Law and Society*, 7(3), 453–469. DOI: 10.1017/als.2020.12

Fügener, A., Grahl, J., Gupta, A., & Ketterformat_quoteCITK, W. (2022). Cognitive Challenges in Human–Artificial Intelligence Collaboration: Investigating the Path Toward Productive Delegation. *Information Systems Research, 33*(2), 678–696. https://doi.org/https://doi.org/10.1287/isre.2021.1079

Fung, C. Y., Su, S. I., Perry, E. J., & Garcia, M. B. (2022). Development of a socioeconomic inclusive assessment framework for online learning in higher education. *Socioeconomic Inclusion During an Era of Online Education*, 23–46. DOI: 10.4018/978-1-6684-4364-4.ch002

Gabriel, F., Marrone, R., Van Sebille, Y., Kovanovic, V., & de Laat, M. (2022). Digital education strategies around the world: Practices and policies. *Irish Educational Studies*, 41(1), 85–106. DOI: 10.1080/03323315.2021.2022513

Gabriel, J. (2024). How Artificial Intelligence (AI) impacts inclusive education. *Educational Research Review*, 19(6), 95–103. DOI: 10.5897/ERR2024.4404

Gardner, H. (1983). *Frames Of Mind: The Theory Of Multiple Intelligences*. Basic Books.

Garibay, O. O., Winslow, B., Matematica, S. A., Antona, M., Bodenschatz, A., Coursaris, C., Falco, G., Fiore, S. M., Garibay, I., Grieman, K., Havens, J. C., Jirotka, M., Kacorri, H., Karwowski, W., Kider, J., Konstan, J., Koon, S., Lopez-Gonzalez, M., Maifeld-Carucci, I., & Xu, W. (2023). Six Human-Centered Artificial Intelligence Grand Challenges. *International Journal of Human-Computer Interaction*, 39(3), 391–437. DOI: 10.1080/10447318.2022.2153320

Geigle, C. (2018). Towards High Quality, Scalable Education: Techniques in Automated Assessment and Probablistic Behavior Modeling. *Department of Computer Science, Ph.D.* file:///C:/Users/sheilarose.darmaraj/Desktop/New folder 1 - IJME/Geigle 2018.pdf

George, B., & Wooden, O. (2023). Managing the Strategic Transformation of Higher Education through Artificial Intelligence. *Administrative Sciences*, 13(9), 1–20. DOI: 10.3390/admsci13090196

Gill, S. S., & Kaur, R. (2023). ChatGPT: Vision and challenges. *Internet of Things and Cyber-Physical Systems*, 3(May), 262–271. DOI: 10.1016/j.iotcps.2023.05.004

Godwin-Jones, R. (2023). Emerging spaces for language learning: AI bots, ambient intelligence, and the metaverse. *Language Learning & Technology*, 27(2), 6–27.

Goksel, N., & Bozkurt, A. (2019). Artificial Intelligence in Education: Current Insights and Future Perspectives. In *Handbook of Research on Learning in the Age of Transhumanism* (pp. 224–236). IGI Global.

Grassini, S. (2023). Shaping the Future of Education: Exploring the Potential and Consequences of AI and ChatGPT in Educational Settings. *Education Sciences*, 13(7), 1–13. DOI: 10.3390/educsci13070692

Haleem, A., Javaid, M., Qadri, M. A., & Suman, R. (2022). Understanding the role of digital technologies in education: A review. *Sustainable Operations and Computers*, 3, 275–285. DOI: 10.1016/j.susoc.2022.05.004

Haleem, A., Javaid, M., & Singh, R. P. (2022). An era of ChatGPT as a significant futuristic support tool: A study on features, abilities, and challenges. *BenchCouncil Transactions on Benchmarks. Standards and Evaluations*, 2(4), 100089. DOI: 10.1016/j.tbench.2023.100089

Hashim, M. A. M., Tlemsani, I., Matthews, R., Mason-Jones, R., & Ndrecaj, V. (2023). Emergent Strategy in Higher Education: Postmodern Digital and the Future? *Administrative Sciences*, 12(4), 196. https://doi.org/https://doi.org/10.3390/admsci12040196. DOI: 10.3390/admsci12040196

Hashimy, S. Q., Jahromi, A., Naaz, I., & Nyamwero, N., & H T, B. (2023). Nurturing Leadership and Capacity Building for Success: Empowering Growth. *International Journal of Rehabilitation and Special Education*, 3(2), 33–46. DOI: 10.48165/ijrse.2023.3.2.5

Hénard, F., & Roseveare, D. (2012). Fostering Quality Teaching in Higher Education. *Policies and Practices.*, (September), 54.

Holmes, W., & Tuomi, I. (2022). State of the art and practice in AI in education. *European Journal of Education*, 57(4), 542–570. DOI: 10.1111/ejed.12533

Hsiao, J. C., & Chang, J. S. (2023). Enhancing EFL reading and writing through AI-powered tools: Design, implementation, and evaluation of an online course. *Interactive Learning Environments*, (May), 1–16. DOI: 10.1080/10494820.2023.2207187

Hsu, C. Y., & Wu, T. T. (2023). Application of Business Simulation Games in Flipped Classrooms to Facilitate Student Engagement and Higher-Order Thinking Skills for Sustainable Learning Practices. *Sustainability (Basel)*, 15(24), 1–18. DOI: 10.3390/su152416867

Hutson, J., & Plate, D. (2023). Enhancing Institutional Assessment and Reporting Through Conversational Technologies : Exploring the Potential of AI- Powered Tools and Natural Language Processing. *Journal of Artificial Intelligence and Robotics*, 1(1), 11–22. https://digitalcommons.lindenwood.edu/faculty-research-papers/483. DOI: 10.59232/AIR-V1I1P102

Hwang, G.-J., Tu, Y.-F., & Tang, K.-Y. (2022). AI in Online-Learning Research: Visualizing and Interpreting the Journal Publications from 1997 to 2019. *International Review of Research in Open and Distance Learning*, 23(1), 104–130. DOI: 10.19173/irrodl.v23i1.6319

Irfan, M., Murray, L., & Ali, S. (2023). Insights into Student Perceptions: Investigating Artificial Intelligence (AI) Tool Usability in Irish Higher Education at the University of Limerick. *Global Digital & Print Media Review*, VI(II), 48–63. DOI: 10.31703/gdpmr.2023(VI-II).05

Ishaq, M., Abid, A., Farooq, M. S., Manzoor, M. F., Farooq, U., Abid, K., & Helou, M. A. (2023). Advances in database systems education: Methods, tools, curricula, and way forward. In *Education and Information Technologies* (Vol. 28, Issue 3). Springer US. DOI: 10.1007/s10639-022-11293-0

Jafar, M., Alfian, R., & Yunus, M. (2023). Improving Student Motor Skills through a Structured Physical Training Program. *J Adv Sport Phys Edu*, 6(5), 82–95. DOI: 10.36348/jaspe.2023.v06i05.003

Jaiswal, A., & Arun, C. J. (2021). Potential of Artificial Intelligence for transformation of the education system in India. [IJEDICT]. *International Journal of Education and Development Using Information and Communication Technology*, 17(1), 142–158. https://eric.ed.gov/?id=EJ1285526

Jantzen, D., Marcellus, L., Vermes, F., Duncan, S., & Maclaren, J. (2022). From Pilot to Established Practice: Reflecting on the 20-Year Journey of Implementing a Collaborative Learning Unit practice education model in Victoria, British Columbia. *Quality Advancement in Nursing Education*, 8(1). Advance online publication. DOI: 10.17483/2368-6669.1305

Jarrah, A. M., Wardat, Y., & Fidalgo, P. (2023). Using ChatGPT in academic writing is (not) a form of plagiarism: What does the literature say? *Online Journal of Communication and Media Technologies*, 13(4), 1–20. DOI: 10.30935/ojcmt/13572

Javaid, M., Haleem, A., Singh, R. P., Khan, S., & Khan, I. H. (2023). Unlocking the opportunities through ChatGPT Tool towards ameliorating the education system. *BenchCouncil Transactions on Benchmarks. Standards and Evaluations*, 3(2), 100115. DOI: 10.1016/j.tbench.2023.100115

Jeon, J., & Lee, S. (2023). Large language models in education: A focus on the complementary relationship between human teachers and ChatGPT. *Education and Information Technologies*. https://doi.org/https://doi.org/10.1007/s10639-023-11834-1

Joamets, K. (2022). Plagiarism as a Legal Phenomenon and Algorithm-Based Decision Making. *TalTech Journal of European Studies*, 12(2), 146–164. DOI: 10.2478/bjes-2022-0015

Jurāne-Brēmane, A. (2023). Digital Assessment in Technology-Enriched Education: Thematic Review. *Education Sciences*, 13(5), 522. https://doi.org/https://doi.org/10.3390/educsci13050522. DOI: 10.3390/educsci13050522

Kamalov, F., Calonge, D. S., & Gurrib, I. (2023). New Era of Artificial Intelligence in Education: Towards a Sustainable Multifaceted Revolution. *Sustainability (Basel)*, 15(16), 12451. https://doi.org/https://doi.org/10.3390/su151612451. DOI: 10.3390/su151612451

Kaminska, D., Zwolinski, G., Laska-Leśniewicz, A. B., Raposo, R., Vairinhos, M. R. M., Pereira, E. T., Urem, F., Hinic, M. L., Haamer, R. E., & Anbarjafari, G. (2023). Augmented Reality: Current and New Trends in Education. *Electronics (Basel)*, 12(16), 3531. https://doi.org/http://dx.doi.org/10.3390/electronics12163531. DOI: 10.3390/electronics12163531

Karadag, N. (2023). The impact of artificial intelligence on online assessment: A preliminary review. *Journal of Educational Technology and Online Learning*, 6(4), 822–837. DOI: 10.31681/jetol.1351548

Karimi, H., & Khawaja, S. (2023). The Impact of Artificial Intelligence on Higher Education in England. *Creative Education*, 14(12), 2405–2415. DOI: 10.4236/ce.2023.1412154

Kasneci, E., Sessler, K., Küchemann, S., Bannert, M., Dementieva, D., Fischer, F., Gasser, U., Groh, G., Günnemann, S., Hüllermeier, E., Krusche, S., Kutyniok, G., Michaeli, T., Nerdel, C., Pfeffer, J., Poquet, O., Sailer, M., Schmidt, A., Seidel, T., & Kasneci, G. (2023). ChatGPT for good? On opportunities and challenges of large language models for education. *Learning and Individual Differences*, 103(March), 102274. Advance online publication. DOI: 10.1016/j.lindif.2023.102274

Khetarpal, K., Riemer, M., Rish, I., & Precup, D. (2022). Towards Continual Reinforcement Learning: A Review and Perspectives. *Journal of Artificial Intelligence Research*, 75, 1401–1476. https://doi.org/https://doi.org/10.1613/jair.1.13673. DOI: 10.1613/jair.1.13673

Kikalishvili, S. (2023). Unlocking the potential of GPT-3 in education: Opportunities, limitations, and recommendations for effective integration. *Interactive Learning Environments*, 1(1), 1–13. DOI: 10.1080/10494820.2023.2220401

Kim, J., Lee, H., & Cho, Y. H. (2022). Learning design to support student-AI collaboration: Perspectives of leading teachers for AI in education. *Education and Information Technologies*, 27(5), 6069–6104. https://doi.org/https://doi.org/10.1007/s10639-021-10831-6. DOI: 10.1007/s10639-021-10831-6

Kolb, D. A. (1984). *Experiential learning: experience as the source of learning and development.* Prentice Hall.

Korchi, A., Messaoudi, F., Abatal, A., & Manzali, Y. (2023). Machine Learning and Deep Learning-Based Students' Grade Prediction. *Operations Research Forum, 4*(4), 1–21. DOI: 10.1007/s43069-023-00267-8

Kostka, I., & Toncelli, R. (2023). *Exploring Applications of ChatGPT to English Language Teaching : Opportunities, Challenges, and Recommendations. 27*(3), 1–19. file:///C:/Users/sheilarose.darmaraj/Desktop/New folder 1 - IJME/Kostka & Toncelli 2023.pdf

Kulik, J. A., & Fletcher, J. D. (2016). Effectiveness of Intelligent Tutoring Systems: A Meta-Analytic Review. *Review of Educational Research*, 86(1), 42–78. DOI: 10.3102/0034654315581420

Lakshman, C., & Gonzalez, J. (2023). From TMT multiculturalism to strategic agility: Business model innovation in MNEs. *Multinational Business Review*, 31(2), 157–175. https://doi.org/https://doi.org/10.1108/MBR-02-2022-0030. DOI: 10.1108/MBR-02-2022-0030

Latif, E., Mai, G., Nyaaba, M., Wu, X., Liu, N., Lu, G., Li, S., Liu, T., & Zhai, X. (2023). Artificial General Intelligence (AGI) for Education. *ArXiv*, 1–34. https://doi.org//arXiv.2304.12479DOI: 10.48550

Laupichler, M. C., Aster, A., Schirch, J., & Raupach, T. (2022). Artificial intelligence literacy in higher and adult education: A scoping literature review. *Computers and Education: Artificial Intelligence*, 3(September), 1–15. DOI: 10.1016/j.caeai.2022.100101

Lee, H. (2023). The rise of ChatGPT: Exploring its potential in medical education. *Anatomical Sciences Education*, (March), 1–6. DOI: 10.1002/ase.2270 PMID: 36916887

Lesage, J., Brennan, R., Eaton, S. E., Moya, B., McDermott, B., Wiens, J., & Herrero, K. (2023). Exploring natural language processing in mechanical engineering education: Implications for academic integrity. *International Journal of Mechanical Engineering Education*. Advance online publication. DOI: 10.1177/03064190231166665

Lo, L. S. (2023). The CLEAR path: A framework for enhancing information literacy through prompt engineering. *Journal of Academic Librarianship*, 49(4), 102720. DOI: 10.1016/j.acalib.2023.102720

Luan, H., Geczy, P., Lai, H., Gobert, J., Yang, S. J. H., Ogata, H., Baltes, J., Guerra, R., Li, P., & Tsai, C. C. (2020). Challenges and Future Directions of Big Data and Artificial Intelligence in Education. *Frontiers in Psychology*, 11(October), 1–11. DOI: 10.3389/fpsyg.2020.580820 PMID: 33192896

Luckin, R., Cukurova, M., Kent, C., & du Boulay, B. (2022). Empowering educators to be AI-ready. *Computers and Education: Artificial Intelligence*, 3, 100076. DOI: 10.1016/j.caeai.2022.100076

Michel-villarreal, R., Vilalta-perdomo, E., & Salinas-navarro, D. E. (2023). *Education sciences Challenges and Opportunities of Generative AI for Higher Education as Explained by ChatGPT*. file:///C:/Users/sheilarose.darmaraj/Desktop/New folder 1 - IJME/Villareal et al 2023.pdf

Mizumoto, A., & Eguchi, M. (2023). Exploring the potential of using an AI language model for automated essay scoring. *Research Methods in Applied Linguistics*, 2(2), 100050. DOI: 10.1016/j.rmal.2023.100050

Mogavi, R. H., Deng, C., Kim, J. J., Zhou, P., Kwon, Y. D., Metwally, A. H. S., Tlili, A., Bassanelli, S., Bucchiarone, A., Gujar, S., Nacke, L. E., & Hui, P. (2023). *Exploring User Perspectives on ChatGPT: Applications, Perceptions, and Implications for AI-Integrated Education*. http://arxiv.org/abs/2305.13114

Moradi, M., & Dass, M. (2022). Applications of artificial intelligence in B2B marketing: Challenges and future directions. *Industrial Marketing Management, 107*(September 2020), 300–314. DOI: 10.1016/j.indmarman.2022.10.016

Naidu, K., & Sevnarayan, K. (2023). ChatGPT: An ever-increasing encroachment of artificial intelligence in online assessment in distance education. *Online Journal of Communication and Media Technologies*, 13(3), e202336. Advance online publication. DOI: 10.30935/ojcmt/13291

Neumann, M., Rauschenberger, M., & Schön, E.-M. (2023). "We Need To Talk About ChatGPT": The Future of AI and Higher Education. *5th International Workshop on Software Engineering Education for the Next Generation (SEENG), November*, 29–32.

Nikolic, S., Daniel, S., Haque, R., Belkina, M., Hassan, G. M., Grundy, S., Lyden, S., Neal, P., & Sandison, C. (2023). ChatGPT versus engineering education assessment: A multidisciplinary and multi-institutional benchmarking and analysis of this generative artificial intelligence tool to investigate assessment integrity. *European Journal of Engineering Education*, 48(May), 559–614. Advance online publication. DOI: 10.1080/03043797.2023.2213169

Olan, F., Arakpogun, E. O., Suklan, J., Nakpodia, F., Damij, N., & Jayawickrama, U. (2022). Artificial intelligence and knowledge sharing: Contributing factors to organizational performance. *Journal of Business Research*, 145, 605–615. https://doi.org/https://doi.org/10.1016/j.jbusres.2022.03.008. DOI: 10.1016/j.jbusres.2022.03.008

Ouyang, F., Wu, M., Zheng, L., Zhang, L., & Jiao, P. (2023). Integration of artificial intelligence performance prediction and learning analytics to improve student learning in online engineering course. *International Journal of Educational Technology in Higher Education*, 20(1), 1–23. DOI: 10.1186/s41239-022-00372-4 PMID: 36683653

Palladino, N. (2023). A 'biased' emerging governance regime for artificial intelligence? How AI ethics get skewed moving from principles to practices. *Telecommunications Policy*, 47(5), 1–20. DOI: 10.1016/j.telpol.2022.102479

Pan, Y., Froese, F., Liu, N., Hu, Y., & Ye, M. (2022). The adoption of artificial intelligence in employee recruitment: The influence of contextual factors. *International Journal of Human Resource Management*, 33(6), 1125–1147. DOI: 10.1080/09585192.2021.1879206

Papert, S. (1980). *Mindstroms Children, Computers, and Powerful Ideas*. Basic Books.

Pavaloaia, V.-D., & Necula, S. (2023). Artificial Intelligence as a Disruptive Technology—A Systematic Literature Review. *Electronics (Basel)*, 12(5), 1102. https://doi.org/https://doi.org/10.3390/electronics12051102. DOI: 10.3390/electronics12051102

Păvăloaia, V. D., & Necula, S. C. (2023). Artificial Intelligence as a Disruptive Technology—A Systematic Literature Review. *Electronics (Basel)*, 12(5), 1–37. DOI: 10.3390/electronics12051102

Pendy, B. (2023). From Traditional to Tech-Infused: The Evolution of Education. *BULLET: Jurnal Multidisiplin Ilmu, 2*(3), 767–777. https://www.journal.mediapublikasi.id/index.php/bullet/article/view/3091

Peters, M. A., Jackson, L., Papastephanou, M., Jandrić, P., Lazaroiu, G., Evers, C. W., Cope, B., Kalantzis, M., Araya, D., Tesar, M., Mika, C., Chen, L., Wang, C., Sturm, S., Rider, S., & Fuller, S. (2023). AI and the future of humanity: ChatGPT-4, philosophy and education–Critical responses. *Educational Philosophy and Theory*, 0(0), 1–35. DOI: 10.1080/00131857.2020.1867108

Poorthuis, A. M. G., & van Dijk, A. (2020). Online Study-Aids to Stimulate Effective Learning in an Undergraduate Psychological Assessment Course. *Psychology Learning & Teaching*, 20(2), 236–249. DOI: 10.1177/1475725720964761

Rajaram, K. (2023). Examining the OECD's perspective on AI in education policy : a critical analysis of language and structure in the 'AI and the future of skills' (AIFS) document and its implications for the higher education. *Learning Intelligence: Innovative and Digital Transformative Learning Strategies*, 3–53. https://doi.org/https://doi.org/10.1007/978-981-19-9201-8_1

Ray, P. P. (2023). ChatGPT: A comprehensive review on background, applications, key challenges, bias, ethics, limitations and future scope. *Internet of Things and Cyber-Physical Systems*, 3, 121–154. DOI: 10.1016/j.iotcps.2023.04.003

Roshanaei, M., Olivares, H., & Lopez, R. R. (2023). Harnessing AI to Foster Equity in Education: Opportunities, Challenges, and Emerging Strategies. *Journal of Intelligent Learning Systems and Applications*, 15(04), 123–143. DOI: 10.4236/jilsa.2023.154009

Ruiz-Rojas, L. I., Acosta-Vargas, P., De-Moreta-Llovet, J., & Gonzalez-Rodriguez, M. (2023). Empowering Education with Generative Artificial Intelligence Tools: Approach with an Instructional Design Matrix. *Sustainability (Basel)*, 15(15), 11524. Advance online publication. DOI: 10.3390/su151511524

Rusmiyanto, R., Huriati, N., Fitriani, N., Tyas, N. K., Rofi'i, A., & Sari, M. N. (2023). The Role Of Artificial Intelligence (AI) In Developing English Language Learner's Communication Skills. *Journal of Education*, 6(1), 750–757. DOI: 10.31004/joe.v6i1.2990

Saaideh, M. (2023). AI-Driven transformations in higher education: Opportunities and challenges. *International Journal of Educational Research and Studies*, 5(1), 29–36. https://www.researchgate.net/publication/370864917

Schumpeter, J. A. (1942). *Capitalism, Socialism, and Democracy*. Harper and Brothers.

Sims, M. L. (2023). Shifting perceptions of socially just writing assessment: Labor-based contract grading and multilingual writing instruction. *Assessing Writing, 57*(October 2022), 100731. DOI: 10.1016/j.asw.2023.100731

Spiker, A., Brock, C., & Kelly, A. (2023). We Never Left Work: Challenges to Sustaining High-Quality Teaching and Learning during COVID-19. *Sustainability (Basel)*, 15(5), 3938. https://doi.org/https://doi.org/10.3390/su15053938. DOI: 10.3390/su15053938

Stige, Å., Zamani, E. D., Mikalef, P., & Zhu, Y. (2023). Artificial intelligence (AI) for user experience (UX) design: a systematic literature review and future research agenda. *Information Technology & People*. https://doi.org/https://doi.org/10.1108/ITP-07-2022-0519

Su, Y., Lin, Y., & Lai, C. (2023). Collaborating with ChatGPT in argumentative writing classrooms. *Assessing Writing*, 57(May), 100752. DOI: 10.1016/j.asw.2023.100752

Sugai, G., & Horner, R. (2009). Sugai & Horner 2009.pdf. In *Handbook of Positive Behavior* (pp. 307–326). file:///C:/Users/sheilarose.darmaraj/Desktop/New folder 1 - IJME/Sugai & Horner 2009.pdf

Taylor, F. W. (1911). *Principles of Scientific Management*. Harper & Brothers.

Tourni, I., Grigorakis, G., Marougkas, I., Dafnis, K., & Tassopoulou, V. (2023). *ChatGPT is all you need to decolonize sub-Saharan Vocational Education. 2*, 1–7. http://arxiv.org/abs/2304.13728

Turing, A. M. (1950). Computing Machinery and Intelligence Author. *Mind, New Series, 59*(236), 433–460. https://www.jstor.org/stable/2251299 Accessed: Tversky, A., & Kahneman, D. (1974). Judgment under Uncertainty: Heuristics and Biases: Biases in judgments reveal some heuristics of thinking under uncertainty. *Science, 185*(4157), 1124–1131. DOI: 10.1126/science.185.4157.1124

Vilà, R., Aneas, A., Rubio, M. J., & Freixa, M.Moving Away from the Regulatory Approach. (2019). The value of student engagement for higher education quality assurance. Moving away from the regulatory approach. *REICE.Revista Electrónica Iberoamericana sobre Calidad, Eficacia y Cambio en Educación*, 17(2), 107–122. DOI: 10.15366/reice2019.17.2.006

Vygotsky, L. S., Cole, M., Jolm-Steiner, V., Scribner, S., & Souberman, E. (1978). *Mind in Society: Development of Higher Psychological Processes*. Harvard University Press., DOI: 10.2307/j.ctvjf9vz4

Wang, T., Lund, B. D., Marengo, A., Pagano, A., Mannuru, N. R., Teel, Z. A., & Pange, J. (2023). Exploring the Potential Impact of Artificial Intelligence (AI) on International Students in Higher Education: Generative AI, Chatbots, Analytics, and International Student Success. *Applied Sciences (Basel, Switzerland)*, 13(11), 6716. https://doi.org/https://doi.org/10.3390/app13116716. DOI: 10.3390/app13116716

Wang, X., Gong, Z., Wang, G., Jia, J., Xu, Y., Zhao, J., Fan, Q., Wu, S., Hu, W., & Li, X. (2023). *ChatGPT Performs on the Chinese National Medical Licensing Examination*. 1–9. file:///C:/Users/sheilarose.darmaraj/Desktop/New folder 1 - IJME/Wang et al 2023.pdf

Wardat, Y., Tashtoush, M. A., AlAli, R., & Jarrah, A. M. (2023). ChatGPT: A revolutionary tool for teaching and learning mathematics. *Eurasia Journal of Mathematics, Science and Technology Education*, 19(7), em2286. Advance online publication. DOI: 10.29333/ejmste/13272

Xin, O. K., Wider, W., & Ling, L. K. (2022). Human Resource Artificial Intelligence Implementation and Organizational Performance in Malaysia. *Asia-Pacific Social Science Review*, 22(3), 18–37. DOI: 10.59588/2350-8329.1461

Zhou, S., Xu, H., Zheng, Z., Chen, J., Li, Z., Bu, J., Wu, J., Wang, X., Zhu, W., & Ester, M. (2022). A Comprehensive Survey on Deep Clustering: Taxonomy, Challenges, and Future Directions. *ArXiv*, 1–35. https://doi.org/https://doi.org/10.48550/arXiv.2206.07579

Chapter 10
Assessing Higher-Order and Critical Skills in the Era of Artificial Intelligence

Doris Chasokela
https://orcid.org/0009-0001-5983-8508
Central University of Technology, Zimbabwe

Joseph Hlongwane
https://orcid.org/0009-0001-2482-4659
National University of Science and Technology, Zimbabwe

ABSTRACT

The rapid development of artificial intelligence has brought about significant changes in the workplace and society, with many tasks being automated and outsourced to AI. As a result, there is a growing need for individuals to develop higher-order and critical thinking skills that cannot be easily replicated by AI. This abstract proposes a study to assess the development and assessment of higher-order and critical thinking skills in the context of AI-enhanced learning environments. The chapter aims to examine the effectiveness of various AI-based educational tools and methodologies in fostering the development of complex cognitive abilities, including problem-solving, critical analysis, and decision-making. and provides insights into how they can be assessed in educational and work settings. It further explores the potential implications of AI on the traditional assessment of higher-order skills and discusses the challenges and opportunities that arise from the integration of AI in educational settings.

DOI: 10.4018/979-8-3693-6351-5.ch010

INTRODUCTION

Integrating AI in the workplace has transformed job roles and skill requirements, emphasizing adaptability, problem-solving, and critical thinking. Higher-order and critical thinking skills are crucial for decision-making and innovation in an increasingly AI-driven world. Traditional assessment methods are now complemented by AI-driven approaches, enhancing personalized and adaptive evaluations. AI-enhanced learning environments foster cognitive skills development. Various AI tools can assist in assessing higher-order thinking skills. Educators play a key role in promoting these skills along with purely humanistic skills like empathy and contextual problem solving which cannot be easily taught using AI. AI–human collaboration offers opportunities for critical thinking development, continuous learning, and novel problem-solving competencies. Educational institutions and workplaces must adapt to these changes, balancing technical and human-centered skills for future success.

The Rise of Artificial Intelligence and the Shift in Workplace Skills

The rapid advancement of AI technologies in recent years has significantly changed the job market and the skills in the highest demand. As AI systems have become increasingly capable of automating a wide range of mundane and routine, repetitive tasks, and some aspects of data analysis, the emphasis on these job skills has diminished, while the demand for new, AI-complementary skills has grown. In education, chatbots like the chat generative pre-trained transformer (ChatGPT) can simulate natural human conversations, regulate language processing and its generation, and go beyond working with the given information to generating new data. Thus educators' roles are shifting from being sources and imparters of knowledge to being facilitators of learning. Since chatbots can engage in human-like conversations with learners and answer many of their general questions in any subject matter, human teachers now have to move on to provide that human touch and empathy devoid of machines and foster natural intelligence that can solve novel problems contextually using on the spot thinking not pre-programmed information, emotions and scientific knowledge (Pavlik, 2023).

ChatGPT is a sophisticated pre-trained AI natural language processor. It can grasp the semantics and syntax of natural language, generate human language text, answer questions, and participate in academic and social dialogues on various topics/ issues. In academic work, it can be used to generate tests, and learning material and generate responses to questions in assignments and thus can be used by students as an aide and by teachers to generate marking guides and assessment tools. It is therefore imperative that educators acquire or develop digital skills to fully utilize this tool to enhance their work output and improve students' learning and creativity (Assaraf, 2022; Kung et al., 2023; Zhai, 2023).

Some Key AI-driven Workplace Skills

Collaborative skills are very important, modern workers should form communities of practice (CoPs) and come together to exchange knowledge, and expertise, and learn from one another's experiences within a shared domain of interest. Within a context of intra-organizational knowledge exchange. CoPs serve as tools for overcoming organizational autocracies that hinder the flow of knowledge, aiming to address advancement issues and share experiences to enhance work efficiency and self-development to keep abreast with socio-economic and technological changes in their field (Sonsupap, Corjon, 2024).

Chatbots lack a deep understanding of human emotions and complexities, leading to responses that can be perceived as insensitive, inappropriate or inhumane, which may affect an individual's self-esteem. Failure to receive adequate or empathetic responses from chatbots during crucial conversations, especially on personal matters can lead to decreased self-confidence among emotionally vulnerable individuals. This is where the human touch leveraging on inter-personal and intra-personal skills is required. Workforce transformations are occurring, emphasizing the creation of hybrid roles that combine human and machine intelligence. Skills such as AI management, ethical AI use, and interdisciplinary knowledge becoming crucial. This calls for new skills from educators, like digital technical skills (e.g., programming, and machine learning) and analytical skills (e.g., data interpretation, and decision-making).

The modern workplace has shown an increased demand for higher cognitive skills that leverage uniquely human cognitive abilities, such as complex problem-solving in novel situations, critical thinking, creativity, and emotional intelligence. Employees who can tackle ambiguous, open-ended challenges are highly sought after. The development, deployment, and maintenance of AI systems has created new job categories, such as data scientists, machine learning engineers, AI ethicists, and AI and Machine Learning (ML) managers. Employees with relevant technical skills in AI technologies are in high demand. Emphasis has shifted to human-AI collaborations. It is thus imperative for human workers to develop skills that are uniquely human and cannot be done by machines so that they can continuously contribute significantly towards this partnership. These skills include effective communication, empathy, and the ability to solve contextual novel problems. Rather than fully replacing human workers, AI is increasingly being deployed to augment and enhance human capabilities. This means that the new market requires people who are capable of utilising AI and controlling it to get the job done more effectively, accurately and efficiently. This chapter envisages a future where AI will not completely replace humans but humans who leverage on AI will replace those who don't. As the job market continues to evolve, the ability to adapt to change, re-skill upskills, and engage in lifelong learning has become increasingly important.

Adapting to the Changing Skill Demands Driven by AI Advancements

To be more productive and remain relevant in the evolving job market, employees should think outside the box and be proactive rather than reactive to change. Adopt a mindset of lifelong learning and skills development to stay ahead of the curve and if possible be less engaged in routine and repetitive tasks and increase engagement in activities that challenge the mind, such as taking on open-ended projects, experimenting with new and modern ways of doing things, and seeking out learning opportunities to improve current skills and also to learn new and relevant skills. This can be achieved by heeding calls from the employer, attending in-house and external workshops and webinars, and through personal research on current industry-related issues. This calls for an employee who is up to date with modern trends within their area of work. Enhance digital fluency and data literacy and strive to become proficient in using various digital tools, software, and technologies relevant to your industry. Explore ways to leverage AI to augment your capabilities, such as using intelligent assistants for research, analysis, or task automation.

How can Organizations Foster a Culture That Encourages Continuous Learning and Adaptability Among Employees?

For industries to prosper in the AI era they should not only concentrate on procuring modern state–of–the–art equipment and hiring external experts to either work or upgrade their systems, but they should also work towards developing their current employees who are keen on up-skilling and re-skilling. Captains of industry have a role to play in identifying knowledge gaps and skills deficits among their employees and critically thinking of and implementing measures to rectify this. Organizations can organize training programs, and workshops, and invest in educational resources to help employees acquire new skills and stay up-to-date with industry trends.

Defining Higher-Order and Critical Thinking Skills in the Era of AI

Due to the divergent views that scholars have on critical thinking, there is currently no unanimously accepted, single definition of critical thinking. Several academics agree that it includes a wide range of qualities and skills like reflection, reasoning, communication, and thoughtful evaluation of arguments and is thus a multifaceted cognitive construct. In the era of rapidly advancing AI technologies, organizations must redefine and prioritize the development of higher-order and critical thinking skills among their workforce. As AI systems become increasingly capable of automating routine tasks and processing large amounts of information, the value of human skills that complement and leverage these technologies becomes paramount.

Problem-Solving and Adaptability

The ability to identify complex problems, analyze multi-faceted issues, and develop novel and innovative solutions. Adaptability and the capacity to thrive in ambiguous, rapidly changing environments by combining human insights with AI-generated data and analytics to generate viable decisions and solutions. AI-driven scenario planning and simulation models can help users explore and adapt to a range of potential future problems, fostering greater adaptability. Augmented reality (AR) and virtual reality (VR) powered by AI can create immersive, interactive environments for practicing problem-solving and adaptability in simulated settings that mimic real-world situations. While this is desired, research has shown that results can be flawed due to the Novelty effect when investigating emerging technologies such as VR This factor can sway the user feedback and result in more positive responses, due to the "wow" effect or negative ones, due to the difficulty and lack of familiarity (Miguel-Alonso, Rodriguez-Garcia, Checa, & Bustillo, 2023).

Creativity and Imagination

This refers to the capacity to think divergently generate novel ideas approach challenges from unconventional perspectives and develop new opportunities, innovations, and process improvements. Blending creative thinking with AI-powered tools to enhance ideation and problem-solving. Virtual Learning Realities(VLEs) including three-dimensional graphical multi-user virtual environments (3DVLE) and simulations are gradually taking centre stage in modern education settings which can facilitate simulated experiential learning Education stakeholders should develop the skills necessary to create and implement VR. This can also assist in the development of higher-order thinking Skills (HOTS) (Jorgensen et al., 2022, Edwards, Brown, 2024).

Critical Evaluation, Analysis, and Judgment

The ability to critically analyze and evaluate information within a given context, and draw thoughtful conclusions showing sound judgment on AI-generated solutions is evidence of human natural intelligence. AI systems may generate solutions that are incomplete, biased, or ambiguous based on their programmers and data sets used in their machine learning process. Modern employees thus should have critical thinking skills and the ability to assess and implement relevant empathy and ethical principles to safeguard against negative impacts of AI technologies like cyberbullying, invasion of privacy, and other cybercrimes. Strategic Thinking and Vision entail the capacity to think strategically, anticipate future trends, and envision long-term, sustainable solutions that can be achieved by aligning AI-driven capabilities with the organization's overall strategic objectives and competitive positioning. AI-based predictive analytics and forecasting models can help organizations anticipate future trends, risks, and opportunities to inform strategic decision-making (Roberts & Patel, 2024).

Assessing Higher-Order and Critical Thinking Skills in the Age of AI: Traditional and Emerging Methods

Traditional assessment methods are being complemented by innovative AI-driven approaches. This section explores various methods for evaluating these cognitive skills, from standardized tests to AI-based assessments. This chapter serves to address the challenge of assessing higher-order thinking skills such as reflective and creative thinking, within the context of virtual learning AI-powered environments. Assessment of these skills requires process-based observations and evaluation, as the output-based methods are insufficient. Virtual learning environments offer a wealth of data on the process, which makes them good candidates for process-based evaluation where learners are credited for each part or step where they show competence and appropriate corrective measures are suggested and implemented (Nowlan et al., 2023).

As the integration of AI-powered tools into learning and development programs becomes more prevalent, it is crucial to consider both traditional and emerging methods for assessing higher-order and critical thinking skills. Here are some key approaches to consider:

Traditional Assessment Methods

These include written Assignments and Essays which evaluate learners' ability to analyze, synthesize, and articulate complex ideas in written form. An assessment of the depth of critical thinking, problem-solving, and reasoning skills demonstrated in their written work. Another popular assessment tool is Oral Presentations and Discussions where learners' ability to communicate their ideas, respond to questions, and engage in collaborative, argumentative discussions is assessed in mostly real-time scenarios. Project-based assessments evaluate learners' ability to apply their knowledge and skills to solve real-world problems through collaborative, hands-on projects and writing detailed project reports.

Emerging Assessment Methods

AI-Powered Performance Monitoring leverages AI-driven learning management systems and adaptive training platforms to continuously monitor learners' engagement, progress, and skill development. Use AI-powered analytics and predictive models to identify areas of strength, weakness, and opportunities for personalized skill-building. AI-generated assessments and Feedback mechanisms apply complex algorithms and machine learning to generate customized, adaptive test questions and evaluation criteria based on learners' individual needs and performance and generate real-time personalized feedback on various types of academic tasks. AI-powered simulations and Scenario-Based Assessments use virtual simulations and interactive scenarios to challenge learners to apply their higher-order thinking skills in dynamic and novel situations to assess learners' problem-solving, decision-making, and adaptability by tracking their actions, decisions, and outcomes within the AI-powered simulation.

AI-Powered Multimodal Assessments combine traditional assessment methods with AI-powered tools that analyze learners' verbal, written, and non-verbal cues (e.g., facial expressions, body language, voice patterns) to holistically evaluate critical thinking and problem-solving skills. These systems utilize both natural and AI to provide a robust assessment tool that incorporates aspects of traditional and modern strategies by selecting and combining best practices from each method.

Accessibility and Inclusivity

Some AI-powered assessment tools and platforms are designed and programmed with accessibility features like screen readers and text-to-speech converters to cater to the visually impaired and auditory learners, video, and picture generators to cater to visual learners and those with eyesight challenges, and several other customizable user interfaces to support learners with diverse needs and abilities. These tend to provide more accurate individuated assessments that traditional methods cannot provide. Advanced AI systems can even assess the attention span and concentration levels of learners by analyzing biometric data such as eye tracking and facial expressions, body language, and vocal pattern algorithms.

The Impact of AI on Critical Thinking Assessment

AI has the potential to enhance the assessment of critical thinking skills by providing more personalized and adaptive evaluation methods. The SDGs and the ethical considerations of generative AI offer unique opportunities to transform and advance traditional pedagogical approaches and promote student collaboration and critical thinking. SDG 4 emphasizes quality education and lifelong learning opportunities for all. AI has the capability of personalizing and enhancing students' learning experiences whilst incorporating ethical concerns such as fairness and transparency in developing AI algorithms. Educators can use AI to create more inclusive and sustainable learning environments by addressing these ethical concerns. Collaborative work and critical thinking are two crucial 21st-century skills that higher education aims to foster in students within virtual Learning Management Systems (LMS) like Google Classroom, Microsoft Teams, and Moodle. These can facilitate communication, teamwork, and problem-solving. Collaborative technologies such as online forums, shared documents (for example in Google Docs), and video conferencing (for example Zoom, and Google Meet), enable students and teachers to easily work together regardless of their physical geographical separation. This creates a global village (UN, 2022, Muca et al., 2022).

Research conducted to assess the development of critical thinking by leveraging AI technologies like ChatGPT reported a significant improvement in student performance and confidence in asking insightful questions, analyzing AI-generated responses, and understanding complicated concepts. Students reported that ChatGPT provided diverse perspectives and challenged their current ways of thinking. This suggests an improvement in critical thinking skills. However, challenges included low-quality student comments and difficulties in validating information sources. This highlights the importance of comprehensive training for educators and access to reliable resources. Future research should focus on training educators in integrating ChatGPT effectively and ensuring student awareness of privacy and security considerations (Guo, Lee, 2023).

However as noted in this chapter, AI is not a god and has its flaws, some studies have shown that chatbot-assisted learning has a medium to high effect on final student outcomes and reported low levels of improvement in critical thinking. This suggests that the impact of AI systems on this cognitive aspect needs further improvement or is very much context dependent thus requiring human intervention in applying general knowledge to specific situations. It should be noted that the quality and accuracy of AI responses are dependent on the programmer, data used for machine training and the specificity and clarity of prompts and questions asked to chatbots (Deng, Yu, 2023).

Developing Cognitive Skills in AI-Enhanced Learning Environments

AI has revolutionized various aspects of daily human life using machine learning algorithms and neural networks to simulate human behaviours and intelligence. AI applies LLMs and the generative pre-trained transformer (GPT) trained on large data sets to provide increasingly highly interactive applications. It can be fine-tuned for specific tasks including translation between different languages, summarising text, and chatting on different subject matter. The development of cognitive skills should be enshrined in the training curriculum of pre-service teachers so that they embrace it and are equipped with relevant skills, knowledge, and the capacity to transfer these skills to their learners who will gain the required 21st-century skills and enhance their capacity to achieve the global 2030 agenda and the SDGs (Lu, Zheng, Gong, et al., 2024). While teaching with conversational AI allows us to explore students' cognitive thinking skills and their relationship with questioning and reflective abilities, these models are mostly confined to specific fields, such as language education. More research is required to extend this to mathematical and scientific fields to provide more accurate scientific arguments and insights that will further drive technological and pedagogical development (Liu et al. 2023).

A crucial connection to the development of higher-order thinking skills in problem-solving within the educational context should be robustly investigated within specific problem-solving frameworks in a quantifiable manner. One study proposed the utilization of Bloom's Taxonomy model to deepen learners' cognitive thinking by examining the process of questioning and reflection within the structured framework of the Taxonomy, determining how the insights gained through questioning and reflective practice can be applied to students' utilization of generative AI due to its ability to facilitate students' questioning and rethinking process, which lies at the heart of interactive learning. It should be noted that AI is here to stay and is being used in all economic spheres and thus should be greatly utilized in education to produce technologically astute graduates fit for the 21st century. (Glanville 2023, Rospigliosi 2023).

These stages occur within a particular real problem-solving context. In the questioning stage, students generate and input their questions based on the six levels of the cognitive domain of Bloom's Taxonomy. During the feedback-receiving process, students receive, analyze, and interpret answers generated by chatbots. Based on their reflection, students generate follow-up questions, referencing the cognitive domain once again. The first three stages repeat in a loop until students are satisfied with the solutions, after which they move on to finalizing the solutions. This argument suggests that AI technologies can reshape and develop the cognitive learning process, but their direct influence on thinking awareness needs to be viewed with caution given the importance of positive self-efficacy, confidence, motivation, and other external forces in using AI technologies (Jia et al., 2024).

Exploring AI Tools for Higher-Order Thinking Assessment

There are currently several AI tools available for assessing and developing higher-order thinking skills, more will be developed in the future as technology keeps advancing. This section reviews some of the most common tools, highlighting their capabilities and limitations.

Large Language Models (LLMs), interactive and generative AI-powered systems like ChatGPT, Co-pilot chatbots on Microsoft Edge, Google Gemini chatbots and Quillbot can be used to assist educators in generating, paraphrasing, correct grammar effective text-based tools and learning materials to develop and assess higher order thinking skills using algorithms that can detect and analyze learners' cognitive and learning abilities/styles. Claude AI can be used to generate text-based tasks as well as coding and creating infographics. Synthesia and Midjourney can be used for creating videos from text using manipulatable avatars and narrations. Tableau is a data visualization AI tool that assists in understanding and visualizing given data. Tools like Character AI, CapCut, Janitor AI and Civitai can be used to creatively generate and interact with virtual and real characters and foster role-play and characterization activities. Some AI tools can also detect plagiarism and therefore help to preserve quality and encourage authentic individual input in academic work. The generative ability of these systems can be used to design assessment tools that can be applied physically or online and can also be used to enhance the higher-order thinking skills in both learners and educators (Earger, Brunton,2023,www.veed.io/learn/best-ai-tools, www.technopedia.com).

Since the days of the COVID-19 pandemic, many governments have included remote learning in their education policies. New technologies leveraging AI have been developed to monitor and assess the effectiveness of online education in terms of learner concentration, active participation acquisition of higher-order thinking skills. For example, the brain-computer interface and eye-tracking systems have the potential to improve the remote learning environment by constantly monitoring the eye movements of the learners and thus determining where their attention is diverted during lessons. Cognitive brain-computer interfaces use complicated algorithms and machine learning to detect which areas of the brain are more active by tracing eye, body movements, and expressions and responses to carefully programmed questions. This can help in the development of a better understanding of brain functions, allowing for the development of more effective learning methodologies and the enhancement of brain-based skills (Jamil, Nasreddine, Lakas, 2022).

Generative AI tools can also be applied in inclusive education setups to develop higher-order cognitive skills among learners with different learning abilities and needs by providing innovative and modern ways of individual and collaborative study with peers and teachers in different geographical locations. Examples include ChatGPT being used to facilitate interactive learning by generating real-time responses to student queries, Canva for creative visualizations of concepts, Google Docs for supporting collaborative writing and feedback, and Zoom and Google Classroom for enhancing virtual communication and collaboration (Lin, 2023). These tools can be creatively combined to develop Intelligent Tutoring Systems (ITS) which can create individualized learning and feedback packages custom-made for particular learners based on their academic history and educational needs. ITS systems use Natural Language Processing (NPL) tools to create Critical Thinking Exercises that engage students in complex problem-solving tasks and evaluation processes. Some systems utilize simulations and gaming learning pedagogies. Predictive and analytic algorithms are used to critically analyze student data identify areas of improvement and suggest appropriate measures that can greatly assist teachers in designing appropriate intervention strategies.

Teaching Strategies for Promoting Higher-Order Skills with AI

This section serves to discuss some strategies employable to teach and promote higher-order cognitive skills, albeit not exhaustible. Educators are at the pinnacle of the learning curve and many learners in their lifetime usually remember how their teacher taught them and made them feel in class more than what they taught them. It is therefore imperative to choose strategies that leave a positive academic impact to stimulate mental growth and foster lifelong learning. Students in the K-12 education phase require active and interactive learning strategies that allow them to experiment and solve problems. They usually lose interest when taught using traditional methods where they are passive participants. Project-based learning and tasks based on solving real societal problems can sharpen their cognitive skills and stimulate research skills to apply knowledge and come up with knowledge-based solutions to problems. Strategies involving collaborative activities, and open-ended questioning can stimulate higher-order thinking skills (Sonsupap & Cojorn, 2024)

AI systems and chatbots can analyze students' current thinking patterns and assist the teacher in designing individualized learning strategies. It is thus pivotal for the student to learn how to generate prompts that will result in the chatbots giving more accurate and relevant responses and for the student to be able to analyze and evaluate the responses because they are not always accurate depending on the training data given to the bot. It is worth noting that students must learn to use AI to enhance their academic output and not to generate information for them to consume without analysis, this kills their critical thinking and problem-solving skills. Education policies should clarify the extent to which AI should be used to avoid turning students into robots that just obtain information from AI systems and regurgitate it in assignments, tests, or problem-solving. Natural Language Processing AI systems often generate text, correct grammar, suggest alternative wording, explain meanings of words, phrases, and mathematical equations, and even suggest sources of information. Used properly these are effective tools for teaching language and communication skills, students should be taught to learn from the corrected prompts to write better text in the future and overly rely on these to correct their written work (Gonzalez, et al., 2024; Green, Taylor, 2024).

AI tools can be used in conjunction with Bloom's taxonomy of six cognitive domains to improve learners' higher-order thinking skills. The interactive platform of AI technologies enables students to elicit information from chatbots and thus enhance their creating, synthesis, and evaluating skills. AI has shown a deficiency in developing the application skill. This is probably because this skill is a criterion, situation and locally based in particular settings that cannot be accurately generalized. After all, a problem at location x may not be a problem at y. This then requires the humanoid skills of critical thinking, problem-solving, creativity, application, and novelty. In this light, AI–human collaboration is required to derive the desired outcomes. Students must be taught to generate appropriate prompts to elicit AI responses that will enable them to fulfill all aspects of Bloom's taxonomy. Educators thus need interactive Learning Environments to enhance their knowledge of AI systems and educational philosophies and pedagogies (Elim, 2024).

The Challenges and Opportunities of AI for Critical Thinking Development

In today's rapidly evolving technological landscape, Artificial Intelligence (AI) is transforming the way we live, work, and interact with each other (Webster & Ivanov, 2020; Goralski & Tan, 2020). While AI has numerous benefits, it also poses significant challenges for critical thinking development (Darwin et al. 2024; Dimitriadou

& Lanitis, 2023; Luckin & Holmes, 2016). As AI takes over routine and repetitive tasks, it is crucial to assess the impact on higher-order and critical skills, such as problem-solving, creativity, and decision-making. This paper aims to explore the challenges and opportunities of AI for critical thinking development, highlighting the importance of adaptability, creativity, and human judgment in the era of AI.

Challenges of AI for Critical Thinking Development

As Artificial Intelligence (AI) becomes increasingly prevalent in various aspects of life, it poses significant challenges to critical thinking development (Abulibdeh et al. 2024; Ocana-Fernandez, et al. 2019). AI can perpetuate a homogenized way of thinking, as machines are programmed to follow established patterns and protocols. This can lead to a loss of diversity in perspectives and ideas. Dependence on data quality of AI's performance is only as good as the data used to train it. If the data is biased, incomplete, or inaccurate, the AI will perpetuate those biases and inaccuracies. AI systems may not fully understand the context in which they are operating, leading to misinterpretation or misapplication of data. Relying too heavily on algorithms can lead to a lack of human judgment and critical thinking, as machines are not capable of understanding nuances and complexities. The threat of job replacement by AI can lead to a fear of change, which can stifle innovation and creativity. The increasing use of AI can lead to a loss of human touch and emotional connection in interactions, which is essential for building trust and understanding. AI systems can perpetuate biases present in the data used to train them, leading to unfair or discriminatory decision-making. AI systems may not provide clear explanations for their decision-making processes, making it difficult to understand and evaluate their outputs. AI requires significant technical expertise to develop, implement, and maintain, which can limit its accessibility and adoption. The increasing use of AI raises cybersecurity concerns, as machines can be vulnerable to hacking and data breaches. These challenges highlight the need for careful consideration when implementing AI solutions and the importance of balancing the benefits of AI with the potential risks and limitations. (Nassar, 2019; Faqih, 2023)

Implications for Critical Thinking Development

The challenges posed by AI for critical thinking development are far-reaching and have many aspects. Some implications include the need for human judgment and critical thinking in evaluating AI outputs, the importance of developing skills that complement AI capabilities, the potential for AI to augment human abilities rather than replace them, the need for diverse perspectives and ideas to counterbalance the homogenizing effects of AI and the importance of transparent decision-making processes in AI systems (Ab Kadir, 2018; Rear, 2017). By acknowledging and addressing these challenges, we can work towards developing critical thinking skills that are complementary to AI capabilities and ensure that humans remain integral components of the decision-making process.

Opportunities of AI for Critical Thinking Development

One of the most significant opportunities presented by AI is the ability to augment human cognition and enhance critical thinking skills (Hassani et al. 2020). According to Jarrahi (2018), AI can process vast amounts of data, analyze patterns, and identify relationships that may not be immediately apparent to humans. By leveraging these capabilities, AI can assist humans in identifying biases, inconsistencies, and logical fallacies, ultimately improving the quality of decision-making. Additionally, AI can provide real-time feedback and suggestions, allowing humans to refine their thinking and make more informed decisions (Hassani et al. 2020). AI can also facilitate personalized learning experiences, tailoring instruction to individual students' needs and abilities. By analyzing learning patterns and identifying knowledge gaps, AI-powered adaptive systems can adapt to a student's strengths and weaknesses, providing targeted support and scaffolding. This personalized approach can help students develop a deeper understanding of complex concepts and improve their critical thinking skills. Furthermore, AI-powered simulations and virtual labs can provide students with immersive and interactive experiences, allowing them to explore complex systems and phenomena in a safe and controlled environment.

AI can also be used to develop more effective communication tools, enabling people to express themselves more clearly and accurately. Natural Language Processing (NLP) algorithms can analyze written and spoken language, providing insights into tone, sentiment, and intent. This technology can be used to develop more nuanced language models, allowing humans to communicate more effectively across linguistic and cultural boundaries. Moreover, AI-powered writing assistants can help individuals craft clear and concise arguments, improving their ability to articulate complex ideas and persuade others. Moreover, AI can facilitate collaboration and teamwork by analyzing team dynamics and identifying areas for improvement. By analyzing communication patterns, conflict resolution strategies, and decision-making processes, AI can provide insights that help teams work more effectively together (Jain et al. 2023; Olan et al. 2022). This technology can also help identify potential biases and conflicts of interest, promoting more inclusive and diverse decision-making processes.

Finally, AI can be used to develop new forms of creative expression, enabling humans to explore novel ideas and perspectives (Long et al. 2019; Shukla, 2023). Generative AI models can create original music, art, and literature, while also inspiring human creatives. By analyzing patterns and trends in human creativity, AI can help identify emerging themes and styles, allowing artists to push the boundaries of their work. In summary, AI offers numerous opportunities for critical thinking development by augmenting human cognition, facilitating personalized learning, developing effective communication tools, facilitating collaboration, and enabling new forms of creative expression. As AI continues to evolve, we must harness its potential to enhance human critical thinking skills and improve decision-making processes.

Assessing Higher-order and Critical Skills

To assess higher-order and critical skills in the era of AI, educators, and employers must focus on developing skills that are complementary to AI capabilities (George, 2023). Assessing higher-order and critical thinking skills is essential to understanding the impact of AI on human cognition and decision-making. Higher-order thinking skills, such as analysis, evaluation, and creation, require individuals to synthesize information, identify patterns, and develop novel solutions (Ghanizadeh et al. 2020). Critical thinking skills, such as problem-solving, decision-making, and argumentation, enable individuals to evaluate evidence, identify biases, and make informed decisions.

AI can help assess higher-order thinking skills by analyzing data and identifying patterns that may not be immediately apparent to humans. For example, AI-powered analytics can identify correlations between variables, detect anomalies, and predict outcomes. By analyzing these patterns, humans can develop a deeper understanding of complex systems and make more informed decisions. AI can evaluate complex systems and decision-making processes by analyzing data and identifying biases. For instance, AI-powered audits can detect potential biases in algorithms, data sets, and decision-making processes. This can help humans identify areas for improvement and develop more equitable decision-making processes. AI can assist in creative tasks by generating ideas, providing inspiration, and suggesting new possibilities. For example, AI-powered brainstorming tools can generate novel combinations of ideas, enabling humans to explore new solutions and approaches.

AI can assess critical thinking skills by evaluating problem-solving strategies and identifying areas for improvement (Su, 2022). For instance, AI-powered simulations can simulate complex scenarios and evaluate human decision-making processes. This can help identify biases, flaws in reasoning, and areas for improvement. AI can analyze decision-making processes by evaluating the quality of evidence-based decisions. For example, AI-powered tools can analyze the reliability of sources, identify biases in arguments, and evaluate the validity of conclusions. AI can also assess critical thinking skills by evaluating the quality of arguments and identifying areas for improvement. For instance, AI-powered debate analysis tools can analyze the structure of arguments, identify fallacies, and provide feedback on logical fallacies.

Challenges in Assessing Higher-order and Critical Skills

Assessing higher-order and critical thinking skills requires considering contextual factors such as cultural background, education level, and socio-economic status. Human judgment is often subjective, making it challenging to develop objective assessment criteria. Assessments may be biased toward certain cognitive styles or abilities. Limited data availability or incomplete information can limit the accuracy of assessments.

Best Practices for Assessing Higher-order and Critical Skills

Several researchers cite best practices for assessing higher-order and critical skills (Abosalem, 2016; Collins, 2014; Darling-Hammond, 2017). Using a combination of assessment methods can help gain a comprehensive understanding of higher-order and critical thinking skills. Consider contextual factors that may impact assessment results. Leverage AI-powered tools to analyze large datasets and identify patterns that may not be immediately apparent to humans. Encourage feedback loops between assessors and students to improve assessment accuracy and effectiveness. By adopting these best practices, we can develop more accurate assessments of higher-order and critical thinking skills, enabling us to better understand the impact of AI on human cognition and decision-making processes. In conclusion, the era of Artificial Intelligence presents both challenges and opportunities for critical thinking development. While AI has the potential to automate routine tasks and perpetuate biases, it also offers opportunities for humans to develop higher-order skills that complement machine capabilities. By focusing on creativity, critical thinking, emotional intelligence, and adaptability, educators and employers can ensure that individuals are equipped to thrive in an increasingly automated world.

Evaluating the Effectiveness of AI in Higher-Order Thinking Education

The effectiveness of AI in higher-order thinking education is a crucial aspect to consider, as it can significantly impact the quality of learning outcomes (Bates et al. 2020). To evaluate the effectiveness of AI in higher-order thinking education, it is essential to assess its ability to enhance critical thinking, problem-solving, and analytical skills. One way to do this is by analyzing the extent to which AI-powered tools and platforms can facilitate the development of complex cognitive skills, such as evaluation, synthesis, and creation. Studies have shown that AI-powered adaptive learning systems can effectively improve cognitive skills development, particularly in subjects such as mathematics and science. According to Balaquiao (2024) and Srinivasa et al. (2022), students who used an AI-powered adaptive math program showed significant improvements in problem-solving skills and mathematical reasoning compared to those who did not use the program. Similarly, a study published in the Journal of Educational Psychology found that AI-powered language learning systems can enhance language proficiency and vocabulary acquisition. To evaluate the effectiveness of AI in higher-order thinking education, it is also essential to measure the transfer of learning to real-world situations. This involves assessing whether students can apply what they have learned in academic settings to real-life problems and scenarios. One way to do this is by using case studies or project-based assessments, which require students to apply their knowledge and skills to complex problems. By evaluating the quality of student solutions and solutions proposed, educators can gain insights into the extent to which AI has facilitated the transfer of learning.

Despite the potential benefits of AI in higher-order thinking education, several limitations and challenges need to be addressed. For instance, AI-powered tools may not always be able to adapt to individual learning needs, leading to frustration or disengagement among students. Additionally, there may be concerns about bias and fairness in AI-driven assessments and grading systems. Furthermore, educators may require training and support to effectively integrate AI-powered tools into their teaching practices. To ensure the effective implementation of AI in higher-order thinking education, educators should follow best practices such as aligning AI-powered tools with learning objectives and outcomes to ensure they are addressing specific cognitive skills. Provide feedback and support to students using AI-powered tools to help them overcome challenges and difficulties. Regularly monitor student progress and adjust instruction accordingly. Encourage collaboration between humans and AI systems to promote active learning and problem-solving. Continuously evaluate the effectiveness of AI-powered tools and adjust instruction accordingly. By following these best practices, educators can effectively implement AI in higher-order thinking education, enhancing cognitive skills development, transfer of learning, and overall student achievement.

Implications for Educational Institutions in the Age of AI

As AI continues to transform the way we learn and work, educational institutions must adapt to ensure that students develop the skills needed to succeed in a rapidly changing world (Jaiswal & Arun, 2021). According to Bates et al. (2020), one crucial aspect of this adaptation is assessing higher-order and critical skills in the era of artificial intelligence. Educational institutions must prioritize the development of these skills to prepare students for a future where machines will perform routine and repetitive tasks, leaving humans to focus on complex problem-solving, creativity, and critical thinking. To assess higher-order and critical skills effectively, educational institutions must reimagine their curriculum and instruction. This may involve integrating AI-powered tools and platforms into teaching practices, as well as incorporating more project-based learning and problem-solving activities that encourage critical thinking and creativity. Instructors should also prioritize developing soft skills, such as communication, collaboration, and time management, which are essential for success in a rapidly changing job market. The rise of AI-powered assessments presents both opportunities and challenges for educational institutions. On one hand, AI can help streamline assessment processes, provide more accurate feedback, and identify areas where students need additional support. On the other hand, AI-powered assessments may raise concerns about bias, fairness, and the potential for over-reliance on technology (Naseer, et al., 2024; Zhai, et al., 2024). Educational institutions must strike a balance between human judgment and AI-driven assessments, ensuring that AI is used to augment human evaluation rather than replace it.

As AI becomes increasingly integrated into education, educational institutions must foster human-AI collaboration. This involves not only teaching students how to work with AI systems but also encouraging instructors to use AI-powered tools in their teaching practices. By promoting human-AI collaboration, educational institutions can help students develop the skills needed to thrive in a future where machines will perform many routine tasks. The shift towards AI-driven education requires educators to upskill and reskill to remain effective. Educational institutions must provide ongoing professional development opportunities, focusing on topics such as AI literacy, data analysis, and pedagogical innovation. By investing in their staff's development, educational institutions can ensure that they are equipped to leverage AI effectively and provide high-quality education to their students.

Finally, educational institutions must prioritize enhancing student outcomes by focusing on higher-order and critical skills development. By prioritizing these skills, students will be better equipped to succeed in a rapidly changing world, where machines will perform routine tasks and humans will focus on complex problem-solving and creativity. By reimagining curriculum and instruction, embracing AI-powered assessments, fostering human-AI collaboration, rethinking professional development, and enhancing student outcomes, educational institutions can thrive in the age of artificial intelligence. In conclusion, assessing higher-order and critical skills in the era of artificial intelligence requires significant changes in educational institutions. By prioritizing these skills, embracing AI-powered assessments, fostering human-AI collaboration, rethinking professional development, and enhancing student outcomes, educational institutions can ensure that students are prepared for success in a rapidly changing world.

Implications for Workplace Hiring and Development Practices

The rise of artificial intelligence (AI) in the workplace has significant implications for hiring and development practices, particularly in assessing higher-order and critical skills (Holm & Lorenz, 2022). As machines take over routine and repetitive tasks, employers must focus on hiring and developing employees who possess uniquely human skills, such as creativity, critical thinking, and problem-solving. In the era of AI, job descriptions and requirements must be rethought to prioritize higher-order skills. Employers should focus on describing the tasks that require human judgment, creativity, and critical thinking, rather than listing specific technical skills that can be automated. This will help attract candidates who possess the skills that are essential for success in a rapidly changing work environment. To ensure that employees possess the skills needed to thrive in an AI-driven workplace, employers must develop new methods for assessing higher-order skills. This may involve using behavioral-based interviews, scenario-based assessments, or simulations, which can help identify candidates' ability to think critically, solve complex problems, and collaborate effectively.

According to Gafni et al. (2024), soft skills such as communication, collaboration, and time management are essential for success in an AI-driven workplace. Employers should prioritize these skills in their hiring and development practices, recognizing that they are just as important as technical skills. By prioritizing soft skills, employers can ensure that employees are equipped to work effectively in teams and communicate complex ideas to stakeholders. To prepare employees for an AI-driven future, employers must provide ongoing development opportunities that focus on higher-order skills. This may involve training programs that emphasize critical thinking, creativity, and problem-solving, as well as opportunities for employees to work on complex projects that require human judgment and expertise.

As AI automates routine tasks, many employees may need to upskill or reskill to remain relevant in the workforce (Li, 2022; Pradhan, & Saxena, 2023). Employers should invest in training programs that help employees develop new skills, such as data analysis, programming, or digital marketing. By providing opportunities for upskilling and reskilling, employers can ensure that employees remain adaptable and competitive in a rapidly changing job market. The effective use of AI requires human-AI collaboration. Employers should provide training programs that teach employees how to work effectively with AI systems, including how to design automation tasks, monitor AI performance, and troubleshoot issues. To measure success in an AI-driven workplace, employers must focus on metrics that go beyond traditional productivity measures. They should track metrics such as innovation, creativity, and employee engagement, which are essential for driving business results in a rapidly changing environment. In conclusion, assessing higher-order and critical skills is crucial for workplace hiring and development practices in the era of artificial intelligence. By rethinking job descriptions and requirements, assessing higher-order skills, prioritizing soft skills, developing employees for an AI-driven future, upskilling and reskilling, fostering human-AI collaboration, and measuring success, employers can ensure that their workforce is equipped to thrive in a rapidly changing job market.

Balancing Human and Artificial Intelligence in the Workplace

In today's workplace, the integration of artificial intelligence (AI) has become an increasingly common phenomenon. While AI has the potential to revolutionize the way we work, it is essential to strike a balance between human capabilities and AI systems to ensure maximum productivity, efficiency, and innovation (Dwivedi, et al., 2021). On one hand, humans possess unique skills and abilities that AI systems cannot replicate, such as creativity, emotional intelligence, and contextual understanding. These human strengths enable us to think critically, make informed decisions, and build strong relationships with colleagues and customers. On the other hand, AI systems excel in areas where humans struggle or are inefficient, such as processing vast amounts of data quickly and accurately, automating routine tasks, and providing insights from complex data sets (Burgess, 2017; Valavanidis, 2023). To achieve a balance between human and AI capabilities, organizations must identify tasks that are best suited for each and design hybrid workflows that combine the strengths of both. This may involve training employees on how to work effectively with AI systems, monitoring performance metrics to identify areas for improvement, and fostering collaboration between humans and machines. By striking this balance, organizations can unlock new levels of innovation, productivity, and growth while also leveraging the unique strengths of both humans and machines. For example, a company may use AI-powered tools to analyze customer data and identify trends, while a human analyst uses their creative skills to develop targeted marketing campaigns that resonate with customers. By combining these strengths, the company can drive business results while also leveraging the unique capabilities of both humans and machines.

Humans possess unique skills and abilities that AI systems cannot replicate (Markauskaite, et al., 2022). Creativity, for instance, allows humans to think creatively, imagine new ideas, and solve complex problems that require original thinking. Emotional intelligence enables humans to understand and empathize with others, build strong relationships, and make informed decisions. Humans also can understand complex contexts, nuance, and subtleties that AI systems may not fully grasp. Furthermore, humans can analyze complex information, evaluate evidence, and make informed decisions that require critical thinking. AI systems excel in areas where humans struggle or are inefficient. For example, AI can process vast amounts of data quickly and efficiently, making it ideal for tasks that require rapid processing and analysis. AI systems can also perform repetitive tasks with high accuracy, reducing errors and increasing productivity. Additionally, AI can analyze complex data sets, identify patterns, and provide insights that inform business decisions. Moreover, AI can automate routine and repetitive tasks, freeing up human resources for more strategic and creative work. To achieve a balance between human and artificial intelligence in the workplace, organizations must first identify tasks that are best suited for each. Some tasks require human expertise in creative problem-solving, and critical thinking, while others are better suited for AI's data analysis and automation capabilities. Organizations must then design hybrid workflows that combine human and AI capabilities to achieve better outcomes. Providing training and development opportunities to employees is also crucial to ensure they can work effectively with AI systems. Monitoring performance metrics is also essential to identify areas where human or AI capabilities need improvement. Furthermore, organizations should foster collaboration between humans and AI systems to promote innovation, creativity, and problem-solving. Addressing potential biases in AI systems by ensuring diverse data sets and regular testing for fairness and accuracy is also crucial. Finally, establishing ethical guidelines for the development, deployment, and use of AI systems is essential to ensure responsible innovation. In conclusion, balancing human and artificial intelligence in the workplace is essential for achieving success in today's rapidly changing business landscape. By understanding the strengths of both humans and machines, organizations can create a harmonious blend of capabilities that drives innovation, productivity, and growth. By leveraging the unique strengths of both humans and AI, organizations can unlock new levels of success and stay ahead of the competition.

Best Practices for Developing Human-Centered Skills in the Age of AI

In the era of artificial intelligence, developing human-centered skills is essential for individuals to remain competitive and relevant in the job market (Abarca & Majluf, 2021). Human-centered skills, such as creativity, critical thinking, and problem-solving, are uniquely valuable in a world where machines can perform routine and repetitive tasks (Andersen, et al., 2022). The best practices for developing these skills include creativity which is a highly sought-after skill in today's job market, and AI has made it more important than ever to develop creative problem-solving skills. Employees can be encouraged to think outside the box and come up with innovative solutions to complex problems. Provide opportunities for employees to work on open-ended projects that require creative thinking and collaboration. Critical thinking is another essential human-centered skill that is critical in an AI-driven world (Balart & Shryock, 2024). Employees can be taught how to analyze complex information, evaluate evidence, and make informed decisions. Encourage critical thinking by providing opportunities for employees to work on projects that require them to evaluate data, identify patterns, and draw conclusions (Cortazar, et al., 2021). Effective communication and collaboration are crucial skills in an AI-driven world. Encourage employees to work together on projects, share ideas, and provide feedback. Provide training on effective communication techniques, such as active listening and clear messaging.

AI has made it possible to automate many routine tasks, but it has also created new challenges and opportunities for learning and development (Dwivedi, et al., 2021; Pedro et al., 2019). Provide employees with opportunities to learn new skills, such as programming languages, data analysis, or digital marketing. Encourage continuous learning by providing access to online courses, training programs, and mentorship opportunities. Adaptability and resilience are essential skills in an AI-driven world. Encourage employees to be open to change, willing to learn from failures, and adaptable to new technologies and processes. Provide opportunities for employees to work on projects that require them to pivot quickly in response to changing circumstances. Rafsanjani & Nabizadeh (2023) and Warnestal (2021), posit that while AI-powered tools can automate many tasks, they can also be used to develop human-centered skills. Use AI-powered tools to provide personalized learning experiences, such as customized training programs or virtual mentors. Use AI-powered tools to analyze employee performance data and provide feedback on areas for improvement. Fostering a culture of continuous improvement is essential for developing human-centered skills. Encourage employees to continuously improve their skills, through self-directed learning, peer-to-peer feedback, or coaching from managers or mentors. Recognize and reward employees who demonstrate a commitment to continuous learning and improvement. In conclusion, developing human-centered skills is essential for individuals to remain competitive and relevant in the job market in the age of AI. By emphasizing creative problem-solving, developing critical thinking skills, fostering collaboration and communication, providing opportunities for learning and development, encouraging adaptability and resilience, using AI-powered tools, and fostering a culture of continuous improvement, individuals can develop the skills needed to succeed in an AI-driven world.

CONCLUSION

In conclusion, the rise of artificial intelligence has brought about a significant shift in the skills required for success in the workplace. As AI takes over routine and repetitive tasks, higher-order and critical thinking skills have become increasingly essential for professionals to remain competitive. This chapter has explored the importance of assessing and developing these skills, particularly in the era of AI. Traditional methods of assessment and teaching must adapt to incorporate emerging AI tools and strategies that promote higher-order thinking. The implementation of AI-enhanced learning environments and AI-powered assessment tools can help educators and organizations develop critical thinking skills in individuals. However, it is crucial to strike a balance between human-centered skills and AI-driven capabilities to ensure that employees can work effectively alongside machines. As we move forward, educational institutions and organizations must prioritize developing human-centered skills, such as creativity, emotional intelligence, and problem-solving, to complement AI-driven technologies. By embracing this balance, we can harness the benefits of AI while preserving the unique strengths of human intelligence, ultimately driving innovation, productivity, and growth in the modern workplace. This comprehensive assessment of higher-order and critical thinking skills in the era of artificial intelligence has explored the transformative impact of AI on the way we approach education and workforce development. From defining the importance of critical thinking skills in the age of AI to exploring emerging methods for assessing and developing these skills, this chapter has provided a nuanced understanding of the challenges and opportunities presented by AI. By examining the impact of AI on critical thinking assessment, developing cognitive skills in AI-enhanced learning environments, and evaluating the effectiveness of AI in higher-order thinking education, we have gained valuable insights into the future of education and workforce development. Moreover, by considering the implications for educational institutions, workplace hiring and development practices, and best practices for developing human-centered skills, we have identified key strategies for navigating the intersection of human and artificial intelligence. Ultimately, this assessment underscores the need for a balanced approach that leverages the strengths of both humans and machines to drive innovation, creativity, and problem-solving in an increasingly complex world.

REFERENCES

Ab Kadir, M. A. (2018). An inquiry into critical thinking in the Australian Curriculum: Examining its conceptual understandings and their implications on developing critical thinking as a "general capability" on teachers' practice and knowledge. *Asia Pacific Journal of Education*, 38(4), 533–549. DOI: 10.1080/02188791.2018.1535424

Abarca, N., & Majluf, N. (2021). *Soft skills for human-centered management and global sustainability*. M. T. Lepeley, & N. J. Beutell (Eds.). London, United Kingdm: Routledge.

Abosalem, Y. (2016). Assessment techniques and students' higher-order thinking skills. *International Journal of Secondary Education*, 4(1), 1–11. DOI: 10.11648/j.ijsedu.20160401.11

Abulibdeh, A., Zaidan, E., & Abulibdeh, R. (2024). Navigating the confluence of artificial intelligence and education for sustainable development in the era of industry 4.0: Challenges, opportunities, and ethical dimensions. *Journal of Cleaner Production*, 437, 140527. DOI: 10.1016/j.jclepro.2023.140527

Andersen, R., Mørch, A. I., & Litherland, K. T. (2022). Collaborative learning with block-based programming: Investigating human-centered artificial intelligence in education. *Behaviour & Information Technology*, 41(9), 1830–1847. DOI: 10.1080/0144929X.2022.2083981

Assaraf, N. (2022). *Chatgpt: Optimizing language models for dialogue*. Retrieved from https://blog.cloudhq.net/openais-chatgpt-optimizinglanguage-models-for-dialogue/

Balaquiao, E. C. (2024). Optimizing Students' Performance through Artificial Intelligence (AI) Technology: A Gamified Approach to Smart Learning Environment. *Journal of Pedagogy and Education Science*, 3(02), 104–114. DOI: 10.56741/jpes.v3i02.515

Balart, T., & Shryock, K. J. (2024, May). A Framework for Integrating AI into Engineering Education, Empowering Human-Centered Approach for Industry 5.0. In *2024 IEEE Global Engineering Education Conference (EDUCON)* (pp. 1-10). IEEE. DOI: 10.1109/EDUCON60312.2024.10578796

Bates, T., Cobo, C., Marino, O., & Wheeler, S. (2020). Can artificial intelligence transform higher education? *International Journal of Educational Technology in Higher Education*, 17(1), 1–12. DOI: 10.1186/s41239-020-00218-x

Best AI Tools. (n.d.). Retrieved from https://www.veed.io/learn/best-ai-tools

Burgess, A. (2017). *The Executive Guide to Artificial Intelligence: How to identify and implement applications for AI in your organization*. Springer.

Cortazar, C., Nussbaum, M., Harcha, J., Alvares, D., López, F., Goñi, J., & Cabezas, V. (2021). Promoting critical thinking in an online, project-based course. *Computers in Human Behavior*, 119, 106705. DOI: 10.1016/j.chb.2021.106705 PMID: 36571081

Darling-Hammond, L. (2017). *Developing and Measuring Higher Order Skills: Models for State Performance Assessment Systems*. Council of Chief State School Officers.

Darwin, R., Rusdin, D., Mukminatien, N., Suryati, N., Laksmi, E. D., & Marzuki, . (2024). Critical thinking in the AI era: An exploration of EFL students' perceptions, benefits, and limitations. *Cogent Education*, 11(1), 2290342. DOI: 10.1080/2331186X.2023.2290342

Deng, X., & Yu, Z. (2023). A Meta-Analysis and Systematic Review of the Effect of Chatbot Technology Use in Sustainable Education. *Sustainability (Basel)*, 15(4), 2940. DOI: 10.3390/su15042940

Dimitriadou, E., & Lanitis, A. (2023). A critical evaluation, challenges, and future perspectives of using artificial intelligence and emerging technologies in smart classrooms. *Smart Learning Environments*, 10(1), 12. DOI: 10.1186/s40561-023-00231-3

Dwivedi, Y. K., Hughes, L., Ismagilova, E., Aarts, G., Coombs, C., Crick, T., Duan, Y., Dwivedi, R., Edwards, J., Eirug, A., Galanos, V., Ilavarasan, P. V., Janssen, M., Jones, P., Kar, A. K., Kizgin, H., Kronemann, B., Lal, B., Lucini, B., & Williams, M. D. (2021). Artificial Intelligence (AI): Multidisciplinary perspectives on emerging challenges, opportunities, and agenda for research, practice and policy. *International Journal of Information Management*, 57, 101994. DOI: 10.1016/j.ijinfomgt.2019.08.002

Eager, B., & Brunton, R. (2023). Promoting Higher Education Towards AI-Augmented Teaching and Learning Practice. *Journal of University Teaching & Learning Practice*, 20(5). Advance online publication. DOI: 10.53761/1.20.5.02

Edwards, S. B. (2024). Teaching Creativity with AI: Innovative Approaches and Classroom Practices. *Journal of Creativity and Innovation in Education*, 16, 190–210.

Elim, E. (2024). Promoting cognitive skills in AI-supported learning environments: the integration of Bloom's taxonomy. *Informa UK Limited, trading as Taylor & Francis Group*, 3-13.

Elme, L. J., Jørgensen, M. L. M., Dandanell, G., Mottelson, A., & Makransky, G. (2022). Immersive virtual reality in STEM: Is IVR an effective learning medium and does adding self-explanation after a lesson improve learning outcomes? *Educational Technology Research and Development*, 70(5), 1601–1626. DOI: 10.1007/s11423-022-10139-3 PMID: 35873274

Faqih, N. (2023, October). Developing Literacy and Critical Thinking with AI: What Students Say. In *Proceeding of Annual International Conference on Islamic Education (AICIED)* (Vol. 1, pp. 16-25).

Gafni, R., Aviv, I., Kantsepolsky, B., Sherman, S., Rika, H., Itzkovich, Y., & Barger, A. (2024). Objectivity by design: The impact of AI-driven approach on employees' soft skills evaluation. *Information and Software Technology*, 170, 107430. DOI: 10.1016/j.infsof.2024.107430

George, A. S. (2023). Preparing students for an AI-driven world: Rethinking curriculum and pedagogy in the age of artificial intelligence. *Partners Universal Innovative Research Publication*, 1(2), 112–136.

Ghanizadeh, A., Al-Hoorie, A. H., & Jahedizadeh, S. (2020). *Higher order thinking skills in the language classroom: A concise guide*. Springer International Publishing. DOI: 10.1007/978-3-030-56711-8

Glanville, M. (2024, March 8). *Why ChatGPT is an Opportunity for Schools*. Retrieved from International Baccalaureate: https://www.ibo.org/news-about-the-ib/why-chatgpt-is-an-opportunity-for-schools/

Gonzalez, M. (2024). Leveraging AI for Critical Thinking and Problem-Solving in K-12 Education. *Journal of Artificial Intelligence in Education*, 34, 85–105.

Goralski, M. A., & Tan, T. K. (2020). Artificial intelligence and sustainable development. *International Journal of Management Education*, 18(1), 100330. DOI: 10.1016/j.ijme.2019.100330

Green, H. (2024). Natural Language Processing in Teaching Writing; Enhancing Higher-Order Skills. *Journal of Applied Linguistics and Educational Technology*, 13, 115–135.

Guo, Y., & Lee, D. (2023). Leveraging ChatGPT for Enhancing Critical Thinking Skills. *Journal of Chemical Education*, 100(12), 4876–4883. DOI: 10.1021/acs.jchemed.3c00505

Hassani, H., Silva, E. S., Unger, S., TajMazinani, M., & Mac Feely, S. (2020). Artificial intelligence (AI) or intelligence augmentation (IA): What is the future? *AI*, 1(2), 8. DOI: 10.3390/ai1020008

Holm, J. R., & Lorenz, E. (2022). The impact of artificial intelligence on skills at work in Denmark. *New Technology, Work and Employment*, 37(1), 79–101. DOI: 10.1111/ntwe.12215

Jain, R., Garg, N., & Khera, S. N. (2023). Effective human–AI work design for collaborative decision-making. *Kybernetes*, 52(11), 5017–5040. DOI: 10.1108/K-04-2022-0548

Jaiswal, A., & Arun, C. J. (2021). Potential of Artificial Intelligence for the transformation of the education system in India. *International Journal of Education and Development Using Information and Communication Technology*, 17(1), 142–158.

Jamil, N., Belkacem, A. N., & Lakas, A. (2023). On Enhancing students' cognitive abilities in online learning using brain activity and eye movements. *Education and Information Technologies*, 28(4), 4367–4397. DOI: 10.1007/s10639-022-11372-2 PMID: 36277512

Jarrahi, M. H. (2018). Artificial intelligence and the future of work: Human-AI symbiosis in organizational decision making. *Business Horizons*, 61(4), 577–586. DOI: 10.1016/j.bushor.2018.03.007

Jia, X., & Tu, J. (2024). Towards a New Conceptual Model of AI-Enhanced Learning for College Students: The Roles of Artificial Intelligence Capabilities. *General Self-Efficacy, Learning Motivation, and Critical Thinking Awareness Systems*, (12), 74.

Kung, T. H., Cheatham, M., Medenilla, A., Sillos, C., De Leon, L., Elepa˜no, C., Madriaga, M., Aggabao, R., Diaz-Candido, G., Maningo, J., & Tseng, V. (2023). Performance of ChatGPT on USMLE: Potential for AI-Assisted medical education using large models. *PLOS Digital Health*, 2(2), e0000198. DOI: 10.1371/journal.pdig.0000198 PMID: 36812645

Li, L. (2022). Reskilling and upskilling the future-ready workforce for Industry 4.0 and beyond. *Information Systems Frontiers*, •••, 1–16. PMID: 35855776

Lin, Z. (2023). Why and how to embrace AI such as ChatGPT in your academic life. *Royal Society Open Science*, 10(8), 11524. DOI: 10.1098/rsos.230658 PMID: 37621662

Long, D., Jacob, M., & Magerko, B. (2019, June). Designing co-creative AI for public spaces. In *Proceedings of the 2019 Conference on Creativity and Cognition* (pp. 271-284). DOI: 10.1145/3325480.3325504

Luckin, R., & Holmes, W. (2016). Intelligence Unleashed: An argument for AI in education.

Markauskaite, L., Marrone, R., Poquet, O., Knight, S., Martinez-Maldonado, R., Howard, S., Tondeur, J., De Laat, M., Buckingham Shum, S., Gašević, D., & Siemens, G. (2022). Rethinking the entwinement between artificial intelligence and human learning: What capabilities do learners need for a world with AI? *Computers and Education: Artificial Intelligence*, 3, 100056. DOI: 10.1016/j.caeai.2022.100056

Miguel-Alonso, I., Rodriguez-Garcia, B., Checa, D., & Bustillo, A. (2023). Countering the novelty effect: A tutorial for immersive virtual reality learning environments. *Applied Sciences (Basel, Switzerland)*, 13(1), 593. DOI: 10.3390/app13010593

Muca, E. C., Cavallini, D., Odore, R., Baratta, M., Bergero, D., & Valle, E. (2022). Are Veterinary Students Using Technologies and Online Learning Resources for Didactic Training? A Mini-Meta Analysis. *Education Sciences*, 12(12), 573. DOI: 10.3390/educsci12080573

Naseer, F., Khalid, M. U., Ayub, N., Rasool, A., Abbas, T., & Afzal, M. W. (2024). Automated Assessment and Feedback in Higher Education Using Generative AI. In *Transforming Education with Generative AI: Prompt Engineering and Synthetic Content Creation* (pp. 433-461). IGI Global. DOI: 10.4018/979-8-3693-1351-0.ch021

Nassar, S. (2019). Future aspects of critical thinking and AI. In *Proceedings of WRFASE International Conference,* Abu Dhabi.

Nowlan, N. (2023). *Higher-order thinking skills assessment in 3D virtual learning environments using motifs and expert data*. Elsevier. DOI: 10.1016/j.cexr.2023.100012

Ocana-Fernandez, Y., Valenzuela-Fernandez, L. A., & Garro-Aburto, L. L. (2019). Artificial Intelligence and Its Implications in Higher Education. *Journal of Educational Psychology-Propositos y Representaciones*, 7(2), 553–568.

Olan, F., Arakpogun, E. O., Suklan, J., Nakpodia, F., Damij, N., & Jayawickrama, U. (2022). Artificial intelligence and knowledge sharing: Contributing factors to organizational performance. *Journal of Business Research*, 145, 605–615. DOI: 10.1016/j.jbusres.2022.03.008

Pavlik, J. V. (2023). Collaborating with ChatGPT: Considering the Implications of Generative Artificial Intelligence for Journalism and Media Education. *J. Mass. Communication Education*, (78), 84–93.

Pedro, F., Subosa, M., Rivas, A., & Valverde, P. (2019). Artificial intelligence in education: Challenges and opportunities for sustainable development.

Pradhan, I. P., & Saxena, P. (2023). Reskilling workforce for the Artificial Intelligence age: Challenges and the way forward. In *The adoption and effect of artificial intelligence on human resources management, Part B* (pp. 181-197). Emerald Publishing Limited.

Rafsanjani, H. N., & Nabizadeh, A. H. (2023). Towards human-centered artificial intelligence (AI) in architecture, engineering, and construction (AEC) industry. *Computers in Human Behavior Reports*, 11, 100319. DOI: 10.1016/j.chbr.2023.100319

Rear, D. (2017). Reframing the debate on Asian students and critical thinking: Implications for Western universities. *Journal of Contemporary Issues in Education*, 12(2). Advance online publication. DOI: 10.20355/C5P35F

Roberts, L. (2024). AI-Driven Pedagogical Strategies for Higher-Order Skills Development. *Educational Assessment Review*, 29, 230–248.

Rospigliosi, P. (2023). Artificial Intelligence in Teaching and Learning: What Questions Should We Ask of ChatGPT? *Interactive Learning Environments*, 31(1), 1–3. DOI: 10.1080/10494820.2023.2180191

Shukla, S. (2023). Creative Computing and Harnessing the Power of Generative Artificial Intelligence. *Journal of Environmental Science and Technology*, 2(1), 556–579.

Sonsupap, K., & Cojorn, K. (2024). Collaborative professional development and its impact on teachers' ability to foster higher order thinking. *Journal of Education and Learning*, 18(2), 561–569.

Srinivasa, K. G., Kurni, M., & Saritha, K. (2022). Harnessing the Power of AI to Education. In *Learning, teaching, and assessment methods for contemporary learners: pedagogy for the digital generation* (pp. 311–342). Springer Nature Singapore. DOI: 10.1007/978-981-19-6734-4_13

Su, K. D. (2022). Implementation of Innovative Artificial Intelligence Cognitions with Problem-Based Learning-Guided tasks to enhance Students' Performance in Science. *Journal of Baltic Science Education*, 21(2), 245–257. DOI: 10.33225/jbse/22.21.245

Top 10 Popular AI Tools. (n.d.). Retrieved from https://www.technopedia.com/top-10-most-popular-ai-tools

United Nations. (2024, March 10). *Sustainable Development Goals (SDGs) and Disability/United Nations.* Retrieved from https://www.un.org/development/desa/disabilities/about-us/sustainable-development-goals-sdgs-and-disability.html

Valavanidis, A. (2023). Artificial Intelligence (AI) Applications. *Department of Chemistry, National and Kapodistrian University of Athens, University Campus Zografou, 15784.*Collins, R. (2014). Skills for the 21st Century: Teaching higher-order thinking. *Curriculum & Leadership Journal*, 12(14), 1–8.

Warnestal, P. (2021, December). Multi-disciplinary Learning and Innovation for Professional Design of AI-Powered Services. In *International Conference on Design, Learning, and Innovation* (pp. 21-36). Cham: Springer International Publishing.

Webster, C., & Ivanov, S. (2020). *Robotics, artificial intelligence, and the evolving nature of work*. Springer International Publishing. DOI: 10.1007/978-3-030-08277-2_8

Zhai, C., Wibowo, S., & Li, L. D. (2024). The effects of over-reliance on AI dialogue systems on students' cognitive abilities: A systematic review. *Smart Learning Environments*, 11(1), 28. DOI: 10.1186/s40561-024-00316-7

Zhai, X. (2023). *ChatGPT for Next Generation Science Learning*. Routledge.

KEY TERMS AND DEFINITIONS

AI-human collaboration: the integration of artificial intelligence and human capabilities to achieve a common goal.

Artificial intelligence: refers to the development of computer systems that can perform tasks that typically require human intelligence, such as learning, problem-solving, and decision-making.

Critical thinking: is the process of analyzing information, evaluating evidence, and making informed decisions.

Higher-order thinking: refers to complex and abstract thinking, such as critical thinking, problem-solving, and decision-making.

Human-centered design: an approach to design that prioritizes the needs, desires, and experiences of humans.

Learning and development: the process of acquiring new knowledge, skills, and abilities through education and training.

Skills assessment: is the process of evaluating an individual's skills, knowledge, and abilities.

Workplace automation: is the use of technology to automate repetitive, routine, or mundane tasks in a workplace setting.

Chapter 11
Mathematics Teaching and Assessment in the Age of Generative AI

Patrick W. Wachira
https://orcid.org/0000-0002-7803-3916
Cleveland State University, USA

ABSTRACT

The advent of generative AI technologies has presented both opportunities and challenges for teaching and assessing mathematics. While there have been several studies that broadly address AI uses in education, few however have examined context specific uses of AI such as ChatGPT in mathematics. This study examined preservice teachers' experiences with using generative AI tools in solving mathematics problems. With students increasingly turning to generative AI tools to aid them in completing assignments, the study also presents a mathematics instructor own experiences with AI in mathematics as he looked to re-imagine teaching and assessment in this environment. Findings indicated that the preservice teachers recognize the potential of AI however they were uncertain on how to integrate it into their teaching of mathematics. Based on these experiences, recommendations for changes needed in assessment of mathematics learning are provided.

INTRODUCTION

Mathematics education today is influenced by several factors that are changing the aims and thereby what math educators consider the goals of mathematical understanding and consequently the assessment of students' learning. One major influence has been advances in and accessibility of technology especially artificial

DOI: 10.4018/979-8-3693-6351-5.ch011

intelligence (AI). The rapid and profound permeation of artificial intelligence technology into all aspects of modern society has led to several significant developments in its widespread adoption and use including in the education field. The advent of generative AI technologies such as ChatGPT, have presented both opportunities and challenges for teaching, learning and assessing mathematics. Several researchers have noted that artificial intelligence (AI) technologies have played an important role in improving learning, teaching, assessment, and educational administration (Chen et al., 2020; Zhang & Aslan, 2021; Chiu et al., 2023). However, while the advent of these generative AI tools has been accompanied by several research projects, there is little discussion of the methods used to assess teaching and learning when teaching and learning in this environment.

This study examined generative AI use in mathematics teaching and assessment. Specifically, the researcher examined preservice teachers' perspectives and experiences with using AI with goal of providing feedback to the instructor on what the capabilities of AI are, while at the same time helping students gain first-hand knowledge of using AI tools within the context of mathematics. Like with any technology, by providing teachers with exposure to the use of AI early in their program, they will be more likely to see its usefulness and relevance. Further, understanding students' experiences and beliefs helps educators understand how teaching and assessment will need to change in response to generative AI. This study also describes a math faculty experiences with AI in mathematics as he mulled with how to rethink assessment of student learning in this environment. As noted by Bower (2023) the ability of ChatGPT and similar generative AI tools to provide students and teachers with often high-quality responses to a wide range of common educational tasks raises fundamental questions about what educators should be teaching and how students should be assessed. Thus, with students increasingly using generative AI tools to aid them in completing tasks, it is essential that AI educators begin to reimagine teaching and assessment in this context.

There have been several studies that broadly address AI uses in education, but few have examined teachers' perceptions and experiences in a context specific area such as mathematics. This study therefore adds to this research literature. The study is important in that for teachers to be able to incorporate technology effectively into their teaching, they first need to understand its value and its potential to enhance learning. Further faculty own experiences with generative AI are also important as this is key to learning how teacher educators can help their pre-service teachers use AI effectively in their future mathematics classrooms.

BACKGROUND

Artificial intelligence (AI) is defined as "computing systems that are able to engage in human-like processes such as learning, adapting, synthesizing, self-correction and use of data for complex processing tasks" (Popenici & Kerr, 2017, p. 2). Generative AI refers to a subset of AI technologies capable of generating new content, ranging from text, images, and music to code and synthetic data (Chiu, 2023, 2024). Unlike typical AI technologies primarily designed for analysis and pattern recognition, Generative AI can create novel outputs based on the data they have been trained on (Barrett & Pack, 2023).

Several research studies have examined-broadly AI uses in education. There are a few that have focused on a mathematics and teachers' perceptions and experiences. For instance, a study by Wardat et al., (2024), investigated Abu Dhabi mathematics teachers' perceptions of implemented AI systems and applications. The study also sought to examine what critical challenges math teachers face when using AI and its applications. Findings indicated that AI could be used as an educational tool to facilitate teaching and develop students' performance. The results also showed the most critical challenge for instance, was the difficulty of applying AI systems and applications. Another challenge was that using AI required additional effort compared to traditional teaching methods, which the researcher attributed to lack of knowledge working with the technology. Findings also revealed significant differences in the perceptions of using AI according to gender, years of experience, and educational qualifications with female teachers tending to have a higher level of technical skills and knowledge.

A study by Bower et. al (2024) examined the views of educators about if and how they believed that generative AI tools such as ChatGPT will impact the impact on teaching and assessment. The study aimed to determine teacher motivations for changing their teaching and assessment practices, and how demographic and contextual factors might influence their beliefs. Findings indicated that the majority of teachers felt that generative AI would have a profound impact on teaching and assessment, though a sizeable minority felt it would have a little or no impact. Teaching level, experience, discipline area, region, and gender all significantly influenced perceived impact of generative AI on teaching and assessment. Higher levels of awareness of generative AI predicted higher perceived impact. Thematic analysis revealed the specific curriculum, pedagogy, and assessment changes that teachers feel are needed as a result of generative AI, centered around learning with AI, higher-order thinking, ethical values, a focus on learning processes and face-to-face relational learning. Teachers were most motivated to change their teaching and assessment practices to increase the performance expectancy of their students and themselves.

Baumanns & Pohl (2024) study with German students aimed to explore how interactions with ChatGPT assist pre-service mathematics teachers (PSTs) in posing problems of various levels of difficulty for middle school students. The preservice teachers were asked to create one easy, moderate, and difficult problem based on a given task. The interactions with ChatGPT were exploratively analyzed using qualitative methods. One of the themes identified was collaboration which was characterized by the mutual use of collaborative language and interactive exchange of ideas. Another theme was pedagogical content knowledge (PCK) in which ChatGPT aimed to activate participants' PCK by formulating questions to encourage students' investigation. However, the researchers found that participants often did not engage deeply with these prompts, indicating a missed opportunity for richer pedagogical discussions. Another theme was support in formulation, in which ChatGPT played the dual role in facilitating the process of refining and adapting task formulations to meet pedagogical objectives. The study concluded that the interactions between PSTs and ChatGPT suggested that AI can play a supportive role in stimulating pedagogical content knowledge and enhancing creating ideas for lesson planning.

In the context of statistics, Stanoyevitch (2024) explored the present landscape and the future of assessment in online courses, considering third party online homework/exam assistance platforms and ChatGPT. The study presented the results of an observational study, using data from an Introductory Statistics course to illustrate the proliferation of cheating methods when exams were administered online versus in person. The researcher analyzed exam score results from the pre and post introduction of ChatGPT periods and found significant increases in exam scores from when exams of similar difficulty were administered in person versus online, underscoring the urgency with which educators and institutions must rethink and reshape assessment methodologies. The instructor for this course had been teaching this course for the last 10 years, therefore was able to make this comparison.

A study by Gatupalli, Maloy & Edwards (2023) compared AI-generated math problem solving hints and strategies with those developed by a research team that comprised of an experienced elementary school teacher with a background in math education, a university teacher educator, and a doctoral student in computer science and education. The researchers sought to investigate the types of strategies AI provide for teachers and students and whether AI generated problem-solving strategies aligned to the knowledge and reading levels of grades 3-6 learners. They also sought to investigate the usefulness and drawbacks of Generative AI as a resource for math teaching and learning in elementary classrooms. The researchers found that when asked to provide hints and strategies for solving math word problems, ChatGPT-4 generated solutions mainly focused on procedural mathematical knowledge. When ChatGPT was prompted to adapt its hints and strategies to make the problem easier to understand and think about for young learners, what it provided was a simplified step-by-step or point-by-point description of how to arrive at a solution. It explained the problem procedurally in conversational language with reminders about what fractions are and how to write them. The hints however offered some conceptual information to expand students' thinking about how to write fractions. The researchers' findings suggested that teachers can utilize AI-generated hints and strategies in conjunction with human-written strategies to enhance math learning for students. They also concluded that AI offers useful ideas that can complement and expand how teachers think about math instruction in classrooms.

In another study with mathematics teachers, Demir & Cimen (2024) aimed at examining the experiences of pre-service teachers in the use of ChatGPT. In this study, 4th grade pre-service mathematics teachers were tasked to prepare a lesson plan in accordance with the 5E learning model using ChatGPT. This process of creating the lesson plan was examined by the researchers. Findings indicated that pre-service teachers started the conversation by asking questions about the model or subject they use when looking at the prompts they gave to ChatGPT. It was found that the pre-service teachers entered extra prompts into ChatGPT and customized the lesson plans prepared by ChatGPT in the way they wanted. The pre-service teachers made changes in the lesson plans presented by ChatGPT in the sections of duration, number of activities, type of activities, expansion/change in the stages of the method used, methods and techniques used in the lesson plan, integrating technology. The study concluded that most of the pre-service teachers wanted to make changes in the entire lesson plan presented by using holistic expressions instead of correcting the parts they found inadequate. In all it was found that pre-service teachers' competencies in using ChatGPT were not strong.

In a study in Italy, Bernardi et al. (2024) conducted a study to examine the extent to which generative AI can be used as a tool in mathematics teachers' professional development, specifically as a tool to enhance classroom discussions and pedagogical strategies. The professional development intervention was designed to engage teachers in producing prompts and analyzing the feedback. Using a problem from the National Standardized Assessment, primary and secondary school teachers were first asked to solve the problem and then asked to explore how ChaptGPT could solve it and if its feedback could be used to enhance mathematical discussions with their students. Findings indicated that when teachers are involved in formulating prompts to be given to ChatGPT and in interpreting its feedback, they can develop Technological Content Knowledge and Technological Pedagogical Knowledge.

A study by Chounta et al. (2022) explored general perceptions of K-12 Estonian teachers about artificial intelligence (AI) as a tool to support teaching in Estonian K-12 education. A survey was administered to K-12 teachers asking them about their understanding and concerns regarding the use of AI in education and the challenges they faced. Findings indicated that teachers had limited knowledge about AI and how it could support them in practice. They however perceived it as an opportunity for education. The findings also indicated that teachers need support in order to be efficient and effective in their practice, and this support could be provided with AI.

A study by Rizos et al. (2024) focused on addressing the research gap in the development and assessment of lesson plans and math worksheets tailored for students with special educational needs in Greece. The researchers designed and conducted a nine-hour teaching intervention in a general mathematics classroom involving two 8th grade students with special educational needs. The intervention utilized worksheets generated by the ChatGPT which were customized based on the current curriculum, as well as the special educational needs and interests of the two participating students. The results indicated that students were actively engaged in the educational process, felt safe and confident, satisfactorily met the learning objectives, and developed positive attitudes towards the mathematics course.

Another study by Beauchamp & Walkington (2024) examined participants' entries into the AI tool, *Magic School.* The teachers used three of Magic School's GenAI tools, *Math Word Problem Maker*, *Make it Relevant,* and *Rewrite* to personalize learning: They chose math word problems from either their state standardized test or from the district curriculum. What was produced by the teachers through the AI tools, including participants' interactions with each other through screen recordings, participants survey responses, and output generated by the AI tool were examined. Participants shared the grade level they teach and information about their classroom to see what Magic School generated regarding ideas for activities. Teachers screen-recorded their usage of each tool while collaborating with a partner. In their findings the researchers noted that the participants were able to identify both positive and negative experiences with the AI tools. For instance, teachers noted that having a variety of word problems generated was a positive outcome. Teachers also noted some limitations including the inability of the AI tools to reflect their students background, ethnicity and interests in a personalized way.

Shakarian et al., (2023) study evaluated the performance of ChatGPT's solving mathematical word problems (MWPs). Specifically, the researchers investigated aspects of math word problems that can indicate the success or failure of ChatGPT on such problems. The study found that ChatGPT's performance changes significantly based on the requirement to show its work. The researchers noted that that the probability of failure increased significantly when the work is not shown. However, when the work was included, ChatGPT performance had fully correct (or rounded) answers 51% of the time but can be viewed and as high as 80% if partially correct answers are included. Further, the researchers found that several factors about MWPs can lead to a higher probability of failure, specifically noting that the probability of failure increases linearly with the number of addition and subtraction operations.

In a comparison study of ChatGPT 's versions, Pelton & Pelton (2024) study explored the evolving role of generative AI specifically ChatGPT, in mathematics education for both pre- and in-service teachers. The study compared responses from ChatGPT-3 and ChatGPT-4 to various prompts, which allowed the researchers to evaluate the progression and current efficacy of generative AI. From the study, responses from ChatGPT-4 suggested a growing "awareness" of its capabilities and limitations, often balancing confidence in its functionalities with cautious acknowledgment of its supportive role in education. The researchers concluded that generative AI is a promising tool for educational support, contingent on careful scrutiny and responsible use by educators and learners.

In an earlier study, Wardat et al., (2023) sought to examine the perspectives of various stakeholders, such as students and educators, on the use of artificial intelligence in teaching mathematics. From the interviews, it was found that the overall sentiment towards ChatGPT in education was positive, with many participants seeing its potential to enhance the learning experience and improve students' mathematical abilities. Many participants highlighted ChatGPT's benefits such as providing instant feedback and support, serving as a personalized learning assistant, adapting to the individual needs and pace of each student, and as a tool to help them to reinforce their understanding of mathematical concepts.

A metanalysis by Hwang, (2022) to examine the effects of AI on elementary students' mathematics achievement, found that the use of AI had a small effect size on elementary students' mathematics achievement. The researcher concluded that AI is an effective mathematics learning method for elementary students, regardless of AI type and organization. The researcher however noted that grade level and topical characteristics related to math learning considerably reduced the impact of AI on math achievement. Another study by Supriyadi & Kuncoro (2023) found that the incorporation of ChatGPT into mathematics pedagogy was significantly associated with an increase in students' mathematical interest.

Dao & Le (2023) studied the impact of ChatGPT on mathematical reasoning and problem-solving in the context of the Vietnamese National High School Graduate Examination. Findings revealed that while ChatGPT had the potential to be an effective instrument for the facilitation of mathematics education, its performance in resolving mathematical problems varied based on the level of difficulty and topic of the problems. ChatGPT success rate significantly decreased as the question difficulty increased showing that it had trouble solving more difficult math problems.

Dabingaya (2022) conducted a study to experimentally examine the efficacy of AI-powered adaptive learning systems in improving mathematics instruction. The researcher's aim was to give an in-depth examination of how different platforms impact student learning results, engagement levels, and overall educational experiences. Specifically, the goal was to discover how they affected student engagement and learning results. The participants were students drawn from various grade levels from two schools in distinct geographic locations. The study assessed engagement metrics and pre- and post-assessment scores among students in both experimental and control groups. The results showed that the experimental group, which used the AI-powered platform, had greater engagement metrics, such as interaction frequency and length, than the control group. Furthermore, the experimental group's post-assessment scores increased significantly, showing better mathematical competency.

In another study, Hidayatullah, Untari, & Fifardin, F. (2024) aimed at evaluating the effectiveness of artificial intelligence (AI) in solving mathematical problems at the high school level by comparing the performance of AI with that of the students. ChatGPT was used to solve a set of 20 mathematics problems encompassing short-answer, multiple-choice, and essay-type questions aligned with the secondary school curriculum. At the same time secondary school students participated in solving the same problems. The results indicated that ChatGPT exhibited a high accuracy in multiple-choice questions (98%) and short-answer questions (95%). However, with essay questions the performance was 75% accurate. In comparison, students demonstrated an average accuracy of 85% for multiple-choice questions, 80% for short-answer questions, and 70% for essay questions, additionally, they also demonstrated higher consistency, particularly in questions requiring complex conceptual understanding. The findings underscore the significant potential of AI as a tool for mathematics learning, even though further development is needed to enhance its ability to comprehend and respond to essay questions, thereby improving conceptual understanding and critical reasoning.

In other content areas, Kolade, Owosen & Egbetokum (2024) study examined the potential impact of ChatGPT on learning and assessment, using the example of academic essays, being a major form of assessment with widespread applications of ChatGPT. In their study ChatGPT was used to generate academic essays in response to a typical assessment brief, and then subjected the essays to plagiarism checks and independent grading. The results indicate that ChatGPT is able to generate highly original, and high quality, contents from distinct individual accounts in response to the same assessment brief. However, ChatGPT was unable to generate multiple original contents from the same account, and it struggled with referencing and provided only ‘placeholder’ or bogus references.

Zhai (2022) conducted a study in the context of science education with the goal of piloting ChatGPT capabilities in meeting several challenges including how to track students’ learning, provide feedback and learning guidance, recommend learning materials, and meet the special needs of students with diverse backgrounds, to meet the expectations of the Next-Generation Science Standards (NGSS). The researcher used a performance expectation of the Next Generation Science Standards to develop a prompt, using which ChatGPT automatically generated a performance-based assessment task. The researcher then supplied a response and asked ChatGPT to grade the response and provide feedback. Further ChatGPT was asked to provide learning guidance and learning materials based on the response. ChatGPT was also asked to recommended specific learning materials for a learner with dyslexia, which It did. Findings suggested that ChatGPT has the potential to tackle the most challenging problems of science learning through automatic assessment development, automatic grading, automatic learning guidance, and automatic recommendation of learning materials. The researcher concluded that with these abilities ChatGPT has the potential to significantly aid educators and school systems, by saving them time and effort in addressing the challenges related to assessment practices in the implementation of the Framework for K-12 Science Education and the NGSS.

STUDY

Using a mixed-methods methodology combining qualitative and quantitative elements (Creswell, 2002), this study explored the use of generative AI in mathematics teaching and assessment by both preservice teachers and a faculty member. With preservice teachers, the study for this chapter, examined preservice teachers' (PSTs) perspectives and experiences with using AI. The study was done within a course in the elementary course sequence for teachers seeking licensure. The participants for this study were elementary school preservice mathematics teachers in a mid-western USA university. A survey was administered to the participants prior to exploration of math problem solving with ChatGPT to gauge previous experiences, if any, with AI use. The instructor then gave students some problems to work on collaboratively in class and then as homework, to use ChatGPT to compare their responses with those generated by AI. The task was to engage in problem solving requiring them to explain their solution in a way that would be comprehensible to an elementary school learner. Since the problems had been done in class, they knew the answers and so could make the comparison with the responses and explanations generated by ChatGPT. The PSTs were asked to then refine and enhance their explanations if they felt that ChatGPT provided a better clearer explanation. A post-survey was also administered in which PSTs wrote to share their experiences after exploring math problems with AI. Additional data was drawn from work samples from their exploration with ChatGPT.

The instructor and the author for this paper was also interested in testing generative AI's effectiveness and efficiency in teaching and assessing mathematics especially problem-solving type problems with the goal of learning the types of tasks and how to pose or modify math tasks in light of the fact that students were increasingly using generative AI tools to aid them in assignments. The instructor therefore tested several mathematics problems with AI, refining, retesting, adding constraints to the prompts with the goal of identifying potential issues. This second part of the study employed an action research framework to investigate the capabilities of generative AI in the context of mathematics teacher education with the goal of informing on how assessment practices need to change. Action research focuses on specific interventions that can be taken in a teaching setting (Samaras & Freese, 2006). Action research is particularly applicable to this study because it is about critically reflecting about one's own practice.

In the analysis, qualitative data was analyzed by a simple thematic analysis. Each data source was analyzed independently by the researcher for patterns, which were coded inductively and sorted for emerging themes. The analysis of the questions from the survey was descriptive in nature. The next section shares themes from teachers' perspectives and experiences as well the faculty experiences with using generative AI in mathematics education.

Preservice Teachers' Perceptions

The survey began by assessing the preservice teachers' familiarity with AI tools. Results indicated that fifty-eight (58%) percent said they were *somewhat familiar* with AI tools, while only 25% of the PSTs surveyed were *familiar* or ***veryfamiliar*** with AI tools such as ChatGPT. When asked about their experiences with generative AI, most of the students indicated that they have used and continue to use it but never in mathematics. Most of them said that they use it in other subjects to help generate ideas when writing papers as well as to improve grammar and other errors. 17% of the students, teachers indicated said they had limited or no experience at all using AI. From the qualitative data two of the teachers commented on how they have used it in other subjects.

I have used AI to help with coming up with writing prompts or to look up how to outline certain essays if the assignment sheet was not clear. However, I elaborated on said prompts and did my own research to go along with it.

I use AI sometimes to look over my papers and find any grammatical errors. I've used AI to help me develop ideas based on whatever I input but I would elaborate more on that myself...

When asked about their perspectives on AI use, 75% of the PSTs believed that AI can be a valuable tool in education and that they believed that it would play an important role in their future classroom 92%. On what benefits they believed AI could bring to mathematics, 58% of the PSTs surveyed indicated that they were unsure of how to use AI in mathematics. This view was collaborated by the qualitative data where they said they were uncertain, of how to use it for teaching mathematics and therefore it may be difficult to integrate it into their teaching. Two of the teachers commented.

I am not sure AI can help with math; I just don't understand how it would help me, but everyone learns different ways, so I'd be open to it

I think it would be hard to use AI in math because I'm not sure how it could be used for math. AI for computer science/coding makes sense but I'm not sure how it would work for mathematics.

Some views of how they could use it in mathematics centered on using AI mostly to check or compare answers. One teacher said they would only allow the use of AI in their classroom "if not just to get an answer but to understand the why and how behind the answer". The few who were more familiar with AI, had some ideas of more specific ways, such as creating word problems, providing a different approach to solving a problem and providing clear explanations for math problems that a teacher did not convey well. One teacher said that

my future students will be allowed to use AI in the classroom but only for specific things. The AI should be monitored and only used for providing them with questions that need to be solved a and helpful step-by-step answers to help them understand how to complete it themselves. If the AI is only giving them the answer it won't help their understanding. AI can be a great tool however, to explain in a way that I may not be able to. Sometimes hearing something but rephrased or from a different angle can help students a lot, which is another reason I think AI would be allowed in the classroom.

Overall, most (92%) of the teachers surveyed, were of the opinion that AI will play an important role in their future classrooms with sixty-seven percent, indicating that they would be interested in learning more about AI and how to integrate it into teaching mathematics.

Preservice Teachers' Experiences with ChatGPT

After engaging in solving mathematics problems with AI, the teachers found AI to be pretty accurate. One of the students commented, "The AI answers are very similar to my own and it is very interesting how accurate they are". Other students did note however that AI can be sometimes inaccurate, while others were unable to judge as they felt they did not have enough knowledge to tell whether it would be as accurate in all cases. One of the teachers, Mike said,

I think AI use in math can be helpful but sometimes can give wrong answer. I would allow students to use AI to compare their answers. Sometimes AI can simplify an explanation they can understand.

Another theme from their experiences was that there was a strengthened understanding of the concept due to ChatGPT's' ability to provide multiple explanations. Almost all the students indicated in their written responses that their level of understanding was better or just about the same. One of the students Rick said, "I would say that the use of ChatGPT helped strengthen my already moderate understanding of the concept."

On how they would use AI, one of the teachers said

I believe AI is good for reinforcing ideas/subjects taught in class, and helpful when trying to get a different perspective. I would allow my students to use AI on HW for completion and when looking for extra help but would recommend not using it in the beginning or until they already have a grasp of the basics of the subject first.

Teachers also indicated that since AI can show a variety of ways to find an answer to a problem and that it can simplify an explanation then they would be open to students using it. Some of the teachers comments were that,

AI could help teachers find different ways to teach a concept if they can't come up with ways on their own. It could help teachers develop example problems.

AI can show a variety of ways instead of just one way so I'd be open to students using it

I believe it can be good for math. I would only allow students to use it to check their answers and get an explanation.

I believe Al could provide clear and concise explanations for mathematical solutions that a teacher may not be able to convey in the same exact way. It could also show students different ways to solve math problems that they may not have thought of on their own, making it easier for them to understand.

A couple of the teachers however were opposed to using AI. One of the teachers said she would not allow her future elementary school students to use it at this level. She felt that it was important for the learners to practice solving problems on their own to build a strong foundation and that relying on AI too soon could keep them from fully understanding the basics or would hinder problem solving and critical thinking skills. Other teachers had the following comments.

I believe that there is always a good and bad side to AI. If we use AI to solve problems for us, it will only decrease our true understanding, and we will lack the knowledge we are supposed to be gaining. However, if AI is used correctly, it can be a great tool. I think it could help us make sense of math concepts and provide helpful problems with in-depth answers that can help us learn how to do it ourselves.

I think it would hinder problem solving and critical thinking skills that are necessary in real life. AI and calculators will not always be available to you and you may not use every math problem in the real world, however, these problem solving skills and critical thinking skills will. And you will only strengthen them by practicing on your own.

Similar concerns were expressed by several others who believed that AI could be used to cheat as AI could be used to solve most of the problems especially at the elementary level where the focus is mostly computational. Generally, 67% of the teachers believed that AI might replace some aspects of teaching.

My biggest concern about using AI for math in the classroom would be that students could use it for cheating or may turn to it as an easier alternative than solving a problem themselves. I do not believe it should be the first option, I think students should attempt the problem without it, and if they still need help, then they can use it as a guide on how to find the correct solution....

I am concerned that with the level of math I would be teaching, it would be easy for AI to solve most of the problems for the students and it would be difficult to regulate this.

In summary, while most of the PSTs said they had used generative AI in other courses to brainstorm ideas for their papers, they were unsure how they could use it in mathematics. Based on their exploration of using AI for solving math problems, they noted that it could be useful as a personal tutor and as a tool to help them to reinforce their understanding of mathematical concepts. They also liked the fact that since AI provided multiple ways of solving a problem, it could be useful in helping learners understand concepts as people learn differently. The most common way they said they could use it is for their students to use it as a tool to compare or check their answers and perhaps just as motivation to stimulate interest in the learners. The PSTs major concern was that AI could undermine students' ability to think on their own especially at the elementary school level they would be teaching where many of the problems were mostly computational. The teachers recognize the potential of AI but indicated that they were uncertain on how to integrate it into their teaching of mathematics. These findings present a gap for educators to help future teachers find ways to harness the potential of generative AI in their teaching and assessment in more meaningful ways.

Instructor Experiences

The author for this chapter was interested in finding out more about the capabilities generative AI tools to solve mathematics problems with the goal of learning how teaching and assessments needed to change in the context of learning in this environment. This section therefore reflects the author's personal experiences as an instructor for the class in which this study took place. One key theme was on conceptual versus a procedural approach to solving problems. While in some instances ChatGPT was able to provide accurate and sound explanations, there were instances where it provided a more procedural approach. For instance, as shown in the output below, when prompted to show how a number line can be used to round a number, ChatGPT displayed a number line and then gave procedural steps for rounding without any reference to how the number line was used, which would be a more conceptual approach that comes before the rule for rounding that learners are exposed to in a more traditional lesson.

ChatGPT output – Rounding the number 3.546 to the nearest hundredths

To round the number 3.546 to the nearest hundredth using a number line, follow these steps:

1. Draw a number line with the number 3.54 marked on it. This is your starting point
2. Identify the hundredths place, which is the second decimal place. In this case, it's the digit 4.
3. Look to the right of the hundredths place (to the digit 6 in this case). If the digit to the right is 5 or greater, you round up. If it's less than 5, you round down.
4. In this case, the digit to the right of the hundredths place is 6, which is greater than or equal to 5.
5. So, round up the hundredths place to the next higher number, which is 5.
6. The rounded number to the nearest hundredth is 3.55.

So, 3.546 rounded to the nearest hundredth is 3.55.

Another problem that the instructor prompted ChatGPT was to compute and explain with aid of a math diagram of base ten blocks how to compute 41-28. Base ten blocks are often used at the elementary school to develop place value as well as multidigit addition and subtraction concepts. As shown in figure 1, ChatGPT was able to provide a step-by-step explanation including how to regroup and subtract. However, the visual used was not that of base ten blocks and would be incomprehensible to a young learner. Further the image generated seemed to be that of an addition problem 41+28. It could be ChatGPT's difficulty with the image for this problem might stem from the precise mathematical terminologies used, such as base ten blocks which it may not be familiar with.

Figure 1. Step-by-step explanation of regrouping and subtraction

Here is a base-ten block drawing illustrating how to solve $41 - 28$. It visually represents each step of the subtraction process:

1. **Starting with 41**: Four tens blocks and one single unit block.
2. **Regrouping**: One ten block is broken into ten single units, leaving three tens blocks and eleven single units.
3. **Subtracting 28**: Two tens blocks and eight single units are removed, leaving one ten block and three single units.

This step-by-step approach helps children understand subtraction and regrouping in a visual and interactive way!

This result suggests that educators should see this as opportunity to engage their preservice teachers in the use of representations and in mathematics problem solving and reasoning as ChatGPT appears to have difficulties with images. It is important to note that for this study, the free version of ChatGPT was used so perhaps with the newer version, the results might be different.

The instructor found, similar to the PSTs experiences, that an advantage of ChatGPT was that it can provide multiple ways of solving a problem. In this task ChatGPT was prompted with another problem common in middle school, that is, integers multiplication. The task was to provide an explanation why a negative times a negative number results in a positive number which most preservice teachers also struggle to explain. As shown in the figure 2, ChatGPT provided a response that included a combination of patterns, algebraic reasoning, and intuition. The algebraic explanation however did not seem accessible to middle school learners so perhaps a tweaking of the prompt would be required to provide an output appropriate for specific grade levels.

Figure 2. Chat gpt responses with patterns and logic

The rule that "a negative times a negative makes a positive" can be understood through several different perspectives, including algebraic reasoning and number patterns.

1. Pattern Observation:

- Consider the multiplication of a number by decreasing positive integers:

$$4 \times 3 = 12$$

$$4 \times 2 = 8$$

$$4 \times 1 = 4$$

$$4 \times 0 = 0$$

- Now, if we continue the pattern by multiplying by negative numbers:

$$4 \times -1 = -4$$

$$4 \times -2 = -8$$

- This pattern shows that multiplying by negative numbers inverts the sign. Extending this reasoning:

$$-4 \times 3 = -12$$

$$-4 \times 2 = -8$$

$$-4 \times 1 = -4$$

$$-4 \times 0 = 0$$

$$-4 \times -1 = 4$$

  - Therefore, when multiplying two negative numbers, the pattern suggests the result should be positive.

2. Algebraic Reasoning:

- Let's use the distributive property, which states:

$$a \times (b + c) = a \times b + a \times c$$

- Consider the expression $(-1) \times (1 + (-1))$:

$$(-1) \times (1 + (-1)) = (-1) \times 0 = 0$$

$$(-1) \times 1 + (-1) \times (-1) = 0$$

  - Since $(-1) \times 1 = -1$, we have:

$$-1 + (-1) \times (-1) = 0$$

$$(-1) \times (-1) = 1$$

  - This algebraic proof shows that multiplying two negative numbers results in a positive number.

3. Intuitive Explanation:

- Think of negative numbers as representing a movement in the opposite direction. If you "reverse" a reversal, you end up moving forward, which corresponds to a positive outcome.

This combination of patterns, algebraic reasoning, and intuition helps explain why a negative

Further ChatGPT was prompted to *"explain to a middle schooler why subtracting a negative number is the same as adding the number"*. This is a rule that is often stated by teachers when teaching integer addition and subtraction, however when the instructor poses this question to preservice teachers, they are not able to explain the reasoning behind it. As shown in figure 3, ChatGPT provided a much-simplified explanation which did not include algebraic means since the prompt included the grade level target, that is middle school. ChatGPT did provide multiple ways which included, using the idea of debt, a real-life context, However, in the explanation that involved a number line instead of providing a visual, ChatGPT simply asked the leaner to imagine the number line. These examples show its limitations, specifically when it came to using images, graphs and other representations. ChatGPT was however able to provide simple explanations accessible to a middle school learner.

Figure 3. Visual of Chat gpt solving a math problem

explain to a middle school learner why subtracting a negative integer is the same as adding the integer

Imagine you're on a number line. Positive numbers move you to the right, and negative numbers move you to the left.

Visualizing Subtraction:

- When you subtract a number, you move to the left on the number line. For example, $5 - 3$ means starting at 5 and moving 3 steps to the left, which lands you at 2.

What Happens with a Negative Number:

- Now, what if you need to subtract a negative number, like $5 - (-3)$? This is like saying, "take away moving left by 3 steps." But taking away moving left actually means you go to the right instead.
- So, subtracting -3 means you move 3 steps to the right, just like adding 3.

Simple Way to Think About It:

- Subtracting a negative number is the same as adding because you're doing the opposite of what the negative number suggests.
- For example:

$$5 - (-3) = 5 + 3 = 8$$

- This happens because the two negatives (the minus sign and the negative number) cancel each other out, turning into a positive.

A Real-Life Analogy:

- Imagine you owe your friend 3 dollars (represented by -3). If someone tells you, "Subtract that debt," it means you're not in debt anymore—instead, you now have 3 extra dollars. So subtracting a negative is like gaining or adding.

In summary, subtracting a negative number is the same as adding because you're reversing the action of the negative, which results in moving to the right on the number line.

The solutions for the integer problems illustrated above shows the advantage of ChatGPT in showing different ways of solving a problem. The availability of different ways of doing or explaining the solution to a problem is important as an educator can choose a method depending on whether they are teaching an elementary class, where students have not had exposure to algebra, or a higher-level class. For instance, the intuitive explanation is something that teachers can build on using a number line, helps elementary school students to understand the concept of adding and subtracting integers. Another advantage of ChatGPT demonstrated by the above examples, is that with the appropriate prompting, ChatGPT could be used to provide explanations that are tailored to the level of the learner, thus differentiating learning.

Another task that the course instructor explored with AI was the creation of word problems set in real-life context. One area that was tested was fractions computations. As many teacher educators would attest, many students often confuse word problems on fraction multiplication, such as $\frac{2}{3}x\frac{1}{2}$ and fraction subtraction such as $\frac{2}{3} - \frac{1}{2}$. The instructor therefore had ChatGPT write some word problems for fraction subtraction and multiplication. An additional prompt asked ChatGPT to write word problems that were culturally relevant. It was found that AI was pretty accurate with creating word problems that clearly distinguished between subtracting and multiplying fractions, as well as the ability write problems that were relevant to teaching urban students. This suggests that this a key area that AI could be leveraged in mathematics, that is, the creation of real-life context word problems as well as adapting these questions to specific subgroups of learners. Assessment items set in real context often provide a much richer environment to assess students' understanding of mathematical concepts than items stated abstractly, however, such items require more time on the part of the instructor to create than typical items, therefore this is another area that AI tools can be of immense help to teachers.

Recommendations - Shifts in Assessment

Based on the preservice teachers' and instructor's experiences with AI, it was concluded that AI poses challenges for assessments especially take-home assignments and tests. With AI being able to do most of the less difficult math problems especially those in the elementary and middle school curriculum, allowing students to take home assignments makes it almost impossible to prevent cheating. Some of the ways the instructor identified that assessment should change included, changing the types of assessment tasks and the modality.

In terms of changing the assessment tasks, an approach this study recommends is to create assessment that avoid computation questions which AI can easily provide an answer for. Problem tasks should be modified to focus more on problem-solving and reasoning types for instance where students are required to show and explain their work. According to NCTM, AI is known to "hallucinate" answers that are untrue or unreasonable. Problem-solving and strong fundamentals (sense making) are essential to develop the intuition for whether an output is reasonable (NCTM, 2024). Thus, by focusing on problem solving, leaners develop a deep understanding of the concept, and with that they are able to verify the correctness of a solution generated by an AI tool.

Further this study found that the ChatGPT version used in this study, had limitations when it came to providing responses that needed diagrams or visuals for explanation. Von Hippel (2023) also noted similar limitations in the context of geometry when ChatGPT's was asked to do other things that math teachers commonly do

In particular, GPT-3 could not describe student misconceptions or catch certain student errors. It couldn't visualize a triangle or do anything equivalent, and it made a surprising computational error when squaring a number. I concluded that, despite the clear disruptive potential of AI for education, GPT-3 had little practical use for teaching geometry and might actually do more harm than good.

In addition, ChatGPT also has difficulty with some precise mathematics terminologies and vocabulary which according to Bailey (2024) stemmed from Large Language Models (LLMs) such as ChatGPT foundational bias towards linguistic rather than mathematical intelligence, a gap further widened by the scarcity of complex math in their training data, limiting their grasp of advanced mathematical concepts. Therefore, one approach to (re)designing assessment items is to take advantage of ChatGPT's current limitations of mathematical images and terminologies and focus on problems that require reasoning with a variety of representations such as diagrams, graphs, and number lines and understanding the relationships among those representations. It is important however to note that generative AI capability and efficiency continues to improve and therefore educators will need to constantly rethink their teaching and assessment.

In terms of changing the modality of assessments, the course instructor felt that that in-class assessments (formative) as well as in-class tests become even more important now to help address the possibility of students completing assessments with the help of AI tools which was found to be accurate for the most part. From his experiences, the instructor for this study has had to shift towards more in person assessments, for instance where students are required to explain or discuss, as the teacher listens or simply to take an in-class proctored test. When it comes to take home assignments and tests, the instructor found it useful to test some of the take-home exam questions on Chat GPT to see how it responds and to gauge the accuracy of that response, and if need be, modify the task or how the task is posed. One advantage was that since learners now have access to generative AI tools to aid with assignments, the instructor is now able to pose more challenging problems where learners can demonstrate a much deeper understanding of the content, rather than simple mostly computational problems.

Another strategy for modifying assessments especially take-home assessments, is to embed AI into the mathematics tasks. For instance, for this study, since an important aspect of teaching is to be able to provide clear explanations, the preservice teachers were asked to use AI to complete their homework and use it to aid them in refining their explanations, so they are clear to a learner. Most of the teachers in this study often struggled with articulating an explanation to how to solve problem and AI was found to very useful to help formulate a clear explanation.

CONCLUSION

Artificial intelligence (AI) when used appropriately has great potential to contribute to mathematical teaching, learning and assessment. In terms of assessment, based on the experiences of the teachers and those of the instructor, this study presented some of the ways to re-imagine assessments given that AI is here to stay and that students will use it to aid in completion of tasks or assignments. The main ways are to change the types of assessments and the modalities of these assessments. In changing the types of assessments, a recommendation is to create assessments that do not just focus on computations, which AI tools are excellent at, but those that encourage problem solving, reasoning and communication using multiple representations. A shift in assessing students' learning is to make in-class assessments even more important including verbal assessments where learners explain how they know they are correct. Further, assessments can ask students to use and to interrelate multiple representations of the same information, and in other cases apply their understanding to new contexts. As noted by NCTM in their position statement, "rather than being threats to math instruction, these tools create positive pressure to avoid the "shallow assessment" trap and create assignments and assessments that blend the fundamentals and creative thinking".

Some important benefits of AI tools as found from experiences in this study is that AI can be incorporated into mathematics to personalize learning by changing the prompts to target specific individual or subgroup of learners. For instance, teachers can use AI to create materials and problems that allow for differentiation in in all three areas namely content, process and product. AI can be used to tailor problems to students' ability levels and interests, providing culturally relevant materials. In terms of learning, students can use AI tools as a personal tutor, helping explain concepts in a different way or in a better way. Thus through, thoughtful incorporation of generative AI tools into teaching strategies, math teachers can help students develop a deep understanding of mathematics and help them communicate their solution processes, thus preparing them for success in mathematics.

However, as the teachers in this study indicated, they still need assistance in finding ways to integrate or incorporate AI tools into their teaching. It is therefore important that educators help preservice teachers learn how to effectively incorporate AI tools into classwork and curriculum. A starting point, as was done in this study, is to provide teachers with opportunities to experience first-hand, mathematics learning activities that incorporate technology tools such as generative AI. Because the results of AI depend on the prompts, educators can also assist preservice teachers harness the power of AI, by helping them in developing prompts, adding constraints, editing and refining the responses generated. The more the prompt is specific, the better the results will be. Such experiences, as with any technology, will enable teachers to think critically about the role the technology will play in their teaching and assessments practices. Once the preservice teachers develop a better understanding of this new technology, then they are more likely to want to leverage its capabilities to enhance their planning, teaching and assessment.

A limitation for this study was that it was done with elementary school preservice teachers. The experiences of using ChatGPT in mathematics with ChatGPT will differ depending on the student population, the level and type of math topics.

REFERENCES

Allison, S. (2024). First Steps in Using the Power of AI in Education. *T-CARE*, XVI, 7.

Bailey, J. (2024). Why AI Struggles with Basic Math (and How That's Changing), AEIdeas. Retrieved on 12.2.2024 from https://www.aei.org/technology-and-innovation/why-ai struggles-with-basic-math-and-how-thats-changing/

Bailey, J. (2024). *Why AI Struggles with Basic Math (and How That's Changing)*. AEIdeas. Retrieved from https://www.aei.org/technology-and-innovation/why-ai-struggles-with basic-math-and-how-thats-changing/

Barrett, A., & Pack, A. (2023). Not quite eye to A.I.: Student and teacher perspectives on the use of generative artificial intelligence in the writing process. *International Journal of Educational Technology in Higher Education*, 20(1), 59. DOI: 10.1186/s41239-023-00427-0

Baumanns, L., & Pohl, M. (2024). *Leveraging ChatGPT for problem posing: an exploratory study of pre-service teachers' professional use of AI*. Proceedings of the 17th ERME Topic Conference MEDA4, 3-6 September 2024, Bari, Italy. P.57-64

Beauchamp, T., & Walkington, C. (2024). Mathematics Teachers Using Generative AI to Personalize Instruction to Students' Interests. *Connections*. Retrieved 12.2.2024 from https://amte.net/sites/amte.net/files/Connections%20%28Beauchamp%29.pdf

Bernardi, C. Faggiano & Troilo (2024). *Teachers exploring the potential of generative AI in mathematics teaching*. Proceedings of the 17th ERME Topic Conference MEDA4, 3-6 September 2024, Bari, Italy. P.57-64

Bower, M., Torrington, J., Lai, J. W. M., Petocz, P., & Alfano, M. (2024). How should we change teaching and assessment in response to increasingly powerful generative Artificial Intelligence? Outcomes of the ChatGPT teacher survey. *Education and Information Technologies*, 29, 15403–15439. DOI: 10.1007/s10639-023-12405-0

Chen, X., Xie, H., Zou, D., & Hwang, G. J. (2020). Application and theory gaps during the rise of artificial intelligence in education. Computers and Education: Artificial Intelligence,1, 100002. . caeai. 2020. 100002DOI: 10. 1016/j

Chiu, T. K. F. (2023). The impact of Generative AI (GenAI) on practices, policies and research direction in education: A case of ChatGPT and Midjourney. *Interactive Learning Environments*, •••, 1–17. DOI: 10.1080/10494820.2023.2253861

Chiu T. K. F. (2024). Future research recommendations for transforming higher education with Generative AI. *Computer & Education: Artificial Intelligence, 6,* 100197. . caeai. 2023. 100197DOI: 10. 1016/j

Chounta, I.-A., Bardone, E., Raudsep, A., & Pedaste, M. (2022). Exploring Teachers' Perceptions of Artificial Intelligence as a Tool to Support their Practice in Estonian K-12 Education. *International Journal of Artificial Intelligence in Education*, 32(3), 725–755. DOI: 10.1007/s40593-021-00243-5

Creswell, J. W. (2002). *Educational research: Planning, conducting, and evaluating quantitative and qualitative research.* Merrill Prentice Hall.

Dabingaya, M. (2022). Analyzing the Effectiveness of AI-Powered Adaptive Learning Platforms in Mathematics Education. *Interdisciplinary Journal Papier Human Review*, 3(1), 1–7. DOI: 10.47667/ijphr.v3i1.226

Dao, X. Q., & Le, N. B. (2023). Investigating the effectiveness of ChatGPT in Mathematical reasoning and problem solving: Evidence from the Vietnamese national high school graduation examination. *ArXiv, 2306*.06331. https://doi.org//arXiv.2306 .06331.DOI: 10.48550

Demir, G., & Cimen, E. (2024). Lesson Plan Preparation Process with ChatGPT in Mathematics Teaching: An Example of Research and Practice. *Technology. Innovation and Special Education Research*, 4(1), 83–98.

Gattupalli, S., Maloy, R. W., & Edwards, S. (2023). *Comparing Teacher-Written and AI Generated Math Problem Solving Strategies for Elementary School Students: Implications for Classroom Learning*. College of Education Working Papers and Reports Series. 5.DOI: 10.7275/8sgx-xj08

Hidayatullah, E., Untari, R., & Fifardin, F. (2024). Effectiveness of AI in solving math problems at the secondary school level: A comparative study with student performance. *Union: Journal Ilmiah Pendidikan Matematika*, 12(2), 350–360. DOI: 10.30738/union.v12i2.17548

Hwang, S. (2022). Examining the effects of Artificial Intelligence on elementary students' mathematics achievement: A Meta-Analysis. *Sustainability (Basel)*, 14(20), 13185. DOI: 10.3390/su142013185

Kolade, O., Owoseni, A., & Egbetokun, A. (2024). Is AI changing learning and assessment as we know it? Evidence from a ChatGPT experiment and a conceptual framework. *Heliyon*, 10(4), e25953. DOI: 10.1016/j.heliyon.2024.e25953 PMID: 38379960

Pelton, T., & Pelton, L. (2024). Using Generative AI in Mathematics Education: Critical Discussions and Practical Strategies for Preservice Teachers, Teachers, and Teacher Educators. In J. Cohen & G. Solano (Eds.), *Proceedings of Society for Information Technology & Teacher Education International Conference* (pp. 1800-1805). Las Vegas, Nevada, United States: Association for the Advancement of Computing in Education (AACE). Retrieved October 25, 2024 from https://www.learntechlib.org/primary/p/224212/

Popenici, S. A. D., & Kerr, S. (2017). Exploring the impact of artificial intelligence on teaching and learning in higher education. *Research and Practice in Technology Enhanced Learning*, 12(1), 1–13. DOI: 10.1186/s41039-017-0062-8 PMID: 30595727

Rizos, I., Foykas, E., & Georgakopoulos, S. V. (2024). Enhancing mathematics education for students with special educational needs through generative AI: A case study in Greece. *Contemporary Educational Technology*, 16(4), ep535. DOI: 10.30935/cedtech/15487

Samaras, A. P., & Freese, A. R. (2006). *Self-study of teaching practices primer*. Peter Lang International Academic Publishers.

Shakarian, P., Koyyalamudi, A., Ngu, N., & Mareedu, L. (2023). An Independent Evaluation of ChatGPT on Mathematical Word Problems (MWP). ArXiv, abs/2302.13814.

Stanoyevitch, A. (2024). Online assessment in the age of artificial intelligence. *Discover Education*, 3(1), 126. DOI: 10.1007/s44217-024-00212-9

Supriyadi, E., & Kuncoro, K. S. (2023). Exploring the future of mathematics teaching: Insight with ChatGPT. *Union J. Ilmiah Pendidik. Mat.*, 11(2), 305–316. DOI: 10.30738/union.v11i2.14898

Von Hippel, P. T. (2024). GPT-4 Is Still Not Ready to Teach Geometry. *Education Next*, 24(4). https://www.educationnext.org/chat-gpt-4-is-still-not-ready to-teach-geometry/

Wardat, Y., Tashtoush, M., Alali, R., & Saleh, S. (2024). Artificial Intelligence in Education: Mathematics Teachers' Perspectives, Practices and Challenges. *Iraqi Journal for Computer Science and Mathematics*, 5(1), 60–77. DOI: 10.52866/ijcsm.2024.05.01.004

Wardat, Y., Tashtoush, M. A., AlAli, R., & Jarrah, A. M. (2023). ChatGPT: A revolutionary tool for teaching and learning mathematics. *Eurasia Journal of Mathematics, Science and Technology Education*, 19(7), em2286. Advance online publication. DOI: 10.29333/ejmste/13272

Xia, Q., Xiaojing, W., Ouyang, F., Lin, T. J., & Chiu, T. K. (2024). A scoping review on how generative artificial intelligence transforms assessment in higher education. *International Journal of Educational Technology in Higher Education*, 2024(21), 40. DOI: 10.1186/s41239-024-00468-z

Zhai (2022). ChatGPT for Next Generation Science Learning, *XDRS, 2*(9), 42-46.

Zhang, K., & Aslan, A. B. (2021). AI technologies for education: Recent research & future directions. *Computers and Education: Artificial Intelligence*, 2, 100025. DOI: 10.1016/j.caeai.2021.100025

Figure 4 – computing 41-28 using base ten blocks

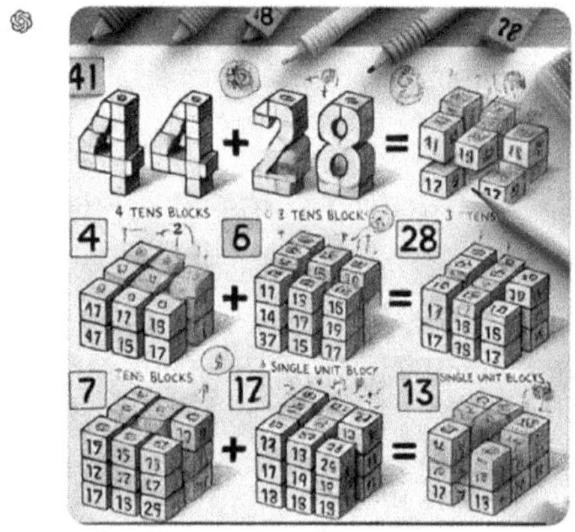

Here is a base-ten block drawing illustrating how to solve 41 − 28. It visually represents each step of the subtraction process:

1. **Starting with 41**: Four tens blocks and one single unit block.
2. **Regrouping**: One ten block is broken into ten single units, leaving three tens blocks and eleven single units.
3. **Subtracting 28**: Two tens blocks and eight single units are removed, leaving one ten block and three single units.

This step-by-step approach helps children understand subtraction and regrouping in a visual and interactive way!

Figure 5: ChatGPT output – subtracting a negative number

The rule that "a negative times a negative makes a positive" can be understood through several different perspectives, including algebraic reasoning and number patterns.

1. Pattern Observation:

- Consider the multiplication of a number by decreasing positive integers:

$$4 \times 3 = 12$$

$$4 \times 2 = 8$$

$$4 \times 1 = 4$$

$$4 \times 0 = 0$$

- Now, if we continue the pattern by multiplying by negative numbers:

$$4 \times -1 = -4$$

$$4 \times -2 = -8$$

- This pattern shows that multiplying by negative numbers inverts the sign. Extending this reasoning:

$$-4 \times 3 = -12$$

$$-4 \times 2 = -8$$

$$-4 \times 1 = -4$$

$$-4 \times 0 = 0$$

$$-4 \times -1 = 4$$

  - Therefore, when multiplying two negative numbers, the pattern suggests the result should be positive.

2. Algebraic Reasoning:

- Let's use the distributive property, which states:

$$a \times (b + c) = a \times b + a \times c$$

- Consider the expression $(-1) \times (1 + (-1))$:

$$(-1) \times (1 + (-1)) = (-1) \times 0 = 0$$

$$(-1) \times 1 + (-1) \times (-1) = 0$$

  - Since $(-1) \times 1 = -1$, we have:

$$-1 + (-1) \times (-1) = 0$$

$$(-1) \times (-1) = 1$$

  - This algebraic proof shows that multiplying two negative numbers results in a positive number.

3. Intuitive Explanation:

- Think of negative numbers as representing a movement in the opposite direction. If you "reverse" a reversal, you end up moving forward, which corresponds to a positive outcome.

This combination of patterns, algebraic reasoning, and intuition helps explain why a negative

Figure 6- Subtracting a negative integer

explain to a middle school learner why subtracting a negative integer is the same as adding the integer

Imagine you're on a number line. Positive numbers move you to the right, and negative numbers move you to the left.

Visualizing Subtraction:

- When you subtract a number, you move to the left on the number line. For example, $5 - 3$ means starting at 5 and moving 3 steps to the left, which lands you at 2.

What Happens with a Negative Number:

- Now, what if you need to subtract a negative number, like $5 - (-3)$? This is like saying, "take away moving left by 3 steps." But taking away moving left actually means you go to the right instead.
- So, subtracting -3 means you move 3 steps to the right, just like adding 3.

Simple Way to Think About It:

- Subtracting a negative number is the same as adding because you're doing the opposite of what the negative number suggests.
- For example:

$$5 - (-3) = 5 + 3 = 8$$

- This happens because the two negatives (the minus sign and the negative number) cancel each other out, turning into a positive.

A Real-Life Analogy:

- Imagine you owe your friend 3 dollars (represented by -3). If someone tells you, "Subtract that debt," it means you're not in debt anymore—instead, you now have 3 extra dollars. So subtracting a negative is like gaining or adding.

In summary, subtracting a negative number is the same as adding because you're reversing the action of the negative, which results in moving to the right on the number line.

Compilation of References

Ab Kadir, M. A. (2018). An inquiry into critical thinking in the Australian Curriculum: Examining its conceptual understandings and their implications on developing critical thinking as a "general capability" on teachers' practice and knowledge. *Asia Pacific Journal of Education*, 38(4), 533–549. DOI: 10.1080/02188791.2018.1535424

Abarca, N., & Majluf, N. (2021). *Soft skills for human-centered management and global sustainability*. M. T. Lepeley, & N. J. Beutell (Eds.). London, United Kingdm: Routledge.

Abbas, M., Jam, F. A., & Khan, T. I. (2024). Is it harmful or helpful? examining the causes and consequences of generative ai usage among university students. *International Journal of Educational Technology in Higher Education*, 21(1), 10. Advance online publication. DOI: 10.1186/s41239-024-00444-7

Abdulghafor, R., Turaev, S., & Ali, M. A. H. (2022). Body Language Analysis in Healthcare: An Overview. *Health Care*, 10(7), 1–35. DOI: 10.3390/healthcare10071251 PMID: 35885777

Abosalem, Y. (2016). Assessment techniques and students' higher-order thinking skills. *International Journal of Secondary Education*, 4(1), 1–11. DOI: 10.11648/j.ijsedu.20160401.11

Abulibdeh, A., Zaidan, E., & Abulibdeh, R. (2024). Navigating the confluence of artificial intelligence and education for sustainable development in the era of industry 4.0: Challenges, opportunities, and ethical dimensions. *Journal of Cleaner Production*, 437, 140527. DOI: 10.1016/j.jclepro.2023.140527

Adams, C., Pente, P., Lemermeyer, G., & Rockwell, G. (2023). Ethical principles for artificial intelligence in K-12 education. *Computers and Education: Artificial Intelligence*, 4, 1–11. DOI: 10.1016/j.caeai.2023.100131

Adeyemo, A., & Omole, O. (2023). *Leveraging AI for Teacher Training in Africa*. Educational Innovations Press.

Adiguzel, T., Kaya, M. H., & Cansu, F. K. (2023). Revolutionizing education with AI : Exploring the transformative potential of ChatGPT. [ARTICLE]. *Contemporary Educational Technology*, 15(3), 1–13. DOI: 10.30935/cedtech/13152

African Union. (2024, July). Continental Artificial Intelligence Strategy Harnessing AI for Africa's Development and Prosperity. https://au.int/sites/default/files/documents/44004-doc-EN-_Continental_AI_Strategy_July_2024.pdf

Ahmad, T. (2019). Scenario based approach to re-imagining future of higher education which prepares students for the future of work. *Higher Education, Skills and Work-Based Learning, 10*(1), 217–238. https://doi.org/https://doi.org/10.1108/HESWBL-12-2018-0136

Ahmed, A. (2024, May). *Meta AI Llama 3 vs ChatGPT 4: A comparative analysis*. PreScouter

Ahmed, M. A. (2023). ChatGPT and the EFL classroom: Supplement or substitute in Saudi Arabia's eastern region. *Information Sciences Letters*, 12(7), 2727–2734. DOI: 10.18576/isl/120704

AI Ethics Lab. (2022). AI Ethics Guidelines. Retrieved from https://aiethicslab.com

Ajgaonkar, S., Neelam, N. G., & Wiemann, J. (2022). Drivers of workforce agility: A dynamic capability perspective. *The International Journal of Organizational Analysis*, 30(4), 951–982. https://doi.org/https://doi.org/10.1108/IJOA-11-2020-2507. DOI: 10.1108/IJOA-11-2020-2507

Akbari, M., Nguyen, H. M., McClelland, R., & Van Houdt, K. (2022). Design, implementation and academic perspectives on authentic assessment for applied business higher education in a top performing Asian economy. *Education + Training*, 64(1), 69–88. DOI: 10.1108/ET-04-2021-0121

Akter, S., Hossain, M. A., Sajib, S., Sultana, S., Rahman, M., Vrontis, D., & McCarthy, G. (2023). A framework for AI-powered service innovation capability: Review and agenda for future research. *Technovation*, 125, 1–17. https://doi.org/https://doi.org/10.1016/j.technovation.2023.102768. DOI: 10.1016/j.technovation.2023.102768

Alabidi, S., AlArabi, K., Alsalhi, N. R., & Al Mansoori, M. (2023). The dawn of ChatGPT: Transformation in science assessment. *Eurasian Journal of Educational Research*, 106(106), 321–337.

Alam, A., & Mohanty, A. (2022). Foundation for the Future of Higher Education or 'Misplaced Optimism'? Being Human in the Age of Artificial Intelligence. *Innovations in Intelligent Computing and Communication. ICIICC 2022.Communications in Computer and Information Science*, 1737, 17–29. DOI: 10.1007/978-3-031-23233-6_2

Aldosari, S. A. (2020). The future of higher education in the light of artificial intelligence transformations. *International Journal of Higher Education*, 9(3), 145. DOI: 10.5430/ijhe.v9n3p145

Aler Tubella, A., Mora-Cantallops, M., & Nieves, J. C. (2024). How to teach responsible AI in higher education: Challenges and opportunities. *Ethics and Information Technology*, 26(1), 3. DOI: 10.1007/s10676-023-09733-7

Allam, H., Dempere, J., Akre, V., & Flores, P. (2023). *Artificial Intelligence in Education (AIED)*. Implications and Challenges., DOI: 10.2991/978-94-6463-286-6_10

Allison, S. (2024). First Steps in Using the Power of AI in Education. *T-CARE*, XVI, 7.

Almusaed, A., Almssad, A., Yitmen, I., & Homod, R. Z. (2023). Enhancing Student Engagement : Harnessing " AIED "' s Power in Hybrid Education — A Review Analysis. *Education Sciences*, 13(7), 1–24. DOI: 10.3390/educsci13070632

Alneyadi, S., & Wardat, Y. (2023). ChatGPT: Revolutionizing student achievement in the electronic magnetism unit for eleventh-grade students in Emirates schools. *Contemporary Educational Technology*, 15(4), ep448–ep448. DOI: 10.30935/cedtech/13417

Alshahrani, A. (2023). The impact of ChatGPT on blended learning: Current trends and future research directions. *International Journal of Data and Network Science*, 7(4), 2029–2040. DOI: 10.5267/j.ijdns.2023.6.010

Alshammari, R. F. N., Arshad, H., Rahman, A. H. A., & Albahri, O. S. (2022). Robotics Utilization in Automatic Vision-Based Assessment Systems From Artificial Intelligence Perspective: A Systematic Review. *IEEE Access : Practical Innovations, Open Solutions*, 10(May), 77537–77570. DOI: 10.1109/ACCESS.2022.3188264

Alshurafat, H., Al Shbail, M. O., Hamdan, A., Al-Dmour, A., & Ensour, W. (2023). Factors affecting accounting students' misuse of ChatGPT: An application of the fraud triangle theory. *Journal of Financial Reporting and Accounting*, 22(2), 274–288. DOI: 10.1108/JFRA-04-2023-0182

Alvarez, S. P., Wan, A. J., & Lee, E. (2021). Workin' languages: Who we are matters in our writing. *Writing Spaces: Readings on Writing, 4*, 1-17. https://writingspaces .org/past-volumes/workin-languages-who-we-are-matters-in-our-writing/

Amabile, T. M. (1996). *Creativity in context*. Westview Press.

Ambrose, S. A., Bridges, M. W., DiPietro, M., Lovett, M. C., & Norman, M. K. (2010). *How learning works: 7 research-based principles for smart teaching*. John Wiley & Sons.

Amer-Yahia, S. (2022). Towards AI-Powered Data-Driven Education. *Proceedings of the VLDB Endowment International Conference on Very Large Data Bases*, 15(12), 3798–3806. DOI: 10.14778/3554821.3554900

Amit, S., Karim, R., & Al Kafy, A. (2022). Mapping emerging massive open online course (MOOC) markets before and after COVID 19: A comparative perspective from Bangladesh and India. *Spatial Information Research*, 2022(5), 655–663. DOI: 10.1007/s41324-022-00463-4

Andersen, R., Mørch, A. I., & Litherland, K. T. (2022). Collaborative learning with block-based programming: Investigating human-centered artificial intelligence in education. *Behaviour & Information Technology*, 41(9), 1830–1847. DOI: 10.1080/0144929X.2022.2083981

Anderson, L. W., & Krathwohl, D. R. (2001). *A taxonomy for learning, teaching, and assessing: A revision of Bloom's taxonomy of educational objectives*. Allyn & Bacon.

Aneja, G. A. (2016). (Non)native speakered: Rethinking (non)nativeness and teacher identity in TESOL teacher education. *TESOL Quarterly*, 50(3), 572–596. DOI: 10.1002/tesq.315

Anshari, M., & Hamdan, M. (2022). Understanding knowledge management and upskilling in Fourth Industrial Revolution: Transformational shift and SECI model. *VINE Journal of Information and Knowledge Management Systems*, 52(3), 373–393. https://doi.org/https://doi.org/10.1108/VJIKMS-09-2021-0203. DOI: 10.1108/VJIKMS-09-2021-0203

Assaraf, N. (2022). *Chatgpt: Optimizing language models for dialogue*. Retrieved from https://blog.cloudhq.net/openais-chatgpt-optimizinglanguage-models-for-dialogue/

Attali, Y., & Arieli-Attali, M. (2015). Gamification in assessment: Do points affect test performance? *Computers & Education*, 83, 57–63. DOI: 10.1016/j.compedu.2014.12.012

Azaria, A., Azoulay, R., & Reches, S. (2023). *ChatGPT is a Remarkable Tool — For Experts*. 1–37. http://arxiv.org/abs/2306.03102

Bacon-Shone. Bolton, K., Lee, S. L., Richards, B., & Bhatia, A. (2019). *The Contribution of Minority Languages and Dialects to Hong Kong's Linguistic Landscape.* Research report. Public Policy Research Funding Scheme. Hong Kong SAR Government.

Bacon-Shone, J., Bolton, K., & Luke, K. K. (2015). *Language use, proficiency and attitudes in Hong Kong*. Social Sciences Research Centre, HKU.

Bai, B., Wang, J., & Zhou, H. (2021). An intervention study to improve primary school students' self-regulated strategy use in English writing through e-learning in Hong Kong. *Computer Assisted Language Learning*, 35(9), 2265–2290. DOI: 10.1080/09588221.2020.1871030

Baidoo-Anu, D., & Owusu Ansah, L. (2023). Education in the Era of Generative Artificial Intelligence (AI): Understanding the Potential Benefits of ChatGPT in Promoting Teaching and Learning. *Journal of AI*, 7(1), 52–62. DOI: 10.61969/jai.1337500

Bai, L., Liu, X., & Su, J. (2023). ChatGPT: The cognitive effects on learning and memory. *Brain-X*, 1(3), e30. Advance online publication. DOI: 10.1002/brx2.30

Bailey, J. (2024). Why AI Struggles with Basic Math (and How That's Changing), AEIdeas. Retrieved on 12.2.2024 from https://www.aei.org/technology-and-innovation/why-ai struggles-with-basic-math-and-how-thats-changing/

Bailey, J. (2024). *Why AI Struggles with Basic Math (and How That's Changing).* AEIdeas. Retrieved from https://www.aei.org/technology-and-innovation/why-ai-struggles-with basic-math-and-how-thats-changing/

Baird, J. S. (1980). Current trends in college cheating. *Psychology in the Schools*, 17(4), 515–522. DOI: 10.1002/1520-6807(198010)17:4<515::AID-PITS2310170417>3.0.CO;2-3

Balaquiao, E. C. (2024). Optimizing Students' Performance through Artificial Intelligence (AI) Technology: A Gamified Approach to Smart Learning Environment. *Journal of Pedagogy and Education Science*, 3(02), 104–114. DOI: 10.56741/jpes.v3i02.515

Balart, T., & Shryock, K. J. (2024, May). A Framework for Integrating AI into Engineering Education, Empowering Human-Centered Approach for Industry 5.0. In *2024 IEEE Global Engineering Education Conference (EDUCON)* (pp. 1-10). IEEE. DOI: 10.1109/EDUCON60312.2024.10578796

Banta, T. W., & Palomba, C. A. (2014). *Assessment essentials: Planning, implementing, and improving assessment in higher education*. Jossey-Bass.

Barana, A., Conte, A., Fissore, C., Marchisio, M., & Rabellino, S. (2019). Learning analytics to improve formative assessment strategies. JE-LKS. *Journal of e-learning and knowledge society, 15*(3), 75-88.

Barkhuus, L., & Wobbrock, J. O. (2020). Empowering people with impairments through conversational access to information. In *Proceedings of the 2020 CHI Conference on Human Factors in Computing Systems* (pp. 1-13).

Baron, S. N. (19 Jan. 2023). How ChatGPT robs students of motivation to think and write for themselves. The Conversation. Retrieved from https://theconversation.com/how-chatgpt-robs-students-of-motivation-to-write-and-think-for-themselves-197875

Barrett, A., & Pack, A. (2023). Not quite eye to A.I.: Student and teacher perspectives on the use of generative artificial intelligence in the writing process. *International Journal of Educational Technology in Higher Education*, 20(1), 59. DOI: 10.1186/s41239-023-00427-0

Bartholomae, D. (1995). Writing with teachers: A conversation with Peter Elbow. *College Composition and Communication*, 46(1), 62–71. DOI: 10.58680/ccc19958754

Basham, J. D., Hall, T. E., Carter, R. A.Jr, & Stahl, W. M. (2016). An operationalized understanding of personalized learning. *Journal of Special Education Technology*, 31(3), 126–136. DOI: 10.1177/0162643416660835

Bastiaens, T., Wood, L., & Reiners, T. (2014). New landscapes and new eyes: The role of virtual world design for supply chain education. *Ubiquitous Learning*, 6(1), 37–49. DOI: 10.18848/1835-9795/CGP/v06i01/40388

Bates, T., Cobo, C., Marino, O., & Wheeler, S. (2020). Can artificial intelligence transform higher education? *International Journal of Educational Technology in Higher Education*, 17(1), 1–12. DOI: 10.1186/s41239-020-00218-x

Baumanns, L., & Pohl, M. (2024). *Leveraging ChatGPT for problem posing: an exploratory study of pre-service teachers' professional use of AI.* Proceedings of the 17th ERME Topic Conference MEDA4, 3-6 September 2024, Bari, Italy. P.57-64

Bauschard, S., & Quidwai, S. (2024). From insight to implementation: How to create your AI school guidance. Available at *SSRN*. DOI: 10.2139/ssrn.4784207

Beauchamp, T., & Walkington, C. (2024). Mathematics Teachers Using Generative AI to Personalize Instruction to Students' Interests. *Connections.* Retrieved 12.2.2024 from https://amte.net/sites/amte.net/files/Connections%20%28Beauchamp%29.pdf

Bernardi, C. Faggiano & Troilo (2024). *Teachers exploring the potential of generative AI in mathematics teaching.* Proceedings of the 17th ERME Topic Conference MEDA4, 3-6 September 2024, Bari, Italy. P.57-64

Berthoff, A. E. (2003). Is Teaching Still Possible? Writing, Meaning, and Higher Order Reasoning. In Villanueva, V. (Ed.), *Cross-Talk in Comp Theory: A Reader* (pp. 329–343). NCTE. Print

Best AI Tools. (n.d.). Retrieved from https://www.veed.io/learn/best-ai-tools

Bewersdorff, A., Seßler, K., Baur, A., Kasneci, E., & Nerdel, C. (2023). Assessing Student Errors in Experimentation Using Artificial Intelligence and Large Language Models: A Comparative Study with Human Raters. *ArXiv Preprint ArXiv:2308.06088.* https://doi.org/https://doi.org/10.48550/arXiv.2308.06088

Bitzenbauer, P. (2023). ChatGPT in physics education: A pilot study on easy-to-implement activities. *Contemporary Educational Technology*, 15(3), 1–10. DOI: 10.30935/cedtech/13176

Bizzell, P. (2006). The Intellectual Work of 'Mixed' Forms of Academic Discourses. In Vandenberg, P., Hum, S., & Clary-Lemon, J. (Eds.), *Relations, Locations, Positions: Composition Theory for Writing Teachers* (pp. 72–83). NCTE. Print

Black, N. B., George, S., Eguchi, A., Dempsey, J. C., Langran, E., Fraga, L., Brunvand, S., & Howard, N. (2024, March). A framework for approaching AI education in educator preparation programs. *Proceedings of the AAAI Conference on Artificial Intelligence*, 38(21), 23069–23077. DOI: 10.1609/aaai.v38i21.30351

Black, P., & Wiliam, D. (1998). Assessment and classroom learning. *Assessment in Education: Principles, Policy & Practice*, 5(1), 7–74. DOI: 10.1080/0969595980050102

Bloom, B. S. (1956). *Taxonomy of Educational Objectives*. Longmans, Green.

Bocala, C., & Parker Boudett, K. (2015). Teaching educators habits of mind for using data wisely. *Teachers College Record*, 117(4), 1–20. DOI: 10.1177/016146811511700409

Bolton, K., Bacon-Shone, J., & Lee, S.-l. (2020). Societal multilingualism in Hong Kong. In Siemund, P., & Leimgruber, J. (Eds.), *Multilingual global cities: Dubai, Hong Kong and Singapore* (pp. 160–184). Routledge. DOI: 10.4324/9780429463860-12

Bolton, K., & Lee, S.-l. (2020). A socio-historical approach to multilingualism in Hong Kong. In Siemund, P., & Leimgruber, J. (Eds.), *Multilingual global cities: Hong Kong, Singapore, and Dubai* (pp. 38–62). Routledge. DOI: 10.4324/9780429463860-4

Bower, M., Torrington, J., Lai, J. W. M., Petocz, P., & Alfano, M. (2024). How should we change teaching and assessment in response to increasingly powerful generative Artificial Intelligence? Outcomes of the ChatGPT teacher survey. *Education and Information Technologies*, 29, 15403–15439. DOI: 10.1007/s10639-023-12405-0

Broadhead, G. (2023, August 25). A Brief Guide To LLM Numbers: Parameter count vs. training size. *Medium*. https://medium.com/@greg.broadhead/a-brief-guide-to-llm-numbers-parameter-count-vs-training-size-894a81c9258

Brown, S., & Race, P. (2012). *Using effective assessment to promote learning*. Routledge. DOI: 10.4324/9780203079690-5

Brown, T., & Smith, J. (2024). The psychological impact of AI on student learning. *Journal of Educational Psychology*, 50(2), 210–225.

Brynjolfsson, E., Li, D., & Raymond, L. (April 2023). Generative AI at work (NBER Working Paper No. W31161). Retrieved from *SSRN*: https://ssrn.com/abstract=4426942 DOI: 10.2139/ssrn.4426942

Budhwar, P., Chowdhury, S., Wood, G., Aguinis, H., Bamber, G. J., Beltran, J. R., Boselie, P., Cooke, F. L., Decker, S., DeNisi, A., Dey, P. K., Guest, D., Knoblich, A. J., Malik, A., Paauwe, J., Papagiannidis, S., Patel, C., Pereira, V., Ren, S., & Varma, A. (2023). Human resource management in the age of generative artificial intelligence: Perspectives and research directions on ChatGPT. '. *Human Resource Management Journal*, 33(3), 606–659. https://doi.org/https://doi.org/10.1111/1748-8583.12524. DOI: 10.1111/1748-8583.12524

Bulger, M. (2016). *Personalized learning: The conversations we're not having* [Working Paper]. Data & Society Research Institute. https://www.datasociety.net/pubs/ecl/PersonalizedLearning_primer_2016.pdf

Burgess, A. (2017). *The Executive Guide to Artificial Intelligence: How to identify and implement applications for AI in your organization*. Springer.

Busch, F., Hoffmann, L., Truhn, D., Palaian, S., Alomar, M., Shpati, K., Makowski, M. R., Bressem, K. K., & Adams, L. C. (2023). International pharmacy students' perceptions towards artificial intelligence in medicine—A multinational, multicentre cross-sectional study. *British Journal of Clinical Pharmacology*, 90(3), 649–661. DOI: 10.1111/bcp.15911 PMID: 37728146

Campbell, H. S. (2023). What is human about writing?: Writing process theory and ChatGPT. *Research Square*. DOI: 10.21203/rs.3.rs-3208562/v1

Cardon, P., Fleischmann, C., Aritz, J., Logemann, M., & Heidewald, J. (2023). The challenges and opportunities of Al-assisted writing: Developing Al literacy for the Al age. *Business and Professional Communication Quarterly*, 86(3), 1–39. DOI: 10.1177/23294906231176517

Carless, D. (2007). Learning-oriented assessment: Conceptual bases and practical implications. *Innovations in Education and Teaching International*, 44(1), 57–66. DOI: 10.1080/14703290601081332

Center for Education Policy Research at Harvard University. (n.d.). *DreamBox learning achievement growth.* Retrieved from https://cepr.harvard.edu/dreambox-learning-achievement-growth

Centre for Learning, Teaching, and Development. (2024). *Guidelines for GAI use in Learning, Teaching, and Research.* University of the Witwatersrand.

Chan, C. K. Y. (2023). A comprehensive AI policy education framework for university teaching and learning. *International Journal of Educational Technology in Higher Education*, 2023(20), 38. DOI: 10.1186/s41239-023-00408-3

Chan, S. D. (2019). From oracy to literacy: the role of Cantonese in the learning of Chinese reading and writing. In Wakefield, J. (Ed.), *Cantonese as a second language: Issues, experiences and suggestions for teaching and learning* (pp. 209–231). Routledge.

Chapelle, C. A., & Chung, Y. R. (2010). The promise of NLP and speech processing technologies in language assessment. *Language Testing*, 27(3), 301–315. DOI: 10.1177/0265532210364405

Chassignol, M., Khoroshavin, A., Klimova, A., & Bilyatdinova, A. (2018). Artificial Intelligence trends in education: A narrative overview. *Procedia Computer Science*, 136, 16–24. DOI: 10.1016/j.procs.2018.08.233

Chauncey, S. A., & McKenna, H. P. (2024, June). Exploring the potential of cognitive flexibility and elaboration in support of curiosity, interest, and engagement in designing AI-rich learning spaces, extensible to urban environments. In *International Conference on Human-Computer Interaction* (pp. 209-230). Cham: Springer Nature Switzerland. DOI: 10.1007/978-3-031-60012-8_13

Chauncey, S. A., & McKenna, H. P. (2023). A framework and exemplars for ethical and responsible use of AI chatbot technology to support teaching and learning. *Computers and Education: Artificial Intelligence*, 5, 100182. DOI: 10.1016/j.caeai.2023.100182

Chechitelli, A. (2023, March 16). *Understanding false positives within our AI writing detection capabilities*. www.turnitin.com. https://www.turnitin.com/blog/understanding-false-positives-within-our-ai-writing-detection-capabilities

Chen, L. (2023, June 23). Hong Kong rolls out first AI curriculum for junior secondary students, including lessons on ChatGPT, with 'lives definitely affected by artificial intelligence'. *South China Morning Post*.

Chen, X., Xie, H., Zou, D., & Hwang, G. J. (2020). Application and theory gaps during the rise of artificial intelligence in education. Computers and Education: Artificial Intelligence,1, 100002. . caeai. 2020. 100002DOI: 10. 1016/j

Chen, X., Xie, H., Zou, D., & Hwang, G.-J. (2020). Application and theory gaps during the rise of Artificial Intelligence in Education. *Computers and Education: Artificial Intelligence, 1*, 1–20. https://doi.org/doi.org/10.1016/j.caeai.2020.100002

Chen, C., Koong, C., & Liao, C. (2022). Influences of Integrating Dynamic Assessment into a Speech Recognition. *Journal of Educational Technology & Society*, 25(1), 1–14. https://www.jstor.org/stable/48647026

Cheng, E. C. K., & Wang, T. (2023). Leading digital transformation and eliminating barriers for teachers to incorporate artificial intelligence in basic education in Hong Kong. *Computers and Education: Artificial Intelligence*, 5, 100171. DOI: 10.1016/j.caeai.2023.100171

Chen, L., Chen, P., & Lin, Z. (2020). Artificial intelligence in education: A review. *IEEE Access : Practical Innovations, Open Solutions*, 8, 75264–75278. DOI: 10.1109/ACCESS.2020.2988510

Chen, X., Zhou, D., Xie, H., Cheng, G., & Liu, C. (2022). Two decades of artificial intelligence in education: Contributors, collaborations, research topics, challenges, and future directions. *Journal of Educational Technology & Society*, 25(1), 28–47.

Chen, X., Zou, D., Xie, H., Cheng, G., & Liu, C. (2022). Two Decades of Artificial Intelligence in Education. *Journal of Educational Technology & Society*, 25(1), 28–47. https://www.jstor.org/stable/48647028

Chhillar, D., & Aguilera, R. V. (2022). An Eye for Artificial Intelligence: Insights Into the Governance of Artificial Intelligence and Vision for Future Research. *Business & Society*, 61(5), 1197–1241. DOI: 10.1177/00076503221080959

Chin, A. C. (2023). A corpus-based approach to learning and teaching Cantonese. In Lee, S. L. (Ed.), *The learning and teaching of Cantonese as a second language* (pp. 184–196). Routledge., DOI: 10.4324/9781003054696

Chiu, T. K. (2023). The impact of generative AI (GenAI) on practices, policies and research direction in education: A case of ChatGPT and Midjourney. *Interactive Learning Environments*, •••, 1–17. DOI: 10.1080/10494820.2023.2253861

Chiu, T. K. F., Meng, H., Chai, C.-S., King, I., Wong, S., & Yam, Y. (2022). Creation and Evaluation of a Pretertiary Artificial Intelligence (AI) Curriculum. *IEEE Transactions on Education*, 65(1), 30–39. DOI: 10.1109/TE.2021.3085878

Chong, L., Zhang, G., Goucher-Lambert, K., Kotovsky, K., & Cagan, J. (2022). Human confidence in artificial intelligence and in themselves: The evolution and impact of confidence on adoption of AI advice. *Computers in Human Behavior*, 127, 107018. DOI: 10.1016/j.chb.2021.107018

Chounta, I.-A., Bardone, E., Raudsep, A., & Pedaste, M. (2022). Exploring Teachers' Perceptions of Artificial Intelligence as a Tool to Support their Practice in Estonian K-12 Education. *International Journal of Artificial Intelligence in Education*, 32(3), 725–755. DOI: 10.1007/s40593-021-00243-5

Chowdhury Niloy, A., Bari, M. A., Sultana, J., Chowdhury, R., Raisa, F. M., Islam, A., Mahmud, S., Jahan, I., Sarkar, M., Akter, S., Nishat, N., Afroz, M., Sen, A., Islam, T., Tareq, M. H., & Hossen, M. A. (2024). Why do students use ChatGPT? Answering through a triangulation approach. *Computers and Education: Artificial Intelligence*, 6, 100208. DOI: 10.1016/j.caeai.2024.100208

Christensen, C. M., & Raynor, M. E. (2024). *The innovator's solution: Creating and sustaining successful growth*. Harvard Business Review Press.

Chu, H.-C., Hwang, G.-H., Tu, Y.-F., & Yang, K.-H. (2022). Roles and research trends of artificial intelligence in higher education: A systematic review of the top 50 most-cited articles. *Australasian Journal of Educational Technology*, 38(3), 22–42. https://doi.org/doi.org/10.14742/ajet.7526

Chui, M., Hazan, E., Roberts, R., Singla, A., Smaje, K., Sukharevsky, A., Yee, L., & Zemmel, R. (2023, June 14), The economic potential of generative AI: The next productivity frontier, *McKinsey Digital*. https://www.mckinsey.com/capabilities/mckinsey-digital/our-insights/the-economic-potential-of-generative-AI-the-next-productivity-frontier#introduction

Chung, J. (2023). AI Luddites: Consumers penalize creative work output generated by artificial intelligence. https://doi.org/DOI: 10.21203/rs.3.rs-3444321/v1

Cingillioglu, I. (2023). *Detecting AI-generated essays: the ChatGPT challenge*. Campus-Wide.

Cingillioglu, I. (2023, May 25). Detecting AI-generated essays: The ChatGPT challenge. *Information Systems*, 40(3), 259–268. DOI: 10.1108/IJILT-03-2023-0043

Conde, J., Reviriego, P., Salvachúa, J., Martínez, G., Hernández, J. A., & Lombardi, F. (2024). Understanding the impact of artificial intelligence in academic writing: Metadata to the rescue. *Computer*, 57(1), 105–109. DOI: 10.1109/MC.2023.3327330

Conference on College Composition and Communication. (2014). *Students right to their own languages.* Retrieved from https://prod-ncte cdn.azureedge.net/nctefiles/groups/cccc/newsrtol.pdf

Consuegra-Fernández, M., Sanz-Aznar, J., Burguera-Serra, J. G., & Caballero-Molina, J. J. (2024). Chatgpt. *Revista de Investigación Educacional*, 42(2). Advance online publication. DOI: 10.6018/rie.565391

Cooper, G. (2023). Examining science education in ChatGPT: An exploratory study of generative artificial intelligence. *Journal of Science Education and Technology*, 32(3), 444–452. DOI: 10.1007/s10956-023-10039-y

Cope, B., Kalantzis, M., & Searsmith, D. (2021). Artificial intelligence for education: Knowledge and its assessment in AI-enabled learning ecologies. *Educational Philosophy and Theory*, 53(12), 1229–1245. DOI: 10.1080/00131857.2020.1728732

Cornell University. (2023, July 18). *Generative artificial intelligence for education and pedagogy.* https://www.cornell.edu

Cortazar, C., Nussbaum, M., Harcha, J., Alvares, D., López, F., Goñi, J., & Cabezas, V. (2021). Promoting critical thinking in an online, project-based course. *Computers in Human Behavior*, 119, 106705. DOI: 10.1016/j.chb.2021.106705 PMID: 36571081

Cosyn, E., Uzun, H., Doble, C., & Matayoshi, J. (2021). A practical perspective on knowledge space theory: ALEKS and its data. *Journal of Mathematical Psychology*, 101, 102512. DOI: 10.1016/j.jmp.2021.102512

Crawford, J., Cowling, M., & Allen, K. A. (2023). Leadership is needed for ethical ChatGPT: Character, assessment, and learning using artificial intelligence (AI). *Journal of University Teaching & Learning Practice*, 20(3), 1–21. DOI: 10.53761/1.20.01.01

Creswell, J. W. (2002). *Educational research: Planning, conducting, and evaluating quantitative and qualitative research.* Merrill Prentice Hall.

Csikszentmihalyi, M. (1990). *Flow: The psychology of optimal experience.* Harper & Row.

Currie, G. M. (2023). Academic integrity and artificial intelligence: Is ChatGPT hype, hero or heresy? In *Seminars in Nuclear Medicine*. WB Saunders., DOI: 10.1053/j.semnuclmed.2023.04.008

Dabingaya, M. (2022). Analyzing the Effectiveness of AI-Powered Adaptive Learning Platforms in Mathematics Education. *Interdisciplinary Journal Papier Human Review*, 3(1), 1–7. DOI: 10.47667/ijphr.v3i1.226

Dai, Y., Liu, A., & Ping, C. (2023). Reconceptualizing ChatGPT and generative AI as a student-driven innovation in higher education. *33rd CIRP Design Conference, 00*, 1–7. DOI: 10.1016/j.procir.2023.05.002

Damasevicius, R., & Sidekerskiene, T. (2024). AI as a teacher: A new educational dynamic for modern classrooms for personalized learning support. In *AI-Enhanced Teaching Methods* (pp. 1–24). IGI Global. DOI: 10.4018/979-8-3693-2728-9.ch001

Darling-Hammond, L. (2017). *Developing and Measuring Higher Order Skills: Models for State Performance Assessment Systems*. Council of Chief State School Officers.

Darwin, R., Rusdin, D., Mukminatien, N., Suryati, N., Laksmi, E. D., & Marzuki, . (2024). Critical thinking in the AI era: An exploration of EFL students' perceptions, benefits, and limitations. *Cogent Education*, 11(1), 2290342. DOI: 10.1080/2331186X.2023.2290342

Datnow, A., & Hubbard, L. (2016). Teacher capacity for and beliefs about data-driven decision making: A literature review of international research. *Journal of Educational Change*, 17(1), 7–28. DOI: 10.1007/s10833-015-9264-2

Davidovitch, N., & Eckhaus, E. (2020). The relationship between students' research motivation, capacity for independent work, and research outputs: Defining the good advisee using natural language processing. *Journal of Education and Learning*, 9(5), 38. DOI: 10.5539/jel.v9n5p38

Davidson, J. (2023). Equity and fairness in AI-driven education. *Journal of Social Equity in Education*, 18(2), 115–130.

Davies, A., Fidler, D., & Gorbis, M. (2011). Future work skills 2020. *Institute for the Future for Apollo Research Institute*. https://uqpn.uq.edu.au/files/203/LIBBY%20MARSHALL%20future_work_skills_2020_full_research_report_final_1.pdf

Davy, T. K. N. G., Luo, W., Chan, H. M. Y., & Chu, S. K. W. (2022). Using digital story writing as a pedagogy to develop AI literacy among primary students. *Computers and Education: Artificial Intelligence*, 3(February), 1–14. DOI: 10.1016/j.caeai.2022.100054

Demetroulis, E. A., Theodoropoulos, A., Antoniou, A., Wallace, M., & Poulopoulos, V. (2023). Collaboration Skills in Educational Robotics: A Methodological Approach—Results from Two Case Studies in Primary Schools. *Education Sciences*, 13(5), 468. https://doi.org/https://doi.org/10.3390/educsci13050468. DOI: 10.3390/educsci13050468

Demir, G., & Cimen, E. (2024). Lesson Plan Preparation Process with ChatGPT in Mathematics Teaching: An Example of Research and Practice. *Technology. Innovation and Special Education Research*, 4(1), 83–98.

Demir, K. A. (2021). Smart education framework. *Smart Learning Environments*, 8(1), 1–36. DOI: 10.1186/s40561-021-00170-x

Denga, E. M., & Denga, S. W. (2024). Revolutionizing education: The power of technology. In *Revolutionizing Curricula Through Computational Thinking, Logic, and Problem Solving* (pp. 167-188). IGI Global.

Deng, L., Bengio, Y., & Frasconi, P. (2020). Guest Editorial: Special Issue on Artificial Intelligence in Education. *IEEE Transactions on Pattern Analysis and Machine Intelligence*, 42(3), 499–501.

Deng, X., & Yu, Z. (2023). A Meta-Analysis and Systematic Review of the Effect of Chatbot Technology Use in Sustainable Education. *Sustainability (Basel)*, 15(4), 2940. DOI: 10.3390/su15042940

Denny, P., Khosravi, H., Hellas, A., Leinonen, J., & Sarsa, S. (2023). Can we trust AI-generated educational content? comparative analysis of human and AI-generated learning resources. arXiv preprint arXiv:2306.10509.

Department for Education Innovation. (2024). *Lecturer's Guide: Leveraging Generative Artificial Intelligence for teaching and Learning Enhancement at the University of Pretoria*. University of Pretoria.

Dergaa, I., Chamari, K., Zmijewski, P., & Ben Saad, H. (2023). From human writing to artificial intelligence generated text: Examining the prospects and potential threats of ChatGPT in academic writing. *Biology of Sport*, 40(2), 615–622. DOI: 10.5114/biolsport.2023.125623 PMID: 37077800

Dewey, J. (1938). *Experience and Education*. Free Press.

Di Battista, S., Pivetti, M., Melotti, G., & Berti, C. (2022). Lecturer Competence from the Perspective of Undergraduate Psychology Students: A Qualitative Pilot Study. *Education Sciences*, 12(2), 139. https://doi.org/https://doi.org/10.3390/educsci12020139. DOI: 10.3390/educsci12020139

Dicheva, D., Dichev, C., Agre, G., & Angelova, G. (2015). Gamification in education: A systematic mapping study. *Journal of Educational Technology & Society*, 18(3), 75–88.

Dimitriadou, E., & Lanitis, A. (2023). A critical evaluation, challenges, and future perspectives of using artificial intelligence and emerging technologies in smart classrooms. *Smart Learning Environments*, 10(1), 12. DOI: 10.1186/s40561-023-00231-3

Ding, A. C. E., Shi, L., Yang, H., & Choi, I. (2024). Enhancing teacher AI literacy and integration through different types of cases in teacher professional development. *Computers and Education Open*, 6, 100178. DOI: 10.1016/j.caeo.2024.100178

Doshi, A. R., & Hauser, O. P. (2024). Generative AI enhances individual creativity but reduces the collective diversity of novel content. *Science Advances*, 10(28), eadn5290. Advance online publication. DOI: 10.1126/sciadv.adn5290 PMID: 38996021

Duah, J. E., & McGivern, P. (2024). How generative artificial intelligence has blurred notions of authorial identity and academic norms in higher education, necessitating clear university usage policies. *Campus-Wide Information Systems*, 41(2), 180–193. Advance online publication. DOI: 10.1108/IJILT-11-2023-0213

Duch, B. J., Groh, S. E., & Allen, D. E. (2001). *The power of problem-based learning: a practical "how to" for teaching undergraduate courses in any discipline*. Stylus Pub.

Dweck, C. S. (2007). *Mindset: The new psychology of success*. Ballantine Books.

Dwivedi, Y. K., Hughes, L., Ismagilova, E., Aarts, G., Coombs, C., Crick, T., Duan, Y., Dwivedi, R., Edwards, J., Eirug, A., Galanos, V., Ilavarasan, P. V., Janssen, M., Jones, P., Kar, A. K., Kizgin, H., Kronemann, B., Lal, B., Lucini, B., & Williams, M. D. (2021). Artificial Intelligence (AI): Multidisciplinary perspectives on emerging challenges, opportunities, and agenda for research, practice and policy. *International Journal of Information Management*, 57, 101994. DOI: 10.1016/j.ijinfomgt.2019.08.002

Dwivedi, Y. K., Kshetri, N., Hughes, L., Slade, E. L., Jeyaraj, A., Kar, A. K., Baabdullah, A. M., Koohang, A., Raghavan, V., Ahuja, M., Albanna, H., Albashrawi, M. A., Al-Busaidi, A. S., Balakrishnan, J., Barlette, Y., Basu, S., Bose, I., Brooks, L., Buhalis, D., & Wright, R. (2023). "So what if ChatGPT wrote it?" Multidisciplinary perspectives on opportunities, challenges and implications of generative conversational AI for research, practice and policy. *International Journal of Information Management*, 71(March), 1–63. DOI: 10.1016/j.ijinfomgt.2023.102642

Eager, B., & Brunton, R. (2023). Prompting Higher Education Towards AI-Augmented Teaching and Learning Practice. *Journal of University Teaching & Learning Practice*, 20(5). Advance online publication. DOI: 10.53761/1.20.5.02

Earl, L. M. (2013). *Assessment as learning: Using classroom assessment to maximize student learning* (2nd ed.). Corwin.

Edwards, S. B. (2024). Teaching Creativity with AI: Innovative Approaches and Classroom Practices. *Journal of Creativity and Innovation in Education*, 16, 190–210.

Elali, F. R., & Rachid, L. N. (2023). AI-generated research paper fabrication and plagiarism in the scientific community. *Patterns (New York, N.Y.)*, 4(3), 1–4. DOI: 10.1016/j.patter.2023.100706 PMID: 36960451

Elbow, P. (1995, February). Being a writer vs. being an academic. *College Composition and Communication*, 46(1), 72–83. DOI: 10.58680/ccc19958755

Elim, E. (2024). Promoting cognitive skills in AI-supported learning environments: the integration of Bloom's taxonomy. *Informa UK Limited, trading as Taylor & Francis Group*, 3-13.

Ellis, E. (2016). "I may not be a native speaker but I'm not monolingual": Reimagining all teachers linguistic identities in TESOL. *TESOL Quarterly*, 50(3), 597–630. DOI: 10.1002/tesq.314

Elme, L. J., Jørgensen, M. L. M., Dandanell, G., Mottelson, A., & Makransky, G. (2022). Immersive virtual reality in STEM: Is IVR an effective learning medium and does adding self-explanation after a lesson improve learning outcomes? *Educational Technology Research and Development*, 70(5), 1601–1626. DOI: 10.1007/s11423-022-10139-3 PMID: 35873274

European Commission. (2020). Digital Education Action Plan 2021-2027. Retrieved from https://ec.europa.eu/education/education-in-the-eu/digital-education-action-plan_en

Falmagne, J. C., Albert, D., Doble, C., Eppstein, D., & Hu, X. (Eds.). (2013). *Knowledge spaces: Applications in education*. Springer Science & Business Media. DOI: 10.1007/978-3-642-35329-1

Faltis, C. J. (2013). Demystifying and questioning the power of academic language. In Arias, M. B., & Faltis, C. J. (Eds.), *Academic language in second language learning* (pp. 3–26). Information Age Publishing.

Fanning, J. (2023). AI-based Assessment in Education (AIBA): evidence review. In B. du Boulay (Ed.), A. Mitrovic (Ed.), K. Yacef (Ed.) *The Handbook of Artificial Intelligence in Education* (pp), Edward Elgar Publishing Ltd. Cheltenham, UK.

Faqih, N. (2023, October). Developing Literacy and Critical Thinking with AI: What Students Say. In *Proceeding of Annual International Conference on Islamic Education (AICIED)* (Vol. 1, pp. 16-25).

Fareed, M. W., Bou Nassif, A., & Nofal, E. (2024). Exploring the potentials of artificial intelligence image generators for educating the history of architecture. *Heritage*, 7(3), 1727–1753. DOI: 10.3390/heritage7030081

Felder, R. M., & Brent, R. (2005). Understanding student differences. *Journal of Engineering Education*, 94(1), 57–72. DOI: 10.1002/j.2168-9830.2005.tb00829.x

Feldstein, M., & Hill, P. (2016). Personalized learning: What it really is and why it really matters. *EDUCAUSE Review*, 51(2), 24–35.

Felix, J., & Webb, L.UK Parliament POST. (2024, January 23). Use of artificial intelligence in education delivery and assessment. *POSTnote*, 712. Advance online publication. DOI: 10.58248/PN712

Fish, S. (24 Aug. 2009). What should colleges teach? *New York Times*, https://archive.nytimes.com/opinionator.blogs.nytimes.com/2009/08/24/what-should-colleges-teach/

Fitzgerald, E., Kucirkova, N., Jones, A., Cross, S., Ferguson, R., Herodotou, C., Hillaire, G., & Scanlon, E. (2018). Dimensions of personalisation in technology-enhanced learning: A framework and implications for design. *British Journal of Educational Technology*, 49(1), 165–181. DOI: 10.1111/bjet.12534

Flores, M. A., Barros, A., Simão, A. M. V., Pereira, D., Flores, P., Fernandes, E., Costa, L., & Ferreira, P. C. (2022). Portuguese higher education students' adaptation to online teaching and learning in times of the COVID-19 pandemic: Personal and contextual factors. *Higher Education*, 83(6), 1389–1408. DOI: 10.1007/s10734-021-00748-x PMID: 34493877

Fortes, P. R. B. (2020). Paths to Digital Justice: Judicial Robots, Algorithmic Decision-Making, and Due Process. *Asian Journal of Law and Society*, 7(3), 453–469. DOI: 10.1017/als.2020.12

Foster, G. (2024). Grading standards in higher education: Trends, Context, and Prognosis. Second Handbook of Academic Integrity, 341-359.

Fowler, G. A. (2023, April 3). We tested a new ChatGPT-detector for teachers. It flagged an innocent student. *Washington Post*. https://www.washingtonpost.com/technology/2023/04/01/chatgpt-cheating-detection-turnitin/

Fowler, D. S. (2023). AI in higher education. Journal of Ethics in Higher Education, (3), 127-143. https://doi.org/DOI: 10.26034/fr.jehe.2023.4657

Frankenberg-Garcia, A. (2020). Combining user needs, lexicographic data and digital writing environments. *Language Teaching*, 53(1), 29–43. DOI: 10.1017/S0261444818000277

Fügener, A., Grahl, J., Gupta, A., & Ketterformat_quoteCITK, W. (2022). Cognitive Challenges in Human–Artificial Intelligence Collaboration: Investigating the Path Toward Productive Delegation. *Information Systems Research, 33*(2), 678–696. https://doi.org/https://doi.org/10.1287/isre.2021.1079

Fung, C. Y., Su, S. I., Perry, E. J., & Garcia, M. B. (2022). Development of a socioeconomic inclusive assessment framework for online learning in higher education. *Socioeconomic Inclusion During an Era of Online Education*, 23–46. DOI: 10.4018/978-1-6684-4364-4.ch002

Gabriel, F., Marrone, R., Van Sebille, Y., Kovanovic, V., & de Laat, M. (2022). Digital education strategies around the world: Practices and policies. *Irish Educational Studies*, 41(1), 85–106. DOI: 10.1080/03323315.2021.2022513

Gabriel, J. (2024). How Artificial Intelligence (AI) impacts inclusive education. *Educational Research Review*, 19(6), 95–103. DOI: 10.5897/ERR2024.4404

Gafni, R., Aviv, I., Kantsepolsky, B., Sherman, S., Rika, H., Itzkovich, Y., & Barger, A. (2024). Objectivity by design: The impact of AI-driven approach on employees' soft skills evaluation. *Information and Software Technology*, 170, 107430. DOI: 10.1016/j.infsof.2024.107430

Gagich, M. (Mar. 2023). Creation and implementation of two GenAI activities. CLE Teaching Collaborative. https://cleteaching.org/gagich-ai/

Gamage, K. A. A., Dehideniya, S. C. P., Xu, Z., & Tang, X. (2023). Chatgpt and higher education assessments: More opportunities than concerns? *Journal of Applied Learning & Teaching*, 6(2). Advance online publication. DOI: 10.37074/jalt.2023.6.2.32

Ganesh, G., Paswan, A., & Sun, Q. (2015). Are face-to-face classes more effective than online classes? An empirical examination. *Marketing Education Review*, 25(2), 67–81. DOI: 10.1080/10528008.2015.1029851

Gao, F., & Gube, J. (2020). Multicultural education: How are ethnic minorities labelled and educated in post-handover Hong Kong? *Migration and Language Education*, 2(3), 51–59. DOI: 10.29140/mle.v1n2.363

Gao, X., Xu, B., Ouyang, G., & Wang, L. (2020). Generative Adversarial Networks for Educational Applications. *IEEE Transactions on Learning Technologies*, 13(1), 6–16.

Garcia, R.. (2023). Self-regulation skills and AI in education. *Learning and Instruction*, 34, 112–130.

Gardner, H. (1983). *Frames Of Mind: The Theory Of Multiple Intelligences*. Basic Books.

Garibay, O. O., Winslow, B., Matematica, S. A., Antona, M., Bodenschatz, A., Coursaris, C., Falco, G., Fiore, S. M., Garibay, I., Grieman, K., Havens, J. C., Jirotka, M., Kacorri, H., Karwowski, W., Kider, J., Konstan, J., Koon, S., Lopez-Gonzalez, M., Maifeld-Carucci, I., & Xu, W. (2023). Six Human-Centered Artificial Intelligence Grand Challenges. *International Journal of Human-Computer Interaction*, 39(3), 391–437. DOI: 10.1080/10447318.2022.2153320

Gattupalli, S., Maloy, R. W., & Edwards, S. (2023). *Comparing Teacher-Written and AI Generated Math Problem Solving Strategies for Elementary School Students: Implications for Classroom Learning*. College of Education Working Papers and Reports Series. 5.DOI: 10.7275/8sgx-xj08

Geigle, C. (2018). Towards High Quality, Scalable Education: Techniques in Automated Assessment and Probablistic Behavior Modeling. *Department of Computer Science, Ph.D.* file:///C:/Users/sheilarose.darmaraj/Desktop/New folder 1 - IJME/ Geigle 2018.pdf

George, A. S. (2023). Preparing students for an AI-driven world: Rethinking curriculum and pedagogy in the age of artificial intelligence. *Partners Universal Innovative Research Publication*, 1(2), 112–136.

George, B., & Wooden, O. (2023). Managing the Strategic Transformation of Higher Education through Artificial Intelligence. *Administrative Sciences*, 13(9), 1–20. DOI: 10.3390/admsci13090196

Gernsbacher, M. A., Soicher, R. N., & Becker-Blease, K. A. (2020, June). Four empirically based reasons not to administer time-limited tests. *Translational Issues in Psychological Science*, 6(2), 175–190. DOI: 10.1037/tps0000232 PMID: 32582819

Getchell, K. M., Carradini, S., Cardon, P. W., Fleischmann, C., Ma, H., Aritz, J., & Stapp, J. (2022). Artificial intelligence in business communication: The changing landscape of research and teaching. *Business and Professional Communication Quarterly*, 85(1), 1–27. DOI: 10.1177/23294906221074311

Ghaffary, S. (2023, September 21). Universities rethink using AI writing detectors to vet students' work. Bloomberg Newsletter.

Ghanizadeh, A., Al-Hoorie, A. H., & Jahedizadeh, S. (2020). *Higher order thinking skills in the language classroom: A concise guide*. Springer International Publishing. DOI: 10.1007/978-3-030-56711-8

Ghufron, M. A., & Rosyida, F. (2018). The role of Grammarly in assessing English as a foreign language (EFL) writing. *Lingua Cultura*, 12(4), 395–403. DOI: 10.21512/lc.v12i4.4582

Gillentine, F. M. (1937). Why do college students cheat? *Peabody Journal of Education*, 15(1), 15–17. DOI: 10.1080/01619563709535395

Gill, S. S., & Kaur, R. (2023). ChatGPT: Vision and challenges. *Internet of Things and Cyber-Physical Systems*, 3(May), 262–271. DOI: 10.1016/j.iotcps.2023.05.004

Glanville, M. (2024, March 8). *Why ChatGPT is an Opportunity for Schools*. Retrieved from International Baccalaureate: https://www.ibo.org/news-about-the-ib/why-chatgpt-is-an-opportunity-for-schools/

Godwin-Jones, R. (2023). Emerging spaces for language learning: AI bots, ambient intelligence, and the metaverse. *Language Learning & Technology*, 27(2), 6–27.

Goff, D., Johnston, J., & Bouboulis, B. (2020). Maintaining academic standards and integrity in online business courses. *International Journal of Higher Education*, 9(2), 248. DOI: 10.5430/ijhe.v9n2p248

Goksel, N., & Bozkurt, A. (2019). Artificial Intelligence in Education: Current Insights and Future Perspectives. In *Handbook of Research on Learning in the Age of Transhumanism* (pp. 224–236). IGI Global.

Gonzalez, M. (2024). Leveraging AI for Critical Thinking and Problem-Solving in K-12 Education. *Journal of Artificial Intelligence in Education*, 34, 85–105.

Goralski, M. A., & Tan, T. K. (2020). Artificial intelligence and sustainable development. *International Journal of Management Education*, 18(1), 100330. DOI: 10.1016/j.ijme.2019.100330

Graham, S., & Perin, D. (2007). *Writing next: Effective strategies to improve writing of adolescents in middle and high schools – A report to Carnegie Corporation of New York*. Alliance for Excellent Education.

Grams, D. (2018). *A quantitative study of the use of DreamBox learning and its effectiveness in improving math achievement of elementary students with math difficulties* [Doctoral dissertation, Northcentral University].

Grassini, S. (2023). Shaping the Future of Education: Exploring the Potential and Consequences of AI and ChatGPT in Educational Settings. *Education Sciences*, 13(7), 1–13. DOI: 10.3390/educsci13070692

Green, H. (2024). Natural Language Processing in Teaching Writing; Enhancing Higher-Order Skills. *Journal of Applied Linguistics and Educational Technology*, 13, 115–135.

Grijalva, T. C., Nowell, C., & Kerkvliet, J. (2006). Academic honesty and online courses. *College Student Journal*, 40(1), 180–185. Retrieved July 31, 2024, from https://www.learntechlib.org/p/101008/

Guo, Y., & Lee, D. (2023). Leveraging ChatGPT for Enhancing Critical Thinking Skills. *Journal of Chemical Education*, 100(12), 4876–4883. DOI: 10.1021/acs.jchemed.3c00505

Haleem, A., Javaid, M., Qadri, M. A., & Suman, R. (2022). Understanding the role of digital technologies in education: A review. *Sustainable Operations and Computers*, 3, 275–285. DOI: 10.1016/j.susoc.2022.05.004

Haleem, A., Javaid, M., & Singh, R. P. (2022). An era of ChatGPT as a significant futuristic support tool: A study on features, abilities, and challenges. *BenchCouncil Transactions on Benchmarks. Standards and Evaluations*, 2(4), 100089. DOI: 10.1016/j.tbench.2023.100089

Hamari, J., Shernoff, D. J., Rowe, E., Coller, B., Asbell-Clarke, J., & Edwards, T. (2016). Challenging games help students learn: An empirical study on engagement, flow and immersion in game-based learning. *Computers in Human Behavior*, 54, 170–179. DOI: 10.1016/j.chb.2015.07.045

Hashim, M. A. M., Tlemsani, I., Matthews, R., Mason-Jones, R., & Ndrecaj, V. (2023). Emergent Strategy in Higher Education: Postmodern Digital and the Future? *Administrative Sciences*, 12(4), 196. https://doi.org/https://doi.org/10.3390/admsci12040196. DOI: 10.3390/admsci12040196

Hashimy, S. Q., Jahromi, A., Naaz, I., & Nyamwero, N., & H T, B. (2023). Nurturing Leadership and Capacity Building for Success: Empowering Growth. *International Journal of Rehabilitation and Special Education*, 3(2), 33–46. DOI: 10.48165/ijrse.2023.3.2.5

Hassani, H., Silva, E. S., Unger, S., TajMazinani, M., & Mac Feely, S. (2020). Artificial intelligence (AI) or intelligence augmentation (IA): What is the future? *AI*, 1(2), 8. DOI: 10.3390/ai1020008

Hattie, J., & Timperley, H. (2007). The power of feedback. *Review of Educational Research*, 77(1), 81–112. DOI: 10.3102/003465430298487

Hazen, H. (2020). Use of oral examinations to assess student learning in the social sciences. *Journal of Geography in Higher Education*, 44(4), 592–607. DOI: 10.1080/03098265.2020.1773418

Heaton, S. (2023, May 6). *The use of AI detection tools in the assessment of student work*. WordPress. https://drsaraheaton.wordpress.com/2023/05/06/the-use-of-ai-detection-tools-in-the-assessment-of-student-work/

Heaven, W. (2023). *GPT-4 is bigger and better than ChatGPT*. MIT Technology Review. https://www.technologyreview.com/2023/03/14/1069823/gpt-4-is-bigger-and-better-chatgpt-openai/

Heffernan, N. T., & Heffernan, C. L. (2014). The ASSISTments ecosystem: Building a platform that brings scientists and teachers together for minimally invasive research on human learning and teaching. *International Journal of Artificial Intelligence in Education*, 24(4), 470–497. DOI: 10.1007/s40593-014-0024-x

Hénard, F., & Roseveare, D. (2012). Fostering Quality Teaching in Higher Education. *Policies and Practices.*, (September), 54.

Henderson, R. R., Adams, C. A., Thomas, L., Gundersen, E., Zaidi, Z., & Hagen, M. (2023). COVID as a catalyst: A qualitative study of professional identity formation among US medical students during COVID-19. *Teaching and Learning in Medicine*, •••, 1–12. PMID: 37592855

Henkel, O., Horne-Robinson, H., Kozhakhmetova, N., & Lee, A. (2024). Effective and Scalable Math Support: Evidence on the Impact of an AI-Tutor on Math Achievement in Ghana. *arXiv preprint arXiv:2402.09809*.DOI: 10.1007/978-3-031-64315-6_34

Hidayatullah, E., Untari, R., & Fifardin, F. (2024). Effectiveness of AI in solving math problems at the secondary school level: A comparative study with student performance. *Union: Journal Ilmiah Pendidikan Matematika*, 12(2), 350–360. DOI: 10.30738/union.v12i2.17548

Holmes, W. (2023). *The unintended consequences of artificial intelligence and education*. Education International.

Holmes, W., Bialik, M., & Fadel, C. (2019). *Artificial intelligence in education: Promises and implications for teaching and learning*. Center for Curriculum Redesign.

Holmes, W., & Tuomi, I. (2022). State of the art and practice in AI in education. *European Journal of Education*, 57(4), 542–570. DOI: 10.1111/ejed.12533

Holm, J. R., & Lorenz, E. (2022). The impact of artificial intelligence on skills at work in Denmark. *New Technology, Work and Employment*, 37(1), 79–101. DOI: 10.1111/ntwe.12215

Hong Kong Government. (2011). *Population census*. Census and Statistics Department, Hong Kong Government.

Hong Kong Government. (2016). *The Hong Kong poverty situation report on ethnic minorities*. Census and Statistics Department, Hong Kong Government.

Hong Kong Government. (2022, December 14). *Using Putonghua as medium of instruction for teaching Chinese Language subject*. [Press release]. https://www.info.gov.hk/gia/general/202212/14/P2022121400322.htm

Horner, B., & Selfe, C. (2013). Translinguality/transmodality relations: Snapshots from a dialogue. Retrieved from University of Louisville website: https://louisville.edu/workingpapers/copy_of_working-papers

Hossain, K. A. (2023). Evaluation of diversified use of artificial intelligence (AI) and consequence of future education.

How do students feel about OpenAI's ChatGPT? (3 Jan. 2023). *Wall Street Journal*. Retrieved from https://www.wsj.com/articles/how-do-students-feel-about-openais-chatgpt-education-openai-exams-testing-essay-learning-plagiarism-cheating-11672780587

Howlin, C., & Lynch, D. (2014). A framework for the delivery of personalized adaptive content. In *2014 International Conference on Web and Open Access to Learning (ICWOAL)* (pp. 1-5). DOI: 10.1109/ICWOAL.2014.7009203

Hsiao, J. C., & Chang, J. S. (2023). Enhancing EFL reading and writing through AI-powered tools: Design, implementation, and evaluation of an online course. *Interactive Learning Environments*, (May), 1–16. DOI: 10.1080/10494820.2023.2207187

Hsu, C. Y., & Wu, T. T. (2023). Application of Business Simulation Games in Flipped Classrooms to Facilitate Student Engagement and Higher-Order Thinking Skills for Sustainable Learning Practices. *Sustainability (Basel)*, 15(24), 1–18. DOI: 10.3390/su152416867

Huang, X., Zou, D., Cheng, G., Chen, X., & Xie, H. (2023). Trends, Research Issues and Applications of Artificial Intelligence in Language Education. *Journal of Educational Technology & Society*, 26(1), 112–131.

Hutson, J. (2024). Rethinking plagiarism in the era of generative AI. *Journal of International Communication*, 4(1), 20–31. DOI: 10.54963/jic.v4i1.220

Hutson, J., & Plate, D. (2023). Enhancing Institutional Assessment and Reporting Through Conversational Technologies : Exploring the Potential of AI- Powered Tools and Natural Language Processing. *Journal of Artificial Intelligence and Robotics*, 1(1), 11–22. https://digitalcommons.lindenwood.edu/faculty-research-papers/483. DOI: 10.59232/AIR-V1I1P102

Hwang, G.-J., Tu, Y.-F., & Tang, K.-Y. (2022). AI in Online-Learning Research: Visualizing and Interpreting the Journal Publications from 1997 to 2019. *International Review of Research in Open and Distance Learning*, 23(1), 104–130. DOI: 10.19173/irrodl.v23i1.6319

Hwang, S. (2022). Examining the effects of Artificial Intelligence on elementary students' mathematics achievement: A Meta-Analysis. *Sustainability (Basel)*, 14(20), 13185. DOI: 10.3390/su142013185

IEEE. (2021). IEEE Global Initiative on Ethics of Autonomous and Intelligent Systems. Retrieved from https://ethicsinaction.ieee.org/

Ifenthaler, D., Eseryel, D., & Ge, X. (2012). Assessment for game-based learning. In *Assessment in game-based learning: Foundations, innovations, and perspectives* (pp. 1–8). Springer New York. DOI: 10.1007/978-1-4614-3546-4_1

Ilkka, T. (2018). *The Impact of Artificial Intelligence on Learning, Teaching, and Education Policies for the future*. Joint Research Centre. Hanover Research (2024, April) Assessment and Generative Artificial Intelligence in Higher Education. Higher Education._https://cms.ahs.uic.edu/

International Telecommunication Union. (2022). *Connecting the world: Internet access in Africa*. International Telecommunication Union. https://www.itu.int

Irfan, M., Murray, L., & Ali, S. (2023). Insights into Student Perceptions: Investigating Artificial Intelligence (AI) Tool Usability in Irish Higher Education at the University of Limerick. *Global Digital & Print Media Review*, VI(II), 48–63. DOI: 10.31703/gdpmr.2023(VI-II).05

Ishaq, M., Abid, A., Farooq, M. S., Manzoor, M. F., Farooq, U., Abid, K., & Helou, M. A. (2023). Advances in database systems education: Methods, tools, curricula, and way forward. In *Education and Information Technologies* (Vol. 28, Issue 3). Springer US. DOI: 10.1007/s10639-022-11293-0

Jackson, N. (2010). *Developing creativity in higher education: An imaginative curriculum*. Routledge.

Jafar, M., Alfian, R., & Yunus, M. (2023). Improving Student Motor Skills through a Structured Physical Training Program. *J Adv Sport Phys Edu*, 6(5), 82–95. DOI: 10.36348/jaspe.2023.v06i05.003

Jain, R., Garg, N., & Khera, S. N. (2023). Effective human–AI work design for collaborative decision-making. *Kybernetes*, 52(11), 5017–5040. DOI: 10.1108/K-04-2022-0548

Jain, S., & Jain, R. (2019). Role of Artificial Intelligence in Higher Education- An Empirical Investigation. *IJRAR-. International Journal of Research and Analytical Reviews*, 6(2), 144–150. https://ijrar.com/

Jaiswal, A., & Arun, C. J. (2021). Potential of Artificial Intelligence for the transformation of the education system in India. *International Journal of Education and Development Using Information and Communication Technology*, 17(1), 142–158.

Jaiswal, A., & Arun, C. J. (2021). Potential of Artificial Intelligence for transformation of the education system in India. [IJEDICT]. *International Journal of Education and Development Using Information and Communication Technology*, 17(1), 142–158. https://eric.ed.gov/?id=EJ1285526

Jamil, N., Belkacem, A. N., & Lakas, A. (2023). On Enhancing students' cognitive abilities in online learning using brain activity and eye movements. *Education and Information Technologies*, 28(4), 4367–4397. DOI: 10.1007/s10639-022-11372-2 PMID: 36277512

Jantzen, D., Marcellus, L., Vermes, F., Duncan, S., & Maclaren, J. (2022). From Pilot to Established Practice: Reflecting on the 20-Year Journey of Implementing a Collaborative Learning Unit practice education model in Victoria, British Columbia. *Quality Advancement in Nursing Education*, 8(1). Advance online publication. DOI: 10.17483/2368-6669.1305

Jarrah, A. M., Wardat, Y., & Fidalgo, P. (2023). Using ChatGPT in academic writing is (not) a form of plagiarism: What does the literature say? *Online Journal of Communication and Media Technologies*, 13(4), 1–20. DOI: 10.30935/ojcmt/13572

Jarrahi, M. H. (2018). Artificial intelligence and the future of work: Human-AI symbiosis in organizational decision making. *Business Horizons*, 61(4), 577–586. DOI: 10.1016/j.bushor.2018.03.007

Javaid, M., Haleem, A., Singh, R. P., Khan, S., & Khan, I. H. (2023). Unlocking the opportunities through ChatGPT Tool towards ameliorating the education system. *BenchCouncil Transactions on Benchmarks. Standards and Evaluations*, 3(2), 100115. DOI: 10.1016/j.tbench.2023.100115

Jenkins, B. D., Golding, J. M., Le Grand, A. M., Levi, M. M., & Pals, A. M. (2023). When opportunity knocks: College students' cheating amid the COVID-19 pandemic. *Teaching of Psychology*, 50(4), 407–419. DOI: 10.1177/00986283211059067

Jeon, J., & Lee, S. (2023). Large language models in education: A focus on the complementary relationship between human teachers and ChatGPT. *Education and Information Technologies*. https://doi.org/https://doi.org/10.1007/s10639-023-11834-1

Jeon, J. (2022). Exploring AI chatbot affordances in the EFL classroom: Young learners' experiences and perspectives. *Computer Assisted Language Learning*. Advance online publication. DOI: 10.1080/09588221.2021.2021241

Jia, F., Sun, D., & Looi, C. K. (2024). Artificial intelligence in science education (2013–2023): Research trends in ten years. *Journal of Science Education and Technology*, 33(1), 94–117. DOI: 10.1007/s10956-023-10077-6

Jia, X., & Tu, J. (2024). Towards a New Conceptual Model of AI-Enhanced Learning for College Students: The Roles of Artificial Intelligence Capabilities. *General Self-Efficacy, Learning Motivation, and Critical Thinking Awareness Systems*, (12), 74.

Ji, H., Han, I., & Ko, Y. (2023). A systematic review of conversational AI in language education: Focusing on the collaboration with human teachers. *Journal of Research on Technology in Education*, 55(1), 48–63. DOI: 10.1080/15391523.2022.2142873

Joamets, K. (2022). Plagiarism as a Legal Phenomenon and Algorithm-Based Decision Making. *TalTech Journal of European Studies*, 12(2), 146–164. DOI: 10.2478/bjes-2022-0015

Johnson, D., Goodman, R., Patrinely, J., Stone, C., Zimmerman, E., Donald, R., & Wheless, L. (2023). Assessing the accuracy and reliability of AI-generated medical responses: an evaluation of the Chat-GPT model. *Research square*. DOI: 10.21203/rs.3.rs-2566942/v1

Jonas, M. (2024). *Mitigating use of artificial intelligence in student assignments*. University of New Hampshire.

Jordan, A. E. (2001). College student cheating: The role of motivation, perceived norms, attitudes, and knowledge of institutional policy. *Ethics & Behavior*, 11(3), 233–247. DOI: 10.1207/S15327019EB1103_3

Jose, J., & Jayaron Jose, B. (2024). Educators' academic insights on artificial intelligence: Challenges and opportunities. Electronic Journal of E-Learning, 00-00. https://doi.org/DOI: 10.34190/ejel.21.5.3272

Josien, L., Seeley, E., Csipak, J. J., & Rampal, R. (2015). Cheating: Students and faculty's perception on potential cheating activity. *Journal of Legal. Ethical and Regulatory Issues*, 18, 21.

Jurāne-Brēmane, A. (2023). Digital Assessment in Technology-Enriched Education: Thematic Review. *Education Sciences*, 13(5), 522. https://doi.org/https://doi.org/10.3390/educsci13050522. DOI: 10.3390/educsci13050522

Kamalov, F., Calonge, D. S., & Gurrib, I. (2023). New Era of Artificial Intelligence in Education: Towards a Sustainable Multifaceted Revolution. *Sustainability (Basel)*, 15(16), 12451. https://doi.org/https://doi.org/10.3390/su151612451. DOI: 10.3390/su151612451

Kaminska, D., Zwolinski, G., Laska-Leśniewicz, A. B., Raposo, R., Vairinhos, M. R. M., Pereira, E. T., Urem, F., Hinic, M. L., Haamer, R. E., & Anbarjafari, G. (2023). Augmented Reality: Current and New Trends in Education. *Electronics (Basel)*, 12(16), 3531. https://doi.org/http://dx.doi.org/10.3390/electronics12163531. DOI: 10.3390/electronics12163531

Kang, B., & Kang, S. (2022). Construction of Chinese Language Teaching System Model Based on Deep Learning under the Background of Artificial Intelligence. *Scientific Programming*, 2022, 1–10. DOI: 10.1155/2022/3960023

Käng, D. B., Goico, S., Ghanbari, S., Bennallack, K., Pontes, T., O'Brien, D. H., & Hargis, J. (2019). Providing an oral examination as an authentic assessment in a large section, undergraduate diversity class. *International Journal for the Scholarship of Teaching and Learning*, 13(2). Advance online publication. DOI: 10.20429/ijsotl.2019.130210

Karadag, N. (2023). The impact of artificial intelligence on online assessment: A preliminary review. *Journal of Educational Technology and Online Learning*, 6(4), 822–837. DOI: 10.31681/jetol.1351548

Karger, H., & Stoesz, D. (2024). *Failing Universities: How Higher Education Became a Commodity and What We Can Do About It*. Bloomsbury Publishing. DOI: 10.5040/9781350383845

Karimi, H., & Khawaja, S. (2023). The Impact of Artificial Intelligence on Higher Education in England. *Creative Education*, 14(12), 2405–2415. DOI: 10.4236/ce.2023.1412154

Karran, A. J., Demazure, T., Hudon, A., Senecal, S., & Léger, P. M. (2022). Designing for confidence: The impact of visualizing artificial intelligence decisions. *Frontiers in Neuroscience*, 16, 883385. DOI: 10.3389/fnins.2022.883385 PMID: 35812230

Kars, M. E. (2023, July 20). *Generative AI in Education. 9th London International Conference, July 11-13, 2023*. Ukey Consulting & Publishing. https://ukey.ilet.in/

Kasneci, E., Sessler, K., Küchemann, S., Bannert, M., Dementieva, D., Fischer, F., Gasser, U., Groh, G., Günnemann, S., Hüllermeier, E., Krusche, S., Kutyniok, G., Michaeli, T., Nerdel, C., Pfeffer, J., Poquet, O., Sailer, M., Schmidt, A., Seidel, T., & Kasneci, G. (2023). ChatGPT for good? On opportunities and challenges of large language models for education. *Learning and Individual Differences*, 103(March), 102274. Advance online publication. DOI: 10.1016/j.lindif.2023.102274

Kaushar, M. (2013). Study of impact of time management on academic performance of college students. *IOSR Journal of Business and Management* (9:6), 59-60.

Kessler, G. (2017). Technology and the future of language teaching. *Foreign Language Annals*, 2018(51), 205–218.

Khalil, M., & Er, E. (2023). Will ChatGPT get you caught? Rethinking of plagiarism detection. arXiv preprint arXiv: 2302.04335. DOI: 10.1007/978-3-031-34411-4_32

Khatri, B. B., & Karki, P. D. (2023). Artificial intelligence (AI) in higher education: Growing academic integrity and ethical concerns. *Nepalese Journal of Development and Rural Studies*, 20(01), 1–7. DOI: 10.3126/njdrs.v20i01.64134

Khetarpal, K., Riemer, M., Rish, I., & Precup, D. (2022). Towards Continual Reinforcement Learning: A Review and Perspectives. *Journal of Artificial Intelligence Research*, 75, 1401–1476. https://doi.org/https://doi.org/10.1613/jair.1.13673. DOI: 10.1613/jair.1.13673

Kikalishvili, S. (2023). Unlocking the potential of GPT-3 in education: Opportunities, limitations, and recommendations for effective integration. *Interactive Learning Environments*, 1(1), 1–13. DOI: 10.1080/10494820.2023.2220401

Kim, H. (2023). The effects of AI on student motivation and learning. *Journal of Educational Psychology*, 45(2), 199–213.

Kim, J., Lee, H., & Cho, Y. H. (2022). Learning design to support student-AI collaboration: Perspectives of leading teachers for AI in education. *Education and Information Technologies*, 27(5), 6069–6104. https://doi.org/https://doi.org/10.1007/s10639-021-10831-6. DOI: 10.1007/s10639-021-10831-6

Kimmerle, J., Timm, J., Festl-Wietek, T., Cress, U., & Herrmann-Werner, A. (2023). Medical students' attitudes toward AI in medicine and their expectations for medical education. *Journal of Medical Education and Curricular Development*, 10, 23821205231219346. Advance online publication. DOI: 10.1177/23821205231219346 PMID: 38075443

Kim, N.-Y., Cha, Y., & Kim, H.-S. (2019). Future English learning: Chatbots and artificial intelligence. *Multimedia-Assisted Language Learning*, 22(3), 32–53.

King, I. (2016). E-learning is the way forward for quality education. *South China Morning Post*, 29 July 2016.

Kluger, A. N., & DeNisi, A. (1996). The effects of feedback interventions on performance: A historical review, a meta-analysis, and a preliminary feedback intervention theory. *Psychological Bulletin*, 119(2), 254–284. DOI: 10.1037/0033-2909.119.2.254

Knewton. (2024). Knewton Alta adaptive learning. Wiley. https://www.wiley.com/en us/education/alta

Kocadere, S. A., & Çağlar, Ş. (2018). Gamification from player type perspective: A case study. *Journal of Educational Technology & Society*, 21(3), 12–22.

Koedinger, K. R., & Corbett, A. (2005). Cognitive Tutors: Technology bringing learning sciences to the classroom. In Sawyer, R. K. (Ed.), *The Cambridge Handbook of the Learning Sciences* (pp. 61–78). Cambridge University Press., DOI: 10.1017/CBO9780511816833.006

Kohnke, L., Moorhouse, B. L., & Zou, D. (2023). ChatGPT for Language Teaching and Learning. *RELC Journal*, 54(2), 537–550. DOI: 10.1177/00336882231162868

Kolade, O., Owoseni, A., & Egbetokun, A. (2024). Is AI changing learning and assessment as we know it? Evidence from a ChatGPT experiment and a conceptual framework. *Heliyon*, 10(4), e25953. DOI: 10.1016/j.heliyon.2024.e25953 PMID: 38379960

Kolb, D. A. (1984). *Experiential learning: experience as the source of learning and development*. Prentice Hall.

Kolb, D. A. (2015). *Experiential learning: Experience as the source of learning and development*. FT Press.

Koraishi, O. (2023). Teaching English in the Age of AI: Embracing ChatGPT to Optimize EFL Materials and Assessment. *Language Education and Technology*, 3(1), 55–72.

Korchi, A., Messaoudi, F., Abatal, A., & Manzali, Y. (2023). Machine Learning and Deep Learning-Based Students' Grade Prediction. *Operations Research Forum, 4*(4), 1–21. DOI: 10.1007/s43069-023-00267-8

Kostka, I., & Toncelli, R. (2023). *Exploring Applications of ChatGPT to English Language Teaching : Opportunities, Challenges, and Recommendations. 27*(3), 1–19. file:///C:/Users/sheilarose.darmaraj/Desktop/New folder 1 - IJME/Kostka & Toncelli 2023.pdf

Krajka, J., & Olszak, I. (2024). "AI, will you help?" How learners use Artificial Intelligence when writing. *XLinguae*, 17(1), 34–48. DOI: 10.18355/XL.2024.17.01.03

Krou, M. R., Fong, C. J., & Hoff, M. A. (2020). Achievement motivation and academic dishonesty: A meta-analytic investigation. *Educational Psychology Review*, 33(2), 427–458. Advance online publication. DOI: 10.1007/s10648-020-09557-7

Kulik, J. A., & Fletcher, J. D. (2016). Effectiveness of Intelligent Tutoring Systems: A Meta-Analytic Review. *Review of Educational Research*, 86(1), 42–78. DOI: 10.3102/0034654315581420

Kumar, Y., Raj, D., Rao, M., Yanambaka, V. P., & Mahajan, S. (2024). Exploring the potential of generative AI in shaping engineering education: Opportunities and challenges. *Journal of Engineering Education Transformations*, 37(2), 439–445. DOI: 10.16920/jeet/2024/v37is2/24072

Kung, T. H., Cheatham, M., Medenilla, A., Sillos, C., De Leon, L., Elepa˜no, C., Madriaga, M., Aggabao, R., Diaz-Candido, G., Maningo, J., & Tseng, V. (2023). Performance of ChatGPT on USMLE: Potential for AI-Assisted medical education using large models. *PLOS Digital Health*, 2(2), e0000198. DOI: 10.1371/journal.pdig.0000198 PMID: 36812645

Lakshman, C., & Gonzalez, J. (2023). From TMT multiculturalism to strategic agility: Business model innovation in MNEs. *Multinational Business Review*, 31(2), 157–175. https://doi.org/https://doi.org/10.1108/MBR-02-2022-0030. DOI: 10.1108/MBR-02-2022-0030

Lamott, A. (2005). Shitty First Drafts. In Eschholz, P., Rosa, A., & Clark, V. (Eds.), *Language Awareness: Readings for College Writers* (9th ed., pp. 93–96). Bedford/St. Martin's.

Lang, J. C. (2024). Embracing generative AI for authentic learning. *Creative Education*, 15(1), 1–20. DOI: 10.4236/ce.2024.151001

Latif, E., Mai, G., Nyaaba, M., Wu, X., Liu, N., Lu, G., Li, S., Liu, T., & Zhai, X. (2023). Artificial General Intelligence (AGI) for Education. *ArXiv*, 1–34. https://doi.org//arXiv.2304.12479DOI: 10.48550

Lau, K. L. (2019). Hong Kong senior secondary students' reading motivation and classical Chinese reading comprehension. *Reading and Writing*, 32(4), 963–982. DOI: 10.1007/s11145-018-9897-7

Laupichler, M. C., Aster, A., Schirch, J., & Raupach, T. (2022). Artificial intelligence literacy in higher and adult education: A scoping literature review. *Computers and Education: Artificial Intelligence*, 3(September), 1–15. DOI: 10.1016/j.caeai.2022.100101

Lee, S. J., & Kwon, K. (2024). A systematic review of AI education in K-12 classrooms from 2018 to 2023: Topics, strategies, and learning outcomes. *Computers and Education: Artificial Intelligence*, 100211.

Lee, A. V. Y., Tan, S. C., & Teo, C. L. (2023). Designs and practices using generative AI for sustainable student discourse and knowledge creation. *Smart Learning Environments*, 10(1), 59. DOI: 10.1186/s40561-023-00279-1

Lee, H. (2023). The rise of ChatGPT: Exploring its potential in medical education. *Anatomical Sciences Education*, (March), 1–6. DOI: 10.1002/ase.2270 PMID: 36916887

Lee, S. L. (2011). [Online components for advanced Chinese reading classes]. *Journal of Technology and Chinese Language Teaching*, 2, 1–22.

Lee, S. L. (2016). E-Learning Readiness in Language Learning: Students' Readiness Survey and Normalization Process. *Journal of Technology and Chinese Language Teaching*, 7(2), 23–37.

Lee, S. L. (2018). Modular approaches in eLearning design. *Journal of Technology and Chinese Language Teaching*, 9, 48–61.

Lee, S. L. (2022). Synchronous online language teaching: a reflection from Hong Kong. In Liu, S. (Ed.), *Teaching the Chinese language remotely: Global cases and perspectives* (pp. 235–251). Palgrave Macmillan. DOI: 10.1007/978-3-030-87055-3_10

Lee, S. L., & Chen, Y. (2024). Discussions of Using AI in Language Education in Hong Kong. In Pan, F. (Ed.), *AI in Language Teaching, Learning, and Assessment* (pp. 133–148). IGI Global. DOI: 10.4018/979-8-3693-0872-1.ch007

Leiter, C., ... (2023). ChatGPT: A meta-analysis after 2.5 months. arXiv preprint arXiv:2302.13795.

Lesage, J., Brennan, R., Eaton, S. E., Moya, B., McDermott, B., Wiens, J., & Herrero, K. (2023). Exploring natural language processing in mechanical engineering education: Implications for academic integrity. *International Journal of Mechanical Engineering Education*. Advance online publication. DOI: 10.1177/03064190231166665

Lieberman, L. (7 Jun. 2024). AI and the death of student writing. *The Chronicle of Higher Education*. Retrieved from https://www.chronicle.com/article/ai-and-the-death-of-student-writing

Li, L. (2022). Reskilling and upskilling the future-ready workforce for Industry 4.0 and beyond. *Information Systems Frontiers*, •••, 1–16. PMID: 35855776

Lim, K. K., & Lee, C. S. (2024, June). Enhancing searching as learning (SAL) with generative artificial intelligence: A literature review. In *International Conference on Human-Computer Interaction* (pp. 143-155). Cham: Springer Nature Switzerland. DOI: 10.1007/978-3-031-61953-3_17

Lin, Z. (2023). Why and how to embrace AI such as ChatGPT in your academic life. *Royal Society Open Science*, 10(8), 11524. DOI: 10.1098/rsos.230658 PMID: 37621662

Liu, O., & Yau, C. (2023, March 22). Who needs a teacher? As ChatGPT takes off in Hong Kong, educationists worry about impact on teaching, learning. *South China Morning Post*.

Liu, X. (2018). A Comparative Study of Language Attitudes in Hong Kong: Towards English, Cantonese and Putonghua. *International Journal of English Linguistics*, 8(3), 195–209. DOI: 10.5539/ijel.v8n3p195

Lo, L. S. (2023). The CLEAR path: A framework for enhancing information literacy through prompt engineering. *Journal of Academic Librarianship*, 49(4), 102720. DOI: 10.1016/j.acalib.2023.102720

Long, D., Jacob, M., & Magerko, B. (2019, June). Designing co-creative AI for public spaces. In *Proceedings of the 2019 Conference on Creativity and Cognition* (pp. 271-284). DOI: 10.1145/3325480.3325504

Lovett, B. J., Lewandowski, L. J., Berger, C., & Gathje, R. A. (2010). Effects of response mode and time allotment on college students' writing. *Journal of College Reading and Learning*, 40(2), 64–79. DOI: 10.1080/10790195.2010.10850331

Luan, H., Geczy, P., Lai, H., Gobert, J., Yang, S. J. H., Ogata, H., Baltes, J., Guerra, R., Li, P., & Tsai, C. C. (2020). Challenges and Future Directions of Big Data and Artificial Intelligence in Education. *Frontiers in Psychology*, 11(October), 1–11. DOI: 10.3389/fpsyg.2020.580820 PMID: 33192896

Luckin, R., & Holmes, W. (2016). Intelligence Unleashed: An argument for AI in education.

Luckin, R., & Cukurova, M. (2019). Designing educational technologies in the age of AI: A review of "I-novels" as a method for co-creation. *British Journal of Educational Technology*, 50(6), 2958–2972.

Luckin, R., Cukurova, M., Kent, C., & du Boulay, B. (2022). Empowering educators to be AI-ready. *Computers and Education: Artificial Intelligence*, 3, 100076. DOI: 10.1016/j.caeai.2022.100076

Luckin, R., Holmes, W., Griffiths, M., & Forcier, L. B. (2016). *Intelligence unleashed: An argument for AI in Education.* Pearson.

Mahligawati, F., Allanas, E., Butarbutar, M. H., & Nordin, N. A. N. (2023). Artificial intelligence in physics education: A comprehensive literature review. *Journal of Physics: Conference Series*, 2596(1), 012080. DOI: 10.1088/1742-6596/2596/1/012080

Makransky, G., Bonde, M. T., Wulff, J. S., Wandall, J., Hood, M., Creed, P. A., & Nørremølle, A. (2016). Simulation based virtual learning environment in medical genetics counseling: An example of bridging the gap between theory and practice in medical education. *BMC Medical Education*, 16(1), 98. Advance online publication. DOI: 10.1186/s12909-016-0620-6 PMID: 27012245

Makransky, G., Terkildsen, T. S., & Mayer, R. E. (2019). Adding immersive virtual reality to a science lab simulation causes more presence but less learning. *Learning and Instruction*, 60, 225–236. DOI: 10.1016/j.learninstruc.2017.12.007

Malik, A. R., Pratiwi, Y., Andajani, K., Numertayasa, I. W., Suharti, S., Darwis, A., & Marzuki, M. (2023). Exploring artificial intelligence in academic essays: Higher education students' perspectives. *International Journal of Educational Research Open*, 5, 100296. DOI: 10.1016/j.ijedro.2023.100296

Mandinach, E. B., & Gummer, E. S. (2016). *Data literacy for educators: Making it count in teacher preparation and practice*. Teachers College Press.

Markauskaite, L., Marrone, R., Poquet, O., Knight, S., Martinez-Maldonado, R., Howard, S., Tondeur, J., De Laat, M., Buckingham Shum, S., Gašević, D., & Siemens, G. (2022). Rethinking the entwinement between artificial intelligence and human learning: What capabilities do learners need for a world with AI? *Computers and Education: Artificial Intelligence*, 3, 100056. DOI: 10.1016/j.caeai.2022.100056

Marsh, J. A., Bertrand, M., & Huguet, A. (2015). Using data to alter instructional practice: The mediating role of coaches and professional learning communities. *Teachers College Record*, 117(4), 1–40. DOI: 10.1177/016146811511700411

Matsuda, P. K. (2006). The myth of linguistic homogeneity in U.S. college composition. *College English, 68*(6), 637-651. Retrieved from https://www.jstor.org/stable/pdf/25472180.pdf?refreqid=excelsior%3A6ae835ff602e9cc74091c0b833274ddbAlvarez, Wan, & Lee, 2021

McCabe, D. L., Treviño, L. K., & Butterfield, K. D. (2012). *Cheating in college why students do it and what educators can do about it* (1st ed.). Johns Hopkins University Press.

McClure, L., & Nickse, R. S.National Institute of Education. (1981). *Competency-based education: Beyond minimum competency testing*. Teachers College Press.

McLaren, P. (2009). Critical pedagogy: A look at the major concepts. A. Darder, M. Baltodano, R.D. Torres (Eds), *The Critical Pedagogy Reader*. New York: NY: Routledge.

McMurtrie, B. (3 Oct. 2024). The future is hybrid. *The Chronicle of Higher Education.* Retrieved from https://www.chronicle.com/article/the-future-is-hybrid

Merchant, Z., Goetz, E. T., Cifuentes, L., Keeney-Kennicutt, W., & Davis, T. J. (2014). Effectiveness of virtual reality-based instruction on students' learning outcomes in K-12 and higher education: A meta-analysis. *Computers & Education*, 70, 29–40. DOI: 10.1016/j.compedu.2013.07.033

Michel-villarreal, R., Vilalta-perdomo, E., & Salinas-navarro, D. E. (2023). *Education sciences Challenges and Opportunities of Generative AI for Higher Education as Explained by ChatGPT*. file:///C:/Users/sheilarose.darmaraj/Desktop/New folder 1 - IJME/Villareal et al 2023.pdf

Miguel-Alonso, I., Rodriguez-Garcia, B., Checa, D., & Bustillo, A. (2023). Countering the novelty effect: A tutorial for immersive virtual reality learning environments. *Applied Sciences (Basel, Switzerland)*, 13(1), 593. DOI: 10.3390/app13010593

Miller, A. (2023). Socioeconomic impacts of AI in education. *International Journal of Educational Development*, 25(4), 277–290.

Mills, A., Bali, M., & Eaton, L. (2023). How do we respond to generative AI in education? Open educational practices give us a framework for an ongoing process. *Journal of Applied Learning and Teaching*, 6(1), 16–30. https://journals.sfu.ca/jalt/index.php/jalt/article/view/843/597

Mizumoto, A., & Eguchi, M. (2023). Exploring the potential of using an AI language model for automated essay scoring. *Research Methods in Applied Linguistics*, 2(2), 100050. DOI: 10.1016/j.rmal.2023.100050

Mogavi, R. H., Deng, C., Kim, J. J., Zhou, P., Kwon, Y. D., Metwally, A. H. S., Tlili, A., Bassanelli, S., Bucchiarone, A., Gujar, S., Nacke, L. E., & Hui, P. (2023). *Exploring User Perspectives on ChatGPT: Applications, Perceptions, and Implications for AI-Integrated Education*. http://arxiv.org/abs/2305.13114

Mollick, E. (2023, September 16). *Centaurs and Cyborgs on the Jagged Frontier*. www.oneusefulthing.org. https://www.oneusefulthing.org/p/centaurs-and-cyborgs-on-the-jagged

Mollick, E., & Mollick, L. (2024). Instructors as innovators: A future-focused approach to new AI learning opportunities, with prompts. *arXiv preprint arXiv:2407.05181*.

Moorhouse, B. L., Wong, K. M., & Li, L. (2023). Teaching with technology in the post-pandemic digital age: Technological normalisation and AI-induced disruptions. *RELC Journal*, 54(2), 311–320. DOI: 10.1177/00336882231176929

Moqbel, M. S. S., & Ai-Kadi, A. M. T. (2023). Foreign Language Learning Assessment in the Age of ChatGPT: A Theoretical Account. *Journal of English Studies in Arabia Felix*, 2(1), 71–84. DOI: 10.56540/jesaf.v2i1.62

Moradi, M., & Dass, M. (2022). Applications of artificial intelligence in B2B marketing: Challenges and future directions. *Industrial Marketing Management, 107*(September 2020), 300–314. DOI: 10.1016/j.indmarman.2022.10.016

Motha, S. (2014). *Race, empire, and English language teaching: Creating responsible and ethical anti-racist practice*. Teachers College Press.

Muca, E. C., Cavallini, D., Odore, R., Baratta, M., Bergero, D., & Valle, E. (2022). Are Veterinary Students Using Technologies and Online Learning Resources for Didactic Training? A Mini-Meta Analysis. *Education Sciences*, 12(12), 573. DOI: 10.3390/educsci12080573

Murray, D. (2003). Teach writing as a process not product. Villanueva, Victor (Ed.) *Cross-Talk in comp theory: A reader*. Urbana, IL: NCTE. 3-6.

Naidu, K., & Sevnarayan, K. (2023). ChatGPT: An ever-increasing encroachment of artificial intelligence in online assessment in distance education. *Online Journal of Communication and Media Technologies*, 13(3), e202336. Advance online publication. DOI: 10.30935/ojcmt/13291

Naseer, F., Khalid, M. U., Ayub, N., Rasool, A., Abbas, T., & Afzal, M. W. (2024). Automated Assessment and Feedback in Higher Education Using Generative AI. In *Transforming Education with Generative AI: Prompt Engineering and Synthetic Content Creation* (pp. 433-461). IGI Global. DOI: 10.4018/979-8-3693-1351-0.ch021

Nassar, S. (2019). Future aspects of critical thinking and AI. In *Proceedings of WRFASE International Conference,* Abu Dhabi.

Nelson, J. (2023, September 29). OpenAI quietly shuts down its AI detection tool. *Decrypt*. https://decrypt.co/149826/openai-quietly-shutters-its-ai-detection-tool

Netcoh, S. (2017). Balancing freedom and limitations: A case study of choice provision in a personalized learning class. *Teaching and Teacher Education*, 66, 383–392. DOI: 10.1016/j.tate.2017.05.010

Neumann, M., Rauschenberger, M., & Schön, E.-M. (2023). "We Need To Talk About ChatGPT": The Future of AI and Higher Education. *5th International Workshop on Software Engineering Education for the Next Generation (SEENG), November*, 29–32.

Ng, D. T. K., Lee, M., Tan, R. J. Y., Downie, J. S., & Chu, S. K. W. (2023). A review of AI teaching and learning from 2000 to 2020. *Education and Information Technologies*, 2023(28), 8445–8501. DOI: 10.1007/s10639-022-11491-w

Ng, D. T. K., Leung, J. K. L., Chu, S. K. W., & Qiao, M. S. (2021). Conceptualizing AI literacy: An exploratory review. *Computers and Education: Artificial Intelligence*, 2, 100041. DOI: 10.1016/j.caeai.2021.100041

Ng, D. T. K., Su, J., Leung, J. K. L., & Chu, S. K. W. (2023). Artificial intelligence (AI) literacy education in secondary schools: A review. *Interactive Learning Environments*, •••, 1–21. DOI: 10.1080/10494820.2023.2255228

Nicol, D. J., & Macfarlane-Dick, D. (2006). Formative assessment and self-regulated learning: A model and seven principles of good feedback practice. *Studies in Higher Education*, 31(2), 199–218. DOI: 10.1080/03075070600572090

Nikolic, S., Daniel, S., Haque, R., Belkina, M., Hassan, G. M., Grundy, S., Lyden, S., Neal, P., & Sandison, C. (2023). ChatGPT versus engineering education assessment: A multidisciplinary and multi-institutional benchmarking and analysis of this generative artificial intelligence tool to investigate assessment integrity. *European Journal of Engineering Education*, 48(May), 559–614. Advance online publication. DOI: 10.1080/03043797.2023.2213169

Nowlan, N. (2023). *Higher-order thinking skills assessment in 3D virtual learning environments using motifs and expert data*. Elsevier. DOI: 10.1016/j.cexr.2023.100012

Noy, S., & Zhang, W. (2023). Experimental evidence on the productivity effects of generative artificial intelligence. *Science*, 381(6654), 187–192. DOI: 10.1126/science.adh2586 PMID: 37440646

Ocana-Fernandez, Y., Valenzuela-Fernandez, L. A., & Garro-Aburto, L. L. (2019). Artificial Intelligence and Its Implications in Higher Education. *Journal of Educational Psychology-Propositos y Representaciones*, 7(2), 553–568.

Ohmann, P. (2019). An assessment of oral exams in introductory CS. *Proceedings of the 50th ACM Technical Symposium on Computer Science Education* (613-619). https://doi.org/DOI: 10.1145/3287324.3287489

Oja, K. J. (2010). Using problem-based learning in the clinical setting to improve nursing students' critical thinking: An evidence review. *The Journal of Nursing Education*, 50(3), 145–151. DOI: 10.3928/01484834-20101230-10 PMID: 21210603

Okolo, C. T. (2023, November 27). The Promise and Perils of Generative AI: Case Studies in an African Context. In *4th African Human Computer Interaction Conference (AfriCHI 2023)*, East London, South Africa. https://doi.org/DOI: 10.1145/3628096.3629066

Olan, F., Arakpogun, E. O., Suklan, J., Nakpodia, F., Damij, N., & Jayawickrama, U. (2022). Artificial intelligence and knowledge sharing: Contributing factors to organizational performance. *Journal of Business Research*, 145, 605–615. https://doi.org/ https://doi.org/10.1016/j.jbusres.2022.03.008. DOI: 10.1016/j.jbusres.2022.03.008

Ouyang, F., Wu, M., Zheng, L., Zhang, L., & Jiao, P. (2023). Integration of artificial intelligence performance prediction and learning analytics to improve student learning in online engineering course. *International Journal of Educational Technology in Higher Education*, 20(1), 1–23. DOI: 10.1186/s41239-022-00372-4 PMID: 36683653

Owan, V. J., Abang, K. B., Idika, D., Etta, E. O., & Bassey, B. A. (2023). Exploring the potential of artificial intelligence tools in educational measurement and assessment. *Eurasia Journal of Mathematics, Science and Technology Education*, 19(8), 1–15. DOI: 10.29333/ejmste/13428

Palladino, N. (2023). A 'biased' emerging governance regime for artificial intelligence? How AI ethics get skewed moving from principles to practices. *Telecommunications Policy*, 47(5), 1–20. DOI: 10.1016/j.telpol.2022.102479

Pane, J. F., Steiner, E. D., Baird, M. D., & Hamilton, L. S. (2015). *Continued Progress: Promising Evidence on Personalized Learning*. RAND Corporation. DOI: 10.7249/RR1365

Pang, R. Y., Yuan, W., Cho, K., He, H., Sukhbaatar, S., & Weston, J. (2024). Iterative reasoning preference optimization. *arXiv preprint arXiv:2404.19733.*

Pan, Y., Froese, F., Liu, N., Hu, Y., & Ye, M. (2022). The adoption of artificial intelligence in employee recruitment: The influence of contextual factors. *International Journal of Human Resource Management*, 33(6), 1125–1147. DOI: 10.1080/09585192.2021.1879206

Papert, S. (1980). *Mindstroms Children, Computers, and Powerful Ideas*. Basic Books.

Partnership on AI. (2019). The Responsible AI Framework. Retrieved from https://partnershiponai.org

Pavaloaia, V.-D., & Necula, S. (2023). Artificial Intelligence as a Disruptive Technology—A Systematic Literature Review. *Electronics (Basel)*, 12(5), 1102. https://doi.org/https://doi.org/10.3390/electronics12051102. DOI: 10.3390/electronics12051102

Pavlik, J. V. (2023). Collaborating with ChatGPT: Considering the Implications of Generative Artificial Intelligence for Journalism and Media Education. *J. Mass. Communication Education*, (78), 84–93.

Pedró, F., Subosa, M., Rivas, A., & Valverde, P. (2019). *Artificial Intelligence and Language Learning: Opportunities and Challenges*. Working Paper on Language Policy. UNESCO. Retrieved from https://unesdoc.unesco.org/ark:/48223/pf0000366994

Pedro, F., Subosa, M., Rivas, A., & Valverde, P. (2019). Artificial intelligence in education: Challenges and opportunities for sustainable development.

Pelton, T., & Pelton, L. (2024). Using Generative AI in Mathematics Education: Critical Discussions and Practical Strategies for Preservice Teachers, Teachers, and Teacher Educators. In J. Cohen & G. Solano (Eds.), *Proceedings of Society for Information Technology & Teacher Education International Conference* (pp. 1800-1805). Las Vegas, Nevada, United States: Association for the Advancement of Computing in Education (AACE). Retrieved October 25, 2024 from https://www.learntechlib.org/primary/p/224212/

Pendy, B. (2023). From Traditional to Tech-Infused: The Evolution of Education. *BULLET: Jurnal Multidisiplin Ilmu, 2*(3), 767–777. https://www.journal.mediapublikasi.id/index.php/bullet/article/view/3091

Perkins, M., Furze, L., Roe, J., & MacVaugh, J. (2024). The Artificial Intelligence Assessment Scale (AIAS): A Framework for Ethical Integration of Generative AI in Educational Assessment. *Journal of University Teaching & Learning Practice*, 21(6). Advance online publication. https://arxiv.org/abs/2312.07086. DOI: 10.53761/q3azde36

Peters, M. A., Jackson, L., Papastephanou, M., Jandrić, P., Lazaroiu, G., Evers, C. W., Cope, B., Kalantzis, M., Araya, D., Tesar, M., Mika, C., Chen, L., Wang, C., Sturm, S., Rider, S., & Fuller, S. (2023). AI and the future of humanity: ChatGPT-4, philosophy and education–Critical responses. *Educational Philosophy and Theory*, 0(0), 1–35. DOI: 10.1080/00131857.2020.1867108

Poorthuis, A. M. G., & van Dijk, A. (2020). Online Study-Aids to Stimulate Effective Learning in an Undergraduate Psychological Assessment Course. *Psychology Learning & Teaching*, 20(2), 236–249. DOI: 10.1177/1475725720964761

Popenici, S. A. D., & Kerr, S. (2017). Exploring the impact of artificial intelligence on teaching and learning in higher education. *Research and Practice in Technology Enhanced Learning*, 12(1), 1–13. DOI: 10.1186/s41039-017-0062-8 PMID: 30595727

Pottle, J. (2019). Virtual reality and the transformation of medical education. *Future Healthcare Journal*, 6(3), 181–185. DOI: 10.7861/fhj.2019-0036 PMID: 31660522

Pradhan, I. P., & Saxena, P. (2023). Reskilling workforce for the Artificial Intelligence age: Challenges and the way forward. In *The adoption and effect of artificial intelligence on human resources management, Part B* (pp. 181-197). Emerald Publishing Limited.

Prince, M. (2004). Does active learning work? A review of the research. *Journal of Engineering Education*, 93(3), 223–231. DOI: 10.1002/j.2168-9830.2004.tb00809.x

Prochaska, E. (2023, January 23). Embrace the bot: Designing writing assignments in the face of AI. *Faculty Focus*. https://www.facultyfocus.com/articles/course-design-ideas/embrace-the-bot-designing-writing-assignments-in-the-face-of-ai/

Queen Mary University of London. (2024). Enhancing Cross-Disciplinary Collaboration: Co-creating AI Skills Enhancement Resources. Retrieved from https://www.qmul.ac.uk/queenmaryacademy/educators/innovation-and-scholarship/innovative-pedagogies/artificial-intelligence/project-profiles/projects/co-creating-ai-best-practices-in-higher-education/

Rafi, M., JianMing, Z., & Ahmad, K. (2019). Technology integration for students' information and digital literacy education in academic libraries. *Information Discovery and Delivery*, 47(4), 203–217. DOI: 10.1108/IDD-07-2019-0049

Rafsanjani, H. N., & Nabizadeh, A. H. (2023). Towards human-centered artificial intelligence (AI) in architecture, engineering, and construction (AEC) industry. *Computers in Human Behavior Reports*, 11, 100319. DOI: 10.1016/j.chbr.2023.100319

Rajaram, K. (2023). Examining the OECD's perspective on AI in education policy : a critical analysis of language and structure in the 'AI and the future of skills' (AIFS) document and its implications for the higher education. *Learning Intelligence: Innovative and Digital Transformative Learning Strategies*, 3–53. https://doi.org/https://doi.org/10.1007/978-981-19-9201-8_1

Ray, P. P. (2023). ChatGPT: A comprehensive review on background, applications, key challenges, bias, ethics, limitations and future scope. *Internet of Things and Cyber-Physical Systems*, 3, 121–154. DOI: 10.1016/j.iotcps.2023.04.003

Rear, D. (2017). Reframing the debate on Asian students and critical thinking: Implications for Western universities. *Journal of Contemporary Issues in Education*, 12(2). Advance online publication. DOI: 10.20355/C5P35F

Rebello, C. M., Siegel, M. A., Freyermuth, S. K., Witzig, S. B., & İzci, K. (2011). Development of embedded assessments for learning in biotechnology: Results and design process for dissemination. *Biochemistry and Molecular Biology Education*, 40(2), 82–88. DOI: 10.1002/bmb.20579 PMID: 22419588

Reich, J., & Ito, M. (2017). *From good intentions to real outcomes: Equity by design in learning technologies*. Digital Media and Learning Research Hub.

Reid, J., & Kroll, B. (1995). Designing and assessing effective classroom writing assignments for NES and ESL students. *Journal of Second Language Writing*, 4(1), 17–41. DOI: 10.1016/1060-3743(95)90021-7

Reynolds, N., Dolmage, J., Bizzell, P., & Herzberg, B. (2012). *A brief history of rhetoric in composition in The Bedford Bibliography for Teachers of Writing* (Reynolds, N., Dolmage, J., Bizzell, P., & Herzberg, B., Eds.).

Richardson, J. E. (2017). *Analysing Newspapers: An Approach from Critical Discourse Analysis*. London: Springer.Rudolph, J., Tan, S., & Tan, S., (2023). ChatGPT: Bullshit spewer or the end of traditional assessments in higher education? *Journal of Applied Learning & Teaching*, 6(1), 342–363.

Ritter, S., Anderson, J. R., Koedinger, K. R., & Corbett, A. (2007). Cognitive Tutor: Applied research in mathematics education. *Psychonomic Bulletin & Review*, 14(2), 249–255. DOI: 10.3758/BF03194060 PMID: 17694909

Rizos, I., Foykas, E., & Georgakopoulos, S. V. (2024). Enhancing mathematics education for students with special educational needs through generative AI: A case study in Greece. *Contemporary Educational Technology*, 16(4), ep535. DOI: 10.30935/cedtech/15487

Roberts, L. (2024). AI-Driven Pedagogical Strategies for Higher-Order Skills Development. *Educational Assessment Review*, 29, 230–248.

Roberts-Mahoney, H., Means, A. J., & Garrison, M. J. (2016). Netflixing human capital development: Personalized learning technology and the corporatization of K-12 education. *Journal of Education Policy*, 31(4), 405–420. DOI: 10.1080/02680939.2015.1132774

Rodriguez-Echeverría, R., Gutiérrez, J. D., Conejero, J. M. & Prieto, Á. E. (2021). Analysis of ChatGPT Performance in Computer Engineering Exams. IEEE Revista Iberoamericana de Tecnologias del Aprendizaje, 19, 71-80, 2024, https://doi:DOI: 10.1109/RITA.2024.3381842

Rose, M. (1985). The language of exclusion: Writing instruction at the university. *College English*, 47(4), 341–359. https://www.jstor.org/stable/376957?origin=JSTOR-pdf. DOI: 10.58680/ce198513275

Roshanaei, M., Olivares, H., & Lopez, R. R. (2023). Harnessing AI to Foster Equity in Education: Opportunities, Challenges, and Emerging Strategies. *Journal of Intelligent Learning Systems and Applications*, 15(04), 123–143. DOI: 10.4236/jilsa.2023.154009

Rospigliosi, P. (2023). Artificial Intelligence in Teaching and Learning: What Questions Should We Ask of ChatGPT? *Interactive Learning Environments*, 31(1), 1–3. DOI: 10.1080/10494820.2023.2180191

Rudolph, J., Tan, S., & Tan, S. (2023). ChatGPT: Bullshit spewer or the end of traditional assessments in higher education? *Journal of Applied Learning & Teaching*, 6(1), 342–263. https://journals.sfu.ca/jalt/index.php/jalt/article/view/689/539

Ruiz-Rojas, L. I., Acosta-Vargas, P., De-Moreta-Llovet, J., & Gonzalez-Rodriguez, M. (2023). Empowering Education with Generative Artificial Intelligence Tools: Approach with an Instructional Design Matrix. *Sustainability (Basel)*, 15(15), 11524. Advance online publication. DOI: 10.3390/su151511524

Rusmiyanto, R., Huriati, N., Fitriani, N., Tyas, N. K., Rofi'i, A., & Sari, M. N. (2023). The Role Of Artificial Intelligence (AI) In Developing English Language Learner's Communication Skills. *Journal of Education*, 6(1), 750–757. DOI: 10.31004/joe.v6i1.2990

Ryan, R. M., & Deci, E. L. (2000). Self-determination theory and the facilitation of intrinsic motivation, social development, and well-being. *The American Psychologist*, 55(1), 68–78. DOI: 10.1037/0003-066X.55.1.68 PMID: 11392867

Saaideh, M. (2023). AI-Driven transformations in higher education: Opportunities and challenges. *International Journal of Educational Research and Studies*, 5(1), 29–36. https://www.researchgate.net/publication/370864917

Sadler, D. R. (1989). Formative assessment and the design of instructional systems. *Instructional Science*, 18(2), 119–144. DOI: 10.1007/BF00117714

Samaras, A. P., & Freese, A. R. (2006). *Self-study of teaching practices primer*. Peter Lang International Academic Publishers.

Sander, P., Sanders, L., & Stevenson, K. (2002). Engaging the learner: Reflections on the use of student presentations. *Psychology Teaching Review*, 10(1), 76–89. DOI: 10.53841/bpsptr.2002.10.1.76

Schildkamp, K., Poortman, C. L., & Handelzalts, A. (2016). Data teams for school improvement. *School Effectiveness and School Improvement*, 27(2), 228–254. DOI: 10.1080/09243453.2015.1056192

Schildkamp, K., Poortman, C. L., Luyten, H., & Ebbeler, J. (2017). Factors promoting and hindering data-based decision making in schools. *School Effectiveness and School Improvement*, 28(2), 242–258. DOI: 10.1080/09243453.2016.1256901

Schmidt, H. G., Rotgans, J. I., & Yew, E. H. (2011, August). The process of problem-based learning: What works and why. *Medical Education*, 45(8), 792–806. DOI: 10.1111/j.1365-2923.2011.04035.x PMID: 21752076

Schmidt, T., & Strasser, T. (2022). Artificial Intelligence in Foreign Language Learning and Teaching: A CALL for Intelligent Practice. *Anglistik: International Journal of English Studies*, 33(1), 165–184. DOI: 10.33675/ANGL/2022/1/14

Schön, E. M., Neumann, M., Hofmann-Stölting, C., Baeza-Yates, R., & Rauschenberger, M. (2023). How are AI assistants changing higher education? *Frontiers of Computer Science*, 5, 1208550. DOI: 10.3389/fcomp.2023.1208550

Schools, K. (2007). The writing process: An overview of research on teaching writing as a process. https://www.ksbe.edu/assets/research/collection/07_0237_.pdf

Schumpeter, J. A. (1942). *Capitalism, Socialism, and Democracy*. Harper and Brothers.

Scott, S. (2008). Perceptions of students' learning critical thinking through debate in a technology classroom: A case study. *The Journal of Technology Studies*, 34(1), 39–44. Advance online publication. DOI: 10.21061/jots.v34i1.a.5

Selwyn, N. (2019). Should robots replace teachers? AI and the future of education. *Polity*.

Shakarian, P., Koyyalamudi, A., Ngu, N., & Mareedu, L. (2023). An Independent Evaluation of ChatGPT on Mathematical Word Problems (MWP). ArXiv, abs/2302.13814.

Shanto, S. S., Ahmed, Z., & Jony, A. I. (2024). Enriching learning process with generative AI: A proposed framework to cultivate critical thinking in higher education using ChatGPT. *Tuijin Jishu/Journal of Propulsion Technology, 45*(1), 3019-3029.

Sharples, J., Oxman, A. D., Mahtani, K. R., Chalmers, I., Oliver, S., Collins, K., Austvoll-Dahlgren, A., & Hoffmann, T. (2017). Critical thinking in healthcare and education. *BMJ (Clinical Research Ed.)*, j2234, j2234. DOI: 10.1136/bmj.j2234 PMID: 28512135

Shaughnessy, M. P. (2003). Diving. In Villanueva, V. (Ed.), *An Introduction to Basic Writing." Cross-Talk in Comp Theory: A Reader* (pp. 311–319). National Council of Teachers of English.

Shaw, C., Yuan, L., Brennan, D., Martin, S., Janson, N., Fox, K., & Bryant, G. (2023, October 23). Tyton Partners. https://tytonpartners.com/time-for-class-2023/GenAI-Update

Sholikah, M., & Anwar, M. A. Muhibbudin, & Sa'diyah, D. F., Hidayati, Y., & Permadi, B. (2019). The Effectiveness of Writing Approach Viewed from Students' Self-Confidence. *Advances in Social Science, Education and Humanities Research*, 349. pp. 322-325. https://doi.org/DOI: 10.2991/iccd-19.2019.85

Shukla, S. (2023). Creative Computing and Harnessing the Power of Generative Artificial Intelligence. *Journal of Environmental Science and Technology*, 2(1), 556–579.

Shute, V. J. (2008). Focus on formative feedback. *Review of Educational Research*, 78(1), 153–189. DOI: 10.3102/0034654307313795

Shute, V. J., & Ventura, M. (2013). *Stealth assessment: Measuring and supporting learning in video games*. MIT Press. DOI: 10.7551/mitpress/9589.001.0001

Sibal, P., Neupane, B., & Orlic, D. (2021). *Artificial intelligence needs assessment survey in Africa*. United Nations Educational, Scientific and Cultural Organization. https://unesdoc.unesco.org/ark:/48223/pf0000375322

Simmons, R. (2024, June). Innovating cybersecurity education through AI-augmented teaching. In *European Conference on Cyber Warfare and Security* (Vol. 23, No. 1, pp. 480-486). DOI: 10.34190/eccws.23.1.2224

Simms, R. C. (2024). Work with ChatGPT, not against. *Nurse Educator*, 49(3), 158–161. DOI: 10.1097/NNE.0000000000001634 PMID: 38502607

Sims, M. L. (2023). Shifting perceptions of socially just writing assessment: Labor-based contract grading and multilingual writing instruction. *Assessing Writing, 57*(October 2022), 100731. DOI: 10.1016/j.asw.2023.100731

Singer, J. (1999). Why can't you be normal for once in your life? From a problem with no name to the emergence of a new category of difference. In Corker, M., & French, S. (Eds.), *Disability Discourse* (pp. 59–67). Open University Press.

Sleegers, P., & Consultancy, B. M. C. (2024). Multi-stakeholder collaboration and co-creation: Towards responsible application of AI in education.

Slim, Z. (2023). The Impact of Artificial Intelligence on Higher Education: An Empirical Study. *European Journal of Educational Sciences*, 10(1), 17–33. DOI: 10.19044/ejes.v10no1a17

Smyth, M. L., & Davis, J. R. (2003). An Examination of Student Cheating in the Two-Year College. *Community College Review*, 31(1), 17–32. DOI: 10.1177/009155210303100102

Sommers, N., & Saltz, L. (2004). The novice as expert: Writing the freshman year. *College Composition and Communication*, 56(1), 124–149. DOI: 10.58680/ccc20043993

Song, N. (2024). Higher education crisis: Academic misconduct with generative AI. *Journal of Contingencies and Crisis Management*, 32(1), e12532. Advance online publication. DOI: 10.1111/1468-5973.12532

Sonsupap, K., & Cojorn, K. (2024). Collaborative professional development and its impact on teachers' ability to foster higher order thinking. *Journal of Education and Learning*, 18(2), 561–569.

Soria Krista, M. (2012). Creating a successful transition for working-class first-year students. *The Journal of College Orientation and Transition*, 20(1), 44–55.

Spiker, A., Brock, C., & Kelly, A. (2023). We Never Left Work: Challenges to Sustaining High-Quality Teaching and Learning during COVID-19. *Sustainability (Basel)*, 15(5), 3938. https://doi.org/https://doi.org/10.3390/su15053938. DOI: 10.3390/su15053938

Srinivasa, K. G., Kurni, M., & Saritha, K. (2022). Harnessing the Power of AI to Education. In *Learning, teaching, and assessment methods for contemporary learners: pedagogy for the digital generation* (pp. 311–342). Springer Nature Singapore. DOI: 10.1007/978-981-19-6734-4_13

Srivastava, A. P., & Agarwal, S. (Eds.). (2024). *Utilizing AI tools in academic research writing*. IGI Global. DOI: 10.4018/979-8-3693-1798-3

Stăiculescu, C., Lacatus, M. L., & Livinti, R. (2021). Employers' expectations and requirements. Case study: Employers of schools of economics and business graduates in Romania. *Proceedings of the International Conference on Business Excellence*, 15(1), 185-195. https://doi.org/DOI: 10.2478/picbe-2021-0018

Stanoyevitch, A. (2024). Online assessment in the age of artificial intelligence. *Discover Education*, 3(1), 126. DOI: 10.1007/s44217-024-00212-9

Stige, Å., Zamani, E. D., Mikalef, P., & Zhu, Y. (2023). Artificial intelligence (AI) for user experience (UX) design: a systematic literature review and future research agenda. *Information Technology & People*. https://doi.org/https://doi.org/10.1108/ITP-07-2022-0519

Storozhyk, M. (2024). Philosophy of future: Analytical overview of interaction between education, science, and artificial intelligence in the context of contemporary challenges. *Futurity Philosophy*, 3(1), 23–47.

Sugai, G., & Horner, R. (2009). Sugai & Horner 2009.pdf. In *Handbook of Positive Behavior* (pp. 307–326). file:///C:/Users/sheilarose.darmaraj/Desktop/New folder 1 - IJME/Sugai & Horner 2009.pdf

Su, J., Guo, K., Chen, X., & Chu, S. K. W. (2023). Teaching artificial intelligence in K–12 classrooms: A scoping review. *Interactive Learning Environments*, •••, 1–20.

Su, K. D. (2022). Implementation of Innovative Artificial Intelligence Cognitions with Problem-Based Learning-Guided tasks to enhance Students' Performance in Science. *Journal of Baltic Science Education*, 21(2), 245–257. DOI: 10.33225/jbse/22.21.245

Sun, Z., Anbarasan, M., & Kumar, D. P. (2021). Design of online intelligent English teaching platform based on artificial intelligence techniques. *Computational Intelligence*, 2021(37), 1166–1180. DOI: 10.1111/coin.12351

Supriyadi, E., & Kuncoro, K. S. (2023). Exploring the future of mathematics teaching: Insight with ChatGPT. *Union J. Ilmiah Pendidik. Mat.*, 11(2), 305–316. DOI: 10.30738/union.v11i2.14898

Su, Y., Lin, Y., & Lai, C. (2023). Collaborating with ChatGPT in argumentative writing classrooms. *Assessing Writing*, 57(May), 100752. DOI: 10.1016/j.asw.2023.100752

Tahir, A., & Tahir, A. (2023). AI-driven advancements in ESL learner autonomy: Investigating student attitudes towards virtual assistant usability. Linguistic Forum. *Journal of Linguistics*, 5(2), 50–56.

Tahir, M. (2024). Role of artificial intelligence in education: A conceptual review. *World Journal of Advanced Research and Reviews*, 22(01), 1469–1475. DOI: 10.30574/wjarr.2024.22.1.1217

Tang, Q. (2024, July 23). *A Case Study on The Application of Artificial Intelligence in Education Industry.* Proceedings of the 2023 3rd International Conference on Modern Educational Technology and Social Sciences (ICMETSS 2023), Advances in Social Science, Education and Humanities Research 784, DOI: 10.2991/978-2-38476-128-9_12

Tang, K. H. D. (2024). Implications of artificial intelligence for teaching and learning. *Acta Pedagogia Asiana*, 3(2), 65–79. DOI: 10.53623/apga.v3i2.404

Taylor, F. W. (1911). *Principles of Scientific Management*. Harper & Brothers.

TeachThought. (2024, August 1). *Bloom's taxonomy verbs: A comprehensive list for critical thinking*. TeachThought. https://www.teachthought.com/critical-thinking/blooms-taxonomy-verbs-2/

The Alan Turing Institute. (2023). Generative AI in Education: Call for Evidence https://www.turing.ac.uk/

The Chinese University of Hong Kong. (2021, 24 August). A 30-minute EEG Test Forecasts Children's Language Development. *CUHK in Touch*. Retrieved from https://cuhkintouch.cpr.cuhk.edu.hk/2021/08/7463/

The Chinese University of Hong Kong. (2023). *Use of Artificial Intelligence Tools in Teaching, Learning and Assessments: A Guide for Students*. Hong Kong: The Chinese University of Hong Kong. Retrieved from https://www.aqs.cuhk.edu

The Hong Kong Polytechnic University. (2023). *Guidelines for Students on the Use of Generative Artificial Intelligence*. Hong Kong: The Hong Kong Polytechnic University of Hong Kong. Retrieved from https://www.polyu.edu.hk/ar/ docdrive/polyu-students/Student-guide-on-the-use-GenAI.pdf

Thomas, A., Hodges, A., & Blair Van Dam, C. (April 2024). An abundance of "resources": Teaching digital literacy & academic integrity to help students navigate a complex information ecosystem. *Conference on College Composition and Communication*, Spokane, WA._https://drive.google.com/file/d/1XvKnbI5QJ_mnDcfq2eOiVnPICU42ed2_/view?usp=sharing

Thomas, J. W. (2000). *A review of research on project-based learning*. Autodesk Foundation.

Thompson, G. (2023). Addressing grade inflation in higher education. *Education Policy Review*, 12(3), 89–102.

Thorp, H. H. (2023). ChatGPT is fun, but not an author. *Science*, 379(6630), 313. DOI: 10.1126/science.adg7879 PMID: 36701446

Top 10 Popular AI Tools. (n.d.). Retrieved from https://www.technopedia.com/top-10-most-popular-ai-tools

Topol, E. J. (2019). High-performance medicine: The convergence of human and artificial intelligence. *Nature Medicine*, 25(1), 44–56. DOI: 10.1038/s41591-018-0300-7 PMID: 30617339

Tourni, I., Grigorakis, G., Marougkas, I., Dafnis, K., & Tassopoulou, V. (2023). *ChatGPT is all you need to decolonize sub-Saharan Vocational Education. 2*, 1–7. http://arxiv.org/abs/2304.13728

Trubek, A. (2016). *The history and uncertain future of handwriting*. Bloomsbury USA, an imprint of Bloomsbury Publishing Plc.

Tsai, C. W., & Fan, Y. T. (2013). Research trends in game-based learning research in online learning environments: A review of studies published in SSCI-indexed journals from 2003 to 2012. *British Journal of Educational Technology*, 44(5), E115–E119. DOI: 10.1111/bjet.12031

Tse, S.-K. (2009). Chinese Language Education in Hong Kong: Twenty Five Years of Educational Research in Hong Kong. *Educational Research Journal*, 24(2), 231–255.

Tuomi, I., Cachia, R., & Villar-Onrubia, D. (2023). *Science for policy report on the futures of technology in education: Emerging trends and policy implications*. Joint Research Centre. https://www.jrc.ec.europa.eu

Turing, A. M. (1950). Computing Machinery and Intelligence Author. *Mind, New Series, 59*(236), 433–460. https://www.jstor.org/stable/2251299 Accessed: Tversky, A., & Kahneman, D. (1974). Judgment under Uncertainty: Heuristics and Biases: Biases in judgments reveal some heuristics of thinking under uncertainty. *Science, 185*(4157), 1124–1131. DOI: 10.1126/science.185.4157.1124

Turnitin. (2023). AI writing detection. Retrieved from https://turnitin.com

Ukwandu, E., Omisade, O., Jones, K., Thorne, S., & Castle, M. (2024). The future of teaching and learning in the context of emerging artificial intelligence technologies. Available at *SSRN* 4852030. DOI: 10.2139/ssrn.4852030

UNESCO. (2019). *Artificial Intelligence in Education: Challenges and Opportunities for Sustainable Development.* Working Papers on Education Policy 07.Paris: United Nations Educational, Scientific and Cultural Organization. https://en.unesco.org/

UNESCO. (2021). Recommendation on the Ethics of Artificial Intelligence. Retrieved from https://unesdoc.unesco.org/ark:/48223/pf0000377897

UNESCO. (2023). *Guidance for generative AI in education and research.* United Nations Educational, Scientific and Cultural Organization. https://www.unesco.org/en/open-access/cc-sa

United Nations. (2024, March 10). *Sustainable Development Goals (SDGs) and Disability/United Nations.* Retrieved from https://www.un.org/development/desa/disabilities/about-us/sustainable-development-goals-sdgs-and-disability.html

Valavanidis, A. (2023). Artificial Intelligence (AI) Applications. *Department of Chemistry, National and Kapodistrian University of Athens, University Campus Zografou, 15784.*Collins, R. (2014). Skills for the 21st Century: Teaching higher-order thinking. *Curriculum & Leadership Journal*, 12(14), 1–8.

Van Dijk, T. A. (2008). *Discourse and context: A Sociocognitive approach.* Cambridge University Press. DOI: 10.1017/CBO9780511481499

Van Mechelen, M., Smith, R. C., Schaper, M. M., Tamashiro, M., Bilstrup, K. E., Lunding, M., Graves Petersen, M., & Sejer Iversen, O. (2023). Emerging technologies in K–12 education: A future HCI research agenda. *ACM Transactions on Computer-Human Interaction*, 30(3), 1–40. DOI: 10.1145/3569897

Vasoya, N. H. (2023). Revolutionizing nano materials processing through IoT-AI integration: Opportunities and challenges. *Journal of Materials Science Research and Reviews*, 6(3), 294–328.

Vesselinov, R., & Grego, J. (2012). *Duolingo effectiveness study: Final report.* https://theowlapp.health/wp-content/uploads/2022/04/DuolingoReport_Final-1.pdf

Vilà, R., Aneas, A., Rubio, M. J., & Freixa, M.Moving Away from the Regulatory Approach. (2019). The value of student engagement for higher education quality assurance. Moving away from the regulatory approach. *REICE.Revista Electrónica Iberoamericana sobre Calidad, Eficacia y Cambio en Educación*, 17(2), 107–122. DOI: 10.15366/reice2019.17.2.006

Von Hippel, P. T. (2024). GPT-4 Is Still Not Ready to Teach Geometry. *Education Next*, 24(4). https://www.educationnext.org/chat-gpt-4-is-still-not-ready to-teach-geometry/

Vos, L. (2023, September 7). *Ai hurts students' writing and communication skills.* eCampus News. https://www.ecampusnews.com/featured/2023/09/21/ai-tools-students-writing-communication-skills/

Vygotsky, L. S. (1978). *Mind in society: The development of higher psychological processes.* Harvard University Press.

Vygotsky, L. S., Cole, M., Jolm-Steiner, V., Scribner, S., & Souberman, E. (1978). *Mind in Society: Development of Higher Psychological Processes.* Harvard University Press., DOI: 10.2307/j.ctvjf9vz4

Wang, T., & Cheng, E. C. K. (2021). An investigation of barriers to Hong Kong K-12 schools incorporating Artificial Intelligence in education. *Computers and Education: Artificial Intelligence, 2*, (2021).

Wang, X., Gong, Z., Wang, G., Jia, J., Xu, Y., Zhao, J., Fan, Q., Wu, S., Hu, W., & Li, X. (2023). *ChatGPT Performs on the Chinese National Medical Licensing Examination.* 1–9. file:///C:/Users/sheilarose.darmaraj/Desktop/New folder 1 - IJME/Wang et al 2023.pdf

Wang, A. I., & Tahir, R. (2020). The effect of using Kahoot! for learning–A literature review. *Computers & Education*, 149, 103818. DOI: 10.1016/j.compedu.2020.103818

Wang, G., Wu, X., & Li, Q. (2021). A bibliometric study of news discourse analysis (1988–2020). *Discourse & Communication*, 16(1), 110–128. DOI: 10.1177/17504813211043725

Wang, H., & Yuan, Z. (2013). The promotion of Putonghua (Mandarin Chinese): An overview. In Li, Y., & Li, W. (Eds.), *The language situation in China* (pp. 27–39). De Gruyter Mouton.

Wang, T., Lund, B. D., Marengo, A., Pagano, A., Mannuru, N. R., Teel, Z. A., & Pange, J. (2023). Exploring the Potential Impact of Artificial Intelligence (AI) on International Students in Higher Education: Generative AI, Chatbots, Analytics, and International Student Success. *Applied Sciences (Basel, Switzerland)*, 13(11), 6716. https://doi.org/https://doi.org/10.3390/app13116716. DOI: 10.3390/app13116716

Wardat, Y., Tashtoush, M. A., AlAli, R., & Jarrah, A. M. (2023). ChatGPT: A revolutionary tool for teaching and learning mathematics. *Eurasia Journal of Mathematics, Science and Technology Education*, 19(7), em2286. Advance online publication. DOI: 10.29333/ejmste/13272

Wardat, Y., Tashtoush, M., Alali, R., & Saleh, S. (2024). Artificial Intelligence in Education: Mathematics Teachers' Perspectives, Practices and Challenges. *Iraqi Journal for Computer Science and Mathematics*, 5(1), 60–77. DOI: 10.52866/ijcsm.2024.05.01.004

Warnestal, P. (2021, December). Multi-disciplinary Learning and Innovation for Professional Design of AI-Powered Services. In *International Conference on Design, Learning, and Innovation* (pp. 21-36). Cham: Springer International Publishing.

Watson, G. R., & Sottile, J. (2010). Cheating in the digital age: Do students cheat more in online courses? *Online Journal of Distance Learning Administration*, 13(1).

Weber, B., & Hertel, G. (2007). Motivation gains of inferior group members: A meta-analytical review. *Journal of Personality and Social Psychology*, 93(6), 973–993. DOI: 10.1037/0022-3514.93.6.973 PMID: 18072849

Webster, C., & Ivanov, S. (2020). *Robotics, artificial intelligence, and the evolving nature of work*. Springer International Publishing. DOI: 10.1007/978-3-030-08277-2_8

Weng, X., Ye, H., Dai, Y., & Ng, O. L. (2024). Integrating artificial intelligence and computational thinking in educational contexts: A systematic review of instructional design and student learning outcomes. *Journal of Educational Computing Research*, 62(6), 07356331241248686. DOI: 10.1177/07356331241248686

Wette, R. (2014). Teachers' practices in EAP writing instruction: Use of models and modeling. *System*, 42, 60–69. DOI: 10.1016/j.system.2013.11.002

Widodo, Y. B., Korwa, R. U., & Nuraini, R. (2023). Artificial intelligence-based decision support system for education management in higher education. Al-Fikrah. *Jurnal Manajemen Pendidikan*, 11(2), 352. DOI: 10.31958/jaf.v11i2.12120

Wiewiora, A., & Kowalkiewicz, A. (2018). The role of authentic assessment in developing authentic leadership identity and competencies. *Assessment & Evaluation in Higher Education*, 44(3), 415–430. DOI: 10.1080/02602938.2018.1516730

Wiggins, G. (1998). *Educative assessment: Designing assessments to inform and improve student performance*. Jossey-Bass.

Wiggins, G. P., & McTighe, J. (1998). *Understanding by design*. Association for Supervision and Curriculum Development.

Wiliam, D. (2011). *Embedded formative assessment*. Solution tree press.

Wiliam, D. (2001). An overview of the relationship between assessment and the curriculum. In Scott, D. (Ed.), *Curriculum and assessment* (pp. 165–182). Greenwood Publishing.

Williamson, B. (2017). Big data in education: The digital future of learning, policy and practice. *Sage (Atlanta, Ga.)*. Advance online publication. DOI: 10.4135/9781529714920

Winkler, R., & Söllner, M. (2018). Unleashing the potential of chatbots in education: A state of-the-art analysis. In *Academy of Management Annual Meeting Proceedings* (Vol. 2018, No. 1). DOI: 10.5465/AMBPP.2018.15903abstract

Wójcik, S., Rulkiewicz, A., Pruszczyk, P., Lisik, W., Poboży, M., & Domienik-Karłowicz, J. (2024). Reshaping medical education: Performance of ChatGPT on a PES medical examination. *Cardiology Journal*, 31(3), 442–450. DOI: 10.5603/cj.97517 PMID: 37830257

World Economic Forum. (2024) Shaping the Future of Learning: The Role of AI in Education 4.0 Insight Report April 2024 https://www3.weforum.org/

Wu, T., & Chang, M. (2021, December). The Cloud-Based Textbook: From Choice to Advantage. In *2021 IEEE International Conference on Engineering, Technology & Education (TALE)* (pp. 01-08). IEEE. DOI: 10.1109/TALE52509.2021.9678553

Wu, T., & Zhang, S. h. (2024). Applications and Implication of Generative AI in Non-STEM Disciplines in Higher Education. In F. Zhao & D. Miao (Eds.), *AI-generated Content. AIGC 2023. Communications in Computer and Information Science,* (vol. 1946, pp. 341 349). Springer, Singapore. DOI: 10.1007/978-981-99-7587-7_29

Wu, C., Hung, C., Shen, C., & Yu, J. (2024). Enhancing the willingness of adopting AI in education using back-propagation neural networks. *Sensors and Materials*, 36(3), 905. DOI: 10.18494/SAM4485

Xiang, J. (2023). Promoting innovation and practice of introduction to artificial intelligence course with curriculum civics as a handle. *Asian Journal of Education and Social Studies*, 41(3), 30–36. DOI: 10.9734/ajess/2023/v41i3897

Xiang, Y. (2023). Analytical assessment design in the age of AI. *Journal of Assessment and Evaluation*, 25(3), 210–230.

Xia, Q., Xiaojing, W., Ouyang, F., Lin, T. J., & Chiu, T. K. (2024). A scoping review on how generative artificial intelligence transforms assessment in higher education. *International Journal of Educational Technology in Higher Education*, 2024(21), 40. DOI: 10.1186/s41239-024-00468-z

Xin, O. K., Wider, W., & Ling, L. K. (2022). Human Resource Artificial Intelligence Implementation and Organizational Performance in Malaysia. *Asia-Pacific Social Science Review*, 22(3), 18–37. DOI: 10.59588/2350-8329.1461

Yaacob, Z., & Saad, N. H. M. (2020). Acceptance of YouTube as a learning platform during the Covid-19 pandemic: The moderating effect of subscription status. *TEM Journal*, 4, 1732–1739. DOI: 10.18421/TEM94-54

Yan, Z., & Brown, G. T. (2021). Assessment for learning in the Hong Kong assessment reform: A case of policy borrowing. *Studies in Educational Evaluation*, 68, 100985. DOI: 10.1016/j.stueduc.2021.100985

Yueng, P. (2019, 31 January). AI will be a game changer for Hong Kong education. *China Daily Hong Kong*.

Zaharia, R. M. (2023). Challenges for competence-oriented education in the context of the development of artificial intelligence systems. *Amfiteatru Economic*, 26(65), 6–11. DOI: 10.24818/EA/2024/65/6

Zai, X., Chu, X., Chai, C. S., Jong, M. S. Y., Istenic, A., & Spector, M. (2021). Liu, J.-B., Yuan, J., & Li, Y. (2021). A review of artificial intelligence (AI) in education from 2010 to 2020. *Complexity*, 2021(1), 8812542. Advance online publication. DOI: 10.1155/2021/8812542

Zakrajsek, T. D. (2022). *The New Science of Learning: How to Learn in Harmony with Your Brain* (3rd ed.). Stylus Publishing LLC.

Zare, P., & Othman, M. (2013). Classroom debate as a systematic teaching/learning approach. *World Applied Sciences Journal*, 28(11), 1506–1513. DOI: 10.5829/idosi.wasj.2013.28.11.1809

Zeb, A., Ullah, R., & Karim, R. (2024). Exploring the role of ChatGPT in higher education: Opportunities, challenges and ethical considerations. *The International Journal of Information and Learning Technology*, 41(1), 99–111. DOI: 10.1108/IJILT-04-2023-0046

Zhai (2022). ChatGPT for Next Generation Science Learning, *XDRS, 2*(9), 42-46.

Zhai, C., Wibowo, S., & Li, L. D. (2024). The effects of over-reliance on AI dialogue systems on students' cognitive abilities: A systematic review. *Smart Learning Environments*, 11(1), 28. DOI: 10.1186/s40561-024-00316-7

Zhai, X. (2023). *ChatGPT for Next Generation Science Learning*. Routledge.

Zhang, B., & Yang, R. R. (2004). Putonghua Education and Language Policy in Postcolonial Hong Kong. In Zhou, M. L., & Sun, H. (Eds.), *Language Policy in the People's Republic of China: Theory and Practice Since 1949* (pp. 143–161). Springer. DOI: 10.1007/1-4020-8039-5_8

Zhang, K., & Aslan, A. B. (2021). AI technologies for education: Recent research & future directions. *Computers and Education: Artificial Intelligence*, 2, 100025. DOI: 10.1016/j.caeai.2021.100025

Zhou, S., Xu, H., Zheng, Z., Chen, J., Li, Z., Bu, J., Wu, J., Wang, X., Zhu, W., & Ester, M. (2022). A Comprehensive Survey on Deep Clustering: Taxonomy, Challenges, and Future Directions. *ArXiv*, 1–35. https://doi.org/https://doi.org/10.48550/arXiv.2206.07579

Zhu, X. (2015). An assessment framework of integrated writing in teaching Chinese as a first language . *Recent developments of Chinese teaching and learning in higher education: Applied Chinese language studies VI*, 108-116.

About the Contributors

Patrick Wachira is a professor in the departments of Mathematics and Teacher Education at Cleveland State University, USA. His teaching experience includes teaching mathematics content and Mathematics education courses for prospective teachers. His main research interests are in the preparation of teachers to teach mathematics in a way that develops understanding facilitated by appropriate and effective integration of technology in learning. Dr. Wachira has co-authored several books focused on technology and assessment in education.

Xiongyi Liu is Associate Professor of Educational Psychology and Research Methods in the Department of Curriculum and Foundations at Cleveland State University, USA. Dr. Liu received a Ph.D. in Educational Psychology from University of Nebraska-Lincoln and previously held a research professor position at University of Maine-Orono. Her research interests include computer-supported collaborative learning, serious games in STEM education, self-regulation and motivation, and technology-facilitated interventions for children with autism spectrum disorder. Dr. Liu has established international collaborations in many of her research endeavors.

Selma Koc is an associate professor of educational technology at Cleveland State University. Her teaching experience includes educational technology, educational psychology and summer institute programs for gifted and talented high school students. Her research interests are in the areas of online learning and assessment, instructional design and development, technology planning and integration in K-12 and higher education

***

Doris Chasokela is a senior lecturer at the National University of Science and Technology (NUST) in Zimbabwe. She holds a Doctorate in Education, a Master of Engineering in Electrical Systems Control and Information Technology; a Bachelor of Technical Education in Electrical and Electronic Engineering; a Diploma in Technical Vocational Education. She has supervised several undergraduate projects and postgraduate dissertations. She has eleven years of experience in higher education. She has published several articles, book chapters and 3 text books. Her interests are higher education, engineering education, artificial intelligence, electrical and electronics, control and e-learning.

Tendai Chigora a holder of Bachelors Degree in Design Education,BDesEd-DTE, DTecVocEd, and NC-TGD. General Certificate of Secondary Education (IGCSE) Design and Technology Teacher.

Liz Giltner has been a dedicated faculty member at the University of Central Florida since 2006. Over her 17 years at UCF, Liz has taught a wide variety of French language courses in face-to-face, online, mixed-mode, and video-live formats. Throughout her career, Liz has demonstrated a strong commitment to excellence in teaching and an enthusiasm for continually developing her pedagogical knowledge and skills. Liz is particularly passionate about motivating students by piquing their curiosity and fostering their growing sense of competence and confidence. She values the opportunity to incorporate evidence-based approaches to enhance her lesson content and teaching techniques.

Joseph Hlongwane is an accomplished Physics educator and examiner with over 15 years of experience including curriculum designing and reviewing. He holds a Master's degree in Physics Education with a distinction in Dissertation and a University Book Prize and is currently a lecturer at the National University of Science and Technology in Zimbabwe where he has spearheaded Physics Laboratory practical work and has successfully supervised Undergraduate and Masters Students, achieving above 80% annual pass rates. Joseph is passionate about Physics, Education, Sustainable Development, and Artificial Intelligence in Education. He is an active researcher with several publications to his name and has made outstanding presentations at International Conferences. Joseph places utmost importance on his students' success and goes above and beyond to ensure that they achieve their full potential, becoming viable 21st-century global citizens with critical thinking and problem-solving skills to achieve the global agenda of 2030.

Edyta Kostanek is a Senior Teaching Fellow at UCL School of Management, University College London. Her research interests span gamification and playfulness in Higher Education, EdTech and AI, project management, and female entrepreneurship.

Siu-lun Lee is Principal Lecturer at the Yale-China Chinese Language Academy, of the Chinese University of Hong Kong, where he teaches courses on Chinese language studies, and Hong Kong language and society. His research interests include applied linguistics, Cantonese studies, Chinese linguistics, sociolinguistics, and language teaching pedagogy. His publications include Modern Cantonese (Vol. 1-3, Routledge, 2023) and The Learning and Teaching of Cantonese as a Second Language (Routledge, 2023).

Fujia (Cliff) Li is a Senior Lecturer in Entrepreneurship and the Director of Education of Innovation, Technology, and Entrepreneurship at the University of Exeter Business School. His research interests span across responsible innovation entrepreneurial resilience, and entrepreneurship education.

Anita Manokore a holder of a degree in Information Technology and a Masters in Software Engineering. Lecturer for E-commerce, Fundamentals of Computer hardware and Secure E-commerce at Harare Institute of Technology (HIT).

Kudakwashe Manokore is pursuing a PhD program with the University of Zimbabwe (UZ) in Educational Assessment. A lecturer in the Art, Design & Technology Education Department at the National University of Science and Technology, Zimbabwe (NUST). A holder of a Master of Education in Teacher Education (MTEd) (UZ). Bachelor of Technical Education Honours Degree (BTEd) (NUST). He has supervised several undergraduates and postgraduate students at university level. Research interests: Assessment in Technical and Vocational Education.

Nathan Pritts is a leader in higher education, specializing in faculty development, instructional innovation, and the integration of emerging technologies in teaching and learning. As Professor and Program Chair for First Year Writing at the University of Arizona Global Campus, he has spearheaded initiatives in strategic implementation of online learning technologies, comprehensive faculty training programs, and the creation of scalable interventions to support both faculty and students in online environments. As author and researcher, Dr. Pritts has published widely on topics including digital pedagogy, AI-enhanced curriculum design, assessment strategies, and the future of higher education including the books Decoherence (Indiana University Press), Film: From Watching to Seeing (3e), Research & Writing (2e), and Essentials of Academic Writing (4e). He also served as editor for, and wrote the introduction to, Living Online: A Digital Fluency Handbook.

Muhammad Usman Tariq has more than 16+ year's experience in industry and academia. He has authored more than 200+ research articles, 120+ case studies,110+ book chapters and several books other than 4 patents. He is founder and CEO of The Case HQ, a unique repository for courses, narrative and video case studies. He has been working as a consultant and trainer for industries representing six sigma, quality, health and safety, environmental systems, project management, and information security standards. His work has encompassed sectors in aviation, manufacturing, food, hospitality, education, finance, research, software and transportation. He has diverse and significant experience working with accreditation agencies of ABET, ACBSP, AACSB, WASC, CAA, EFQM and NCEAC. Additionally, Dr. Tariq has operational experience in incubators, research labs, government research projects, private sector startups, program creation and management at various industrial and academic levels. He is Certified Higher Education Teacher from Harvard University, USA, Certified Online Educator from HMBSU, Certified Six Sigma Master Black Belt and has been awarded PFHEA, SMIEEE, and CMBE.

Laurie Uttich an experienced educator of composition and creative writing, Laurie joined the UCF teaching center in 2023. Laurie was also the director of the UCF Literary Arts Partnership where she recruited, trained, and supported UCF students to lead poetry and storytelling workshops in community settings, including Title One schools, residential treatment facilities, juvenile delinquency centers, and memory care facilities. She is an active part of the Florida Prison Education Project and has taught multiple creative writing courses at an Orlando correctional center for men.

Kevin Yee is the director of UCF's teaching center. In the classroom, he believes the science of learning provides a crucial foundation for instructors, influencing everything from course design and assessment structure, to classroom management and lesson planning. He is an avid believer in interactive teaching, and has curated a popular list of interactive techniques since 1992. More recently, he's been developing resources for faculty related to AI Fluency and how to use generative AI (such as ChatGPT) in the college classroom, as well as ways faculty can use AI in their day job.

Index

A

B

C

D

www.ingramcontent.com/pod-product-compliance
Lightning Source LLC
LaVergne TN
LVHW080343011026
849161LV00009B/2168